THE AIR PILOT'S MANUAL

Volume 2

Aviation Law
Aeromedicine and Safety
Meteorology

Exercises & Answers
for Vols. 2, 3 & 4

Trevor Thom

Airlife
England

Nothing in this manual supersedes any legislation, rules, regulations or procedures contained in any operational document issued by Her Majesty's Stationery Office, the Civil Aviation Authority, the manufacturers of aircraft, engines and systems, or by the operators of aircraft throughout the world.

Text, Copyright © 1987 Trevor Thom.
Original Illustrations & Diagrams, Copyright © 1987
Trevor Thom & Robert Johnson.

Thom, Trevor
    Air pilots manual.—Rev. 2nd ed.
    Vol. 2: Aviation law and meteorology
    1. Airplanes—Piloting   2. Private
    flying
    I. Title
    629.132′5217   TL710

    ISBN 1-85310-015-3

First edition published 1987
by Airlife Publishing Ltd.

This second revised edition published 1987.

Printed in England by Livesey Ltd., Shrewsbury.

Airlife Publishing Ltd.

7 St. John's Hill, Shrewsbury, England.

THE AIR PILOT'S MANUAL Vol. 2

CONTENTS

PERSONAL PROGRESS TABLE	
Theory	Exercises

CONTENTS
(continued)

EDITORIAL TEAM

Trevor Thom.

A current Boeing 727 Captain with Ansett Airlines of Australia, Trevor is active in the *International Federation of Airline Pilots' Associations (IFALPA)*, based in London, and is a member of the *IFALPA Aeroplane Design and Operations Group.* He was recently appointed IFALPA representative to the *Society of Automotive Engineers (SAE) – Aerospace,* a body which makes recommendations to the aviation industry, especially the manufacturers. Prior to his airline position Trevor worked as a lecturer in Mathematics and Physics, and also as an Aviation Ground Instructor and a Flying Instructor. He is a double degree graduate from the University of Melbourne and also holds a Diploma of Education.

Bill Ryall.

A highly experienced Pilot, Bill is currently Editor of *Pooley's Flight Guides,* having retired from the RAF in 1980 after 38 years' service. He flew *Lancasters* during the war, followed by a spell on transport aircraft and twelve marvellous years with Overseas Ferry Command, during which he flew a great variety of aircraft, from *Dakotas* to twin jets. Later, he became a VIP Pilot and an Instrument Rating Examiner, and was decorated for distinguished flying and awarded the *QCVSA.* Bill's experience was broadened by tours of duty as an APP/Radar Controller and on the editorial staff of No.1 AIDU Northolt. He still holds a Pilot's Licence and flies *Chipmunks* regularly with the RAFVR.

John Fenton.

A Flying Instructor since 1970, John is joint proprietor and assistant CFI of Yorkshire Flying Services at Leeds/Bradford. He is a PPL Examiner and recently received the Bronze Medal from the Royal Aero Club for his achievements and contributions to air rallying. John has made considerable contributions to the field of flying instruction in this country and pioneered the use of audio tapes for flight training.

Edward Pape.

Director of the Manchester School of Flying and a former Chief Flying Instructor of the Lancashire Aero Club, Ed has over 3000 instructional flying hours and is dedicated to Private Pilot training.

Ronald Smith.

A senior Aviation Ground Instructor, Ron's twenty years in aviation include considerable time as a flying instructor, specialised flying in remote areas, fish-spotting, and a period operating his own Air Taxi Service. He is an active member of *California Wheelchair Aviators* and holds a Commercial Pilot's Licence.

Robert Johnson.

An experienced aviator, Bob drew most of the diagrams, designed the cover, and prepared the final sub-edit and layout of the manuals for printing. His aviation experience includes flying a *Cessna Citation* executive jet, a *DC-3* and light aircraft as Chief Pilot for an international University based in Switzerland, and seven years as a First Officer on *Fokker Friendship, Lockheed Electra* and *McDonnell Douglas DC-9* airliners. Prior to this he was an Air Taxi Pilot and also gained technical experience as a Draughtsman on Airborne Mineral Survey work in Australia. In this volume Bob took the cloud photos, Figs.C6-1 to -9.

ACKNOWLEDGEMENTS

We greatly appreciate the input of the following:

The Civil Aviation Authority; numerous Flying Schools throughout the UK; RFD Inflatables Ltd., Beaufort Air Sea Equipment Ltd., Stephen Burt for the excellent colour slides of Cumulonimbus, Ac Castellanus and Lenticular clouds (Chapter C6); Peter Godwin, Peter Grant; and of course Airtour International Ltd. and Robert Pooley Ltd.

'Good, clear Knowledge
minimises
Flight Training Hours'

Part (A)

AVIATION LAW

A1

RULES OF THE AIR

The Rules of the Air have been established to allow aircraft to operate as safely as is reasonably possible. Air safety depends to a large extent upon all Pilots understanding the basic rules and operating within them.

The Rules were established under Article 64 of a document known as the 'Air Navigation Order' (ANO) and are listed in Civil Aviation Authority publication **CAP 393, 'Air Navigation: the Order and the Regulations'**. The Rules are known by their numbers; Rule 5, for example, concerns 'Low Flying'. They are referred to, where applicable, throughout this section on Aviation Law. In this chapter we will be dealing with those topics covered in the Rules which are applicable to aerial operations by a Private Pilot.

The Rules of the Air apply to:
- all aircraft in the UK (including the neighbourhood of offshore installations, where the low flying rule is concerned); and
- to all UK-registered aircraft wherever they may be.

The Rules may be departed from to the extent necessary for avoiding immediate danger or for complying with the law of any other country in which the aircraft might be. When a Rule is departed from for safety reasons the circumstances must be reported afterwards to the competent authority.

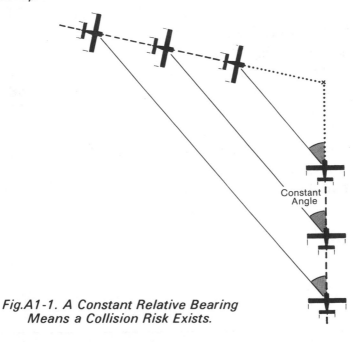

Fig.A1-1. A Constant Relative Bearing Means a Collision Risk Exists.

COLLISION AVOIDANCE IN THE AIR (Rule 17).

With many aircraft sharing the same airspace, it is often necessary to take collision avoidance action. A collision risk exists when the other aircraft is at the same level or approaching it, its range is decreasing and its relative bearing remains constant, *(Fig.A1-1)*.

Some basic rules understood by all Pilots, and applied when necessary, are essential to avoid aerial collisions.

General.

- Regardless of any ATC clearance it is the duty of the Commander of an aircraft to take all possible measures to see that he does not collide with any other aircraft.
- An aircraft must not fly so close to other aircraft as to create a danger of collision.
- Aircraft must not fly in formation unless the commanders have agreed to do so.
- An aircraft which is obliged to give way to another aircraft must avoid passing over, or under, or crossing ahead of, the other aircraft (unless passing well clear of it).
- An aircraft with right of way should maintain its course and speed.
- For the purposes of this Rule a glider and a machine towing it are considered to be a single aircraft under the command of the commander of the towing machine.

Approaching Head-On.

- When two aircraft are approaching head-on or nearly so, and there is danger of collision, each must turn right, *(Fig.A1-2a.)*

Fig.A1-2a. Each Turns Right to Avoid a Collision.

Overtaking.

- An aircraft which is being overtaken in the air has right-of-way and the overtaking aircraft, whether climbing, descending or level, must keep out of the way by turning right. A glider overtaking another glider may, however, turn either right or left, *(Fig.A1-2b.)*

Fig.A1-2b. Overtaking, Keep Right.

3

Converging Aircraft.

- An aircraft in the air must give way to other converging aircraft as follows:
    - flying machines must give way to airships, gliders and balloons;
    - airships must give way to gliders and balloons;
    - gliders must give way to balloons.
- Subject to the above paragraph, when two aircraft are converging at about the same altitude, the aircraft which has the other on its right must give way. Powered aircraft must give way, however, to those towing other aircraft or objects such as banners.

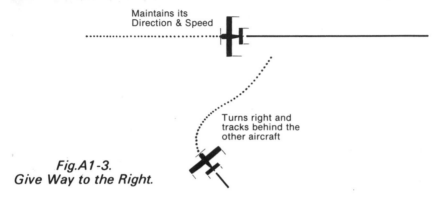

Maintains its
Direction & Speed

Turns right and
tracks behind the
other aircraft

Fig.A1-3.
Give Way to the Right.

FLIGHT IN THE VICINITY OF AN AERODROME (Rules 17 & 35).

A flying machine, glider or airship flying in the vicinity of an aerodrome or moving on an aerodrome shall, unless the aerodrome's ATC unit otherwise authorises:

- conform to the pattern of traffic formed by other aircraft intending to land at that aerodrome, or keep clear of the airspace in which the pattern is formed;
- make all turns to the left unless ground signals otherwise indicate.

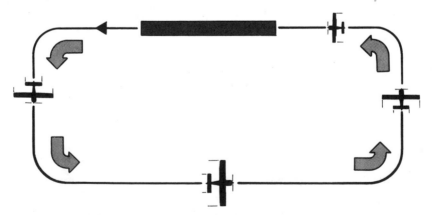

Fig.A1-4. Make Left-Hand Circuits Unless Right-Hand Circuits are Indicated.

Order of Landing.

- An aircraft landing or on final approach has right-of-way over others in flight or on the surface.
- In the case of two or more flying machines, gliders or airships approaching any place for landing, the lower aircraft has right-of-way (although it must not cut in front of, or overtake, another which is on final approach); provided that:
  - when ATC has given any aircraft an order of priority for landing they must approach to land in that order; and
  - when the commander of an aircraft is aware that another is making an emergency landing he must give way, and at night (even if he already has permission to land) must not attempt to land until given further permission.

Landing and Take-Off.

- A flying machine, glider or airship must take-off and land in the direction indicated by ground signals or, in their absence, into wind unless good aviation practice demands otherwise;
- A flying machine or glider must not land on a runway which is not clear of other aircraft, unless an aerodrome ATC unit otherwise authorises;
- Where take-offs and landings are not confined to a runway:
  - a flying machine or glider when landing must leave clear on its left any aircraft which has landed, or is already landing, or is about to take-off, (i.e. keep to the right of other aircraft). If such a flying machine or glider is obliged to turn when taxying on the landing area, it shall turn to the left after the Commander has satisfied himself that such action will not interfere with other traffic movements; and
  - a flying machine about to take-off must manoeuvre so as to leave clear on its left any aircraft which has taken-off, or is about to take-off.

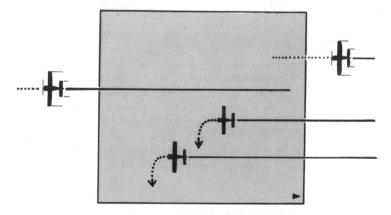

Fig.A1-5. Turn Left After Landing
When Operations Are Not Confined to a Runway.

- A flying machine must after landing move clear of the landing area as soon as possible unless the aerodrome ATC unit otherwise authorises.

Use Radio in an Aerodrome Traffic Zone.

A Pilot in an Aerodrome Traffic Zone must maintain appropriate radio (or other) communication with the aerodrome authority (Air Traffic Control, Aerodrome Flight Information Service or Air/Ground radio).

NOTE: Explanations of Airspace terminology such as 'Aerodrome Traffic Zone' are contained in Chapter A4 – Airspace.

RIGHT-HAND TRAFFIC RULE (Rule 19).

An aircraft flying in sight of the ground and following a road, railway, canal, coast or other line feature shall keep the line feature on its left, except where it is instructed to do otherwise by the appropriate Air Traffic Control authority. This will ensure separation from aircraft flying in the opposite direction and following the same line feature.

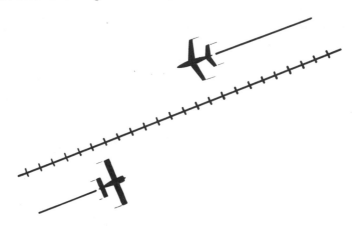

Fig.A1-6. Keep to the Right (and Keep the Line Feature on your Left).

LIGHTS ON AIRCRAFT (Rules 9 to 15).

The direction of flight of aircraft is more difficult to determine by night than by day. To assist in the identification of aircraft position and heading by night, aircraft must display such lights as are specified for the particular category of aircraft. These lighting requirements generally apply when the aircraft is moving on the ground also. No other lights may be displayed that would impair the effectiveness of the required lights.

If any required light fails in flight and cannot be repaired or replaced at once the aircraft must **land** as soon as it can safely do so unless ATC authorises continuation of the flight.

Knowing the arcs of the basic aircraft navigation lights helps in assessing collision risk. On flying machines and airships the **green main navigation light on the right (or starboard) wing** and **red main navigation light on the left (or port) wing** show through 110 degrees from dead ahead out to their respective sides. The white tail-light shows through 70 degrees either side of dead astern. An anti-collision light, where carried on an aircraft, is a flashing red light showing in all directions.

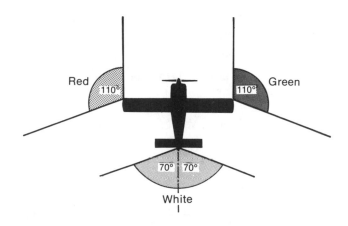

Fig.A1-7. Aeroplane Lights.

If at night you see the red navigation light of an approaching aircraft out to the left, then your paths will not cross (i.e. red to red is safe). A red light out to the right, however, could mean that the risk of a collision exists.

The situation is reversed for the green light of an approaching aircraft – out to the right it is safe, out to the left there is a risk of collision. Green to green is safe.

If both the red and green lights are visible, then the other aeroplane is flying directly towards you. If the white light is visible, it is flying away from you.

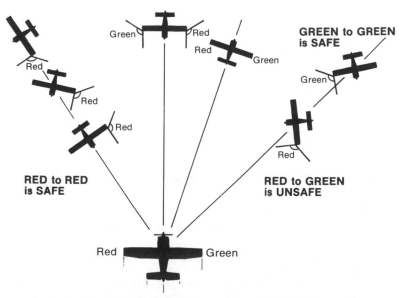

Fig.A1-8. Using Navigation Lights to Avoid Collision.

7

In the case of airships there is also a white nose-light showing through 110 degrees either side of dead ahead. A glider may show either the basic lights for a flying machine, as just described, or a steady red light visible in all directions. Free balloons are required to show a steady red light visible in all directions.

Night is defined for the Rules of the Air as being:
- from 30 minutes after sunset;
- until 30 minutes before sunrise.

This differs from the definition of *Night* required for **Night Training Flights,** which is when the Sun exceeds twelve (12) degrees below the horizon; (reference Air Navigation Order, Schedule 9).

LOW FLYING REGULATIONS (Rule 5).

The following restrictions apply to low flying in all cases other than the exceptions specified below.

Flight Over Congested Areas.

A congested area in relation to a city, town or settlement, means any area which is substantially used for residential, industrial, commercial or recreational purposes.

An aircraft (other than a helicopter) must not fly over a **congested area**:
- below a height that would allow it to **land clear** of the area and without danger to people or property if an engine fails; or
- less than **1500 feet above the highest fixed object within 2000 feet of the aircraft**, whichever is the higher.

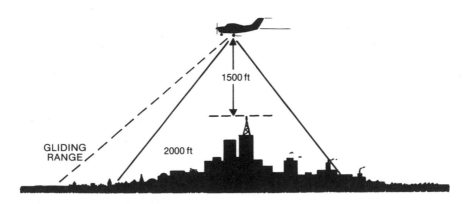

Fig.A1-9. 'Land Clear' and 1500 ft Clearance Over Congested Areas.

Large Open-Air Gatherings.

No aircraft may fly over or within **3000 feet** of an open-air gathering of more than 1000 people except with the permission in writing of the Authority (i.e. the CAA) and in accordance with any conditions specified, and with the written consent of the organisers; nor may it fly below a height that would enable it to **land clear** of the assembly if an engine failed.

(In the case of inadvertent contravention of this rule, it may be a good defence to show that the particular flight was made at a reasonable height and for a purpose not connected with the assembly.)

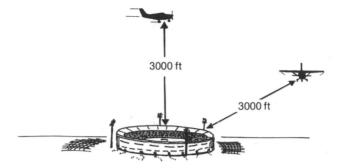

Fig.A1-10. Maintain 3000 ft Clearance From Large Open-Air Gatherings.

The 500 ft Rule.

An aircraft must not fly closer than 500 feet to any person, vessel, vehicle or structure. (Exceptions to this rule are included below.)

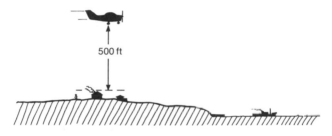

Fig.A1-11. Maintain 500 ft Clearance.

Helicopters.

A helicopter must not fly below a height that would allow it to land without danger to people or property if an engine fails. Neither (except with the written permission of the Authority) may it fly over a congested area at less than 1500 feet above the highest fixed object within 2000 feet, or over a specified area of Central London below a height that would enable it to land clear of that area if an engine fails.

NOTE: The general requirement for all aircraft to be able to land clear is the responsibility of the Pilot-in-Command, and not of ATC. If an ATC clearance is given which would not permit the requirement to be met, e.g. a Special VFR Clearance at 1000 feet, say, in a single-engined aircraft over London, the clearance should not be accepted by the Pilot-in-Command.

Exceptions.

The proviso stipulating '1500 feet above the highest fixed object within 2000 feet' does not apply on routes notified for the purposes of the Low Flying Regulations (Rule 5), or on Special VFR flights made in accordance with ATC instructions.

The '3000 ft' and '500 ft' rules specified above do not apply to flights over or within 3000 feet of an assembly gathered for an aircraft race, contest or display if the aircraft is part of the event and the Pilot-in-Command has the written consent of the organisers.

The '500 ft' rule specified above does not apply to any aircraft landing or taking-off in accordance with normal aviation practice, nor to a glider which is hill-soaring.

None of the above rules apply when flying as necessary to save life or during take-off, landing, practice approaches and Navaid checking at a Government, Authority or licensed aerodrome. Practice approaches must, however, be made in airspace customarily used for landing or taking-off. Note that the '1500 feet' prohibition specified above **does** apply to flight after take-off or before landing at **unlicensed** aerodromes.

REPORTING HAZARDOUS CONDITIONS (Rule 4).

The Commander of an aircraft must report as soon as possible (to ATC) any hazardous flight conditions encountered, giving details pertinent to the safety of other aircraft. Typical situations worthy of reporting are severe windshear or turbulence, rapidly deteriorating visibility or an unserviceable runway.

AEROBATICS (Rule 18).

Aerobatics are not permitted over a congested area. (A 'congested area' is one which is substantially used for residential, industrial, commercial or recreational purposes within a city, town or settlement.) Within controlled airspace aerobatics may be permitted with the specific approval of the controlling authority.

SIMULATED INSTRUMENT FLIGHT (Rule 6).

When simulated instrument flying is taking place (i.e. a Pilot is flying the aircraft with his external field of view artificially restricted) the aircraft must have dual flying controls, and a second Pilot must be present who can assist the other (note that a Student Pilot does not qualify for this assistant role). If necessary, a third person is to be carried as an observer to ensure an adequate look-out.

PRACTICE INSTRUMENT APPROACHES (Rule 7).

A Pilot practising instrument approaches in Visual Meteorological Conditions (VMC) must tell ATC and carry a safety look-out.

MISUSE OF SIGNALS AND MARKINGS (Rule 3).

Signals and markings specified in the Rules for a particular meaning or purpose must not be used except with that meaning or for that purpose. Signals which may be confused with a specified signal must not be made, and military signals must not be used except with the necessary authority.

☐ Now complete **Exercises A1 – Rules Of The Air.** The Exercises are located in Part (D), at the end of this Volume.

A2

AERODROMES

An aerodrome is an area of land or water used for the taking-off and landing of aircraft. There are various categories of aerodrome depending upon their use. The Aerodrome (AGA) section of the UK Aeronautical Information Publication (AIP) contains an aerodrome directory giving specific information on physical characteristics, local hazards and flying restrictions.

LIMITATIONS ON THE USE OF AERODROMES.

Certain restrictions apply at some aerodromes and not at others.

At Military Aerodromes, and at Civil Aerodromes with an Ordinary Licence, **prior permission to land** is needed from the aerodrome authority, and at Unlicensed Aerodromes the **prior permission of the owner or person in charge**. This may be designated in documents as **'PPR'**, which stands for Prior Permission Required. Permission to use a military aerodrome must be obtained before taking-off for the aerodrome concerned.

The civil use of Military Aerodromes is restricted to the normal hours of watch, and to aircraft on inland flights. At some Military Aerodromes, civil use is further restricted to certain classes of traffic (e.g. scheduled services, charter flights, or private aircraft).

The above restrictions on aerodrome use would not apply in the case of an in-flight emergency. Aerodromes not listed in AIP-AGA (AGA section of the Aeronautical Information Publication) may be used in an **emergency** or if **prior permission** from the owner or operator is obtained.

For further reading on the hazards in using disused and partially disused aerodromes, you are directed to Aeronautical Information Circular AIC 11/1983 (Pink 41).

CUSTOMS FACILITIES.

Designated Customs and Excise Airports for the purposes of international travel are listed in the AGA section of the UK AIP, together with hours of attendance and special requirements.

AERONAUTICAL LIGHT BEACONS.

Aeronautical light beacons are installed at various civil and military aerodromes in the UK. Their hours of operation vary, but broadly speaking they can be expected to be on at night and by day in bad visibility, whenever the aerodrome is operating.

Aeronautical Light Beacons include:
- **'Identification Beacons'** which flash a two-letter morse group every 12 seconds (**green** at civil aerodromes and **red** at military aerodromes); and
- **'Aerodrome Beacons'** which give an alternating-colour flash signal instead (usually **white/white** or (less commonly) **white/green**). They are not normally provided in addition to an identification beacon.

AERODROME TRAFFIC ZONES (ATZs).

A certain amount of airspace surrounding most aerodromes in the UK has been designated as Aerodrome Traffic Zones, usually because of the intensity of aerial activity.

The dimensions of an ATZ are:
- from ground level to 2000 ft Above Aerodrome Level;
- within the area bounded by a circle of radius:
   (i) 2 nm, where length of longest runway is 1850 m or less; or
   (ii) 2·5 nm, where longest runway is greater than 1850 m;
   – the centre of the circle being the mid-point of the longest runway.

NOTE: Some 2 nm ATZs are expanded to 2·5 nm radius to provide at least 1·5 nm clearance from the end of all runways. Such exceptions are notified in the list of ATZs published in AIP RAC 3-2.

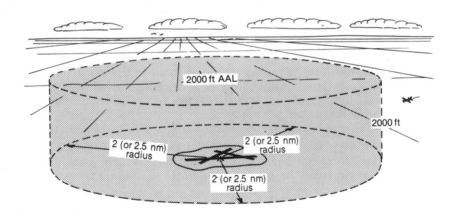

Fig.A2-1. Dimensions of an Aerodrome Traffic Zone (ATZ).

MOVEMENT OF AIRCRAFT ON AERODROMES (Rule 31).

An aircraft must not taxi on the apron or the manoeuvring area of an aerodrome without the permission of the aerodrome authorities. The **manoeuvring area** of an aerodrome is that part of the aerodrome provided for the take-off and landing of aircraft and for the movement of aircraft on the surface (i.e. taxying), excluding aprons and maintenance areas. An **apron** is a paved area of an airfield used for purposes such as loading and unloading of aircraft, aircraft turnaround operations, maintenance and repair, and any other approved purpose other than flight operations.

ACCESS ON AERODROMES (Rule 32).

A person shall not, without permission, go onto a part of an aerodrome provided for the use of aircraft. This applies to any part that is not a Public Right of Way.

RIGHT OF WAY ON THE GROUND (Rule 33).

1. Regardless of any ATC clearance it is the duty of an aircraft commander to do all possible to avoid collision on the ground with other aircraft or vehicles.

2. Aircraft on the ground must give way to those taking-off or landing, and to any vehicle towing an aircraft.

3. When two aircraft are approaching head-on, or nearly so, each must turn right.

4. When two aircraft are converging, the one which has the other on its right must give way, avoiding crossing ahead of the other unless passing well clear.

5. An aircraft which is being overtaken by another has right-of-way, and the overtaking aircraft must keep out of the way by turning left until past and well clear.

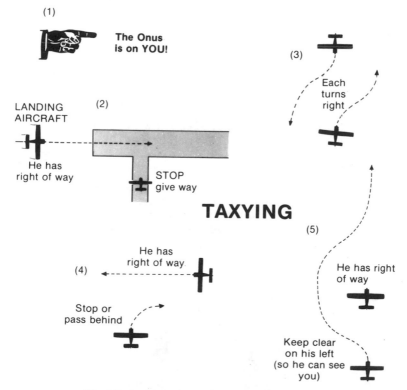

Fig.A2-2. Five Rules for Taxying on the Manoeuvring Area of an Aerodrome.

AERODROME SIGNALS AND MARKINGS
(Rules 41-45)

A SIGNALS AREA is positioned near the control tower at aerodromes to allow messages to be passed to a Pilot without the use of radio:
- **in-flight**, by signals laid out on the ground; and
- **on the ground**, by signals hoisted up a mast located in the signals area.

SIGNALS AND MARKINGS IN THE SIGNALS AREA.
Direction Of Take-Off And Landing.
A **white 'T'** signifies that aeroplanes and gliders taking-off or landing shall do so parallel with the shaft of the 'T' and towards the cross arm, unless otherwise authorised by the appropriate ATC unit.

A White Disc at the head of the 'T' means that the direction of landing and the direction of take-off do not necessarily coincide. This latter situation may also be indicated by **a Black Ball suspended from the mast**.

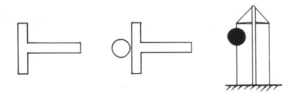

Fig.A2-3. Direction of Take-Off and Landing.

Use Hard Surfaces Only.
A **white dumb-bell** signifies that movements of aeroplanes and gliders on the ground shall be confined to paved, metalled or similar hard surfaces. The addition of black strips in each circular portion of the dumb-bell, at right angles to the shaft, signifies that aeroplanes and gliders taking-off or landing must do so on a runway, but that movement on the ground is not confined to hard surfaces.

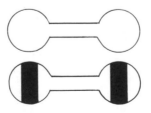

Fig.A2-4. Use Of Hard Surfaces Signals.

Right-Hand Circuit.

A **red and yellow striped arrow bent through 90 degrees** around the edge of the signals area and pointing in a clockwise direction means that a right-hand circuit is in force.

Where the circuit direction at an aerodrome is variable (left-hand or right-hand) **a red flag** on the signals mast indicates that a left-hand circuit is in operation. **A green flag** signifies that the circuit is **right-hand.**

Fig.A2-5. Right-Hand Circuit Indicator.

Special Precautions.

A **red square panel with a single yellow diagonal stripe** means that the state of the manoeuvring area is poor and that Pilots must exercise special care when landing.

Fig.A2-6. Special Precautions Signal.

Landing Prohibited.

A **red square panel with a diagonal yellow cross** signifies that the aerodrome is unsafe for the movement of aircraft and that landing is prohibited.

Fig.A2-7. Landing Prohibited Signal.

Helicopter Operations.

A **white 'H'** in the signals area means that helicopters must take-off and land only within a designated area (that area itself being marked by a much larger white 'H').

(a) a white letter H is displayed in the signals area:

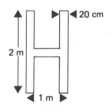

(b) a white letter H indicates the area to be used by helicopters:

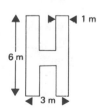

Fig.A2-8. Helicopter Operations Markers.

Gliding.

A **double white cross and/or two red balls** suspended from a mast, one above the other, signify that glider-flying is taking place at the aerodrome. (A similar but much larger signal is used to mark an area on the aerodrome which is to be used only by gliders).

A **yellow cross** indicates the tow-rope dropping area.

Tow-ropes, banners, etc can only be picked up or dropped at an aerodrome, and then only as directed by the aerodrome authority, or in the designated area (yellow cross) with the aircraft flying in the direction appropriate for landing. (ANO Article 39 & Rule of the Air 34.)

Fig.A2-9. Gliding In Progress.

SIGNALS ON PAVED RUNWAYS AND TAXIWAYS.

Unserviceable Portion of Runway or Taxiway.

Two or more white crosses along a section of runway or taxiway, with the arms of the crosses at an angle of 45 degrees to the centreline of the runway or taxiway at intervals of not more than 300 metres, signify that the section of the runway or taxiway marked by them is unfit for the movement of aircraft.

Fig.A2-10. Unfit Section of Runway or Taxiway.

Orange and white markers as illustrated below, spaced not more than 15 metres apart, signify the boundary of that part of a paved runway, taxiway or apron which is unfit for the movement of aircraft. Each marker comprises a base board supporting a slatted vertical board, both striped orange-white-orange.

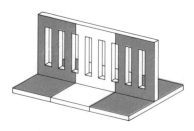

Fig.A2-11. Boundary of Unserviceable Area Marker.

Holding Point on Paved Taxiway.

Two close parallel yellow lines – one continuous and the other broken – across a taxiway, signify a holding point beyond which no part of an aircraft or vehicle may proceed, in the direction of the runway, without ATC permission. (Until recently holding points were marked with white lines.)

NOTE: Of the two lines, **the broken yellow line** is marked on the runway side, enabling the Pilot to determine if the holding point affects him. Moving in the reverse direction towards a holding point, e.g. having turned-off the runway after landing, the holding point does not require a clearance to cross it.

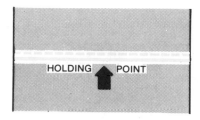

Fig.A2-12. Holding Point on Paved Taxiway.

MARKERS ON UNPAVED MANOEUVRING AREAS.

Aerodrome Boundary Markers.

Orange/white striped wedge-shaped markers (like elongated wheel-chocks in shape), placed not more than 45 metres apart, indicate the boundary of an aerodrome. These are supplemented by flat orange/white markers, also placed 45 metres apart, on any structures which lie on the boundary.

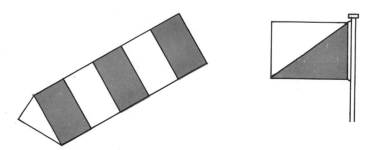

Fig.A2-13. Boundary Marker.

Unserviceable Portion.

The orange/white striped wedge-shaped markers shown above are also used to mark the boundary of an unpaved area which is unserviceable for aircraft movement. These alternate with square flags showing equal orange and white triangular areas. Within this marked area the bad ground is itself marked with one or more white crosses (as described above).

Runway/Stopway Boundary Markers.

White, flat rectangular markers, flush with the surface and placed not more than 90 metres apart, indicate the boundary of an unpaved runway or of a stopway. (A stopway is a prepared rectangular area of ground at the end of a runway, in the direction of take-off, designated as a suitable area in which an aircraft can be stopped in the case of an interrupted take-off).

Light Aircraft Area.

A **white letter 'L'** indicates a part of the manoeuvring area to be used only for the taking-off and landing of light aircraft.

If a dumb-bell displayed in the aerodrome signals area has a **red 'L'** superimposed, it means that light aircraft are allowed to take-off and land either on a runway or on the area designated by the white 'L'.

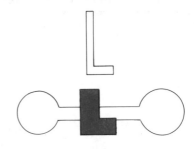

Figs.A2-14 & 15.
Light Aircraft Areas.

Runway To Be Used.

A **white 'T'** as described above (placed on the left side of a runway when viewed from the landing direction) indicates that *it* is the runway to be used. Where there is no runway it indicates the direction for take-off and landing.

Landing Dangerous.

A **white cross displayed at each end of a runway** indicates that landing is dangerous and that the aerodrome is used for storage purposes only.

Fig.A2-16. Landing Dangerous.

Emergency Use Only.

A **white cross and a single white bar displayed at each end of the runway** at a disused aerodrome indicates that the runway is fit for emergency use only. Runways so marked are not safe-guarded and may be temporarily obstructed.

Fig.A2-17. Emergency Use Only.

Land In Emergency Only.

Two vertical yellow bars on a red square on the Signals Area indicate that the landing areas are serviceable but the normal safety facilities are not available. Aircraft should land in emergency only.

Fig.A2-18. Land in Emergency Only.

SUMMARY OF AERODROME SIGNALS VISIBLE ONLY WHEN ON THE GROUND.

In The Signals Area.

1. **A black ball** on a mast signifies that the directions of take-off and landing are not necessarily the same.

2. **Two red balls** on a mast signify that gliding is taking place.

3. **A rectangular red/yellow chequered flag or board** means that aircraft may move on the manoeuvring area and apron only with the permission of ATC.

Fig.A2-19a. ATC In Operation.

4. If the circuit direction at the aerodrome is variable, and a **left-hand circuit** is in operation, a **red flag** will be flown from the mast. **A green flag** on the mast signifies that a **right-hand circuit** is in force at the aerodrome. (The colours of the flags for left and right circuits are the same as for navigation lights on an aircraft.)

Away From the Signals Area.

5. A **square yellow board bearing a black 'C'** indicates the position at which a Pilot can report to ATC or other aerodrome authority.

Fig.A2-19b. Location of the Aerodrome Authority.

Fig.A2-20. Example of Signals Area Display at Wycombe (WP).

Clockwise from bottom LH corner – Special Precautions; Gliding in Progress; (white dash symbol is part of dumb-bell not in use); RH Circuits; and in Centre: T/O & Landing Direction (towards the cross-arm).

MEANING OF LIGHTS & PYROTECHNIC SIGNALS
(Rule 46)

Characteristic and colour of light beam or pyrotechnic	From an aerodrome		From an aircraft in flight to an aerodrome
	to an aircraft in flight	to an aircraft or vehicle on the aerodrome	
(a) Continuous red light	Give way to other aircraft and continue circling.	Stop.	–
(b) Red pyrotechnic light, or red flare	Do not land; wait for permission.	–	Immediate assistance is requested.
(c) Red flashes	Do not land; aerodrome not available for landing.	Move clear of landing area.	–
(d) Green flashes	Return to aerodrome; wait for permission to land.	To an aircraft: You may move on the manoeuvring area and apron. To a vehicle: You may move on the manoeuvring area.	–
(e) Continuous green light	You may land.	You may take off.	–
(f) Continuous green light, or green flashes, or green pyrotechnic light	–	–	By night: May I land? By day: May I land in direction different from that indicated by landing T?
(g) White flashes	Land at this aerodrome after receiving continuous green light, and then after receiving green flashes, proceed to the apron.	Return to starting point on the aerodrome.	I am compelled to land.
(h) White pyrotechnic lights Switching on and off the navigation lights Switching on and off the landing lights	–	–	I am compelled to land.

Fig.A2-21. Meaning of Lights and Pyrotechnic Signals – (excerpt from the CAA Publication CAP 85).

MARSHALLING SIGNALS
(Rules 47 & 48)

FROM MARSHALLER TO PILOT (Rule 47).

Fixed Wing.

(a) Right or left arm down, the other arm moved across body and extended to indicate position of the other marshaller.

Meaning of Signal:
- Proceed under guidance of another marshaller.

Fig.A2-22.

(b) Arms repeatedly moved upward and backward, beckoning onward.
- Move ahead.

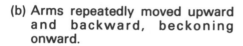

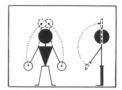

Fig.A2-23.

(c) Right arm down, left arm repeatedly moved upward and backward. The speed of arm movement indicates the rate of turn.
- Open up starboard engine or turn to port.

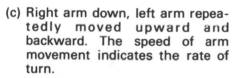

Fig.A2-24.

(d) Left arm down, the right arm repeatedly moved upward and backward. The speed of arm movement indicates the rate of turn.
- Open up port engine or turn to starboard.

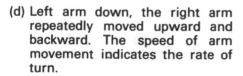

Fig.A2-25.

(e) Arms repeatedly crossed above the head. The speed of arm movement indicates the urgency of the stop.
- Stop.

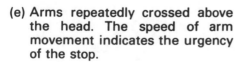

Fig.A2-26.

(f) A circular motion of the right hand at head level, with the left arm pointing to the appropriate engine.

  • Start engines.

Fig.A2-27.

(g) Arms extended, the palms facing inwards, then swung from the extended position inwards.

  • Chocks inserted.

Fig.A2-28.

(h) Arms down, the palms facing outwards, then swung outwards.

  • Chocks away.

Fig.A2-29.

(j) Either arm and hand placed level with the chest, then moved laterally with the palm downward.

  • Cut engines.

Fig.A2-30.

(k) Arms placed down, with the palms towards the ground then moved up and down several times.

  • Slow down.

Fig.A2-31.

(l) Arms placed down, with the palms towards the ground, then either the right or left arm moved up and down indicating that the motors on the left or right side, as the case may be, should be slowed down.

  • Slow down engines on indicated side.

Fig.A2-32.

´(m) Arms placed above the head in a
    vertical position.
- This bay.

Fig.A2-33.

(n) The right arm raised at the elbow
    with the arm facing forward.
- All clear – marshalling finished.

Fig.A2-34.

Rotary Wing.

(o) Arms placed horizontally
    sideways.

    Meaning of signal:
- Hover.

Fig.A2-35.

(p) Arms placed down and crossed in
    front of the body.
- Land.

Fig.A2-36.

(q) Arms placed horizontally
    sideways with the palms up
    beckoning upwards. The speed of
    the arm movement indicates the
    rate of ascent.
- Move upwards.

Fig.A2-37.

(r) Arms placed horizontally
    sideways with the palms down
    beckoning downwards. The
    speed of arm movement indicates
    the rate of descent.
- Move downwards.

Fig.A2-38.

(s) Appropriate arm placed horizontally sideways, then the other arm moved in front of the body to that side, in the direction of the movement, indicating that the helicopter should move horizontally to the left or right side, as the case may be, repeated several times.

Fig.A2-39.

- Move horizontally.

(t) Arms placed down, the palms facing forward, then repeatedly swept up and down to shoulder level.

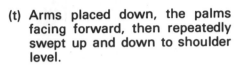

Fig.A2-40.

- Move back.

(u) Left arm extended horizontally forward then right arm making a horizontal slicing movement below left arm.

Fig.A2-41.

- Release lead.

(v) Raise arm, with fist clenched, horizontally in front of the body, then extend fingers.

Fig.A2-42.

- Release brakes.

(w) Raise arm and hand, with fingers extended, horizontally in front of body, then clench fist.

Fig.A2-43.

- Engage brakes.

(x) Left hand overhead with the number of fingers extended, to indicate the number of the engine to be started, and circular motion of right hand at head level.

Fig.A2-44.

- Start engine(s).

(y) Point left arm down, move right arm down from overhead, vertical position to horizontal forward position, repeating right arm movement.

- Back aircraft tail to starboard.

Fig.A2-45.

(z) Point right arm down, move left arm down from overhead, vertical position to horizontal forward position, repeating left arm movement.

- Back aircraft tail to port.

Fig.A2-46.

FROM PILOT TO MARSHALLER (Rule 48).

Fixed Wing.

(a) Raise arm and hand with fingers extended horizontally in front of face, then clench fist:
- Brakes engaged.

(b) Raise arm with fist clenched horizontally in front of face, then extend fingers:
- Brakes released.

(c) Arms extended palms facing outwards, move hands inwards to cross in front of face:
- Insert chocks.

(d) Hands crossed in front of face, palms facing outwards, move arms outwards:
- Remove chocks.

(e) Raise the number of fingers on one hand indicating the number of the engine to be started. For this purpose the aircraft engines shall be numbered in relation to the marshaller facing the aircraft, from his right to his left.

For example, No.1 engine shall be the port outer engine, No.2 shall be the port inner, No.3 shall be the starboard inner, and No.4 shall be the starboard outer.

- Ready to start engines.

☐ Now complete **Exercises A2 — Aerodromes**, located in the exercises section at the end of this volume.

A3

ALTIMETER SETTING PROCEDURES

Atmospheric pressure decreases as altitude is gained. The altimeter, the flight instrument that is used to determine the vertical position of an aeroplane, is a barometer that measures atmospheric pressure, but which has a scale calibrated in feet rather than the unit for pressure.

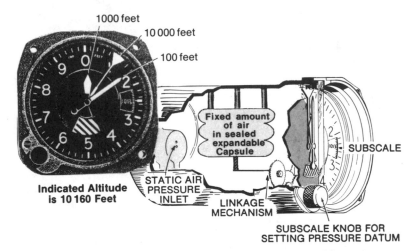

Fig.A3-1. The Altimeter is a Pressure-Sensitive Instrument.

The pressure at the Earth's surface changes from time to time and from place to place, so it is necessary to have some means of selecting the base level pressure from which height will be measured. To achieve this, altimeters have a **subscale** which can be altered with a knob – the 'subscale setting knob'.

The pressure set on the subscale determines the pressure level from which the altimeter will indicate height.

The usual pressure references are:

- **QNH**: the Mean Sea Level pressure at that time causing the altimeter to indicate **altitude** – the vertical distance Above Mean Sea Level (AMSL). This is useful when separation from terrain is of concern, since the ground and obstacles are shown as heights AMSL on maps.

  QNH varies from time to time and place to place as pressure systems move across the face of the Earth, so the Pilot needs to update it on the altimeter subscale, both periodically and as he flies from region to region.

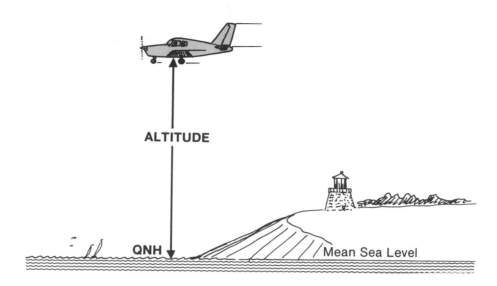

Fig.A3-2. Altitude is Measured from Mean Sea Level.

- **QFE**: the pressure level at the aerodrome elevation (which is the highest point on the landing area) causing the altimeter to indicate **height** – the vertical distance above a specified datum, usually chosen to be Above Aerodrome Level (AAL). This is useful when the only concern is height above the aerodrome and so QFE is a common setting to use for take-offs, circuits and landings.

QFE at an aerodrome will vary with time, information of any changes being passed to the Pilot by ATC. QFEs at different aerodromes will differ depending upon elevation and the pressure pattern;

- Pressure – 1013.2 millibars (or hectoPascals – see Note below) causing the altimeter to read **Pressure Altitude** (PA), which is useful for vertical separation from other aircraft on the same setting at the higher cruising levels where terrain clearance is no longer a problem.

Setting Standard Pressure avoids the need to periodically update QNH with changes in time and/or location. To avoid confusing *'Pressure Altitude'* with *'altitude'*, PA generally has the last two zeros removed and is then referred to as a Flight Level, e.g. PA 3500 is FL35.

NOTE: The term *'hectoPascal'* has been proposed as the ICAO standard for the unit of atmospheric pressure, however the UK has decided to continue using *'millibar'*, at least for the time being. HectoPascals will be used increasingly in other countries. The unit size is identical, i.e. **1 mb = 1 hPa.**

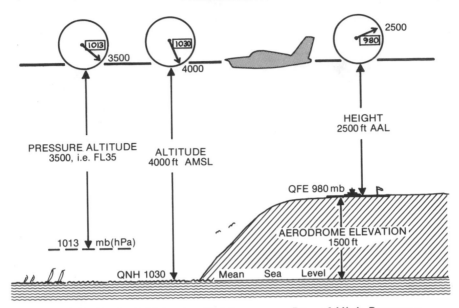

Fig.A3-3. Typical Altimeter Settings on a Day of High Pressure.

The UK is divided into twenty **Altimeter Setting Regions** (ASRs) so that, once en route, all aircraft flying on QNH in the same region will have the appropriate **Regional QNH** set, allowing the Pilots to ensure vertical separation between their aircraft. The Pilot must be aware which Altimeter Setting Region he is in, and when he changes from one Region to another. The Regional QNH is also known as the **Regional Pressure Setting**.

The actual QNH will vary throughout the region depending upon the pressure pattern. The Regional QNH is the lowest forecast QNH value for each hour, thereby ensuring that the Pilot will be at, or slightly higher than, the altitude indicated. Regional QNH is updated each hour by the Air Traffic Service (ATS) and as the pilot passes from one Altimeter Setting Region to another. No Aerodrome QNH in that region should be lower than the value of the Regional QNH. If desired, QNH values can be advised one hour in advance by ATC, any Meteorological Office or the Flight Information Service.

VERTICAL SEPARATION FROM TERRAIN AND FROM OTHER TRAFFIC.

Altitude information is useful both for separation from terrain (since height on charts is given Above Mean Sea Level) and from other aircraft, so when flying reasonably low, QNH (sea level pressure) is set in the subscale as the reference datum.

The **Transition Altitude is the altitude below which vertical position of aircraft is controlled by reference to altitude**, the Pilots having QNH set on their altimeter subscales. Transition Altitude is 3000 ft AMSL over most of the UK. Exceptions beneath certain airspace are listed in the UK Aeronautical Information Publication and in Pooley's *Pilots Information Guide.*

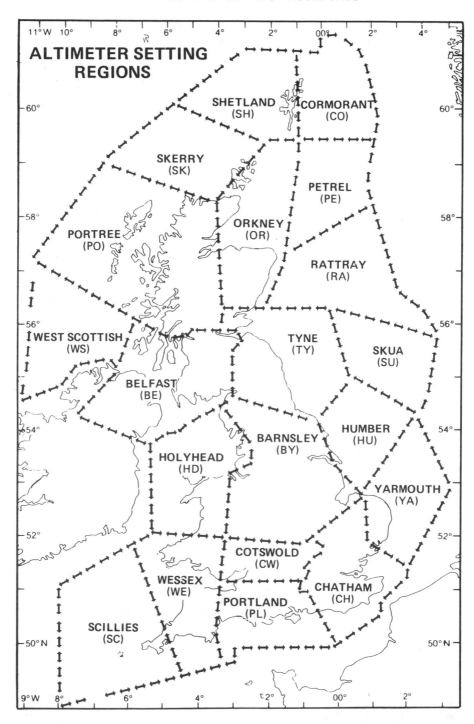

Fig.A3-4. The Altimeter Setting Regions in the United Kingdom (ASRs).

When flying at a level well above the terrain where separation from other traffic is the consideration, a standard pressure setting can be used as the reference datum. **Standard Pressure** is defined as 1013.2 mb(hPa), which is sea level pressure on a 'standard day'. This avoids the need to update the QNH continually. A Vertical Distance measured by an altimeter above the 1013 mb(hPa) pressure level is referred to as a **Pressure Altitude** (e.g. PA 5500 ft), or, by removing the last two zeros, as a **Flight Level** (e.g. FL55).

Above the Transition Altitude, the term Flight Level is used, so Standard Pressure (1013) should be set on the altimeter subscale. To ensure safe vertical separation between Instrument Flight Rules (IFR) traffic, 1013 is used (subject to some exceptions, as specified in the UK Aeronautical Information Publication) by all aircraft in controlled airspace, or above 3000 ft in Uncontrolled Airspace.

Transition Level is the lowest Flight Level available for cruising above the Transition Altitude, the airspace between them being known as the **Transition Layer**.

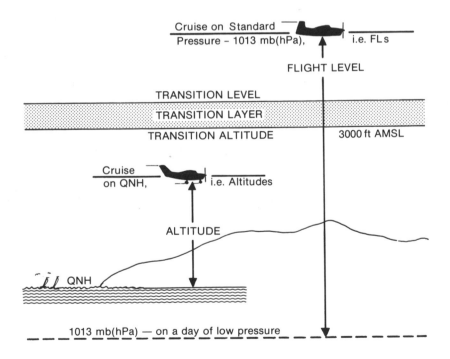

Fig.A3-5. Transition from Altitudes to Flight Levels.

Since the altimeter subscale setting will normally be changed when entering the Transition Layer, it is usual to express vertical displacement in terms of Flight Level after climbing through the Transition Altitude and in terms of altitude after descending through the Transition Level.

In a flight plan:
- **Altitudes** should be specified for that part of the flight below the Transition Altitude; and
- **Flight Levels** for that part of the flight above Transition Level.

Cruising levels should be chosen so that:
- adequate terrain clearance is assured;
- any Air Traffic Service requirements are met; and
- to comply with the Quadrantal or Semi-circular Rules as specified for Instrument Flight Rules, if appropriate. This is covered shortly.

A TYPICAL CROSS-COUNTRY FLIGHT.

Altimetry procedures are much easier in practice than it seems when you read the regulations. A typical cross-country flight between two aerodromes and remaining in uncontrolled airspace and probably not above 3000 ft AMSL is illustrated below.

The main points are:
- Regional QNH is set en route so that the altimeter indicates height Above Mean Sea Level; and
- In the circuit area at each aerodrome, the altimeter subscale is set, according to the Pilot's preference, to either:
    - Aerodrome QFE, so that the altimeter indicates height above the aerodrome; or
    - Aerodrome QNH, so that the altimeter indicates height AMSL (i.e. altitude).

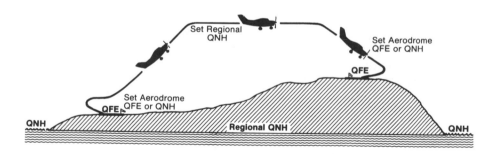

Fig.A3-6. A Typical Cross-Country Flight.

TAKE-OFF AND CLIMB.

There are two altimeter readings that can be of value to a Pilot for take-off and climb:
- **Height Above Aerodrome Level** (with QFE set) – useful for flying in the circuit, e.g. when a 1000 ft circuit is flown 1000 ft is indicated on the altimeter;
- **Altitude** (i.e. Height Above Mean Sea Level with QNH set) – useful for terrain and obstacle clearance;

31

Within Controlled Airspace, where Air Traffic Control has a responsibility to separate air traffic, a Pilot may use:

- any subscale setting for **take-off**. If the aircraft is fitted with two altimeters one should be set to aerodrome QNH to assist Air Traffic Control with vertical separation from other aircraft and the Pilot with separation from terrain. (In other words first altimeter to Aerodrome QNH, second altimeter either to the same setting or to Aerodrome QFE);

- Aerodrome QNH during **climb** to, and while at or below, the Transition Altitude. Vertical position will be expressed as altitude on Aerodrome QNH.

After clearance to climb above the Transition Altitude has been given and the climb commenced, vertical position will (unless specially requested otherwise by ATC) be expressed as Flight Level, *provided* that the aircraft is no more than 2000 ft below Transition Altitude. Flight Levels are based on Standard Pressure 1013 mb(hPa) at all times and so are useful for vertical separation from other traffic using the same subscale setting. This occurs above the **Transition Level**.

Outside Controlled Airspace a Pilot may use any desired altimeter setting for take-off and climb (which, in practical terms, means either Aerodrome QNH or QFE). Vertical position should be reported as altitude. When under Instrument Flight Rules, however, vertical position must be expressed as a Flight Level (based on 1013) after climbing through the Transition Altitude.

NOTE: Flights in Special Rules Airspace (which is not controlled, but is 'regulated' to some extent) should follow the procedures used in controlled airspace as specified above. Details on airspace delineation are covered in the next Chapter (A4.)

Pilots taking-off at aerodromes beneath Terminal Control Areas (TMAs) and Special Rules Areas (SRAs) should use Aerodrome QNH when flying below the Transition Altitude and beneath these areas (to assist in vertical separation from them), except that aerodrome QFE may be used within the circuit.

EN ROUTE.

It is important to update the Regional QNH periodically, and when you enter a new Altimeter Setting Region.

If you are flying into an area of lower pressure, then the aeroplane will gradually descend if the original QNH is not altered. If you are flying from a high pressure area to a low pressure area, **beware below!**

Another effect results from a decreasing temperature because it increases the air density, the result being that a given pressure level is lower in cold air than in warm air. Thus, flying from a warm area to a cold area, the aeroplane will gradually descend.

In a very cold air mass, the aeroplane may be 10% lower than the height indicated on the altimeter. The aeroplane should still be flown at a level according to the altimeter but, as the Pilot-in-Command, you should consider *"when flying from High to Low, Beware Below"*.

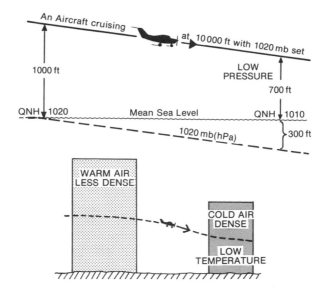

Fig.A3-7. When Flying From High to Low, Beware Below; (valid for both Low Temperatures and Low Pressures.)

In areas of low pressure, the 1013 mb(hPa) pressure level is below Mean Sea Level and so FLs will be lower than at first thought. For example, if the QNH is 997 mb(hPa), the 1013 mb(hPa) pressure level is almost 500 ft below MSL. FL40 will therefore be only 3500 ft AMSL.

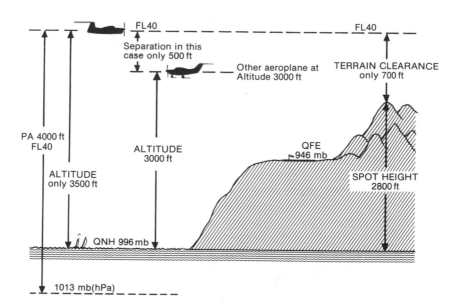

Fig.A3-8. Select the Minimum Suitable Flight Level Carefully, Especially When QNH is Low.

If the intention is to be separated by 1000 ft vertically from traffic or terrain at 3000 ft AMSL, then FL45 is the minimum suitable Flight Level, since it will (in this pressure situation) equate to an altitude of 4000 ft.

If needed, a chart **to convert Altitudes to Flight Levels** (and vice versa) is in the UK Aeronautical Information Publication (AIP RAC 2-4) and Pooley's *Pilots Information Guide*.

FLIGHT LEVEL GRAPH

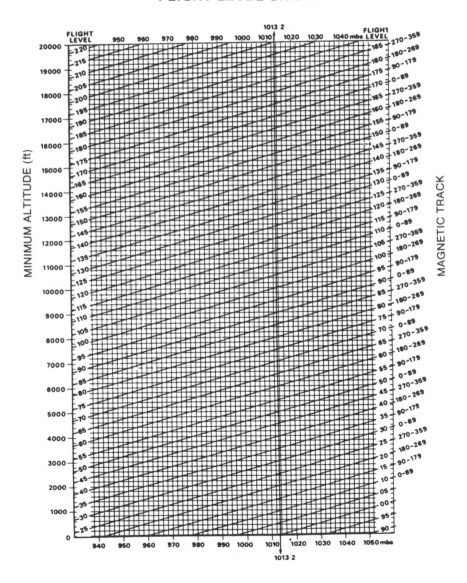

Fig.A3-9. The Flight Level / Altitude Conversion Chart.

To use this chart *(Fig.A3-9)*:
- take a vertical line upwards from the QNH reading along the bottom axis until it meets the appropriate (sloping) Flight Level line; then
- read horizontally across to the equivalent Altitude.

Operations Within Controlled Airspace.

Above 3000 ft AMSL, or above the appropriate Transition Altitude, whichever is the higher, en route aircraft are flown at *Flight Levels* (i.e. with standard pressure 1013 mb set on the subscale), to assist in separation from other traffic.

Regional QNH is to be used en route, usually on the second altimeter, for checking terrain clearance. Aircraft flying in a Control Zone (CTR) or Terminal Control Area (TMA or TCA) at or below the Transition Altitude will be given the appropriate QNH in their ATC clearance to enter.

Operations Outside Controlled Airspace.

At or below 3000 ft AMSL, Pilots may use any altimeter subscale setting. The most logical one to use when cruising is **Regional QNH**.

Pilots flying **beneath a Terminal Control Area (TMA) or a Special Rules Area (SRA),** however, should use the **QNH of an aerodrome** situated beneath that area when flying below Transition Altitude. This will not differ greatly from the Regional QNH and will be the same setting that aeroplanes above in the TMA or SRA are using.

When penetrating a Military Air Traffic Zone (**MATZ**) where military aircraft may be landing and taking-off with QFE set, the Pilot will be given the **Aerodrome QFE** to enable vertical separation between aeroplanes to be applied. If there is more than one aerodrome in a combined MATZ, the QFE of the aerodrome with the highest elevation will be given. This is known as the *'Clutch QFE'.*

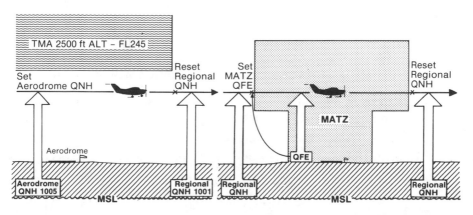

Fig.A3-10. Aerodrome QNH (rather than Regional QNH), or Aerodrome QFE, may be Required En Route.

Outside controlled airspace vertical position in flight plans and communications with the Air Traffic Service Unit is to be expressed as altitude. At or below 3000 ft AMSL on an Advisory Route, the **Regional QNH** should be set. Flights in Special Rules Airspace, since it is regulated to some extent by Air Traffic Control, should follow the same procedures as for controlled airspace.

In level flight above 3000 ft AMSL (or above the appropriate Transition Altitude, whichever is the higher), Pilots flying under the **Instrument Flight Rules** (IFR) must have 1013 mb(hPa) set on an altimeter and conform to the **Quadrantal Rule** when selecting cruising levels. Vertical position will then be expressed as a *'Flight Level'*. Regional QNH should be used for checking terrain clearance.

VFR traffic above 3000 ft AMSL (or above the Transition Altitude) may operate on Regional QNH (for example, when the flight involves various headings and/or cruise heights), however, en route flights choosing to fly quadrantal levels **must** set the standard altimeter setting, 1013 mb(hPa).

The Quadrantal Rule (Rule 26) is a means of vertically separating traffic flying in different directions. Whilst it is required for IFR traffic below FL245 (i.e. Pressure Altitude 24,500), it is **strongly suggested for VFR flights** as well. *The Quadrantal Rule* is based on **Magnetic Track** (rather than heading) since, in strong crosswind conditions, fast and slow aircraft maintaining identical tracks will have significantly different headings.

MAGNETIC TRACK	CRUISING LEVEL
000 – 089	Odd Thousands of Feet
090 – 179	Odd Thousands plus 500 Feet
180 – 269	Even Thousands of Feet
270 – 359	Even Thousands plus 500 Feet

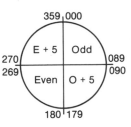

Fig.A3-11a. The Quadrantal Rule for Determining Cruise Levels below FL245.

Example 1: For an aircraft **tracking** 330°M, a suitable level is FL45.

Example 2: For an aircraft **heading** 085°M and experiencing 10° right drift, a suitable level is FL55 (since its **magnetic track** is 095°M).

Above FL245, the **Semi-Circular Rule** applies, where vertical separation is increased because of the inaccuracies that creep into the altimeter.

MAGNETIC TRACK	CRUISING LEVEL
000 – 179	FL250, 270, 290, 330, 370.
180 – 359	FL260, 280, 310, 350, 390.

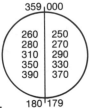

Fig.A3-11b. The Semi-Circular Rule Applies Above FL245.

ALTIMETRY PROCEDURES ON APPROACH AND LANDING.

When an aircraft is descending from a Flight Level to an Altitude preparatory to commencing approach for landing, ATC will pass the **Aerodrome QNH** (which may differ slightly from the Regional QNH, but should never be less than it).

On vacating the cruising Flight Level, the Pilot will change to the QNH unless further Flight Level reports have been requested, in which case the QNH will be set after the final Flight Level report is made. Thereafter the Pilot will continue on the Aerodrome QNH until established on final approach, when QFE or any other setting may be used. The only logical settings, of course, are either Aerodrome QNH or Aerodrome **QFE**.

On a **Radar Final Approach** where the Radar Controller issues tracking and descent guidance, he will assume that an aircraft is using QFE and heights passed by the Controller will be related to QFE (i.e. heights above the runway). A reminder of the assumed setting will be included in the radio phraseology.

To ensure safety it is recommended that all Pilots use QFE, but if a Pilot advises that he is using QNH, heights will be amended by the Radar Controller as necessary and *'altitude'* (i.e. height AMSL) will be substituted for *'height'* in the radio calls.

Vertical positioning of aircraft during approach will, below Transition Level, be controlled by reference to altitudes (QNH) and then to heights (QFE). **Pilots landing beneath TMAs and SRAs should use Aerodrome QNH** when below the Transition Altitude and beneath these areas, except that the Aerodrome QFE may be used within the circuit.

MISSED APPROACH.

On a Missed Approach (i.e. a *'Go-Around'*) Pilots may continue with the altimeter setting selected for final approach, but reference to vertical position should be in terms of altitude on Aerodrome QNH, unless otherwise instructed by ATC.

☐ You can now tackle **Exercises A3 — Altimeter Setting Procedures.**

A4

AIRSPACE

The basic division of UK airspace is into the **London** and **Scottish** *Flight Information Regions* (abbreviated FIRs).

Fig.A4-1. London and Scottish FIRs.

The London and Scottish Flight Information Regions (FIRs) extend upwards to 24 500 feet (Flight Level 245). Above this the airspace is known as *Upper Airspace* and abbreviated as *UIR* for *Upper Information Region*.

Within the confines of the FIR structure, airspace is further divided into various categories, basically according to the intensity of aeronautical activity. For example, the areas around London must be treated differently to the airspace over the Outer Hebrides. More comprehensive Air Traffic Services are provided in the busier airspace.

CATEGORIES OF AIRSPACE IN THE UNITED KINGDOM.

- **Uncontrolled Airspace** (which varies from being totally 'Open FIR' to more regulated airspace – explained below);
- **Controlled Airspace** (in which Air Traffic Control governs the movement of aircraft in the vicinity of certain Aerodromes, Terminal Areas, and along Airways).

UNCONTROLLED AIRSPACE

Uncontrolled Airspace in the United Kingdom comprises:

1. **Special Rules Airspace** (in which traffic is required to operate in accordance with specific regulations);
2. **Advisory Airspace** (in which information regarding the movement of other aircraft is provided by designated Air Traffic Service Units);
3. **Aerodrome Traffic Zones** (ATZs);
4. **Military Aerodrome Traffic Zones** (MATZs);
5. The remaining airspace (approximately 60% of all UK airspace), which can be described as **'Open FIR'**.

In Uncontrolled Airspace a **Flight Information and Alerting Service** (FIS) is available to all aircraft in the Flight Information Regions (FIRs) through *"London Information"* and *"Scottish Information"* Air Traffic Service Units (ATSUs), as appropriate to the FIR. **Radar Services** are also available, on request, in Open FIR. These take the form of a *Radar Advisory Service (RAS)* and a *Radar Information Service (RIS),* and are explained in the next chapter.

NOTE:
**All chart excerpts shown here
are for study purposes only.**

*Fig.A4-2. Boundary between London and Scottish FIRs –
1:500 000 Chart.*

Air Traffic Services are explained in the next chapter, however in relation to Uncontrolled Airspace the Service includes:
- information and warnings on meteorological conditions;
- changes of serviceability in navigational and approach aids;
- condition of aerodrome facilities;
- aircraft proximity warnings; and
- other information pertinent to the safety of air navigation.

1. SPECIAL RULES AIRSPACE.

Although not classified as controlled airspace, Special Rules Airspace is (to some extent) **'regulated' by Air Traffic Control**. Special Rules Airspace may be established around certain aerodromes that are busy or which have occasional airline traffic, but insufficient to justify the establishment of Controlled Airspace.

Aircraft in Special Rules Airspace are required to comply with ATC instructions and any other regulations (for example, visibility criteria) applicable to that airspace. Special Rules Airspace exists at such aerodromes as Aberdeen, Glasgow, Southampton, Southend, Bristol and Newcastle.

Special Rules Airspace is divided into:
- **Special Rules Areas (SRAs)**, which extend upwards from a specified altitude or flight level to an upper limit.

- **Special Rules Zones (SRZs)**, which extend upwards from ground level to a specified altitude or flight level.

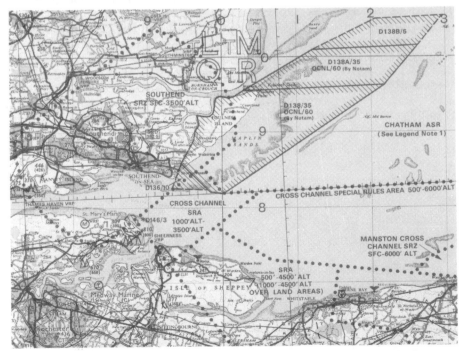

Fig.A4-3. Southend SRZ and Associated SRAs to the South-East.

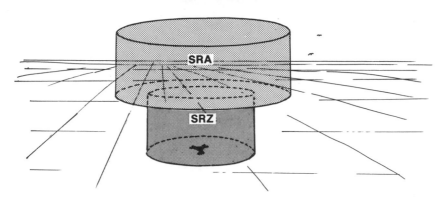

Fig.A4-4. An SRZ and Associated SRA.

NOTE: In many cases, a Special Rules Zone can co-exist with a Control Zone – examples being Cardiff, East Midlands, Edinburgh, Luton and Stansted. (This is explained later under *'Controlled Airspace'*.)

2. ADVISORY AIRSPACE.

In well-used Uncontrolled Airspace, Advisory Airspace has been established to provide an **Air Traffic Advisory Service** to all participating aircraft (in addition to the basic Flight Information Service, described above).

The Service mainly provides traffic separation information, however as it only involves participating traffic, it is not a perfect service. Since many types of aircraft, including airliners, are likely to be in Advisory Airspace, the more Pilots that utilise the Service, the better it is.

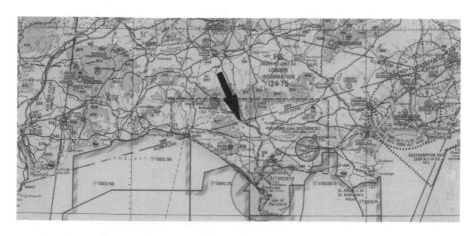

Fig.A4-5. Advisory Route 'Delta Red Eight' (DR8) from Southampton to Dawly, as shown on the Southern England 1:500 000 Aeronautical Chart (not to scale).

Advisory Airspace consists of **Radar Advisory Service Areas** (RASAs) and **Advisory Routes** (ADRs). The latter are Advisory Service Areas in the form of Routes between specified locations. An ADR is deemed to be 10 nm wide and extends from a specified level, with an upper limit. For example, such a route exists between Southampton and Dawly on the south coast (see previous Figure). To utilise the Air Traffic Advisory Service **on an Advisory Route**, the Pilot must file a Flight Plan.

Fig.A4-6. Part of Cardiff Radar Advisory Service Area as shown on the UK 1:500,000 Chart.

3. AERODROME TRAFFIC ZONE (ATZ).

The airspace surrounding most aerodromes listed in the UK is designated as an Aerodrome Traffic Zone. The dimensions of an ATZ are:
- from ground level to 2000 ft Above Aerodrome Level;
- within the area bounded by a circle of radius:
  (i) 2 nm, where length of longest runway is 1850 m or less; or
  (ii) 2·5 nm, where longest runway is greater than 1850 m;
  – the centre of the circle being the mid-point of the longest runway.

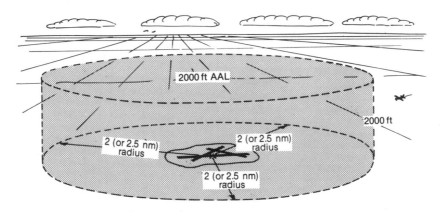

Fig.A4-7. Dimensions of an Aerodrome Traffic Zone (ATZ).

NOTE: Some 2 nm ATZs are expanded to 2·5 nm radius to provide at least 1·5 nm clearance from the end of all runways. Such exceptions are notified in the list of ATZs published in AIP RAC 3-2.

The Rules Designed To Enable Safe Flight in an ATZ.

An aircraft must not fly within an ATZ unless the Commander:
- has the permission of the appropriate Air Traffic Control (ATC) unit; or
- where there is no ATC, has obtained sufficient information from the Flight Information Service (AFIS) unit to enable flight within the zone to be made safely; or
- where there is no an ATC or AFIS unit, has obtained information from the Air/Ground (A/G) radio station at the aerodrome to enable the flight to be made safely.

Aircraft flying in an ATZ must:
- maintain a continuous watch on the appropriate radio frequency notified for communications at the aerodrome or, if this is not possible, keep a watch for visual instructions;
- where the aircraft has radio, give position and height to the aerodrome ATC or AFIS unit or air/ground radio station, as the case may be, on entering and leaving the zone;
- make any other standard calls or requested calls.

These requirements apply at:
- a Government aerodrome at such times as are notified (usually H24);
- an aerodrome having ATC or an AFIS unit, during the hours of watch;
- a licensed aerodrome having A/G radio communication with aircraft, during the hours of watch, and whose hours of availability are detailed in the AIP.

The location and details (ATZ radius, hours of operation and radio frequency) are listed in AIP RAC 3-2. ATZs are also shown on new UK 1:500,000 and CAA 1:250,000 aeronautical charts.

4. MILITARY AERODROME TRAFFIC ZONE (MATZ).

A Military Aerodrome Traffic Zone (MATZ) is the airspace surrounding certain military aerodromes:
- from the surface up to 3000 feet Above Aerodrome Level within a radius of 5 nm; and
- with a stub (or stubs), width 4 nm, extending out a further 5 nm along final approach path(s) for the main instrument runway(s) between 1000 and 3000 ft Above Aerodrome Level (AAL).

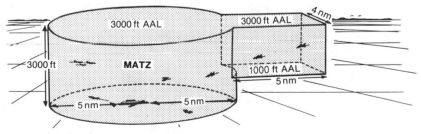

Fig.A4-8. Dimensions of a Typical Military Air Traffic Zone (MATZ).

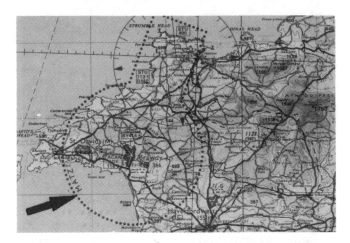

Fig.A4-9.
Brawdy MATZ,
as shown on
the 1:250 000
Aeronautical
Chart.

Note that even if a Pilot should choose to ignore the MATZ (which technically is non-regulated airspace) there is, within the MATZ, an Aerodrome Traffic Zone (ATZ) which he must observe at all times.

Pilots of civil aircraft wishing to penetrate a Military Air Traffic Zone (MATZ) are strongly advised to do so under the control of the MATZ ATC authorities in accordance with published procedures.

5. 'OPEN FIR'.

This term applies to that Uncontrolled Airspace not taken up by the various 'regulated' airspace described above. About 60% of all UK Uncontrolled Airspace is Open FIR.

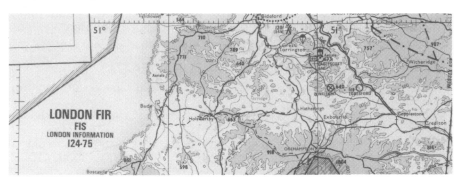

Fig.A4-10. 'Open FIR' in the London Flight Information Region (FIR).

The **Flight Information and Alerting Service (FIS)** is available to flights throughout the UK FIRs. Over much of the UK, Radar Services are also available, either:

- The **Radar Advisory Service (RAS),** which provides traffic information and advisory avoiding action; or
- The **Radar Information Service (RIS),** which provides traffic information only.

These services are explained in more detail in the next chapter.

CONTROLLED AIRSPACE

Controlled Airspace in the UK comprises **'Control Zones', 'Control Areas', 'Terminal Control Areas'** and **'Airways'**.

A CONTROL ZONE (CTR) is the airspace around certain aerodromes in which Air Traffic Control (ATC) is provided to all flights. A CTR extends from ground level to a specified altitude or flight level. Control Zones exist at most of the principal aerodromes in the UK, such as Heathrow, Edinburgh, Manchester, Belfast and Cardiff.

A CONTROL AREA (CTA) is a portion of airspace in which Air Traffic Control is provided, and which extends upwards from a specified altitude or flight level. In the UK CTAs have an upper limit expressed as a flight level.

A TERMINAL CONTROL AREA is a control area established at the confluence of Air Traffic Service routes in the vicinity of one or more major aerodromes. *Terminal Control Area* is sometimes abbreviated as *TCA,* but more commonly as **'TMA'** (from the earlier designation *Terminal Manoeuvring Area).*

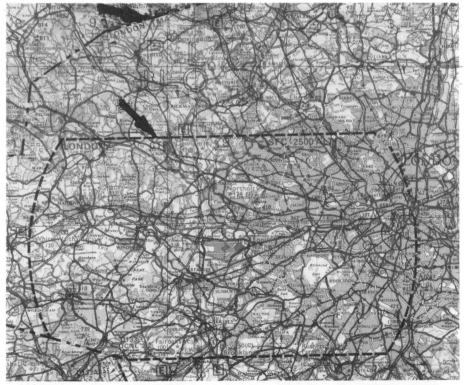

Fig.A4-11. London TMA and CTR (excerpt from a 1:250 000 Chart).

AN AIRWAY is a Control Area in the form of a corridor and is delineated by radio navigation aids. Each Airway has a colour and number identification, and extends 5 nm each side of a straight line joining certain places, and has specified vertical limits.

Airways are used by airliners (and other Instrument Flight Rules traffic) travelling between the principal aerodromes. As the aerodromes are approached, the lower level of the Airway may descend to provide controlled airspace protection for air traffic on climb or descent.

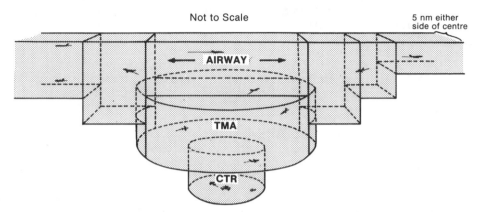

Fig.A4-12. A Control Zone (CTR), Terminal Control Area (TMA) and An Airway.

Controlled Airspace is depicted on aeronautical charts. A fuller description of the boundaries and vertical extent of CTRs, TMAs and Airways is given in the UK Aeronautical Information Publication (AIP) and Pooley's *Pilots Information Guide.*

Of the various types of Controlled Airspace (CTRs, CTAs, TMAs and Airways), the holder of a basic Private Pilot Licence (i.e. without an IMC or Instrument Rating) may only enter **certain** Control Zones, and then only under specific circumstances.

'RULE 21 AIRSPACE'.

Some controlled airspace has been specified (in *Rule 21* of the Rules of the Air) as being restricted to *Instrument Flight Rules* (IFR) only. Pilots wishing to operate in *Rule 21 Airspace* must hold a valid Instrument Rating and their aircraft must be suitably equipped for flight under IFR.

With Two (2) Exceptions, a basic PPL holder (i.e. no IMC or Instrument Rating) is permanently excluded from *'Rule 21 Controlled Airspace'*. The two exceptions are:
1. In accordance with a *'Special VFR Clearance'* from the appropriate ATC unit, **in the case of Control Zones only** (explained in more detail below).
2. Those *'Rule 21 Control Zones'* where provision is made for VFR flights **within 'Access Lanes'**, e.g. to Denham Aerodrome in the London Control Zone (London CTR).

NOTE: In **Access Lanes** special local flying and/or entry/exit procedures exist to avoid the need for an ATC clearance. Your Flying Training Organisation will brief you thoroughly on the specific operating details should you be involved in flying in an Access Lane.

'NON RULE 21' AIRSPACE (i.e. Not Exclusive to IFR Flights).

Non Rule 21 Controlled Airspace is a little less restrictive. A basic PPL holder may enter *Non Rule 21* Control Zones (CTRs) either:
- in accordance with the Visual Flight Rules, provided he remains in sight of the surface (no ATC clearance required); or
- under the conditions specified in a *Special VFR Clearance,* issued by the appropriate ATC unit.

The Special VFR Clearance (SVFR).

The issue of an SVFR Clearance is dependent upon the existence of suitable weather and traffic conditions (as determined by the appropriate ATC unit), and is designed to facilitate flights that would otherwise be restricted.

A Special VFR Clearance will only be issued for flights in Control Zones* and **not** in Control Areas, Terminal Control Areas, or on Airways, (i.e. in CTRs, but **not** in CTAs, TMAs or Airways). Additionally, SVFR Clearances are applicable to certain Special Rules Airspace.

Note that the issue of a 'Special VFR Clearance' by ATC to fly in a Control Zone does **not** absolve the Pilot from his responsibilities to observe the Rules of the Air, where applicable. For example, if a Special VFR Clearance was accepted to fly across London at 1000 ft in the London CTR it may cause an aircraft to contravene the 'Land Clear' requirements of Rule 5.

COMBINED CONTROLLED and SPECIAL RULES Airspace.

At some of the busier aerodromes, where there is a significant volume of public transport activity, combined Controlled/Special Rules airspace has been established. This is marked on aeronautical charts as CTR/SRZ or CTA/SRA, and operates as a combined portion of airspace.

The provision of controlled airspace ensures that VFR flights are conducted in reasonably good weather conditions, thereby easing separation problems. The application of Rule 36 (Special Rules airspace) secures a known traffic environment for ATC in all weather conditions, bearing in mind that aircraft could otherwise operate in controlled airspace (outside ATZs) under VFR without contacting ATC.

CROSSING AN AIRWAY.

Crossing the Base of an Airway.

A basic PPL holder (i.e. no IMC or Instrument Rating) may fly **at right-angles across the base** of an en-route section of Airway **where the lower limit is defined as a Flight Level** (and not an *'altitude'*, i.e. height AMSL) but must not enter the Airway. For example, if the lower limit of an Airway running North-South is FL70, then the Pilot may cross it by flying East or West not above FL70.

*Rule 21 CTRs, or Non Rule 21 CTRs where weather conditions are below VFR.

Penetrating an Airway.

A Pilot who holds a valid Instrument Rating, even in an aeroplane not fully-equipped for IFR flight, may penetrate and cross an Airway in Visual Meteorological Conditions (VMC) by day provided he:

• files a Flight Plan either before departure or when airborne; and
• requests a *"crossing clearance"* from ATC when at least 10 minutes from the intended crossing point, and subsequently receives that ATC crossing clearance.

Except where otherwise authorised by ATC, aircraft are required to cross an Airway by the shortest route (normally at right angles) and to be in level flight at the cleared level on entering the Airway.

AIRSPACE RESTRICTIONS AND HAZARDS

The UK Aeronautical Information Publication (AIP) contains **the Chart of United Kingdom Airspace Restrictions and Hazardous Areas** and a tabulation of the full details for each area depicted. Amendments are notified by NOTAM (Notice to Airmen) and AIC (Aeronautical Information Circular).

Aeronautical Charts also depict Airspace Restrictions and Hazards, the manner of presentation varying slightly with the chart used. Each chart will have a **'Legend'** listing the various features and how they are depicted. Specific types of restriction or hazard of interest to the Private Pilot are given below.

PROHIBITED AREAS.

A Prohibited Area is defined airspace in which flight is prohibited.

Fig.A4-13. Prohibited Area P311, up to 2200 ft (1:250 000 Chart).

RESTRICTED AREAS.

A Restricted Area is defined airspace in which flight is restricted according to certain conditions.

DANGER AREAS.

A Danger Area is defined airspace in which activities dangerous to flight may occur. They are specified in the RAC section of the UK Aeronautical Information Publication (AIP) and on the **'Chart of Airspace Restrictions and Hazardous Areas'**, where they are shown as:
- **Solid red** outline if they are active in published hours (i.e. scheduled);
- **Pecked red** outline if they are inactive unless notified by NOTAM Class 1.

A Danger Area designated as *D129/1·75* indicates that it is:
- located between 51°N–52°N latitudes, as shown by the first number; (a *'0'* would indicate a Danger Area that is just North of 50°N, and a *'6'* that it is just North of 56°N); and
- extends from the surface to 1750 ft AMSL (as shown by the *'1·75'*; *'1-2·5'* would indicate a Danger Area that extends from 1000–2500 ft AMSL).

On other aeronautical charts Danger Areas may be depicted differently, and you should refer to the legend on the particular chart in use.

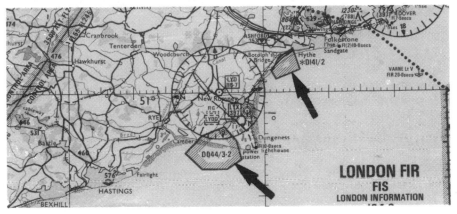

Fig.A4-14. Danger Areas D044 and D141 as shown on the 1:500 000 Chart.

AIR NAVIGATION OBSTRUCTIONS.

Details of structures which reach a height of **300 feet Above Ground Level** (AGL) are published in the UK AIP. They are also shown on certain aeronautical charts. Obstructions which are over **500 feet AGL** are lit. Those between 300 and 500 feet may (or may not) be lit.

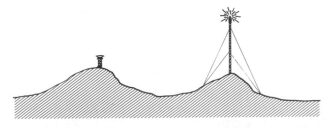

Fig.A4-15. Air Navigation Obstructions May, or May Not, Be Lit.

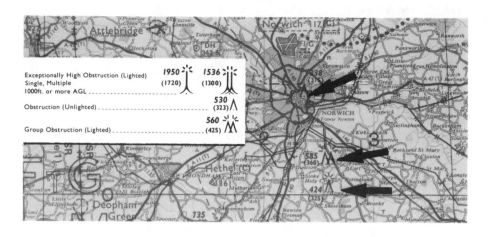

Fig.A4-16. Lit and Unlit Obstructions Depicted on the 1:250000 Chart.

AERODROME OBSTRUCTIONS.

Obstructions on or near aerodromes and which are considered hazardous to aircraft landing or taking-off are listed in the UK AIP and are shown on Instrument Approach and Landing charts.

GLIDER LAUNCHING SITES.

Glider launching may take place from aerodromes or other sites. Pilots are warned that a winch-launched glider may carry the cable up to a height of 1500 feet before releasing it. At a few sites this height may be exceeded.

PILOTLESS AIRCRAFT.

Pilotless aircraft operate and manoeuvre in certain Danger Areas. The aircraft are orange or red and may be flown by day and night in all weather conditions. These aircraft may operate up to 60 000 feet, under radar control.

Details of the Danger Areas concerned are given in the UK AIP (primarily West Wales). Pilots should note that, because pilotless aircraft are less manoeuvrable in the landing configuration than manned aircraft, care should be taken to avoid that part of Danger Areas in which recovery of pilotless aircraft takes place. This can be ascertained by contacting the controlling authority.

PARACHUTE TRAINING BALLOONS.

Captive balloons used for military parachute training may be flown without notification. They will not be flown above 1000 feet AGL, and will be flown in a horizontal visibility of not less than 3 nm and a separation from cloud of not less than 1000 feet.

FREE-FALL PARACHUTING SITES.

Regular free-fall parachuting up to FL150 takes place at the sites and during the periods listed in the UK AIP. Some Government and licensed aerodromes where regular parachuting occurs are included in the list but parachuting may also take place during daylight hours at any Government or licensed aerodrome.

All parachutists are required to operate only in weather conditions which will enable them to remain clear of cloud, in sight of the surface and in a flight visibility of at least 3 nautical miles.

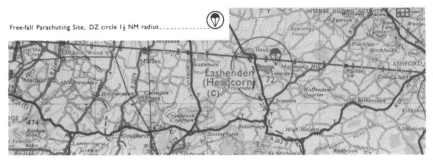

Fig.A4-17. Free Fall Parachute Site.

AREAS OF INTENSE AIR ACTIVITY AND MILITARY LOW FLYING.

The UK AIP gives details of areas of intense air activity and of the military low flying system. Pilots should be extremely vigilant when operating in areas of intense air activity. Military low flying occurs in many parts of the UK at heights up to 2000 feet above the surface. As **the greatest concentration** is between 250 and 500 feet AGL **Civil Pilots** are strongly recommended to avoid this height band whenever possible.

TARGET TOWING TRIALS.

Aircraft towing targets on up to 2000 feet of cable may be flown in daylight, in Visual Meteorological Conditions (VMC) only, at up to 10000 feet. The areas in which these trials take place are given in the UK AIP.

HIGH INTENSITY RADIO TRANSMISSIONS.

The UK AIP lists certain sources of high intensity radio and radar transmissions. Flight within the specified areas may lead to interference with communication and navigational equipment, and flight within some areas could endanger health.

BIRD HAZARDS.

Bird concentration areas are shown in the UK AIP together with the location of bird sanctuaries. Pilots should avoid flying below 1500 feet over areas where birds are known (or are likely) to concentrate. Where it is essential to fly lower, Pilots should bear in mind that the risk of a bird strike increases with speed.

A 'Prior Warning' is issued by NOTAM Class II when there are indications that migration or mass flocking is imminent. A 'Bird Movement Warning Message' is issued by NOTAM Class I when mass flocking is observed and when flocks have started to move.

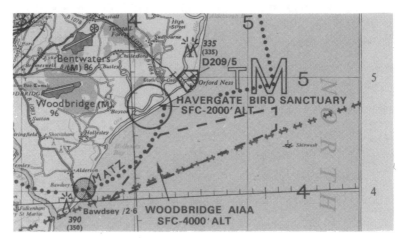

Fig.A4-18. Havergate Bird Sanctuary as depicted on the 1:250 000 Chart.

HANG GLIDING SITES.

Thermalling hang-gliders may be at heights up to the cloud base or the base of controlled airspace, whichever is the lower. Known hang-gliding sites are listed in the UK AIP and *Pooley's Flight Guide,* and are depicted on aeronautical charts.

At certain sites hang gliders may be launched by winch or auto-tow, and cables may be carried up to 2000 ft AGL.

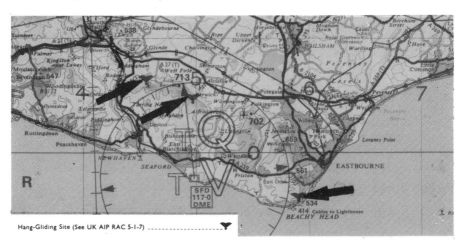

Fig.A4-19. Hang-Gliding Indicated on the 1:250 000 Chart.

MICROLIGHT FLYING SITES.

These areas at which **intensive flying** by microlight aeroplanes may take place are listed in the UK AIP, *Pooley's Flight Guide,* and are also shown on aeronautical charts.

PARASCENDING.

Because of the low-speed characteristics of parascenders, and the difficulty in seeing them in certain conditions, they are a potential hazard to other airspace users. Known parascending sites are therefore listed in the UK AIP.

Parascenders in thermals may be at heights up to the cloud base or base of Controlled Airspace, whichever is lower. Launch cables may be carried up to 2000 feet AGL.

ROYAL FLIGHTS.

A 'Royal Flight' is a civil or military flight over the UK carrying one or more of the principal members of the Royal Family. The special conditions applying to such flights vary depending on whether the Royal Flight is by fixed wing or helicopter:

- **Fixed Wing**: Royal Flights are conducted where possible within existing controlled airspace. Where this is not possible temporary Controlled Airspace (known as 'Purple Airways') is established along the route. Irrespective of the weather conditions, all controlled airspace used (whether existing or temporary) is treated as **'Rule 21 Airspace'** (i.e. is *'notified'* as being *Instrument Flight Rules only).* Details are promulgated by NOTAM.

- **Helicopter**: No special ATC procedures are employed, but details are promulgated by NOTAM. Pilots should keep a sharp look out for the aircraft and keep well clear. In the event of getting into close proximity, however, the normal right of way rules apply.

☐ Now attempt **Exercises A4 — Airspace.**

A5

AIR TRAFFIC SERVICES

There are many Air Traffic Service Units (ATSUs) spread throughout the UK whose function it is to assist the passage of aircraft by providing information prior to flight and in maintaining radio contact during flight.

AIR TRAFFIC CONTROL CENTRE (ATCC) SERVICES.

An Air Traffic Control Centre (ATCC) provides the following Air Traffic Services:
- an Air Traffic Control Service to aircraft operating on Airways (IFR flights);
- an Air Traffic Advisory Service to aircraft flying on Advisory Routes;
- a Flight Information Service (FIS) and Alerting Service;
- a Distress and Diversion service.

AERODROME TRAFFIC SERVICES.

Air Traffic Control (ATC).

ATC at an aerodrome is responsible for the **control** of aircraft in the air in the vicinity of the aerodrome, and all traffic on the manoeuvring area. All movements on the manoeuvring area are subject to the prior permission of ATC.

The total Air Traffic Control responsibility is shared between **Aerodrome Control** and **Approach Control**. Aerodrome Control is responsible for aircraft on the manoeuvring area except runways in use.

The point dividing the responsibilities of Aerodrome Control and Approach Control for aircraft on runways in use and in the air may vary with weather conditions or other considerations, but it is the normal rule that departing aircraft contact Aerodrome Control first and arriving aircraft contact Approach Control first.

Non-radio aircraft may be given instructions or information by **lamp or pyrotechnics** from the control tower and by **ground signals** in the aerodrome signals area. Lamp and pyrotechnic signals may be made to any aircraft, radio-equipped or otherwise, from a subsidiary control point such as a runway control van.

Aerodrome Flight Information Service (AFIS).

AFIS is provided at some aerodromes which do not have ATC to give information relevant to the safe and efficient conduct of flights in the ATZ. The Aerodrome Flight Information Service is not permitted to give instructions at any time as AFIS is not a *'control'* service but an *'information only'* service. When AFIS is provided the callsign suffix *"Information"* is used; for example *"Rochester Information"*.

Air/Ground Radio Station.

There are some aerodromes which provide neither Air Traffic Control (ATC) nor Aerodrome Flight Information Service (AFIS) but which do have an Air/Ground (A/G) radio station through which aircraft and the aerodrome authority can communicate. It should be kept in mind that such facilities are operated by people without ATC qualifications. The callsign suffix *"Radio"* is used to distinguish them, for example *"Nottingham Radio"*.

AIR TRAFFIC SERVICES IN THE 'OPEN FIR'.

The Lower Airspace Radar Service (LARS).

When flying in UK unregulated airspace up to and including FL95 within the limits of radio/radar coverage Pilots are recommended to use the Lower Airspace Radar Service (LARS). LARS is a structured national system whereby nominated civil and military ATSUs provide the Radar Advisory Service (RAS) or the Radar Information Service (RIS), on request, within approximately 30 nm of each unit. If three attempts to establish radio contact with a LARS station are made without success, it may be assumed that the station is not operating.

(a) The Radar Advisory Service (RAS) is available on request from a Pilot. The Radar Controller will use radio communications to provide:
• traffic information; and
• advisory avoiding action necessary to maintain separation from all other aircraft.

VFR Pilots should not accept an instruction that would take them into cloud. The Radar Controller should be told immediately of any instructions (heading or level changes) that are not acceptable to the Pilot, in which case the Pilot becomes responsible for his own avoiding action. Any self-initiated changes in heading or altitude by the Pilot should be immediately advised to the Radar Controller, since it may affect separation from other aircraft.

(b) The Radar Information Service (RIS) is available on request from a Pilot. The Radar Controller will use radio communications to provide:
• traffic information only (no avoiding action will be offered).

This service is useful in good VMC conditions, where the Radar Controller can provide the Pilot with an extra pair of eyes, without repeated avoiding action which may be unnecessary in the good conditions and time-wasting for the flight. The Pilot should advise the Radar Controller if he is changing level, level-band or route.

Both **RAS** and **RIS** are mainly utilised through *LARS* units but are also available from some other ATSUs, on request by the Pilot.

The Flight Information Service (FIS) existed before the advent of the radar services and is still available. The service provides local information on weather, serviceability of radio navaids, aerodrome conditions and other reported traffic.

The Procedural Service is a non-radar ATC service mainly used to separate IFR traffic by time and/or distance using an approach control service, and for aircraft flying along advisory routes.

THE FLIGHT PLAN.

The Flight Plan is an ATC message, compiled by, or on behalf of, the Aircraft Commander (the Pilot-in-Command) to a set CAA format and then transmitted by the appropriate ATS authority to organisations concerned with the flight. It is the basis on which ATC clearance is given for the flight to proceed.

Correct use of the CAA Flight Plan Form (form CA48) is most important – particularly in these days of automatic data processing. Incorrect completion may well result in a delay in processing and consequently a delay to the flight. Full instructions for completion of the Flight Plan Form are contained in an Aeronautical Information Circular (AIC), and in Part 4 of Pooley's *'Pilots Information Guide'*.

Note that a Pilot intending to make a flight must in any case contact ATC (or other authority where there is no ATC) at the aerodrome of departure. This is known as '**Booking Out**' and is a separate and additional requirement to that of filing a Flight Plan.

Also note that where an aerodrome is notified as 'Prior Permission Required' (PPR) the filing of a Flight Plan does **not** constitute prior permission.

Private Pilots may, if they wish, file a Flight Plan for any flight. They are advised to file a Flight Plan if intending to fly **more than 10 nm from the coast or over sparsely populated or mountainous areas**.

All Pilots *must* file a Flight Plan for flights:
- within Controlled Airspace 'notified' as IFR only (i.e. Rule 21 controlled airspace);
- within Controlled Airspace, in Instrument Meteorological Conditions (IMC) or at night, excluding Special VFR (SVFR);
- within Controlled Airspace in Visual Meteorological Conditions (VMC) if the flight is to be conducted under the Instrument Flight Rules (IFR);
- within certain Special Rules Airspace, irrespective of weather conditions;
- within Scottish and London Upper Information Regions (UIRs) – i.e. above FL245 ;
- where the destination is more than 40 km (21·6 nm) from departure and maximum total weight authorised exceeds 5700 kg;
- to or from the UK which will cross a UK Flight Information Region (FIR) boundary;
- during which it is intended to use the Air Traffic Advisory Service on an Advisory Route (ADR).

NOTE: The fact that **night flying** is conducted in accordance with IFR procedures does not, of itself, require that a Flight Plan be filed. Equally, IFR flight in the open FIR, by day or night, does not of itself require a Flight Plan.

Flight Plans must be filed at least 30 minutes before requesting taxi or start-up clearance (60 minutes in certain cases where the controlling authority is London, Manchester or Scottish Control).

If a Pilot who has filed a Flight Plan lands at an aerodrome other than the destination specified, the Air Traffic Service Unit (ATSU) at the specified destination must be told within **30 minutes** of the estimated time of arrival.

METEOROLOGY.

At aerodromes with suitable communication facilities (facsimile, AFTN – Aeronautical Fixed Telecommunications Network – and telex) full flight forecast documentation is available in chart or text form. These are issued by designated *Forecast Offices* throughout the UK – the graphic charts via facsimile networks, and the text messages through AFTN or telex following the *AIRMET* area forecast system.

The weather information will cover flights within the UK and near Continent and consist of:

- Area Forecasts of weather between the surface and 15,000 ft AMSL, with winds and temperatures up to at least 18,000 ft;
- Terminal Aerodrome Forecasts (TAFs) and/or Aerodrome Reports (METARs).

For flights outside the area of coverage of the above area forecast systems *(facsimile* or *AIRMET)*, **Special Forecasts** will be provided by the designated Forecast Offices, as listed in the UK AIP (MET section). Requests for such forecasts should include details of the route, the period of the flight, the height to be flown and the time at which the forecast is to be collected.

At least **4 hours** notice should be given for flights over 500 nm, and at least **2 hours** for shorter flights. At less notice the best possible service will be given in the time available, but it may be only a briefing, without documentation. A UK area forecast relevant to the flight will also have to be obtained.

A recorded AIRMET Service is available via the **Public Telephone Network,** providing Area Forecasts for Pilots flying below 15,000 ft AMSL. Forecasts are given in a standard format to aid copying onto a special form (or *'proforma'*) produced for the purpose. TAFs and METARs for relevant aerodromes may be obtained by telephoning the appropriate Forecast Office and speaking with meteorological personnel (although it is intended to automate this aspect also, at a later date). Details of areas, telephone numbers and procedures are in the MET section of the UK AIP, and in *Pooley's Flight Guide.*

Regular **Volmet** broadcasts of weather reports and tendency at certain aerodromes are made on specific VHF frequencies.

Broadcasts of recorded information for certain aerodromes are made on selected VHF-NAV radio frequencies or on discrete VHF-COM radio frequencies to relieve congestion on Air Traffic Control communication frequencies. This is known as the **Automatic Terminal Information Service** (ATIS). At larger airports the ATIS may be split into arrivals and departures, each broadcast on separate frequencies.

ATIS frequencies, where the service is available, are listed in the COM section of the AIP and in the aerodrome directory of the *Pooley's Flight Guide.*

FACILITATION.

Facilitation is the simplification of formalities in moving aircraft across international boundaries.

Private Aircraft on International Flights.

Aircraft leaving or entering the UK must do so via a Customs Airport unless permission to do otherwise has been obtained from the Commissioners of Customs and Excise.

Before a registered aircraft leaves the country the owner must present to the Customs Officer a Department of Transport licence for the export of the aircraft. This requirement is waived if the aircraft is leaving temporarily provided that the Pilot produces a *Carnet de Passage en Douane* or a *Customs Form C42,* undertaking that the aircraft will return within a month.

If an aircraft has to force land while flying to or from abroad at any place other than a Customs Airport the Pilot must report the landing to the Customs or Police, produce the documents relating to the flight and must not (without consent of a Customs Officer) unload goods or let people leave the vicinity of the aircraft except for emergency reasons.

Documentary requirements for private flights are as for scheduled flights (refer to the FAL Section of the UK AIP for these) except that only one copy of the General Declaration is needed. So long as a private aircraft is not carrying any fare-paying passengers or cargo, however, these documents need not be delivered on arrival or departure provided a Carnet is carried and the appropriate import/export voucher is presented.

No documents need be delivered to the Immigration Officer on arrival/departure if the Pilot presents himself, with any passengers, to that Officer. It should be noted that the PPL is not acceptable for establishing identity, and Private Pilots must carry Passports and Visas.

The Airport Medical Officer may examine the following, and take any necessary measures for protecting public health:
(a) people entering the UK who are suspected of suffering from or of having been exposed to an infectious disease, or suspected of being verminous;
(b) people proposing departure from the UK if there are reasonable grounds for believing them to be suffering from a quarantinable disease.

The Medical Officer may require the production of an International Certificate of Vaccination against Smallpox by people entering the UK from certain areas. People without a Certificate may be offered vaccination and may be put under surveillance or in isolation.

'EUROCONTROL' En Route Navigation Services.

Charges for en route navigation services (i.e. other than those provided in connection with the use of an aerodrome) in the London and Scottish FIRs and UIRs may be levied in respect of private aircraft. Certain flights are exempted, notably those:
- made entirely under VFR;
- starting and finishing at the same aerodrome;
- made by aircraft with a maximum total authorised weight of less than 2000 kg.

☐ **Exercises A5 — Air Traffic Services,** should now be completed.

A6

VISUAL FLIGHT RULES
(Rule 23)

Visual reference to the outside environment both for attitude reference and to navigate the aeroplane is necessary for the visual Pilot, (i.e. the Pilot holding a basic PPL, without either an IMC Rating or an Instrument Rating).

If visual reference is lost – for example, by inadvertently entering cloud, or by flying in conditions of reduced visibility – then the results may be disastrous. To avoid this, certain requirements have been established which involve minimum distances from cloud and a minimum flight visibility. These are known as the Visual Flight Rules (VFR).

The starting point for the Visual Flight Rules is:
- **a minimum flight visibility of 5 nm; and**
- **a distance from cloud of at least 1 nm horizontally and 1000 ft vertically.** Under certain conditions, these requirements are reduced.

1. OUTSIDE 'REGULATED AIRSPACE', i.e. Outside Controlled Airspace and Special Rules Airspace.

(a) **Above 3000 feet AMSL** an aircraft may fly under VFR provided it is able to remain at least:
- 1 nm horizontally and 1000 feet vertically away from cloud; and
- in a flight visibility of at least 5 nm.

(b) An aircraft (other than a helicopter) may fly under VFR **at or below 3000 feet AMSL** at greater than 140 knots Indicated Air Speed provided it:
- remains at least 1 nm horizontally and 1000 ft vertically from cloud; and
- in a flight visibility of at least 3 nm.

(c) An aircraft (other than a helicopter) may fly under VFR **at or below 3000 feet AMSL at 140 knots or less Indicated Air Speed** provided it:
- remains clear of cloud;
- in sight of the surface;
- in a flight visibility of at least 1 nm*.

*NOTE: If the Pilot does not hold an Instrument Rating or IMC Rating the flight visibility limit set in the privileges of the PPL (Aeroplanes) is 1.5 nautical miles without passengers, and 3 nautical miles with.

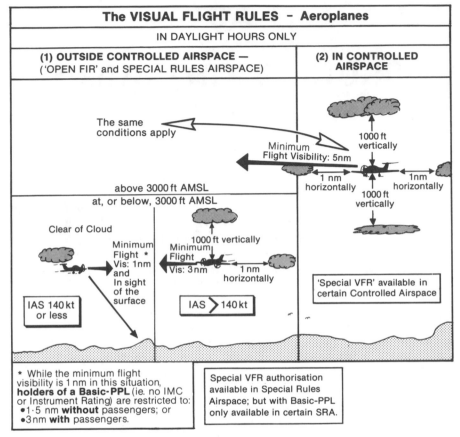

Fig.A6-1. The Main Conditions for VFR Flight in an Aeroplane.

(d) **Helicopters** at or below 3000 feet AMSL must remain either clear of cloud and in sight of the surface or at least 1 nm horizontally and 1000 feet vertically from cloud in a flight visibility of at least 3 nm.

NOTE: Under VFR, **the Pilot is solely responsible for the safety of the flight**, separation from other aircraft, terrain clearance, and remaining at a satisfactory distance from cloud in adequate flight visibility.

2. IN CONTROLLED AIRSPACE.

An aircraft may fly under VFR by day in *Non Rule 21 Controlled Airspace* (i.e. **not** notified exclusively IFR), if it is able to remain:
- at least 1 nm horizontally and 1000 feet vertically away from cloud;
- in a flight visibility of at least 5 nm; and
- in sight of the surface.

In addition, certain *Rule 21 Airspace* can be entered by a basic PPL holder (i.e. no IMC or Instrument Rating) under a Special VFR clearance (see below) or in notified Access Lanes.

3. IN SPECIAL RULES AIRSPACE (i.e. Rule 36 Airspace).

On flights for which a *'Special VFR (SVFR) Clearance'* has been given (see para 4 below) the aircraft must, in addition to complying with the applicable visibility minimum, be flown clear of cloud, within sight of the surface and in accordance with any instructions given by ATC.

Any other flight in Special Rules Airspace must be operated in accordance with the conditions for flight outside Regulated Airspace (i.e. outside Controlled or Special Rules Airspace).

4. SPECIAL VFR (SVFR) FLIGHTS (see also RAC 1-7 of UK AIP).

An SVFR flight is one made under VFR (as outlined below) within a control zone in Instrument Meteorological Conditions (IMC), or at night, or at any time in a notified *'Rule 21 Control Zone'* (IFR at all times), or in certain Special Rules Airspace where provision is made for such flights. In all cases SVFR flights are subject to prior authorisation by the appropriate ATC unit.

'Special VFR' allows the relaxation by ATC, in certain circumstances, of some of the restrictions to facilitate an operation without lowering flight safety to an unacceptable level. SVFR is usually applied by ATC in **Control Zones and Special Rules Airspace**, when weather and traffic conditions permit, to allow Private Pilots access to aerodromes within them. SVFR Flights will not, however, be permitted in Airways, CTAs or the London TMA.

A flight plan is not required for an SVFR Flight, but ATC approval is. A request for a *Special VFR Clearance* may be made in flight, but will not necessarily be granted by ATC.

Authorisation for an **SVFR flight is a concession granted by ATC** only when weather and traffic conditions permit. An SVFR Clearance absolves the Pilot from complying with:
- the full requirements of Instrument Flight Rules (IFR); and
- with the requirement to maintain a height of 1500 feet above the highest fixed object within 2000 feet of the aircraft if the height limitation specified in the ATC clearance makes compliance with this requirement impossible. (It does **not** absolve the Pilot from any other Rule requirements, in particular the *'ability to land clear in the event of engine failure'* requirement of the Low Flying Rule.)

All ATC instructions must be obeyed.

It is entirely the Pilot's responsibility to ensure that flight conditions (i.e. forward visibility and distance from cloud) will enable the aircraft to remain clear of all obstructions. It is implicit in all SVFR clearances, therefore, that the aircraft remains clear of cloud and in sight of the surface. Flight visibility must be at least 5 nm (unless the Pilot holds an IMC Rating, when the minimum flight visibility required is 1.5 nautical miles).

At some aerodromes in control zones there are designated **Access Lanes** in which aircraft may fly in Instrument Meteorological Conditions (IMC) without complying with the full Instrument Flight Rules (IFR) procedures, and in most cases without having to obtain clearance. The procedures for flying in these lanes are given in the UK Aeronautical Information Publication (AIP) and in Pooley's *Pilots Information Guide*.

COMBINED SPECIAL RULES AIRSPACE AND CONTROLLED AIRSPACE.

Special Rules airspace (Rule 36) has been established around a number of aerodromes that are busy with airline traffic, but do not yet justify the establishment of Controlled airspace. Special Rules Airspace allows a mix of traffic, both Visual Flight Rules (VFR) and Instrument Flight Rules (IFR). The Visual Meteorological Conditions minima that apply to VFR operations in Special Rules Airspace are those labelled (1) in the diagram. These minima are not very restrictive. In certain situations (for instance, in Special Rules Airspace at or below 3000 ft AMSL at a speed of less than 140 kt), a VFR Pilot only requires a flight visibility of 1 nm, and to be clear of cloud and in sight of the surface. In busy airspace, such marginal conditions do not allow for good *'see and be seen'* protection where some Pilots are flying visually and others are on instruments.

At some of the busier Special Rules aerodromes (e.g. Stansted, Luton, Birmingham, and the like), these marginal weather conditions are considered inadequate to provide sufficient protection for air transport movements. In such airspace, the CAA has increased the VMC minima for VFR Pilots to those labelled (2) in the diagram, and which apply in Controlled airspace.

The required VMC minima for VFR Pilots in this *'combined Special Rules and Controlled Airspace'* are the same as in Controlled airspace:
- flight visibility increased to 5 nm; and
- the aeroplane must remain at least 1 nm horizontally and 1000 ft vertically from cloud.

If conditions are worse than these, then the aeroplane must operate under the Instrument Flight Rules (IFR) or Special VFR (SVFR).

If conditions are better than these, then the aircraft can fly in the airspace under VFR, provided that ATC permission has been obtained from the appropriate Air Traffic Service Unit on the notified frequency prior to entering the airspace, and radio communication is maintained as required in Special Rules airspace.

NOTES ON THE VISUAL FLIGHT RULES.

In interpreting the Visual Flight Rules it is essential to remember that a Pilot must at all times fly within the privileges of the licence which is held. In particular, Private Pilots should refer to the distance from cloud and visibility requirements at the beginning of this chapter.

In the interest of safety, Pilots are **advised** to select cruising levels in accordance with the Quadrantal or Semi-Circular Rule as applicable, even when under VFR. However, it is perfectly acceptable, especially when manoeuvring, to fly on the Regional QNH pressure setting above 3000 ft when under VFR.

There is **no VFR flight at night**, or in **notified airspace**, (i.e. notified under Rule 21 as being restricted to Instrument Flight Rules traffic only). **'Night'** is defined in the Air Navigation Order as meaning the time between 30 minutes after sunset and 30 minutes before sunrise, as measured at surface level.

☐ Now complete **Exercises A6 — Visual Flight Rules.**

A7

INSTRUMENT FLIGHT RULES
(Rules 24 - 28)

Flight under the Visual Flight Rules is very restrictive if, for instance, a regular air service is to be achieved. For this reason, Flight and Navigation Instruments have been developed that allow a properly trained Pilot to operate in cloud and other conditions not suitable for visual flight. The rules that apply to this category of flight are known as the **Instrument Flight Rules** (IFR).

THE MINIMUM HEIGHT RULE (Rule 25).

Subject to the usual low flying requirements (Rule 5), an aircraft operated according to the Instrument Flight Rules, both inside and outside controlled airspace, must not fly at less than 1000 feet above the highest obstacle within 5 nm except:

(a) on a route notified for the purposes of this Rule or otherwise authorised by the competent authority, (this may include controlled airspace such as certain Terminal Control Areas and Airways with particular high obstacles such as a radio mast underlying them and giving less than 1000 ft clearance from the base of the controlled airspace);

(b) as necessary for take-off or landing;

(c) when flying at 3000 feet AMSL or below, clear of cloud and in sight of the surface.

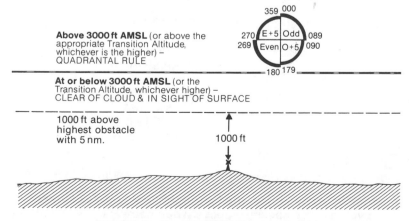

Fig. A7-1. General IFR Requirements.

IFR FLIGHTS CRUISE AT QUADRANTAL LEVELS (Rule 26).

In level flight above 3000 ft AMSL (or above the appropriate Transition Altitude, whichever is the higher), Pilots must select cruising levels according to the Quadrantal Rule (or Semi-Circular Rule above FL245). Flight Levels are based on the standard altimeter setting **1013·2** mb(hPa).

The Quadrantal and Semi-Circular Rules require an aircraft to be flown at a cruising level appropriate to its **magnetic track** as shown below.

IFR FLIGHTS AT LEVELS BELOW 24500 FEET

Magnetic Track	Cruising Level
000 – 089 degrees	Odd thousands of feet
090 – 179 degrees	Odd thousands of feet + 500 feet
180 – 269 degrees	Even thousands of feet
270 – 359 degrees	Even thousands of feet + 500 feet

IFR FLIGHTS AT LEVELS ABOVE 24500 FEET

Magnetic Track	Cruising Level
000 – 179 degrees	25000 feet (lowest usable) 27000 feet 29000 feet and higher levels at intervals of 4000 ft
180 – 359 degrees	26000 feet (lowest usable) 28000 feet 31000 feet and higher levels at intervals of 4000 ft

Figs.A7-2 & 3. IFR Cruising Levels Below & Above 24500 ft.

An aeroplane operating under the Instrument Flight Rules may cruise at a different level to those specified above when complying with instructions given by an ATC unit or with notified holding procedures.

FLIGHT PLAN and ATC CLEARANCE (Rule 27).

(a) In order to comply with the IFR, before any flight within controlled airspace the aircraft commander must file a flight plan (irrespective of whether IMC or VMC exist) and obtain an ATC clearance based upon it. The flight must be made in accordance with the clearance and with the notified holding and approach procedures at destination unless otherwise instructed by ATC.

(b) Except when in Rule 21 Airspace (i.e. controlled airspace that is *'notified'* in the sense that Rules 27 and 28 – Flight Plan, ATC Clearance and Position Reports – apply at all times in both Instrument Meteorological Conditions and Visual Meteorological Conditions), a Pilot flying IFR in Controlled Airspace may cancel IFR (and therefore switch to VFR) provided that:
  • he can maintain VMC whilst in controlled airspace; and
  • he informs ATC accordingly, asking them to cancel IFR.

(c) ATC must be told as soon as possible if, to avoid immediate danger, any departure has to be made from the requirements of this Rule.

(d) Except when the Flight Plan has been cancelled an aircraft commander must inform ATC when the aircraft lands within or leaves controlled airspace.

POSITION REPORTS (Rule 28).

An aircraft under IFR which flies in or intends to enter controlled airspace must report its time, position and level at such reporting points or at such intervals of time as may be notified or directed by ATC.

A typical position report is:

(Aircraft Identification)	*Golf Alfa Echo Sierra Echo*
(Position and Time)	*Wicken Four Seven*
(Level)	*Flight Level Three Three Zero*
(Next Position and Estimate)	*Marlow Five Seven*

APPLICABILITY (Rule 24).

(a) Rules 25 and 26 apply outside controlled airspace.

(b) Rules 25, 27 and 28 apply within controlled airspace.

☐ **Exercises A7 — Instrument Flight Rules.**

A8

DISTRESS, URGENCY, SAFETY AND WARNING SIGNALS
(Rules 49-50)

DISTRESS SIGNALS.

If a Pilot feels that the aeroplane is in grave and imminent danger and wants immediate help then the following signals, either together or separately, before a message will alert others to the fact.

Radio Telephony (RTF): on the frequency in use or on the emergency service frequency 121·5 MHz – *"MAYDAY MAYDAY MAYDAY"* followed by the message.

> MAYDAY MAYDAY MAYDAY
> GOLF – ALFA BRAVO CHARLIE DELTA
> ENGINE HAS FAILED
> MAKING A FORCED LANDING
> FIVE MILES NORTH OF THE FIELD
> THREE THOUSAND FEET AND DESCENDING
> HEADING TWO EIGHT ZERO
> STUDENT PILOT*

Visual Signalling can be made with lights, pyrotechnics or flares to indicate *distress:*
- *S-O-S* in morse code: *dit-dit-dit   dah-dah-dah   dit-dit-dit;*
- a succession of pyrotechnic single reds fired at short intervals; or
- a red parachute flare.

Sound Signalling (other than Radio Telephony) can be used to indicate *distress:*
- *S-O-S* in morse code: *dit-dit-dit   dah-dah-dah   dit-dit-dit;*
- a continuous sound, with any apparatus.

---

* NOTE: Although not an international (ICAO) requirement, inclusion of *Pilot Qualification* in an emergency message enables the controller to plan a course of action best suited to the Pilot's ability.

Also, inexperienced Civil Pilots are invited to use the term *"TYRO"* when transmitting an emergency message on a military frequency to indicate to the controller lack of experience. This will ensure that instructions are not issued which the Pilot may have difficulty following.

URGENCY AND SAFETY SIGNALS.

The following signals, either together or separately before a message, mean that an aircraft is in difficulties which compel it to land, but the Pilot considers that he does not need immediate assistance:
- a succession of white pyrotechnics;
- repeated switching *ON* and *OFF* of landing lights;
- repeated switching *ON* and *OFF* of navigation lights (in a manner distinguishable from normal flashing navigation lights).

The following, either together or separately, mean that the aircraft has an **urgent** message to transmit concerning the safety of a ship, aircraft, vehicle or other property, or of a person on board or within sight of the aircraft from which the signal is given:
- Radio Telephony (RTF): on the frequency in use or on the emergency service frequency 121.5 MHz, *"PAN PAN – PAN PAN – PAN PAN"*.

  PAN PAN – PAN PAN – PAN PAN
  CRANFIELD APPROACH
  GOLF BRAVO CHARLIE DELTA ECHO
  AN AIRCRAFT HAS FORCE-LANDED IN A FIELD TWO MILES
  SOUTH OF OLNEY
  OCCUPANTS APPEAR TO BE SAFE AND HAVE EVACUATED
  THE AIRCRAFT

- **Visual Signalling**: *X-X-X* in morse code:
  "dah-dit-dit-dah   dah-dit-dit-dah   dah-dit-dit-dah".
- **Sound Signalling** (other than by Radio): *X-X-X* in morse code:
  "dah-dit-dit-dah   dah-dit-dit-dah   dah-dit-dit-dah".

WARNING SIGNALS.

In the UK, by day or by night, **a series of projectiles** fired from the ground at intervals of 10 seconds, each showing, on bursting, **red and green lights or stars** indicates to a Pilot that his aircraft is in, or is about to enter, an active Danger Area, Restricted Area or Prohibited Area and that immediate action is to be taken:
- to leave the area by the shortest route and without changing level; or
- to change course to avoid it.

☐ Now complete **Exercises A8 — Distress, Urgency, Safety and Warning Signals**.

A9

SEARCH AND RESCUE (SAR)

Search and Rescue in the event of a mishap is controlled by a Rescue Co-ordination Centre (RCC), who will act upon reports received from any source. A joint Civil/Military response may result.

A continuous listening watch is held on the aeronautical **Emergency VHF Frequency 121·5 MegaHertz** so, if a Pilot is unable to transmit a MAYDAY (Emergency), PAN PAN (Urgency) or 'Lost' call on the frequency that he is already using, then a call on 121·5 MHz should be made.

Aircraft desirous of a constant SAR watch can **file a Flight Plan** with Air Traffic Control and this is advised if:
- flying more than 10 nm from the coast;
- flying over remote or hazardous areas *('remote areas'* including Northern Scotland and almost all of the west coast down to Cornwall);
- flying an aircraft not fitted with a suitable radio.

If an aircraft is expected at an aerodrome, the Pilot must inform the Air Traffic Control Unit or other Authority at that aerodrome as quickly as possible of either:
- any change in intended destination; and/or
- any estimated delay in arrival of 45 minutes or more.

This is Rule 20(1), and its intent applies to delays prior to departure caused by technical problems, weather deterioration, late passengers, etc., say for a flight for which a flight plan has already been submitted.

If a Pilot decides en route **not** to land at the planned destination, but at another airfield, then he must inform ATC at the original destination (or request that they be informed) prior to his **'planned ETA plus 30 minutes'** at that field, otherwise SAR action will commence.

SEARCH AND RESCUE SIGNALS.

If an aeroplane makes a forced landing, then survivors should, if thought necessary, make a call on the radio if it is still functioning or use some or all of the following methods of attracting attention when search aircraft or surface craft are seen or heard.

(a) Fire off distress flares or cartridges.

(b) Use some object with a bright flat surface as a heliograph to flash sunlight at the searching craft.

(c) Flash a light.

(d) Fly anything in the form of a flag and, if possible, make the international distress signal by flying a ball, or something resembling a ball, above or below it.

(e) Blow whistles.

(f) Deploy fluorescent markers to leave a trail in the sea.

(g) Lay out the following ground-air visual signals (as appropriate), forming the symbols as large as possible (at least two or three metres long) with materials which contrast with the background:

   (i) Need assistance: V

   (ii) Need medical help: X

   (iii) Proceeding in this direction: →

   (iv) Yes: Y

   (v) No: N

□ **Exercises A9 — Search And Rescue (SAR).**

A10

ACCIDENT INVESTIGATION REGULATIONS

An accident must be notified if, between the time when anyone boards an aircraft with the intention of flight, and such time as all have left it:

- **anyone is killed or seriously injured** while in or on the aircraft, or by direct contact with any part of the aircraft (including any part which has become detached from it) or by direct exposure to jet blast, except when the death or serious injury is from natural causes, is self-inflicted or is inflicted by other persons or is suffered by a stowaway hiding outside the areas normally available in flight to the passengers and crew; or
- the aircraft incurs damage or structural failure, other than:
  - engine failure or damage, when the damage is limited to the engine, its cowling or accessories;
  - damage limited to propellers, wing tips, antennae, tyres, brakes, fairings, small dents or punctured holes in the aircraft skin; which adversely affects its structural strength, performance or flight characteristics and which would normally require major repair or replacement of the affected component; or
- the aircraft is missing or is completely inaccessible.

When a notifiable accident occurs the **Aircraft Commander** (or, if he is killed or incapacitated, the Operator) must notify:

- the **Department of Transport Accident Investigation Branch** by the quickest available means; and
- where the accident occurs in or over the UK the **local police authority**.

For further reading on this subject you are directed to Aeronautical Information Circulars 66/1984 (Pink 63) and 21/1984 (Pink 53), and Pooley's *Pilots Information Guide*.

☐ Complete **Exercises A10 — Accident Investigation Regulations.**

A11

AVIATION DOCUMENTS

ICAO — THE INTERNATIONAL CIVIL AVIATION ORGANISATION.

In a fine example of international ço-operation, the *International Civil Aviation Organisation (ICAO)* was formed with headquarters in Montreal, Canada to collaborate in the standardisation of aviation rules and procedures wherever possible. The United Kingdom, along with most other nations of the world, is an active member of ICAO.

Standardisation has occurred to a remarkable degree since the signing of the *'Chicago Convention'* in 1944 although, as is always the case in international affairs, some *differences* still remain. For example, cruising levels in Western nations are based on **feet**, whereas in Eastern Europe and the U.S.S.R. they are based on **metres**; many countries are currently introducing the 'hectoPascal' as the unit for pressure on ICAO recommendation, whereas the UK has decided to retain the 'millibar' for the forseeable future. These *differences* however do not detract from the fact that the basic rules and procedures are very similar throughout the world.

AVIATION LAW IN THE UNITED KINGDOM.

Aviation Law in the United Kingdom is enacted by Parliament and published in statutory documents – the main one for the Private Pilot being the **Air Navigation Order**. Another is the **Air Navigation (General) Regulations**.

The authority responsible for Civil Aviation in the United Kingdom is the **Civil Aviation Authority** (CAA), often referred to in the documents as *'the Authority'*. One of its main functions is to provide an **Aeronautical Information Service** (AIS) to collect and disseminate the information necessary for safe and efficient air navigation. It does this through three documentation channels:

1. The United Kingdom **Aeronautical Information Publication** (UK AIP) which contains essential information or instructions of a lasting character. The UK AIP is published in three volumes with a regular amendment service and contains information under the following headings:
(a) AGA – Aerodromes and Ground Aids;
(b) COM – Radio Communication and Navigation Facilities;
(c) MET – Meteorological Services;
(d) RAC – Rules of the Air and Air Traffic Services;
(e) FAL – Facilitation (Customs/Immigration, Airport Formalities & Public Health);
(f) SAR – Search and Rescue;
(g) MAP – relevant Maps and Charts;
(h) GEN – general items.

2. **NOTAMs**, which are NOTices to AirMen, containing information on any aeronautical facility, service, procedure or hazard, timely knowledge of which is required by people concerned with flight operations and which may be given either:
(a) a **NOTAM Class I** distribution by teleprinter for urgent matters; or
(b) a **NOTAM Class II** distribution through the post for less urgent matters.

3. **Aeronautical Information Circulars** (AICs). These are published monthly and concern administrative matters and advance warnings of operational changes, and draw attention to and advise on matters of operational importance, e.g. the availability of aeronautical charts, corrections to these charts and amendments to the Chart of UK Airspace Restrictions.

- AICs directly associated with **Air Safety** are printed on **pink paper**;
- Administrative AICs are on white paper;
- Operational and Air Traffic Services AICs are on yellow paper;
- UK Restrictions Charts AICs are on mauve paper; and
- Maps/Charts AICs are on green paper.

Note that the Aviation Law examination may refer to the contents of a specific AIC. You should read the more important pink AICs which will certainly be available in a folder at your Flying Training Organisation. These include:
- AIC 37/1987: Low Altitude Windshear;
- AIC 36/1987: The Effect of Thunderstorms and Associated Turbulence on Aircraft Operations;
- AIC 14/1987: Aeronautical Charts for Civil Aviation;
- AIC 89/1982: Frost, Ice and Snow on Aircraft;
- AIC 52/1985: Take-off, Climb and Landing Performance of Light Aeroplanes;
- AIC 90/1986: Wake Turbulence;
- AIC 77/1984: The Effect of Drugs and Alcohol.

Explanatory Publications.
Since all the documents detailed above must cover the full range of aviation activity, their contents in total are quite daunting for a Private Pilot. To present vital matters in a simpler form, the CAA has available subsidiary Civil Aviation Publications (CAP) including:
- CAP 53 on Private Pilot licensing and associated Ratings;
- CAP 85, a guide to Aviation Law; and
- CAP 413 on Radio Telephony (RTF) procedures.

There are also some non-CAA documents that are particularly valuable in clarifying matters of aviation law and operational practices, such as Pooley's *Pilots Information Guide (PIG)*, available at Flying Schools throughout the UK.

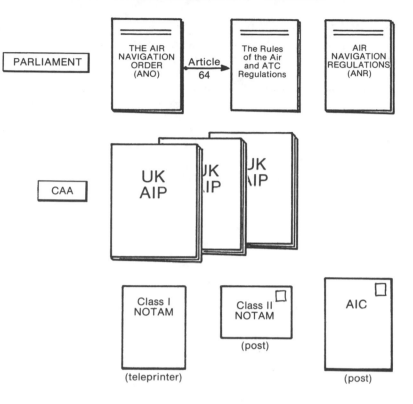

Fig.A11-1. The Regulatory Documents.

THE AIR NAVIGATION ORDER

The Air Navigation Order (also referred to as the *'Order'* or as the *'ANO')* is a *'Statutory Instrument'* that was enacted by Parliament to form the basis of civil aviation in the UK.

'PARTS' AND 'ARTICLES' IN THE ANO.

The Air Navigation Order is arranged in '**Parts**', each relating to an item of major importance, e.g. Part (viii) – Control of Air Traffic.

The *Parts* of the ANO each contain a number of '**Articles**' and these are numbered consecutively from the start of the ANO, dealing with particular subjects within the broader scope of the Part. For example, Part (viii) commences with **Article 64, Rules of the Air and Air Traffic Control**.

Although the Rules themselves are listed in a separate 'Statutory Instrument' with this name ('The Rules of the Air and Air Traffic Control Regulations'), their basis is Article 64 of the ANO.

'APPENDICES' IN THE ANO.

Further detail in the ANO is given in a series of Appendices to the Order, known as **'Schedules'**, e.g. Schedule 5, Aircraft Equipment. An Operator would refer to this to determine the minimum equipment necessary when fitting his aeroplane out for a particular task.

People concerned with planning and developing flight operations will constantly refer to the ANO, e.g. to determine requirements in such matters as equipment, licensing of crew members, documents and records, registration of aircraft and their operation. The Private Pilot, however, will probably find that only occasional reference to specific Articles in the ANO is sufficient, although some knowledge of the contents is required.

GENERAL.

Penalties (Article 90).

Pilots who contravene the Air Navigation Order (ANO) or Regulations made under the Order are held liable, and this Article defines the extent of liability and the maximum penalties which may be imposed if convicted of such contraventions.

Interpretation (Article 96).

This article gives the legal definitions for the terms used in the ANO, many of which concern the Private Pilot and some of which are commonly misconstrued. It also acts as a glossary to the ANO.

☐ **Exercises A11 — Aviation Documents.**

A12

REGISTRATION AND AIRWORTHINESS

REGISTRATION AND THE MARKING OF AIRCRAFT.

The Registration of Aircraft (Articles 3 and 4; Schedule 1).
To all intents and purposes, the Private Pilot must not fly in the UK unless
the aircraft is registered, either in the UK or elsewhere, and displays the
appropriate registration markings.

United Kingdom		
Civil Aviation Authority		

Certificate of Registration of Aircraft

*Certificate Number*_____

1 Nationality or Common Mark and Registration Mark	2 Manufacturer and Manufacturer's Designation of Aircraft	3 Aircraft Constructor's Serial Number

4 Name of Registered Owner or Charterer

5 Address of Registered Owner or Charterer

Fig.A12-1. A Certificate of Registration.

Fig.A12-2. Registration Markings.

In applying for registration, the aeroplane must be properly described
according to the **'General Classification of Aircraft'** specified in Schedule
1 of the Air Navigation Order (ANO).

75

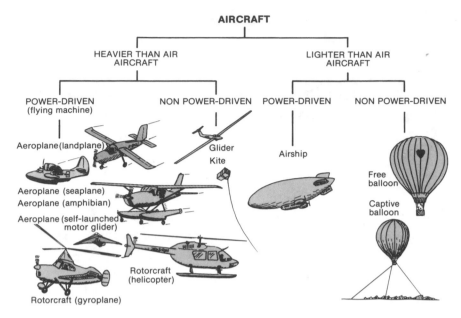

Fig.A12-3. The General Classification of Aircraft.

It is the responsibilty of Owners (and Part-owners) to inform the CAA in writing of any change in the particulars shown on the original application for registration of an aircraft, e.g. change of ownership or part-ownership, its destruction or permanent withdrawal from use.

Gliders and hang-gliders need not be registered. In some circumstances, a powered-aeroplane need not be registered, e.g. experimental or test aeroplanes, and aeroplanes undergoing certification-testing, or carrying out a demonstration flight.

If a Pilot does fly an unregistered aircraft, he is accountable for any other offences against the ANO made during the flight, just as if the aircraft were registered.

AIRWORTHINESS AND EQUIPMENT.

The Airworthiness of Aircraft (Articles 7-11, Schedule 2).

A Certificate of Airworthiness (CofA) is issued by the CAA in respect of each aeroplane determined to be airworthy, following consideration of design, construction, workmanship, materials, essential equipment and the results of flying trials and other tests. **In the UK a CofA usually lasts for 3 years** and will have a validity period specified on it. Certification, especially of a new aeroplane type, is a very important process and a major function of the CAA.

A **Flight Manual** will form part of the CofA and will specify requirements, procedures and limitations with respect to the operation of the aeroplane. In the case of foreign-manufactured aircraft, the CAA may attach a supplement to the original Flight Manual, which amends the manner in which the aeroplane should be operated.

United Kingdom Civil Aviation Authority

CERTIFICATE OF AIRWORTHINESS

No. _____

Nationality and Registration Marks	Constructor and Constructor's Designation of Aircraft	Aircraft Serial No. (Constructor's No.)
G-KILT	Grumman American Aviation Corporation AA-5A	AA5A-0763
CATEGORY	Transport Category (Passenger)	

This Certificate of Airworthiness is issued pursuant to the Convention on International Civil Aviation dated 7 December 1944, and to the Civil Aviation Act, 1949, and the Orders and Regulations made thereunder, in respect of the above-mentioned aircraft which is considered to be airworthy when maintained and operated in accordance with the foregoing and the pertinent operating limitations. A Flight Manual forms part of this Certificate.

This certificate is valid for the period(s) shown below		Official Stamp and Date
From	to	
From 1st October 1984	to 30th September 1987	C.A.A.
From	to	
From	to	
From	to	
From	to	
From	to	

FLIGHT MANUAL

G—KILT

Fig.A12-4.
The Flight Manual.

Fig.A12-5.
A CofA.

In general, a Private Pilot may only fly within the UK in an aeroplane that has **a current CofA** valid under the law of the country in which it is registered and then only **according to the conditions specified**, e.g. to tow a glider legally, the CofA must be so endorsed (Article 39). The CofA will specify the **categories** (Transport, Aerial Work, Private, or Special) in which the aeroplane may be operated (ANO Article 8, Schedule 3).

In some circumstances, an aeroplane that does not have a current CofA may be issued with a 'Permit to Fly' by the CAA, subject to certain conditions. (See "A and B Conditions" in ANO Schedule 2.) This could apply to an aeroplane undergoing tests.

MAINTENANCE (Articles 9, 10, 11).

If an aircraft has a CofA in either the *transport* or *aerial work* categories, then the aircraft and its equipment must be maintained to a schedule approved by the CAA and it must have a valid **Certificate of Maintenance Review**.

A **Technical Log** must also be kept for such aircraft to record aircraft flight times, unserviceable items, maintenance carried out, etc.

NOTE: Flying Training is classified as aerial work and hired aeroplanes fall into the transport category, so this requirement applies to aeroplanes that a Private Pilot is likely to fly.

An aircraft must have, in addition to a CofA, a **Certificate of Release to Service** if it (or any part of it or such of its equipment as is necessary for its airworthiness) has been overhauled, repaired, replaced, modified or otherwise maintained. Only certain persons are allowed by the ANO to issue such a certificate, although the ANRs specify minor repairs or replacements which may be made by a Pilot, such as changing tyres, completing an oil change, changing spark splugs and setting their gaps, etc.

Provision is also made for the Pilot of an aeroplane that is **away from base** to confirm that a minor adjustment to a control has been satisfactorily performed and to sign the second part of a Duplicate Inspection Certificate.

Engine and Propeller Logbooks (Article 15 and Schedule 7). In addition to the previously mentioned documents, the Operator is required to keep:
(a) an Aircraft Logbook;
(b) an Engine Logbook;
(c) a Variable Pitch Propeller Logbook (if applicable).

All logbooks have to be preserved for two (2) years after the particular aircraft, engine or propeller has been destroyed or permanently withdrawn from use.

WEIGHT AND BALANCE (Article 16).

An important part of the Certificate of Airworthiness is the **Aircraft Weight Schedule**, which approves certain weight limitations and specifies the allowable range for the position of the Centre of Gravity (CG).

ANO Article 16 requires that an aeroplane must be weighed at its Basic Weight (or other approved weight) and have the position of its Centre of Gravity determined at that weight. A Weight Schedule must then be prepared by the operator. Following the next occasion the aircraft is officially weighed for the purposes of this Article and a new Weight Schedule prepared, **the earlier Weight Schedule should be preserved for a period of 6 months** even though it has expired.

FLY WITHIN THE CERTIFICATE OF AIRWORTHINESS SPECIFICATIONS.

Operating the aircraft outside the conditions specified in the CofA (which includes the Flight Manual) may seriously degrade the safety of the flight and renders the CofA invalid, e.g. flying a non-permitted operation or manoeuvre or exceeding Weight and Balance limitations. **This has very serious legal implications**, making the Pilot liable to a fine or imprisonment, rendering the insurance policies invalid and invalidating any warranties or guarantees on the aircraft and its equipment.

A Pilot should always operate an aeroplane within the specifications of its CofA.

Equipment of Aircraft (Articles 13 and 14, Schedules 5 and 6).

Many aircraft are lavishly equipped, but there is a certain minimum standard specified in the ANO below which an aeroplane should not be flown (general aircraft equipment being detailed in ANO Schedule 5, and radio communication and radio navigation equipment being detailed in Schedule 6).

Pilots must be familiar with the minimum equipment requirements for their particular operation, e.g. when carrying out aerobatic manoeuvres, a suitable safety harness or safety belt must be fitted; when night flying in helicopters, parachute flares must be carried; an unserviceable Attitude Indicator (Artificial Horizon) may not render the aeroplane unserviceable, whereas an unserviceable Clock may do so.

☐ **Exercises A12 – Registration and Airworthiness.**

A13

OPERATION
OF AIRCRAFT

The Air Navigation Order contains certain instructions and information regarding the operation of aeroplanes, some of which are considered below.

PRE-FLIGHT ACTIONS.

Pre-flight Actions of the Pilot-in-Command (Article 32).

The Pilot-in-Command must satisfy himself before each flight:

- that the flight can be made safely, taking into account the latest information available as to route and aerodromes to be used, weather reports and forecasts available, and options open if the flight cannot be completed as planned;
- that equipment (including radio) required by regulation is carried and working and that appropriate maps and charts and navigational equipment is carried;
- that the aircraft is fit for the flight and has a valid Certificate of Maintenance Review where required;
- that any load is safe in terms of weight, distribution and security;
- that enough fuel, oil, coolant and ballast (if appropriate) is carried, including a margin for safety;
- that, with regard to its performance, the aircraft is capable of safely taking-off, reaching and maintaining a safe height and making a safe landing at the intended destination.

  (In very approximate terms, a 10% increase in weight will increase Take-Off Distance Required by 20%, a tailwind component of 10% of the take-off speed – usually about 5 knots – will increase Take-Off Distance required by 20%, a 10°C rise in temperature or 1000 ft rise in elevation will increase Take-Off Distance Required by about 10%. Precise consideration, of course, requires reference to the Take-Off and Landing Charts or Tables);
- that all required pre-flight checks have been carried out.

AIR TRAFFIC.

Authority of the Commander of Aircraft (Article 51).

Everyone on board must obey all lawful commands which the Aircraft Commander gives for the purpose of the safety of the aircraft and of people or property carried, or for the safety, efficiency or regularity of air navigation.

Crew Composition (Article 18).

An aircraft must not fly unless the crew composition meets the legal requirements of the country of registration. (UK requirements are stated in ANO Article 18).

Pilots to Remain at Controls (Article 33).

The commander of a flying machine or glider is responsible for ensuring that:
- one pilot is at the controls at all times in flight;
- both pilots are at the controls during take-off and landing if the aircraft is required to carry two pilots under the Order;
- each pilot at the controls wears a safety belt or a safety harness. Note that a harness must be worn during take-off and landing when one is required to be provided by Article 13.

Method of Carriage of Persons (Article 45).

No one must be in or on any part of an aircraft in flight not designed for the accommodation of people, nor be in or on any object (other than a glider or flying machine) towed or attached to an aircraft in flight, except for temporary access to any part of an aircraft:
- for the purpose of taking action necessary for the safety of the aircraft or of any person, animal or goods on board;
- in which cargo or stores are carried and which is designed to enable a person to have access during flight.

Smoking in Aircraft (Article 50).

Notices indicating when smoking is prohibited in any part of an aircraft must be exhibited so as to be visible from each passenger seat and obeyed.

It is good airmanship to observe *'no smoking'* during take-off, landing and low flying especially, however smoking is not specifically prohibited at any time except when the *'no smoking'* sign is displayed. The Pilot has the authority to ban smoking at all times if he so desires, bearing in mind that cigarette smoke in the cockpit may impair performance and cause distress to certain persons.

Drunkenness in Aircraft (Article 49).

A person shall not enter an aircraft when drunk, or be drunk on any aircraft. A person must not, when acting as a crew member or being carried for the purpose of so acting, be under the influence of drink or a drug to such an extent as to impair his capacity so to act. Although no exact times are specified in the ANO, it is reasonable for a Pilot to not fly until at least 8 hours after any alcohol has been imbibed and, if excessive amounts have been consumed, for this time to be considerably extended.

Imperilling the Safety of Aircraft, Persons or Property (Articles 47 and 48).

A person must not, recklessly or negligently, either act in a manner likely to endanger an aircraft or anyone in it, or cause or permit an aircraft to endanger anyone or any property, e.g. a person deliberately damaging an aeroplane or a Pilot flying excessively low, carrying inadequate fuel, etc., would be in contravention of this Article.

Operation of Radio in Aircraft (Article 35).

Anyone operating an aircraft's radio equipment must hold an appropriate radiotelephony (RTF) licence – (covered in more detail in the next chapter). The radio equipment itself must be licensed and operated only in accordance with the conditions of that licence.

Flight Recording Systems (Article 37 and Schedule 5).

Although this article will not usually apply to a Private Pilot, aeroplanes over 5700 kg and helicopters over 2700 kg Maximum Take-Off Weight Authorised are required, in certain circumstances, to carry and operate flight recording systems, and to preserve the records from them for a specified time.

Carriage of Weapons and Munitions of War (Article 43).

No weapon may be carried on board an aircraft unless:
* the consent of the Operator is obtained;
* the weapon is unloaded in the case of a firearm; and
* the weapon is carried in a part of the aircraft not accessible to passengers.

Munitions of war (including weapons, ammunition, explosives or noxious substances) shall not be carried without the written permission of the CAA and then only in accordance with any conditions relating thereto.

Carriage of Dangerous Goods (Article 44).

The Secretary of State can classify certain articles and substances as dangerous goods. As a Pilot, you should be aware that goods which may be fairly innocuous at ground level and/or in the open air, may be very dangerous in flight where atmospheric pressure is reduced and persons are restricted to the confined space of the aircraft cabin.

Many dangerous goods are not permitted in aircraft and those permitted to be carried by air are subject to special conditions of handling, loading, packing, labelling and documentation. Classification lists and conditions are published in the form of regulations made from time to time by the Secretary of State.

As a commonsense practice, Private Pilots should make a habit of checking the things being carried by those in their aircraft for obviously dangerous items, e.g. certain types of matches and lighters, any compressed gases, corrosives or flammable substances. As a general rule, *if in doubt, leave it out!*

Towing Gliders (Article 38).

An aircraft in flight may not tow a glider unless its Certificate of Airworthiness includes an express provision that it may. The Article also specifies safety requirements with regard to signals, take-off techniques, and length and condition of tow-ropes.

Towing, Picking Up and Raising of Persons and Articles (Article 39).

An aircraft in flight may not tow, pick up or raise anything unless expressly permitted by its Certificate of Airworthiness. The Article also contains specific requirements concerning the several types of activity which fall under the its heading, e.g. banner-towing and loads slung from helicopters.

Dropping of Articles and Animals (Articles 40, 41 and 42).

Articles and animals whether or not attached to a parachute must not be dropped, projected or lowered so as to endanger people or property and should not be dropped, projected or lowered in other circumstances without **written CAA approval,** except for certain articles in certain situations, e.g. dropping a life raft to save lives, or jettisoning of items to lighten the load in an emergency.

Pilots involved in crop-spraying operations are directed to Article 42 and the requirement to obtain an *'Aerial Application Certificate'*. Also, if the Certificate of Airworthiness for a helicopter expressly allows it, then the lowering of any person, animal or article to the surface is permitted.

Dropping of Persons (Article 41) – (Parachuting).

Except for escaping in an emergency, no one must drop to the surface or jump from an aircraft in flight without the **written permission of the CAA** and then only in such a manner as not to endanger people or property. In the case of parachuting, the Certificate of Airworthiness of the aircraft must include a provision that it may be so used and the aircraft must be operated in accordance with the Parachuting Manual which the holder of a *'CAA Permission to Drop'* has to maintain.

Rules of the Air (Article 64).

This Article is the legal basis for the large subject *'Rules of the Air and Air Traffic Control Regulations'*. These are *'The Rules'* referred to throughout this section on Aviation Law, mainly in the the first chapter. Article 64 of the ANO also lists when the Rules of the Air may be departed from, and to what extent.

Inadvertent Infringement of a Restricted or Prohibited Area (Article 69).

If any aircraft inadvertently enters an area notified as Restricted or Prohibited or as a Danger Area the Pilot-in-Command must, unless otherwise instructed by radio or by one of the prescribed visual signals by Air Traffic Control (ATC) or the airspace authority, **leave the area as quickly as possible, not descend whilst over the area and land at the nearest suitable aerodrome.**

Consideration should be given at this time to making a distress call by radio or one of the prescribed visual signals (e.g. flashing of landing lights).

A series of projectiles fired from the ground at intervals of 10 seconds, each showing red and green lights or stars on bursting, is an indication that the aeroplane is in or is about to enter an active Danger Area or a Prohibited or Restricted Area and that action is to be taken to leave the area or to change course to avoid it.

Prohibited and Restricted Areas are shown on aeronautical charts. Refer to the legend of the chart in use to ascertain how they are depicted and described.

Balloons, Kites and Airships (Article 70).

There are specific limitations for the flying of captive balloons and kites with regard to the method of mooring, location and height.

A captive balloon or kite shall not be flown:
- at a height of more than 60 metres AGL (Above Ground Level);
- within 60 metres of any vessel, vehicle or structure;
- within 5 km of an aerodrome.

A balloon, either captive or free, exceeding 2 metres in any linear dimension (including any basket, etc.) must not be flown in controlled airspace.

An airship shall not be moored.

NOTE: Each of these limitations may be varied by request and with written permission of the CAA, subject to conditions which will accompany the permission.

DOCUMENTATION AND RECORDS.

Documents to be Carried (Article 57 and Schedule 12).

On an **aerial work** flight, the documents to be carried are:
- the aircraft's Radio Licence;
- the Certificate of Airworthiness (CofA);
- the Certificate of Registration (if the flight is international, i.e. beyond the bounds of the UK, Channel Islands and Isle of Man);
- Flight Crew Licence(s);
- one copy of each Certificate of Maintenance Review in force;
- the Technical Log (if any and if required); and
- although not a requirement, it is good practice to carry the insurance documents.

NOTE: The requirement to carry full documentation on an aerial work flight is **waived** when it is intended to take-off and land at the **same aerodrome** and remain **within UK airspace.** Also, with the CAA's approval a Flight Manual need not be carried if an Operations Manual, which contains the specified information, is carried.

A **private** flight need only carry the first four documents listed above if international air navigation is involved but, for flights totally within the confines of the UK, Channel Islands and Isle of Man, no documents need be carried.

Production of Documents (Article 59).

The Commander of an aircraft shall, within a reasonable time after being requested to do so by an authorised person (a Constable, or anyone authorised by the Secretary of State or the CAA in a manner appropriate to the case), produce:
- the Certificates of Registration and Airworthiness in respect of the aircraft;
- the Licence(s) of its Flight Crew and the personal flying logbooks (for up to two years after the date of the last entry in any book); and
- such other documents that the aircraft should carry when in flight.

Offences in Relation to Documents and Records (Article 63).

It is an offence to:
- use a forged, altered, revoked or suspended document issued under the Order, or to use one to which you are not entitled;
- lend a document issued under the Order, or otherwise allow it to be used by anyone else, with intent to deceive;
- forge or render illegible any logbook or record required by the Order, or to make a false entry or material omission, or to destroy it during the period for which it is required to be preserved (all entries in such documents must be made in ink or indelible pencil).

NOTE: The CAA can revoke or vary any licence or document that it has issued.

AERODROMES.

Use of Aerodromes for Instruction in Flying (Article 71).

Aeroplanes and rotorcraft are restricted to take-off and land only at a licensed aerodrome, a Government aerodrome, or an aerodrome owned or managed by the Authority, whenever engaged in both flying instruction and flying tests for the purpose of qualifying for a pilot's licence, aircraft rating or night rating.

Gliders are similarly restricted if engaged in flying instruction, except where they are flown under club arrangements. **Self-launched motor gliders** are exempted from the restriction when being used for gliding instruction or pilot testing, if flown under club arrangements. **Microlights** are exempted from the restriction when flown under club arrangements.

Aviation Fuel at Aerodromes (Article 82).

No person shall cause or permit any fuel to be used in an aircraft if he knows or has reason to believe that it is not fit for such use. Fuel must not be used in aircraft unless it has been dealt with in accordance with certain stipulations for the storage and sampling of aviation fuel stocks at aerodromes.

NOTE: as a guide to Pilots and others, and in an attempt to avoid refuelling with the wrong type of fuel, **AVGAS equipment at aerodromes is usually marked in red.** You are directed to Aeronautical Information Circular 19/1981.

Notification of Arrival and Departure (Rule 20).

If an aircraft is expected at an aerodrome the commander must inform the authorities at the aerodrome as soon as possible if the destination is changed or arrival will be delayed by 45 minutes or more. This is to avoid any unnecessary *'overdue action'*.

Wherever possible an aircraft's commander must report upon arrival, and prior to departure, to the appropriate authority at an aerodrome.

AIRMISS REPORTING PROCEDURE.

When a Pilot considers that the aircraft may have been endangered by the proximity of another aircraft within UK airspace the incident must be reported as an *'Airmiss'*. This is a requirement stated in Article 85 (Mandatory Reporting) of the ANO.

An initial report should be made by radio to the Air Traffic Service Unit (ATSU) with which the aircraft is in communication. If it is impossible to report by radio, a report should be made by telephone or other means to any ATSU, but preferably to an Air Traffic Control Centre (ATCC) immediately after landing. Reports made by telephone or radio must be confirmed within 7 days on CA Form 1094.

☐ **Exercises A13 – Operation Of Aircraft.**

A14

THE PRIVATE PILOT LICENCE

LICENCES AND RATINGS
(Articles 18, 19, 20 and Schedule 9).

THE STUDENT PILOT.

A Student Pilot may commence training without a licence under the supervision of a suitably qualified Flying Instructor. During the course of his training for a Private Pilot Licence, he may (without a licence) act as Pilot-in-Command (PIC) and fly solo if:
- he is at least 17 years of age;
- he holds a Medical Certificate validated by an approved Authorised Medical Examiner (AME) and complies with any restrictions stated thereon (e.g. a requirement to wear spectacles if decided by the AME);
- flights are restricted to the United Kingdom, Channel Islands or Isle of Man;
- no other person is carried in the aircraft;
- he acts in accordance with instructions given by a suitably qualified Flying Instructor.

THE GRANTING OF A PRIVATE PILOT LICENCE (PPL).

The CAA only grants a PPL when it is satisfied that the applicant is a fit person to hold the licence and is qualified by reason of knowledge, experience, competence, skill, physical fitness and mental fitness. The minimum age for holding a Private Pilot Licence is 17 years.

In addition to holding a valid medical certificate, the Applicant for a Private Pilot Licence must produce evidence to the CAA that he has, within the 6 months preceding the granting of the licence, passed:
- **four ground examinations:** (1) Aviation Law, Flight Rules and Procedures (for which this Section has prepared you); (2) Navigation; (3) Meteorology; and (4) Aircraft (General); (plus an examination in Radio Telephony);
- **a flight test,** which will also involve an oral examination: Aircraft (Type).

The Private Pilot Licence, when granted by the CAA, is not valid until it is signed in ink by the holder. There is no maximum period of validity although, for the holder to exercise its privileges, the licence must be renewed periodically with either a Certificate of Experience (CofE) or a Certificate of Test (CofT), each of which is valid for 13 months.

THE PRIVILEGES ACCORDED TO A PRIVATE PILOT.

A Private Pilot Licence holder may fly as Pilot-in-Command (PIC) (often stated as *'Aircraft Commander')* or as Co-Pilot in any of the aeroplane types or groups specified in the aircraft rating in the licence, provided:

- he has included in his personal flying book (logbook), a Certificate of Test (CofT) or Certificate of Experience (CofE) valid for the type of aircraft to be flown;

- he has a valid medical certificate issued by an Authorised Medical Examiner (AME);

- he does not fly an aeroplane for the purpose of public transport (i.e. the carriage of persons or cargo for hire or reward, either promised or given) or aerial work (i.e. flight for hire and reward for purposes not involving public transport) other than aerial work which consists of:

  - the giving of flying instruction, in which case his licence must be endorsed with a Flying Instructor's Rating or an Assistant Flying Instructor's Rating; or

  - the conducting of tests for the purposes of the ANO.

NOTE: In either case the aerial work would have to be done in an aircraft owned, or operated under arrangements entered into, by a flying club of which the person instructing or conducting the test and the person being instructed or undergoing the test are both members.

- he is not remunerated for services as a Pilot other than for such instructing or conducting of flying tests;

- unless he has obtained (and the licence includes) an Instrument Rating (IR) or Instrument Meteorological Conditions (IMC) rating, he does not fly as Pilot-in-Command.

  (i) when outside controlled airspace:

    - in a flight visibility (i.e. visibility forward from the cockpit) less than 1·5 nautical miles (nm) when flying alone; or

    - when a passenger is carried and the aeroplane is flying either above 3000 feet AMSL in Instrument Meteorological Conditions (IMC) or at or below 3000 ft in a flight visibility of less than 3 nm;

    - out of sight of the surface.

  (ii) on a Special VFR (SVFR) flight in a control zone in a flight visibility of less than 5 nm except on a route or in an Aerodrome Traffic Zone (ATZ) notified for the purpose;

  (iii) out of sight of the surface;

- he does not fly as Pilot-in-Command at night on which a passenger is carried or instruct in flying at night unless:

  (i) his licence includes a Night Rating; and

  (ii) his licence includes an Instrument Rating (IR) or he has within the immediately preceding 6 months carried out as Pilot-in-Command not less than 5 night take-offs and 5 night landings with the Sun at least 12° below the horizon, (i.e. in darkness, following the time when the brighter stars are clearly discernible and large unlit objects on the Earth's surface become difficult to distinguish). (This differs from the ANO definition of *'night'*, which is from half an hour after sunset to half an hour before sunrise.)

The minimum conditions for flight on a basic Private Pilot Licence (i.e. without an IMC Rating or an Instrument Rating) are best explained diagramatically (Fig.A14-1 below).

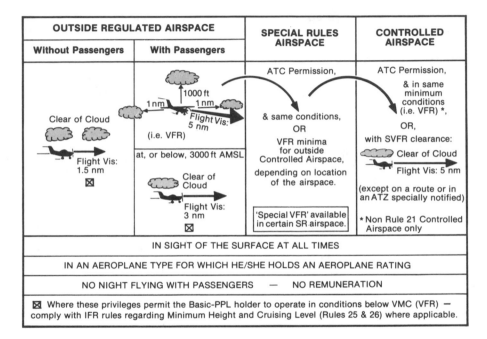

Fig.A14-1. Minimum Conditions for Flight on a Basic PPL.

PPL (Helicopters and Gyroplanes).

In addition to the usual requirements, a holder must not:

- fly as Pilot-in-Command of a gyroplane at night on a flight on which a passenger is carried or instruct in flying at night unless a Night Rating is held and 5 night take-offs and 5 night landings have been made as Pilot-in-Command in the last 90 days;

- fly as Pilot-in-Command of a helicopter at night on a flight on which a passenger is carried or instruct in flying at night unless both a Night Rating and an Instrument Rating are held or, as an alternative to the Instrument Rating, 5 flights at night have been made as Pilot-in-Command in the last 90 days, each consisting of a take-off, a transition from hover to forward flight, a climb to at least 500 feet and a landing.

NOTE: If you do not hold a particular licence or rating, you cannot undertake any of the functions to which that licence or rating relates.

THE FLIGHT RADIOTELEPHONY OPERATOR'S LICENCE.

To operate radio equipped aircraft, a Private Pilot should hold a **Flight Radiotelephony Operator's (FRTO) Licence** (although Student Pilots have a dispensation). Training and assessment for the FRTO is now combined with that for the PPL and your flying training organisation can give you guidance on how to obtain this licence. Reference can also be made to AIC 38/1986 (White 196), for more details.

PPL (BALLOONS and AIRSHIPS).

A holder may fly as Pilot-in-Command of any aircraft type specified in Part 1 of the aircraft rating in the licence and Co-Pilot of any type specified in the rating provided he has a valid Medical Certificate and does not fly for the purpose of public transport or aerial work, other than aerial work which is instruction in flying or the conducting of flying tests.

In either case the aerial work would have to be done in an aircraft owned, or operated under arrangements entered into, by a flying club of which the person instructing or conducting the test and the person being instructed or undergoing the test are both members.

Although PPL (Balloons and Airships) licence holders are not required by law to hold a valid Certificate of Test or Certificate of Experience, they are not entitled to exercise the privileges of the licence unless during the previous 13 months they have made 5 flights as PIC or have satisfactorily completed a flight test.

VALIDITY OF THE CERTIFICATE OF TEST and CERTIFICATE OF EXPERIENCE.

A Certificate of Test (CofT) is valid for 13 months from the date of the flight test which it certifies.

A Certificate of Experience (CofE) must relate to experience gained within the 13 months preceding its signing, and it is valid for 13 months from the date it is signed. There should be at least 5 hours flying in the logbook signed-off and stamped by a PPL Examiner.

In all cases it is the holder's responsibility to ensure that renewals are made within the appropriate time limit if licence privileges are to be maintained. If the 13 months is exceeded without a Certificate of Experience extending the licence, a flight test is required to renew the privileges. Beyond 26 months certain flight training is required prior to the flight test, and beyond 4 years the CAA will handle each case individually, determining what flight training is required by the Pilot prior to the test.

VALIDITY OF MEDICAL CERTIFICATES.

The periods of validity for medical certificates issued on or after 1 January 1986 are as follows:

Age	Validity
less than 40	5 years or until the age of 42 (the lesser thereof)
40 to 50	2 years
50 to 70	1 year
more than 70	6 months

NOTE: An alternative form of Medical Certificate is available for flight of Balloons and Airships (or Microlight Aircraft) only. It has a **Declaration of Health** to be signed by the applicant and countersigned by his or her General Practitioner, or an AME. The certificate is only valid if so countersigned. Its period of validity is the same as for the standard certificate.

In all cases, it is the licence holder's responsibility to ensure that renewals are made within the appropriate time limits if licence privileges are to be maintained.

A Pilot is not entitled to act as flight crew if he knows or suspects that he is **medically unfit** for it. This includes:
• injury affecting his ability to act as flight crew;
• any illness involving incapacity to undertake his flight crew functions for a period of 20 days or more; or
• a belief that she is pregnant, in the case of a woman.

The CAA must be advised in writing as soon as possible in the case of injury or pregnancy, and as soon as the period of 20 days has elapsed in the case of illness. The medical certificate is deemed to be suspended from the date of the occurrence until such time as the individual is re-examined and certified medically fit again.

RATINGS.

The Private Pilot Licence will include one or more **ratings** specifying the aircraft types that the holder may fly and any additional privileges that the holder has obtained.

Aircraft Ratings entitle holders to pilot aircraft of the type, group or class specified (provided that a valid and appropriate CofT or CofE is held). For Private Pilots, aeroplanes are sub-divided into the following aircraft rating groups:
- **Group A**: all single-engined aeroplanes not exceeding 5700 kg maximum total weight authorised;
- **Group B**: all multi-engined aeroplanes not exceeding 5700 kg maximum total weight authorised;
- **Group C**: aeroplanes whose maximum total weight authorised exceeds 5700 kg.
- **Group D**: microlight aeroplanes, i.e. having an empty weight (i.e. no fuel, Pilot, passengers or cargo) not exceeding 150 kg, a wing area not less than 10 square metres, a wing loading not exceeding 10 kg per square metre at empty weight, and designed to carry not more than 2 people.

The **IMC Rating (Aeroplanes)** entitles holders to be Pilot-in-Command of an aeroplane without being subject to the flight visibility restrictions stated earlier, provided:
(i) they do not fly on a Special Visual Flight Rules (SVFR) flight in a control zone in a flight visibility of less than 1.5 nm;
(ii) they do not act as such when the aeroplane is taking-off or landing at any place if the flight visibility below cloud is less than 1 nm.

The **Instrument Rating (Aeroplanes)** entitles the holder to be Pilot-in-Command or Co-Pilot of an aeroplane flying in controlled airspace in circumstances which require compliance with the Instrument Flight Rules (IFR).

The **Night Rating (Aeroplanes)** entitles holders to be Pilot-in-Command at night of an aeroplane in which a passenger is carried.

The **Flying Instructor's Rating** entitles the holder to give instruction in flying (in the type, group or class specified in the rating) to any person who is flying with him for the purpose of becoming qualified for the grant of a pilot's licence or the inclusion or variation of any rating in the licence.

The **Assistant Flying Instructor's Rating** entitles holders to instruct in flying aircraft of types specified in the rating provided that:

(i) instruction is given under the supervision of a holder of a flying instructor's rating present during the take-off and landing at the aerodrome at which the instruction is to begin and end; and

(ii) no direction or authorisation is given to students regarding their first solo or first cross-country flight, whether by day or by night (a cross-country flight being one that is properly pre-planned with a route, turning points and destination, proceeding more than 3 nm from the departure aerodrome, and of suitable duration and distance as to require in-flight track adjustments).

The Instrument Rating (Helicopters) entitles holders to be Pilot-in-Command or Co-pilot of a helicopter in controlled airspace in circumstances which require compliance with Instrument Flight Rules (IFR).

The Night Rating (Helicopters and Gyroplanes) entitles holders to be Pilot-in-Command at night of a helicopter or gyroplane in which a passenger is carried.

PERSONAL FLYING LOGBOOKS (Article 22).

A personal flying logbook must be kept by qualified pilots and those flying to obtain or renew a licence. The following particulars shall be recorded:

- the name and address of the licence holder;
- the details of the licence;
- the details of each flight made as a member of a flight crew or for the purpose of obtaining or renewing a licence including:
  - the date, the places at which the holder embarked and disembarked and the time spent during the flight in either of the capacities mentioned;
  - the type and registration marks of the aircraft;
  - the capacity in which the holder acted in flight (with a Flight Instructor on board, the time is logged as *'dual';* when solo or Pilot-in- Command, the time is logged as *'in command');*

- details of any special conditions including night flying, instrument flying and in particular the training exercises specified in the PPL qualifying requirements;
- particulars of any test or examination undertaken whilst in flight;
- particulars of flight simulator tests.

Date	AIRCRAFT		CAPTAIN	Holder's Operating Capacity	JOURNEY or Nature of Flight		Departure (G.M.T.)	Arrival (G.M.T.)
	Type	Registration			From	To		
AUG 2	AA-5A CHEETAH	G-KILT	SELF	P1	ELSTREE	ELSTREE	12.20	13.50
AUG 8	SLINGSBY T67	G-BKTZ	SELF	P1	LEAVESDEN	BIRMINGHAM	07.30	08.55
AUG 8	"	G-BKTZ	SELF	P1	BIRMINGHAM	CRANFIELD	12.45	13.15
AUG 8	"	G-BKTZ	SELF	P1	CRANFIELD	LEAVESDEN	17.00	17.45
AUG 24	AZTEC	G-ARBN	R GODWIN	P1 US	ELSTREE	LOCAL	12.05	13.15

60			02			05	Hrs.	Totals Brought Forward
25			15			30	Mins.	

(1)	(2)	(3)	(4)	(5)	(6)	(7)	(8)	(9)	(10)	
DAY				NIGHT						FLYING TIMES
Single-Engine		Multi-Engine		Single-Engine		Multi-Engine		Instrument Flying	Simulated Instrument Flying	REMARKS
In Command	Dual or P.2	In Command	Dual or P.2	In Command	Dual or P.2	In Command	Dual or P.2			Including counter-signature for P.1/S
1.30										
1.25										
.30										
.45										
		1.10								

Fig.A14-2. Typical Logbook Entries.

NOTE: The Commander of an aircraft is required to produce his logbook, within a reasonable time after being requested to do so by an authorised person, for up to **2 years** from the date of the last entry.

INSTRUCTION IN FLYING (Article 23).

The total flying training required to obtain a PPL (Private Pilot Licence) is 43 hours, made up of at least 30 hours dual and 10 hours solo, although certain Training Organisations have been approved by the Civil Aviation Authority to reduce the requirements to 38 hours under certain conditions.

Flying instruction for the grant of a licence or rating must generally only be given by those who hold a licence entitling them to act as Pilot-in-Command for that purpose and in the circumstances under which the instruction is to be given. The licence must include a Flying Instructor's or Assistant Flying Instructor's Rating.

☐ Finally, for this Section (Aviation Law), complete **Exercises A14 – The Private Pilot Licence.**

Part (B)

AEROMEDICINE AND SAFETY

B1

ARE YOU FIT TO FLY?

PHYSICAL FITNESS.

As a Pilot, you should maintain a reasonable degree of physical fitness. It allows better physical and mental performance during flight and in the long term, and quite apart from flying, improves your chances of a long and healthy life.

Keeping fit takes some effort and this effort must be continuous for fitness to be retained, but it can also be good fun and very recreational. Walking, jogging, digging in the garden, cycling, swimming – in fact anything that steadily raises your pulse rate will improve your fitness.

If you are grossly unfit or obese, then allow yourself several diet-conscious months with moderate exercise that is gradually increased, and consider medical supervision. It might seem like a long haul, but the quality of life and your perception of yourself will improve along with your fitness. Physical activity also promotes a hunger for healthy foods as well as encouraging good sleeping patterns.

Physical fitness helps a Pilot cope better with stress, tiredness, fatigue and the reduced availability of oxygen at higher levels in the atmosphere.

MENTAL FITNESS.

Flying an aeroplane involves physical activity but the main workload on a Pilot is intellectual. Mental fitness is vital to safe flying, but it can be degraded by:

- medication;
- drugs, including alcohol and cigarettes;
- excessive stress;
- personal or family problems;
- lack of sleep or poor eating habits; and
- fatigue or allowing oneself to get over-tired.

ILLNESS AND DRUGS (Including Alcohol and Smoking).

A reasonably innocuous complaint on the ground (such as the common cold) may have serious effects under the stress of flying and high altitudes.

Medical drugs taken to combat an illness may impair flying activity and physical comfort in flight. *'Recreational Drugs'* such as alcohol, marijuana, LSD, etc., must never be mixed with flying and a person dependent upon these may not be fit to hold a Pilot's licence.

Smoking also significantly decreases a Pilot's capacity to perform by reducing the amount of oxygen carried in the blood, replacing it with the useless and potentially poisonous byproducts of cigarette smoke. A Pilot does not have to be the active smoker to suffer the effects; smoke from any person in the cockpit will affect everyone.

MEDICAL CHECKS.

Regular checks by an Aviation Medical Examiner hopefully will establish your general good health, both physical and mental.

Major items in the medical test include checks of the Central Nervous System (including eyesight), the Cardiovascular System (including heart and blood pressure), correct functioning of the kidneys (using a urine test), hearing ability and, finally, the Respiratory System (ears, nose, throat and lungs), especially the Eustachian Tubes for their ability to allow pressures to equalise either side of the ear drums.

Regular medical checks verify your general health and fitness, but occasional bouts of sickness or injury may make you temporarily unfit to fly, particularly if medication is involved. **If in doubt** consult an Aviation Medical Examiner.

It is a requirement that any licence holder who suffers an illness involving an incapacity to fly for a period of twenty days or more, or injury affecting their ability to fly or, in the case of women, have reason to believe that they are pregnant, must advise the Civil Aviation Authority in writing. The medical certificate is deemed to be suspended until such time as the individual is re-examined and certified medically fit again.

Pilots carry a heavy responsibility to themselves and to the general community and so medical fitness in general and on the day of flight in particular is most important.

The period of validity of a medical check, provided it is not interrupted by injury, illness or pregnancy, is:

- at an age less than 40 years – 5 years, except that it will certainly have to be renewed at age 42 years as for the requirement below;
- at 40 to 50 – 2 years;
- at 50 to 70 – 1 year;
- at greater than 70 years of age – 6 months.

MEDICATION.

Until cleared by a doctor, it is safest to assume that any drug or medication will temporarily ground you.

A list of common medications considered incompatible with flying includes:

- antibiotics (e.g. penicillin) used to combat infection;
- tranquillisers, anti-depressants and sedatives;
- stimulants (caffeine, amphetamines) used to maintain wakefulness or suppress appetite;
- anti-histamines, often used to combat colds and hay fever;

- drugs for the relief of high blood pressure;
- analgesics to relieve pain;
- anaesthetics (used for local, general or dental purposes) usually require about 24 hours before returning to flight.

It is also recommended that active Pilots do not donate blood. Whilst this is a very worthwhile contribution to the community, it does reduce, at least temporarily, the ability to move energy-giving oxygen around the body.

ALCOHOL.

A Pilot who has *'had a drink'* is obliged not to fly if under the influence of alcohol or any drug which will impair his ability to perform his duties – Air Navigation Order: Article 47(2).

Even small quantities of alcohol in the blood can impair one's performance, with the added danger of relieving anxiety so that the person thinks he is performing marvellously. Alcohol severely affects a person's judgement and abilities. High altitudes, where there is less oxygen, worsen the effect.

It takes time for the body to remove alcohol and, as a general rule, a Pilot should not fly for at least 8 hours after drinking small quantities of alcohol and increase this time if greater quantities are consumed. After heavy drinking, alcohol may still be in the blood 30 hours later. Sleep will not speed up the removal process, in fact it slows the body processes down and the removal of alcohol may take even longer.

Persons who are dependent upon alcohol (i.e. *'alcoholics')* should not hold a Pilot's licence.

A drunk person should not be permitted on board an aeroplane as a passenger (Air Navigation Order: Article 47).

ALCOHOL AND FLYING SHOULD NEVER BE MIXED!

Fig.B1-1. Alcohol is Dangerous.

UPPER RESPIRATORY TRACT PROBLEMS.

The common cold, hay fever, sinusitis, tonsilitis or any similar condition can lead to blocked ears, which can mean trouble for a Pilot. When air is unable to pass through the Eustachian Tubes and equalise pressures either side of the ear drums (e.g. with changes in altitude and therefore in pressure), great pain and ultimately permanent damage to the ear drums can be caused.

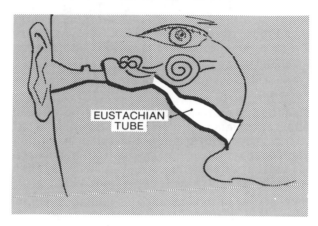

Fig.B1-2. Eustachian Tubes Equalise Pressure Either Side of the Ear Drums.

During a climb, atmospheric pressure on the outer parts of the body decreases. The now greater pressure from within the inner ear forces the ear drum out and also causes air to flow from the inner ear through the Eustachian Tubes into the throat to release this greater pressure.

Most training aeroplanes only have a low rate of climb, so air can readily flow out of the Eustachian Tubes, which means that ear problems during the climb are generally not serious. During descent, however, difficulties with the ears may be more serious.

As atmospheric pressure on the outer parts of the body increases during a descent, it pushes the ear drums in. Ideally, some air will flow from the throat via the Eustachian Tube into the inner ear and equalise the pressure.

The nature of the Eustachian Tubes is such that air will not move into them as readily as it moves out and so any swelling or blocking of or around them can lead to problems. High rates of descent worsen the situation and the pain can be very severe.

Problems can also arise in the sinuses, which are cavities in the head connected by narrow tubes to the nasal/throat system. Blockages can cause great pain, especially during descent.

Blocked ears can sometimes be cleared by holding your nose and blowing, by chewing, swallowing or yawning. The best advice is, however, **if you have a cold, do not fly.**

CARBON MONOXIDE POISONING.

Carbon monoxide is a colourless, odourless and tasteless gas for which haemoglobin in the blood has an enormous affinity. The prime function of haemoglobin is to transport oxygen from the lungs throughout the body to act as *'fuel'*. Carbon monoxide molecules breathed into the lungs along with *'air'* will attach themselves to the haemoglobin (being more attractive to haemoglobin than oxygen) and so the body and brain suffer oxygen starvation even though oxygen is present in the air.

The performance of a Pilot in a carbon monoxide environment will be seriously impaired and recovery, even on pure oxygen, may take several hours. **Carbon monoxide poisoning is serious and can be fatal!**

Carbon monoxide is produced during the combustion of fuel in the engine and is also present in cigarette smoke, both of which can sometimes be found in the cockpit.

Many cabin heating systems use warm air from around the engine and the exhaust manifold as their source of heat. **Any leaks in the exhaust system** can allow carbon monoxide to enter the cabin in the heating air and possibly through open windows and cracks. To minimise the effect of any carbon monoxide that enters the cockpit in this way, fresh air should always be used in conjunction with cabin heat.

Regular checks and maintenance are essential. Even though carbon monoxide is odourless, it may be assocated with other exhaust gases that do have an odour. **'Engine smells' in the cabin are a warning that carbon monoxide may be present.**

The symptoms of carbon monoxide poisoning may include headache, dizziness, nausea, deterioration in vision and slower breathing rate. If carbon monoxide is suspected in the cabin, shut-off cabin heat, stop all smoking, increase the supply of fresh air through vents and windows and don oxygen masks if available.

FOOD POISONING.

Food poisoning may result from an improperly prepared meal and its onset may be almost immediate following consumption of the food, or it may not become evident for some hours but, even then, its onset may be very sudden. The stomach pains, nausea, diarrhoea, vomiting, etc., that accompany food poisoning can make it physically impossible for a Pilot to perform his duties.

It is a good practice, for the half day prior to flight, to avoid foods that are often the cause of food poisoning, including shellfish, fish, mayonnaise, creams, over-ripe and thin-skinned fruits, uncooked foods such as salads and raw foods, and old food (e.g. food that has been cooked and stored for some time).

If you suspect that some effects of food poisoning are imminent from something bad that you have eaten, **do not fly!**

EYESIGHT AND SPECTACLES.

If you are required by the Aviation Medical Officer to wear glasses to correct your sight, then it is good airmanship to wear them as required. It is also compulsory to carry a spare pair of spectacles.

For further reading on this subject, you are directed to Aeronautical Information Circular (AIC) 58/1983 (Pink 46).

SMOKING.

Smoking is prejudicial to good health, both in the short term and in the long term.

In the short term, carbon monoxide which is present in cigarette smoke is absorbed into the blood in preference to oxygen. This reduces the body's ability to produce energy (including in the brain). The diminished supply of oxygen to the body and brain becomes very noticeable at higher altitudes where cigarette smoke in the cabin can significantly decrease the Pilot's performance (even if he is not actually smoking the cigarette!).

In the long term, it is now generally accepted that cigarette smoking plays a role in cardiovascular (heart) and other diseases. If you want to live a long and healthy life and not smell like an old rag, then cigarette smoke should vanish from your life.

As a point of interest and worthy of note, cigarette smoking in the cockpit is banned by many Airline Captains.

FATIGUE AND SLEEP DEPRIVATION.

Fatigue, tiredness and sleep deprivation can lower a Pilot's mental and physical capacity quite dramatically. The nature of flying is such that a Pilot must train himself to cope with moderate levels of these complaints, and to recognise when his **personal limits** are being approached. A fatigued Pilot should not be flying!

Fatigue can become deep-seated and chronic if psychological or emotional problems are not solved, resulting in deep rest or sleep not occurring over a prolonged period. Chronic fatigue will be cured when the problems are solved, or at least being coped with, and the person can relax and unstress. A Pilot should prohibit himself or herself from flying until this is the case.

Short-term fatigue is caused by overwork, mental stress, an uncomfortable body position, a recent lack of sleep, **'living it up'** a bit too much, lack of oxygen or lack of food. Sleep and rest are needed!

To guard against fatigue that is prejudicial to flight safety, a Pilot should:

- have his psychological and emotional life under control;
- be reasonably fit;
- eat regularly;
- ensure he is not deprived of adequate sleep;
- ensure that cockpit comfort is optimised and that energy foods and drink are available on long flights;
- exercise his limbs occasionally and land to stretch his legs at least every four (4) hours, if practicable.

☐ Now complete **Exercises B1 — Are You Fit To Fly?**

B2

IN-FLIGHT MEDICAL FACTORS

FITNESS MAY NOT BE SUFFICIENT PROTECTION AGAINST AEROMEDICAL PROBLEMS.

Whilst fitness and good health are a very good starting point for a Pilot, he still must protect himself against potential problems such as lack of oxygen, food poisoning, fatigue and carbon monoxide poisoning.

LACK OF OXYGEN (Hypoxia).

The Atmosphere is Held to the Earth by Gravity.

The atmosphere surrounding the Earth consists mainly of nitrogen (80%), oxygen (20%) and water vapour, with very small quantities of carbon dioxide and inert gases. The mixture is known familiarly as **'Air'**.

The atmosphere is held to the Earth by the force of Gravity, and the great mass of air pressing down causes air pressure and air density to be greater at the lower levels of the atmosphere. The atmospheric pressure *'pushing'* on our bodies is greatest at sea level, and our bodily tissues and fluids have adjusted to this and *'push back'* with the same pressure.

Air Pressure Decreases With Altitude.

As an aeroplane climbs, the air pressure drops and therefore less pressure is exerted on the human body. It will react to this lower pressure in various ways, e.g. the Eustachian Tubes will allow a small amount of air to flow through them to equalise the pressures either side of the ear drums. Colds and other infections that cause blockages can prevent this from happening.

Air Density Decreases With Altitude, Resulting In Less Oxygen Per Breath.

At higher altitudes, the air density (i.e. the number of molecules per unit volume) will be less than at sea level, therefore each lungful of air will contain fewer oxygen molecules and the body and brain will have to function with less energy-giving oxygen.

Air Temperature Decreases With Altitude — Beware of Hypothermia.

On average the temperature falls about 2°C for every 1000 feet gained in altitude. This will vary from place to place and from time to time, sometimes being greater and sometimes less, but in general, temperature decreases with altitude. The human body does not function all that well when it is extremely cold and, in a *'standard atmosphere'* with a sea level temperature of +15°C, the temperature at 10 000 ft will be –5°C.

Respiration Brings Oxygen Into The Body And Removes Carbon Dioxide.

By muscular action of the diaphragm, the lungs are expanded and air is drawn in through the nose and mouth and into the lungs. The oxygen diffuses across the membranes in the millions of small air sacs in the lungs and becomes attached to haemoglobin in the red blood corpuscles.

The diffusion across the lung membranes depends upon the partial pressure of oxygen and when it is low (e.g. at high altitudes), less oxygen enters the blood. The blood transports this oxygen right throughout the body where it is used in a burning process to produce energy.

Carbon dioxide is produced as a waste product in the burning process and it is transported back to the lungs, where it is expelled in the breath. The amount of waste carbon dioxide in the returning blood is sensed by the brain, which responds by altering the respiration (breathing) rate. If carbon dioxide is present in larger amounts than normal (e.g. during strenuous exercise), the brain senses this and speeds up the rate of respiration.

The average capacity of the lungs is about 5 litres and the average breath when at rest is about ½ litre, using only a fraction of the lung capacity to provide about 8 litres/minute. Strenuous activity may increase this to 60 litres/minute.

Respiration At High Altitudes Brings Less Oxygen Into The Body.

At high altitudes, even though the percentage of oxygen in the air does not change greatly, the lower air pressure and lower partial pressure of oxygen will reduce the number of oxygen molecules that diffuse across the lung membranes and attach themselves to the haemoglobin in the red blood corpuscles. Less oxygen is then transported around the body and less energy is generated (including in the brain). In this condition a Pilot is less able to think clearly and less able to perform physically.

Hypoxia — The Lack Of Oxygen.

Whereas food can be stored in the body, oxygen needs to be continually supplied. The lack of sufficient oxygen to the body (and brain) is called Hypoxia.

Above 8000 feet, the effects of oxygen deprivation may start to become apparent in some Pilots, especially if the Pilot is active or under stress. At 10000 feet, most people can still cope with the diminished oxygen supply, but above 10 000 feet supplemental oxygen is required (i.e. oxygen supplied through a mask) if a marked deterioration in performance is not to occur.

At 14000 feet, performance will be very poor and at 18000 feet the Pilot may become unconscious – (lower if he is a smoker, unfit or fatigued).

The initial symptoms of Hypoxia may hardly be noticeable to the sufferer, in fact, they include feelings of euphoria. The brain is affected quite early, so a false sense of security and well-being is present. Physical movements will become clumsy, but the Pilot may not notice this.

Drowsiness, giddiness, a headache, deterioration of vision, a high pulse rate, blue lips and blue finger nails may all follow, ending in unconsciousness. Throughout all of this the Pilot will probably feel that he is doing a great job. Hypoxia is subtle and it sneaks up on you!

Pressurised Cabins Can Lead To Hypoxia If They Depressurise.

Advanced aeroplanes have pressurised cabins that allow the cabin to hold air at higher pressure than in the outside atmosphere. For instance, an aeroplane flying at 30 000 feet may have a cabin that is pressurised *(pumped up)* to 4000 feet, hence there is no need for the Pilot and passengers to be wearing oxygen masks – a significant improvement in comfort and convenience.

This, of course, changes if the aeroplane depressurises for some reason and the cabin air escapes, reducing the partial pressure of oxygen in the air available to the Pilot. Supplementary oxygen then becomes vital and is usually obtained through a mask until the Pilot descends to a lower altitude (below 10 000 feet) where there is sufficient oxygen available and the mask can be discarded if desired.

The Time Of Useful Consciousness.

If a person is suddenly deprived of an adequate supply of oxygen, unconsciousness will follow. This is a very important consideration for a high flying pressurised aircraft that suffers depressurisation.

The time available for Pilots to perform useful tasks without a supplemental oxygen supply is known as the *'Time of Useful Consciousness'*, which gets shorter and shorter the higher the altitude. The Pilots **must** get the masks on and receive oxygen well within this period if flight safety is to be preserved.

Altitude (ft) above sea level	Sudden Failure of Oxygen Supply	
	moderate activity	minimal activity
22 000	5 minutes	10 minutes
25 000	2 minutes	3 minutes
28 000	1 minute	1½ minutes
30 000	45 seconds	1¼ minutes
35 000	30 seconds	45 seconds
40 000	12 seconds	15 seconds

Fig.B2-1. Time Of Useful Consciousness Following Failure of Oxygen.

Consciousness of the Pilot is paramount, even if the passengers become unconscious for a short period. The Pilot must think of himself first, since the safety of all on board depends upon his well-being.

How To Avoid Hypoxia.

To avoid Hypoxia it is best to be reasonably fit, to have no cigarette smoke in the cockpit, and to ensure that you use supplemental oxygen at the higher altitudes and most definitely above 10 000 feet. Remember that lack of oxygen can lead to a feeling of euphoria and a lack of judgement (a similar effect perhaps to alcohol) and self-discipline must be imposed and the oxygen mask donned when the altitude approaches 10 000 ft.

For further reading on *'Hypoxia'*, you are directed to AIC 60/1984 (Pink 59).

HYPERVENTILATION – AN EXCESS OF OXYGEN.

Hyperventilation occurs when the body *'over-breathes'* for some reason such as fear, anxiety, excitement or in a mistaken attempt by a person trying to improve performance by forced breathing (e.g. prior to an underwater swimming attempt).

The balance of oxygen and carbon dioxide in the body is upset, causing symptoms similar to those of Hypoxia to occur (e.g. giddiness, numbness, tingling sensations, increasing breathing rate and pulse rate). Hyperventilation may lead to blurred vision, muscle spasms and unconsciousness.

If these symptoms occur, it is essential to establish whether the problem is Hyperventilation (too much oxygen) or Hypoxia (too little oxygen) before it can be remedied:

• Hyperventilation can be remedied by slowing down the breathing rate (talking is a good way of doing this), or by breathing into and out of a bag to increase the level of carbon dioxide in the blood back to more normal levels; but:

• if recovery is not evident, then assume that Hypoxia rather than Hyper-ventilation is the problem and use oxygen.

DECOMPRESSION SICKNESS CAN FOLLOW SCUBA DIVING.

Scuba diving and flying do not mix very well. When the body is deep under water it is acted on by strong pressures and certain gases, such as nitrogen, are absorbed into the blood. The deeper and longer the diving, the more this occurs.

If the pressure on the body is then reduced – for example, by returning to the surface from a great depth or, even worse, by flying in an aeroplane at high cabin altitudes – the gases may come out of the blood solution as bubbles. One sees this effect when the top is removed from gaseous drinks and bubbles of gas come out of solution.

Gas bubbles in the blood will cause great pain and immobilisation in the shoulders, arms and joints. This serious complaint is known as *'the bends'*. The remedy is to return the body to the region of high pressure for a lengthy period of time (say in a decompression chamber) and gradually return it to normal pressures over a period of hours or days.

In an aeroplane, the best you can do if the presence of the *'bends'* is suspected is to descend to a low altitude or to land. Even that may not provide a sufficient pressure increase to remedy the problem. Medical assistance should be sought without delay.

Diving at depths below 20 feet for long periods should not be considered prior to flying!

LOW TEMPERATURES CAN CAUSE HYPOTHERMIA.

Low temperatures can decrease Pilot performance, so it is important that the cabin temperature is kept comfortable. This applies when climbing to high altitudes, but it can also apply on the ground in cold climates.

VERTIGO.

Vertigo is generally experienced as a feeling of rotation, when in fact no rotation is actually occurring (or vice versa).

Vertigo can be caused by disease, by accelerations that disturb the delicate balance mechanisms in the inner ear and by sudden pressure changes in the inner ear. Strong blowing of the nose or sneezing can do this quite violently and bring on a spell of *'dizziness'*.

If you wish to experience Vertigo on the ground, you can bring it on by spinning around about 20 times with your head held low and then trying to walk in a straight line. Similar forces occur when an aeroplane is manoeuvring, especially when high *'g-loadings'* are pulled in steep turns, spins, spiral dives, etc., and Vertigo can occur, especially if there is no visual reference to the horizon.

Non Instrument-Rated (i.e. Visual) Pilots are asking for trouble if they enter cloud!

MOTION SICKNESS.

Air sickness is generally caused by the balance mechanisms of the inner ear continually being over-stimulated by accelerations. This can be caused by turbulence, or manoeuvres such as steep turns or spins, in which forces other than the normal **'1g'** (that the body is used to) will be experienced. A hot, smelly cockpit does not help!

Psychological aspects can also play a role in the onset of motion sickness, e.g. a fear of flying or apprehension at seeing the horizon at different angles.

To avoid airsickness:

- fly the aeroplane smoothly and in balance;

- avoid manoeuvres where unusual g-forces are pulled;

- ventilate the cabin with a good supply of fresh air;

- involve a potentially airsick passenger in the operation, especially if this involves looking outside the aeroplane and into the distance (e.g. to help identify ground references);

- as a last resort, recline the passenger's seat to reduce the effect of the vertical accelerations and keep a sick bag handy.

SPATIAL DISORIENTATION.

Spatial disorientation is said to occur when the pilot is unsure of his precise attitude in space, i.e. where is *'up'* and where is *'down'*. Vertigo *'dizziness'* need not necessarily be present although it may be.

Spatial disorientation can occur when a non Instrument-Rated Pilot loses reference to the natural horizon by, for example, flying into cloud, or flying over sloping terrain or a sloping cloud layer, or when flying in restricted visibility. Flashing strobe lights or the Sun flashing through the propeller can also have a destabilising effect and cause a Pilot to become disoriented or suffer Vertigo.

To prevent spacial disorientation, a Pilot should avoid flying in the above conditions, avoid looking directly at the Sun or any strobe light, and should gain some expertise at flying on instruments. The Flight Instruments will allow a Pilot to spacially orientate himself even when his sensory images (sight and balance) of the outside world are false.

☐ Now complete **Exercises B2 — In-Flight Medical Factors**.

B3

SAFETY AND CARE
OF PASSENGERS

The Pilot is responsible for the safety of his aeroplane and passengers. As well as being properly prepared for the flight himself, he must ensure that the passengers are adequately briefed on safety matters.

PRIOR TO BOARDING.

The Pilot should inform the passengers that at various times throughout the flight he will have important duties to perform which will require his full attention. For this reason, he may occasionally request that there be no interruptions and no excessive conversation during the periods he is concentrating on *'vital actions'*.

Correct clothing is important to passenger comfort. Most aircraft cabins can be kept warm (or cool) in flight. Overcoats and other very heavy clothing need not be worn, although they should remain accessible in the event of an emergency evacuation. Passengers are forbidden to fly when drunk and should not fly if sick or affected by an upper respiratory complaint such as a cold.

Pressure changes will occur as the aeroplane climbs and descends and, if the ears do not automatically adjust, chewing, yawning or holding the nose whilst blowing with a closed mouth may assist. Blocked nasal passages can hinder this process. The higher noise level and possible turbulence may be a little disconcerting. Passengers should be reminded that there are no toilet facilities on board.

Baggage should be checked to ensure that it is not overweight and does not contain dangerous goods such as aerosol cans, pressurised cigarette lighters and matches, none of which should be carried.

It is inadvisable to smoke or have any naked flame near aircraft, especially if refuelling is in progress.

Passengers should be warned to remain well clear of propellers, since even a stationary propeller can spring to life, and a rotating propeller may hardly be visible. For this reason, children must be very closely supervised. The safest approach to an aeroplane is from the left and behind with passengers remaining in a single group under the supervision of the Pilot.

Various attachments on the aeroplane, such as the pitot tube and radio aerials are fragile and should not be used for support. Care should be taken when entering the aeroplane not to step where the wing or any part of the aeroplane structure could be damaged.

ON BOARD.

Ensure that your passengers are comfortably seated and confirm that the front-seat passenger will not restrict full movement of any control with bags, cameras or legs. Any metallic or magnetic objects should be stored well away from the magnetic compass.

Seat belts will consist of a lap-strap and sometimes a shoulder harness. The lap-strap should be fastened and adjusted until it is firm but comfortable, followed by the shoulder harness if one is fitted. The passenger must be shown how to fasten, adjust and release his seat belt.

The passengers should know how to close, lock and then open the **doors and windows** or canopy. Once a door is closed by the Pilot, the position of the lock and handle should not be altered.

Aircraft cabins can become stuffy, so ensure that there is **adequate ventilation** and each passenger knows how to adjust the appropriate vent to maximise his comfort.

The **Intercom**, if one is to be used, should be explained. The radio volume should be adjusted to a comfortable level.

Passengers need not be passive, but can actively assist in some aspects of flight, such as maintaining a good **Look Out** for other aircraft and for landmarks, as well as passing the sandwiches around!

LIFE-JACKETS.

Before flying over any expanse of water in a single-engined aircraft (e.g. the English Channel), all occupants should don **life-jackets**. There are various types and the Pilot must be familiar with their use. Most life-jackets are designed to be worn uninflated inside the aeroplane so that their bulk is minimised, both for comfort and for ease of departing the cabin.

The Pilot should explain how to don the life-jacket, which is usually by fitting it over your head with the main part of the jacket in front of your body, then passing the straps around your back and tieing them in front. Some jackets may require a different fitting technique for children.

The passenger must understand how to inflate the life-jacket and use any attached items such as a light or whistle. It should be emphasised that it is best to inflate the life-jacket **after** having exited from the cabin so that the evacuation is unhindered.

Inflation is generally achieved by pulling a release on a small gas cylinder attached to the front of the life-jacket. If the gas pressure provides insufficient inflation, there is a tube through which the passenger can blow and further inflate the life-jacket.

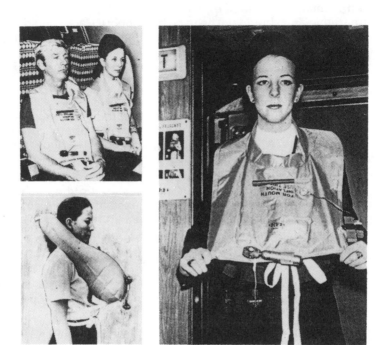

Fig.B3-1. Use of a Life-Jacket (RFD 102).

LIFE-RAFTS.

Immersion in the seas surrounding the UK could result in death within a few hours; in some extreme temperatures and winds within a few minutes. Whilst life-jackets are useful for flotation, they will not protect the body from icy water. For this reason, it is prudent, on overwater journeys, to carry a **life-raft** in which the occupants can be sheltered from exposure and remain fairly dry.

Most life-rafts suitable for light aircraft are stored in a small bag and weigh 10-15 kg. The raft must be inflated outside the aircraft, usually by removing it from its bag, ensuring that its cord is firmly held and placing or throwing the uninflated raft into the water. It may be advisable to swim a short distance from the aircraft before inflating the life-raft to avoid any danger of holing it.

Pulling the release cord should then activate the gas cylinder and inflate the raft. A sea anchor (bucket) can be used to prevent the raft drifting too far from the aircraft, which will assist in the search.

The raft will have associated equipment such as paddles, a canopy (very important in minimising exposure) ropes, knife, dies, flares, light, first aid kit and possibly emergency rations.

Fig.B3-2. Typical Life-Raft (Beaufort 4 person).

FIRE

Fire is a hazard to aviation and is to be avoided at all costs.

Three things are necessary for a fire to occur:
- a fuel (e.g. AVGAS, oil, papers, fabric, cabin seating, etc.);
- oxygen (present in the air);
- a source of ignition (cigarettes, matches, electrical sparks, etc., but bear in mind that once a fire is burning it is itself a source of ignition.

Prevention is by far the best cure, and Pilots are advised to pay attention to items and situations that are a potential cause of, or contributor to, fire. Any possible 'fuel' and any possible source of 'ignition' should be kept separate. For example, when refuelling ensure that no person is smoking in the vicinity, that the aeroplane and refuelling equipment are adequately grounded to avoid the possibility of a static electricity build-up causing a spark, and that no fuel is spilled. As a precaution when refuelling, a suitable fire extinguisher should be readily available.

In flight, if the Pilot permits any passenger to smoke, then he must ensure that no hot ash or cigarette butt comes in contact with papers or even the cabin seating, which may smoulder or burn, possibly unnoticed for some time. The risk of fire, as well as the detrimental effects of carbon monoxide in the blood, is another reason to discourage smoking in aircraft.

Cockpit fires can also be caused by faulty electrical circuits, which can often be recognised by a peculiar smell. Further development of an electrical fire may be prevented by switching off the electrical power (Master Switch *OFF,* or pulling the appropriate circuit breaker).

The usual method of extinguishing a fire once it is burning is to eliminate one or more of these items (fuel, oxygen, source of ignition), e.g. blanketting a fire with dry chemical from a fire extinguisher to starve the fire of oxygen. If it appears that a fire has not yet started but is imminent, and the fuel and ignition source cannot be separated, it may be advisable to starve the area of oxygen by using an extinguisher.

FIRE EXTINGUISHERS.

The CAA requires that Public Transport aircraft carry fire extinguishers, however for Private Category aeroplanes this is only a **recommendation** and not a requirement.

Many light aircraft are indeed fitted with a small fire extinguisher that is securely stowed where the Pilot may reach it in flight. The usual extinguishants contained in these are BCF (Halon) and Dry Chemical, both of which are capable of handling most types of fires. Other extinguishants in use include Carbon Dioxide, Water and Foam. There is a standard graphic code to differentiate between the suitability of fire extinguishers in fighting certain types of fire, and this is usually displayed on the extinguisher with an indication of its suitability for the specific categories.

PAPER,	INFLAMMABLE	LIVE
WOOD,	LIQUIDS	ELECTRICAL
TEXTILES	& GASES	EQUIPMENT

Fig.B3-3. Graphic Code in use on many Fire Extinguishers.

Typically, a stored gas pressure discharges the extinguishant when a trigger is pressed. Each particular brand of fire extinguisher may have special requirements (such as to break a seal by twisting a handle, or by releasing a handle, or by breaking a lockwire), so the Pilot should read the instructions and become familiar with the extinguisher that he might have to use at short notice. Some of the more common types of fire extinguishers are discussed below.

Some fire extinguishers are re-usable either by recharging the cylinder or by placing the trigger and head mechanism onto a new cylinder, whereas others may have to be discarded once used. A serviceability check of the fire extinguisher may require checking pressure on a gauge which may be colour-coded, or on an indicator disc which, if it can be pressed in, indicates that the pressure is low and the fire extinguisher unserviceable. There may also be a weight check to determine that no extinguishant has been lost, but this check is more likely to be done by an Engineer during his periodic inspections.

BCF (Halon).

BCF extinguishers contain Halon 1211 (**B**romo**C**hlorodi**F**louromethane), and are often found in light aeroplanes. BCF is a very versatile extinguishant and is capable of combatting most types of fires, including fuel, fabric and electrical. BCF is stored as liquified gas, which comes out as a fine jet of fluid and develops into a spray. Its toxicity is low (so will not poison the Pilot or passengers) and can be safely used in the cockpit, although it is advisable to avoid inhaling excessive amounts of fuel and smoke.

Bearing in mind that the BCF extinguishant gas will exclude oxygen to some extent, **the cabin should be well ventilated once the fire is extinguished.** A significant advantage of BCF is that (unlike Dry Chemical) it does not leave any residue, and so the cabin and instruments will not require cleaning after its use.

Dry Chemical.

A Dry Chemical fire extinguisher contains dry powder and carbon dioxide. It is very effective against most types of fire, including electrical and fuel, but is less effective than BCF against material fires (paper, textiles, wood).

Unfortunately, Dry Chemical has several disadvantages. During its use it may restrict visibility in the cockpit and cause breathing difficulties, so **ventilating the cabin is important once the fire is out.** After it has been used, a powdery residue will remain which is corrosive to aluminium alloys and can be damaging to instruments, therefore thorough cleaning is necessary after Dry Chemical has been used.

CO2 Fire Extinguishers.

Carbon Dioxide fire extinguishers contain liquified CO_2 which can be discharged as a gas and used to combat electrical fires, engine fires on the ground and other fires. When sprayed at the base of the fire, the CO_2 blankets the fire and starves it of oxygen. A typical CO_2 fire extinguisher will have a trigger with a lock-wire that must be broken before use (an intact lockwire is also a check for serviceability), and a nozzle that should be raised before the CO_2 is discharged with the trigger. The nozzle pipe should not be held with the bare hands, since it will become very cold as the gas vaporises, and skin could be frozen to it. CO_2 will cause breathing difficulties and is best not used in the cockpit (unless oxygen masks are available).

Water Fire Extinguishers.

"Wet" water fire extinguishers generally contain distilled water with an anti-freeze agent to retain serviceability at low temperatures and a "wetting" agent. Water is suitable for extinguishing material fires (e.g. a smouldering cabin seat), but definitely should not be used for electrical fires or fuel fires.

Foam Fire Extinguishers.

Foam fire extinguishers are generally designed for outside use. One common type is inverted just prior to use, causing chemicals to mix and form foam under pressure which can then be directed at the base of the fire.

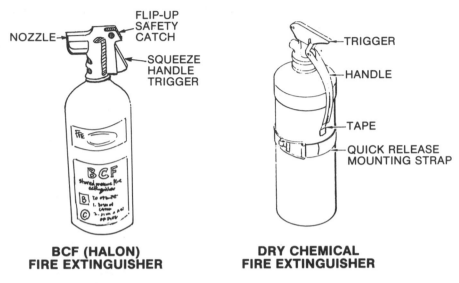

**BCF (HALON)
FIRE EXTINGUISHER**

**DRY CHEMICAL
FIRE EXTINGUISHER**

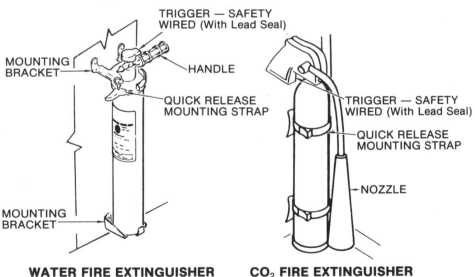

WATER FIRE EXTINGUISHER   **CO₂ FIRE EXTINGUISHER**

Fig.B3-4. Typical Fire Extinguishers in Aviation Use.

☐ **Exercises B3 — Safety and Care of Passengers.**

B4

FIRST AID

First Aid is what its name suggests – the initial care of the sick or injured. It can preserve life, protect the unconscious, prevent worsening of a condition and promote recovery. First Aid lasts until medical aid (doctor, nurse or ambulance officer) arrives or until the casualty recovers.

First Aid is useful knowledge for all citizens, but is especially useful for those who may find themselves in remote areas well away from medical aid (e.g. following a forced landing in an aircraft). The St.John's Ambulance Association specialises in First Aid and is highly recommended for their manuals and courses.

MINOR PROBLEMS THAT MAY OCCUR IN FLIGHT

Minor medical problems may occur in flight and can often be handled without much difficulty. It is most important, however, that this does not distract you from flying the aeroplane and adequately controlling its flight path, which is your principal responsibility.

AIRSICKNESS AND NAUSEA.

Airsickness may occur in flight, especially if the person is passive, in a hot stuffy cabin and is experiencing unusual motion, such as in manoeuvres or turbulence. Generally, passengers are more passive than the Pilot, although it is not unknown for a Pilot to become airsick. The affected person may feel poorly, *'hot and cold'* and nauseous, but will often feel better after having vomited.

To manage a person who feels airsick (ensuring that you, as Pilot, do not neglect your prime responsibilities in controlling the flight path of the aeroplane):
- loosen clothing;
- ensure plenty of fresh air;
- lay him down or recline the seat;
- place a cool cloth on his forehead;
- comfort and reassure;
- have a *'sick bag'* handy in case of vomiting.

113

FAINTING.

Insufficient blood reaching the brain may cause a person to faint and possibly lose consciousness temporarily. A temporary disturbance of the nervous control of the blood vessels can be caused by nervous shock (such as a fright or a horrifying sight), an injury, being passive in a hot stuffy environment or by a sudden postural change (like standing up after having been sitting for a long period).

A person who is about to faint may feel weak and giddy, 'hot and cold', and have a pale, clammy skin, experience blurred vision and a desire to yawn.

To manage a person who has fainted, or is about to faint:
- lay the casualty down if possible, with the legs raised; otherwise recline the seat;
- loosen clothing;
- ensure plenty of fresh air;
- allow the casualty to rest;
- have a *'sick bag'* handy in case of vomiting.

NOSE BLEEDING.

Nose bleeding may result from injury, high blood pressure or excessive blowing of the nose. It usually occurs from just inside the nose on the central cartilagenous partition below the bone.

Instruct the casualty:
- not to blow his nose;
- to breathe through his mouth;
- to apply finger and thumb pressure on the flaps of the nostrils (just below the bony part of the nose) for at least 10 minutes;
- to sit up, with the head slightly forward and to loosen any tight clothing; and
- to keep cool with a good supply of fresh air and with cold towels on the neck and forehead.

MORE SERIOUS PROBLEMS THAT MAY OCCUR IN FLIGHT

Anything that prejudices the health and well-being of the Pilot in flight may end in disaster. **Food poisoning**, for instance, can totally disable a Pilot quite quickly, even though symptoms may not appear until several hours after an ill-prepared meal. Also, the onset of symptoms, when they do appear, can be quite sudden! Diarrhoea is certainly not helpful to safe flight. Passengers, as well as the Pilot, can experience medical problems (fainting, heart attack, stroke, etc.).

It is up to the Pilot to decide how to manage the problem, either in flight or on the ground following a landing (ideally at an aerodrome, but in a nearby field if urgency demands it).

FIRST AID FOLLOWING AN ACCIDENT

The Pilot is responsible for the safety of the aeroplane and its occupants at all times. On rare occasions, accidents do occur and the Pilot must be capable of managing subsequent events adequately. The welfare of the group must take precedence over that of any individual and, if possible, the safety of the flight (whilst it lasts) should not be prejudiced.

PREVENTION IS THE BEST CURE!

Preventing an accident or incident is of course best. Food poisoning, for instance, can be avoided by careful choice of food. Pilot welfare is best achieved by staying on the ground if someone has diarrhoea or nausea, or if an upper respiratory or hearing complaint is being experienced.

Some good points of airmanship (common sense) in *Prevention* are as follows:
• have the seat belts fastened;
• do not allow careless smoking; and
• guard against fumes and carbon monoxide in the cabin by ensuring a good supply of fresh air.

IF AN ACCIDENT OCCURS AND PASSENGERS ARE INJURED.

In the event of an accident actually taking-place do everything in your power to stop the situation worsening. Secure the aeroplane and evacuate uninjured passengers, taking any useful emergency equipment and supplies. Consider the welfare of injured passengers and whether or not they should be moved. Do not forget the welfare of the non-injured members of the party.

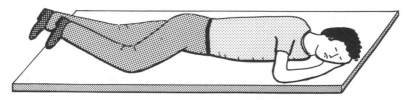

Fig.B4-1. The 'Coma Position'.

If an unconscious passenger is evacuated, then it should be done gently and firmly, with the casualty being placed in the *'Coma Position'*. This is a comfortable position that aids blood supply to the brain and allows any vomit to escape without blocking the breathing passages.

HEAD INJURIES.

Head injuries are potentially very serious as they can result in brain damage, altered consciousness, spinal injury, bleeding, breathing difficulties, vision and balance difficulties. Even mild head injuries should be treated seriously.

Indications of head injury may include headache, nausea, memory loss, blurring of vision, weakness on one side of the body, wounds, bleeding, bruising, clear fluid escaping from the nose or ear, twitching, noisy breathing, incoherent speech, congestion on the face, vomiting, dilated pupils or pupils becoming unequal in size, strange behaviour and abnormal responses of the injured person to commands and to touch.

Treat a casualty suffering head injury as if he were unconscious. Consider placing him in the *Coma Position* so that any bleeding, discharge or vomit can drain away. An open airway is vital. Ensure that the tongue or dentures do not obstruct the passages. Breathing should be monitored and assisted if necessary.

BLEEDING.

Bleeding is loss of blood from the blood vessels and may be either internal or external. In either case blood is lost to the circulation and the ability to carry energy-giving oxygen around the body and to the brain is reduced. Blood loss can lead to faintness, dizziness, nausea, thirst, a weak and rapid pulse, cold and clammy skin, and rapid breathing.

Fortunately, bleeding will often stop of its own accord but, if it does not, severe bleeding can lead to shock and eventually to death. Severe bleeding therefore is extremely serious and must be controlled before less serious injuries are attended to.

External bleeding is best controlled by placing a bulky dressing (or your hand if nothing more suitable is available) over the wound and applying firm pressure to it for 10 minutes or more. Raise the injured part and rest it to decrease the blood flow.

Profuse bleeding may be reduced by pressing the sides of the wound together or by applying a constrictive bandage or hand pressure to block the blood flow through the arteries (say above the elbow or knee). This should be a last resort and the pressure should be released every 10 minutes or so to ensure some blood supply to the area.

Bleeding from the palm of the hand may be serious and can best be treated by clasping a firm pressure pad (e.g. a bandage roll, a handkerchief wrapped around a stone, or two or three fingers of the other hand) and elevating the hand above the head to reduce the blood flow to it.

Internal bleeding may result in pain, tenderness, tight stomach muscles and the above-mentioned signs of blood loss. To manage internal bleeding, rest the casualty completely. Elevate the legs comfortably (if not broken), loosen tight clothing and allow no food or drink. Seek urgent medical assistance.

FRACTURES.

A fracture is a broken or cracked bone. There will be bleeding, either internally or through an open wound, causing a loss of blood to the circulation. The area where the break has occurred may be painful, tender, mis-shapen or swollen, bruised and unable to be used normally.

In managing a casualty with a fracture:

• control bleeding and cover wounds with a sterile or clean dressing;

- immobilise and support the fracture with a sling, bandage or splint and preferably support the injured limb in an elevated position:
  - splints: use any suitable material that is long, wide and firm enough to give support and to immobilise the joints above and below the fracture. Use can be made of the upper body to splint a fractured arm and of a good leg to splint a fractured leg.
  - padding: may protect the skin and bony points and may allow the splint to fit snugly.
  - bandages: in general should be broad and supportive.
- check frequently to ensure that blood circulation to a fractured limb is not impaired, that bandages have not loosened, and that splints are still supportive, and look for signs of shock.

BURNS.

Burns are a serious injury. Extensive burns to the body or to the respiratory tract (due to breathing hot air or fumes) are potentially dangerous and may be fatal.

To manage a casualty with burns, first extinguish the fire if possible and/or remove the casualty from danger, making sure that you do not become a burns casualty yourself.

Put out burning clothing by smothering with a non-inflammable blanket or jacket, or possibly a dry chemical fire extinguisher (directed away from the eyes).

Remove or cut away any clothing near the burnt area unless it is stuck to it, in which case it should be left alone. Remove any rings, bracelets, watch bands, etc., before swelling starts. Cool the injured area if possible under cold, gently running water – (cooling make take up to 10 minutes).

Do not prick blisters and avoid touching the burnt area. Do not apply any lotions, ointments, oily dressings or fluffy material. Apply a sterile non-stick dressing and bandage lightly.

A conscious casualty seriously burnt should be given frequent small amounts of water, weak tea or milk (about ½ cup every 10 minutes) to minimise the effect of fluid loss from the burnt tissues. Do not give alcohol. **Seek medical aid urgently.**

DEEP SHOCK.

Shock can range from fainting (nervous shock) to deep shock that may follow serious injuries and illnesses, especially where there is severe bleeding, pain or loss of fluid from burns. Deep shock can be a life-threatening condition. Insufficient circulation of blood to the brain and other body tissues may lead to a collapse of the circulatory system and death.

Shock is progressive and may take some hours to become obvious and the symptoms should be carefully watched for. A casualty experiencing shock may be faint or dizzy, restless and apprehensive, nauseous and thirsty. The pulse may be very weak and rapid. The face and lips may be pale and the skin pale and clammy, the extremities becoming bluish. Breathing may be rapid and the casualty may become dull, drowsy, apathetic, confused or unconscious.

To treat a person in shock:

- increase the blood supply to the brain if possible by laying the patient down with the head low;
- control any external bleeding, dress any wounds or burns, immobilise any fractures and loosen any tight clothing;
- keep the casualty warm, but do not overheat him as this draws blood away from the vital organs;
- if thirsty, moisten the lips or allow the casualty to suck an ice cube;
- monitor breathing and pulse;
- if breathing is difficult, or vomiting likely or if consciousness is lost, lay the casualty on the side with the mouth slightly down;
- seek urgent medical assistance.

FIRST AID KITS.

Although aeroplanes flying for a purpose other than public transport (e.g. for training or for private flights) are not required to carry a First Aid Kit, (whereas public transport aircraft are required to do so), it is good airmanship for the Operator of the aeroplane to provide one. ANO Schedule 5, Scale B provides a guide to the contents of a suitable First Aid Kit.

Scale B

(i) First-Aid equipment of good quality, sufficient in quantity, having regard to the number of persons on board the aircraft, and including the following—

Roller bandages, triangular bandages, adhesive plaster, absorbent gauze, cotton wool (or wound dressings in place of the absorbent gauze and cotton wool), burn dressings, safety pins;
Haemostatic bandages or tourniquets, scissors;
Antiseptic, analgesic and stimulant drugs;
Splints, in the case of aeroplanes the maximum total weight authorised of which exceeds 5,700 kg.;
A handbook on First Aid.

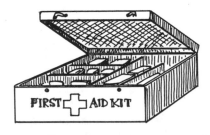

Fig.B4-2.

□ **Exercises B4 — First Aid.**

Part (C)

AVIATION METEOROLOGY

C1

THE ATMOSPHERE

The solid Earth is surrounded by a mixture of gases which are held to it by the force of Gravity. This mixture of gases we know as **air** and the space it occupies around the Earth we call the **atmosphere**. The atmosphere is of particular importance to Pilots because it is the medium in which aeroplanes fly.

AIR DENSITY DECREASES WITH ALTITUDE.

The force of Gravity exists between each individual air molecule and the Earth. This has the effect of drawing them together, causing the air molecules to crowd around the surface of the Earth and squeeze closer together than at altitude. Therefore, there are more molecules per unit volume of air at sea level than at higher altitudes. For example, at 40 000 ft altitude, the number of molecules in a cubic metre of air is only about half that at sea level.

Density is the mass per unit volume and, on average, the density of air at sea level is 1,225 grammes per cubic metre.

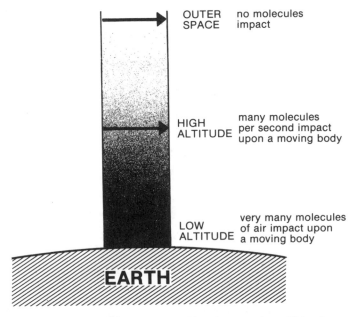

Fig. C1-1. Air Density Decreases With Increasing Altitude.

Three reasons why air density is so important to Pilots are that:
- the Lift force supporting the aeroplane's Weight is generated by the flow of air around the wings;
- engine power is generated by burning fuel and air; and
- we need to breathe air in order to live.

In air that is dense:
- the required Lift can be generated at a lower True Air Speed (V);
- greater engine power is available;
- a person's breathing is easier and more oxygen is taken into the lungs.

THE ATMOSPHERE EXTENDS FURTHER ABOVE THE EQUATOR THAN ABOVE THE POLES.

The Earth spins on its axis, carrying the atmosphere with it and tending to throw the air to the outside. For this reason, the atmosphere extends further into space above the Equator than above the Poles.

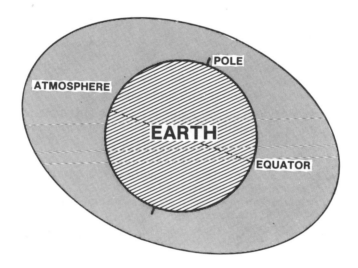

Fig.C1-2. The Atmosphere Extends Further Above the Equator than Above the Poles.

THE SUBDIVISION OF THE ATMOSPHERE.

The atmosphere is divided vertically into four regions – the *Troposphere*, the *Stratosphere*, the *Mesosphere* and the *Thermosphere*. Light aircraft flying occurs in the Troposphere, although high flying jets may cruise in the Stratosphere – the boundary between the two regions being known as the **Tropopause**.

The Tropopause occurs at a height of about 20000 ft over the poles, and at about 60 000 ft over the tropics. In the 'average' International Standard Atmosphere it is assumed to occur at 36 000 ft. Most of the 'weather' occurs in the Troposphere.

There are some significant differences between the Stratosphere and the Troposphere:

- Temperature falls with height gained in the Troposphere, but is constant in the Stratosphere (at least in general terms) at about –57°C.
- There is marked vertical movement of air in the Troposphere, with warm air rising and cool air descending, both on a large and a small scale.
- The Troposphere contains almost all of the water vapour in the atmosphere and so cloud formation rarely extends beyond the Tropopause (although occasionally large cumulonimbus clouds with strong and fast vertical development may push into the Stratosphere).

THE ATMOSPHERE IS A MIXTURE OF GASES AND CARRIES WATER VAPOUR.

'Air' is a mixture of gases, the main ones being:

Oxygen	(21% by volume)
Nitrogen	(78%)
Water Vapour	
Other gases	(1%)
.... Total	(100%)

Air always contains some water vapour. This is most important because it is water vapour that condenses out to form clouds, from which we get the precipitation (rain, snow, hail, etc.) that is vital to life on Earth.

Air over an ocean (known as *maritime air*) will absorb moisture from the body of water and will, in general, contain more water vapour than the air over a continent (known as *continental air*), particularly if the land mass consists largely of desert areas.

In other words, a maritime air mass is moister than a continental air mass, and so an air mass moving in across the UK from over the Atlantic Ocean is likely to carry more moisture than an air mass whose origin is continental Europe/Asia.

Whilst nitrogen is the main constituent of air, the other constituents vital to aviation are:

- oxygen (to support life and combustion);
- water vapour (to produce *weather*).

HUMIDITY.

The water molecule (H_2O) is a relatively light molecule and its presence in large numbers in an air mass lowers its density, which affects both the aerodynamic performance of an aeroplane and the power production from the engine, making performance slightly poorer on a damp day compared with a dry day. This is a consideration when operating in conditions of **high relative humidity**.

Another consideration in relation to operating in conditions of high relative humidity is the possiblity of ice forming in the carburettor as the air is cooled by expansion whilst mixing with the vapourising fuel.

☐ **Exercises C1 — The Atmosphere**, (located in Part (D) at the end of this volume).

C2

HEATING EFFECTS IN THE ATMOSPHERE

THE SUN RADIATES ENERGY.

The source of energy on Earth is the Sun, which radiates electromagnetic energy (light, radio waves, etc.). We experience this solar radiation as **heat** and **light**.

The wave-lengths of solar radiation are such that a large percentage penetrates the Earth's atmosphere and is absorbed by the Earth's surface, causing its temperature to increase. The ground in turn heats that part of the atmosphere which is very close to it, with the result that any parcel of air warmer than the surrounding air will then rise.

THE EARTH IS IN ORBIT AROUND THE SUN.

The Earth orbits around the Sun once in every year and, because the Earth's axis is tilted, this gives rise to the four seasons. The solar radiation received at a place on Earth is more intense in Summer than in Winter, when its surface is presented to the Sun at a more oblique angle.

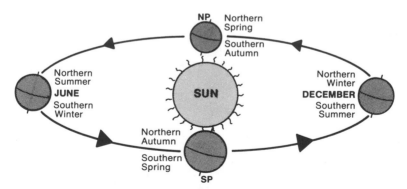

Fig.C2-1. Solar Radiation Received at the Earth's Surface is More Intense in Summer.

HEATING FROM SOLAR RADIATION IS GREATEST IN THE TROPICS.

Solar radiation is like a torch beam that produces more intense light on a perpendicular surface than on an oblique surface. Since solar radiation strikes tropical regions from directly overhead, or almost directly overhead, right throughout the year, the heating is quite intense.

In contrast, the Sun's rays strike polar regions of the Earth at an oblique angle and, during the winter situation (the northern summer is shown in the diagram), they may not strike the polar regions at all.

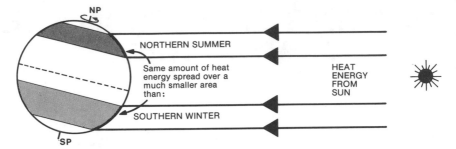

Fig.C2-2. Surface Heating Is Greatest In The Tropics and Least At High Latitudes.

WARMED AIR RISES AND COOL AIR SINKS.

The greater heating of the Earth's surface in the tropics causes the air in contact with it to become relatively warm. This leads to the air expanding, becoming less dense in the process and thus commencing to rise, which in turn causes it to spread out in the upper regions of the atmosphere. As a result, new air moves in across the Earth's surface to replace the air which has risen.

In contrast, the cooler air over the polar regions sinks down, creating a large scale vertical circulation pattern in the Troposphere. This process is known as the **general circulation** pattern and consists of three main *'cells'*:
- the polar cell;
- the mid-latitude cell; and
- the tropical cell.

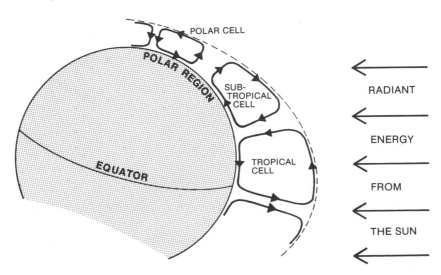

Fig.C2-3. The General Circulation Pattern.

The hot and less dense air rising over the tropics creates a band of low pressure at the Earth's surface known as the **Equatorial Trough**, into which other surface air will move (known as *'convergence'*).

The cool and dense air subsiding in the polar regions creates a high pressure area at the Earth's surface in the very high latitudes and the surface air will spread outwards (known as *'divergence'*).

TERRESTRIAL RADIATION.

Heat energy in the Earth's surface is re-radiated into the atmosphere but, because its wave-length is longer than solar radiation, it is more readily absorbed in the atmosphere, especially by water vapour and carbon dioxide. It is this absorption of heat from the Earth that is the main process which causes weather.

In summary:
- solar radiation penetrates the atmosphere and heats the Earth's surface; then
- the Earth re-radiates this energy and heats the lower levels of the atmosphere.

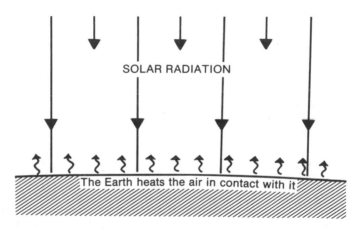

SOLAR RADIATION

The Earth heats the air in contact with it

Fig.C2-4. Indirect Heating of the Atmosphere by the Sun.

THE EARTH ROTATES ON ITS AXIS.

The Earth rotates on its axis once every 24 hours, causing the *'apparent'* motion of the Sun across the sky, which results in day and night on the Earth.

Solar heating of the Earth's surface occurs only by day, but terrestrial re-radiation of heat energy occurs continually through both the day and the night. The net result is that the Earth's surface heats up by day, reaches its maximum temperature about mid-afternoon (3.00 pm) and cools by night, reaching its minimum temperature around sunrise.

This continual heating and cooling on a daily basis is called the **diurnal variation of temperature** – a typical daily pattern of heating and cooling that is most extreme in desert areas and more moderate over the oceans.

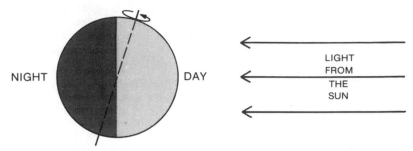

Fig.C2-5. The Earth's Rotation Causes Day and Night.

DIFFERENT SURFACES HEAT DIFFERENTLY.

The heating of various surfaces and the temperatures which they reach depends upon a number of factors:

1. **The Specific Heat of the Surface**. Water requires more heat energy to raise its temperature by 1°C than land, therefore land will heat more quickly (and also cool more quickly). Compared with the sea, land is warmer by day and cooler by night. Scientifically we say water has a higher Specific Heat than land.

2. **The Reflectivity of the Surface**. If the solar radiation is reflected from the surface it can, obviously, **not** be absorbed. Snow and water surfaces have a high reflectivity and so will not be heated as greatly as absorbent areas such as a ploughed field or a dense jungle.

3. **The Conductivity of the Surface**. Ocean currents transfer heat through water motion, causing the sea to be heated to a greater depth than a land surface.

CLOUD COVER CAN AFFECT SURFACE HEATING AND COOLING.

Cloud coverage by day stops some of the solar radiation penetrating to the Earth's surface, resulting in reduced heating of the Earth and lower temperatures. The air in contact with the surface will therefore be subject to less heating by day.

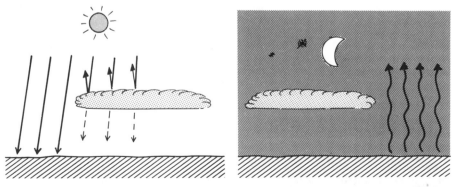

Fig.C2-6. Cloud Reduces Surface Heating By Day and Cooling By Night.

By night, however, cloud coverage causes the opposite effect and prevents some of the heat energy escaping from the Earth's surface. The atmosphere beneath the cloud will experience less cooling and higher temperatures will result.

THE TRANSFER OF HEAT ENERGY.

Heat energy may be transmitted from one body to another, or redistributed in the one body by a number of means, including:

1. **Radiation**. All bodies transmit energy in the form of electromagnetic radiation, the higher the temperature of the body, the shorter the wave-length of the radiation. Radiation from the Sun is therefore of shorter wave-length than the re-radiation from the Earth, which is much cooler.

2. **Absorption**. Any body in the path of radiation will absorb some of its energy. How much it absorbs depends upon both the nature of the body and of the radiation. A densely forested area will absorb more solar radiation than snow-covered mountains.

3. **Conduction**. Heat energy may be passed within the one body, or from one body to another in contact with it, by conduction. Iron is a good conductor of heat – wood is not a good conductor, and nor is air. A parcel of air in contact with the Earth's surface is heated by conduction, but will not transfer this heat energy to neighbouring parcels of air. This is a very significant factor in the production of *weather systems.*

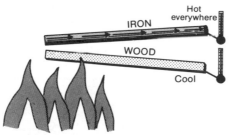

Fig.C2-7. Some Things Are Good Conductors of Heat; Others Are Not.

4. **Convection**. A body in motion carries its heat energy with it. A mass of air that is heated at the Earth's surface will expand, becoming less dense, and rise. As it rises, it will carry its heat energy higher into the atmosphere – which is the process called *convection.*

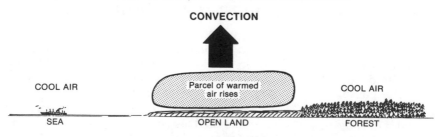

Fig.C2-8. Convection.

5. Advection. When air moves in to replace air that has risen by convection, this horizontal motion of air is known as *advection*. The air mass, moving horizontally by advection, will of course bring its heat energy (and moisture content) with it.

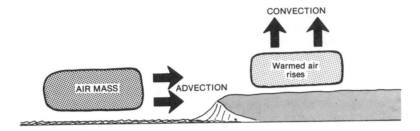

Fig.C2-9. Advection Is The Horizontal Transfer Of Air And Heat Energy.

The general vertical circulation pattern of air flow that occurs on a large scale around the Earth also happens on a smaller scale in localised areas.

THE SEA BREEZE BY DAY.

The process known as a *Sea Breeze* occurs on sunny days, when the land heats more quickly than the sea. The air above the land becomes warmer and rises (usually by mid- to late-afternoon). This sets up the situation for a vertical circulation pattern with the cooler air from offshore moving in to replace the air from over the land which has risen due to surface heating.

The vertical extent of a Sea Breeze is usually only 1000 or 2000 ft.

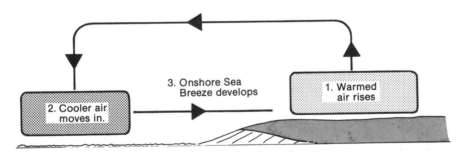

Fig.C2-10. The Sea Breeze – A Small Circulation Cell.

Sea Breezes may have a significant effect on aerodromes near a coastline. If the Sea Breeze opposes the general wind pattern it is quite possible that the wind velocity at circuit height will be quite different to that at ground level. Windshear and some turbulence may be experienced as the aeroplane passes from one body of air to the other.

The cooler air moving in over the land as a Sea Breeze may bring Fog or Mist with it, causing visibility problems. This could be the situation if a Sea Fog exists and, as the day progresses and the land heats up, an onshore Sea Breeze develops, moving the Fog in across the land.

THE LAND BREEZE BY NIGHT.

By night, the land cools more quickly than the sea, causing the air above it to cool and subside. The air over the sea is warmer and will rise.

A Land Breeze could hold a Sea Fog offshore early in the day but, as the land warms, the Land Breeze could die out and a Sea Breeze develop, bringing the Sea Fog in and possibly causing visibility problems at coastal aerodromes.

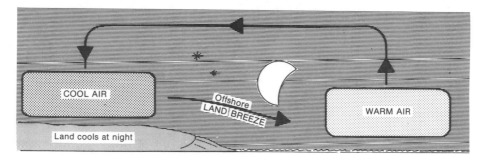

Fig.C2-11. The Land Breeze Blows Offshore at Night.

THE 'KATABATIC WIND' BLOWS DOWN MOUNTAIN SLOPES AND VALLEYS AT NIGHT.

During night-time the Earth's surface loses a lot of heat through terrestrial radiation and cools down. This is particularly the case on clear, cloudless nights. The air in contact with the ground loses heat to it by conduction, cools down, becomes denser and starts to sink.

In mountainous regions the cool air will flow down the sides of the mountain slopes and into the valleys, creating what is called a **Katabatic Wind**. In certain areas, Katabatic Winds of 30 knots or so can be flowing down the slopes of large mountains into the valleys by sunrise.

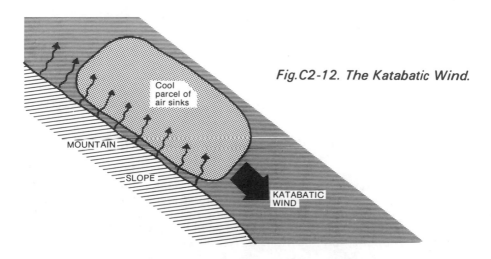

Fig.C2-12. The Katabatic Wind.

THE ANABATIC WIND DRIFTS UP A MOUNTAIN SLOPE BY DAY.

Heating of a mountain slope by day causes the air mass in contact with it to warm, decreasing its density and causing it to flow up the slope. Since its flow uphill is opposed by Gravity, the daytime Anabatic Wind is generally a weaker flow than the night-time Katabatic Wind.

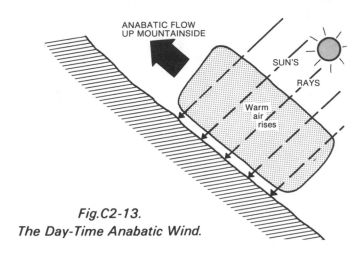

ANABATIC FLOW
UP MOUNTAINSIDE

SUN'S

RAYS

Warm
air
rises

Fig.C2-13.
The Day-Time Anabatic Wind.

TEMPERATURE INVERSIONS.

The general pattern of temperature distribution in the atmosphere is that **temperature decreases with height**. In the International Standard Atmosphere (ISA), which is a purely theoretical model of the atmosphere used as a measuring stick, the temperature is assumed to fall by 2°C for each 1000 ft climbed in the stationary air mass.

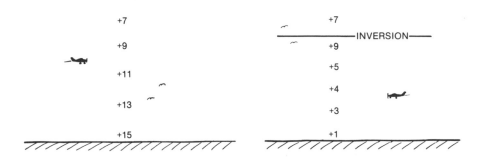

Fig.C2-14. The Normal Temperature Situation and
The Temperature Inversion.

On clear nights when the Earth loses a great deal of heat by terrestrial radiation and cools down, the air in contact with its surface also cools by conduction. The cooler air tends to sink and not mix with air at the higher levels. This will lead to the air at ground level being cooler than the air at altitude, a phenomenon known as a *'Temperature Inversion'*.

The Temperature Inversion may exist only for twenty feet or a few hundred feet, but it is important as it can have by-products such as ground fog or windshear. As a Pilot passes through the Inversion Layer he may experience a slight *'bump'*.

TEMPERATURE IS A MEASURE OF HEAT ENERGY.

As a body of matter absorbs heat energy its molecules become more agitated. This agitation and motion is measured as temperature, which can be used as a measure of heat energy. The temperature at which molecular agitation would theoretically be zero is known as Absolute Zero, i.e. zero on the scientific *'Absolute Scale of Temperature'*, and this occurs at –273°C.

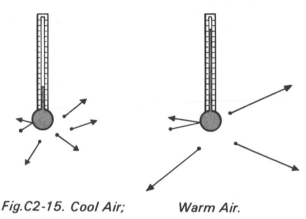

Fig.C2-15. Cool Air;   Warm Air.

THE DIFFERENT TEMPERATURE SCALES IN USE AROUND THE WORLD.

There are various scales used to measure temperature, but the one most widely used in Aviation and Meteorology is the **Celsius** scale, which divides the temperature difference between the boiling point and the freezing point of water into 100 degrees, water boiling at 100°C and freezing at 0°C.

Although most of the World is now using *'degrees Celsius'* (°C), the United States of America is still using the *Fahrenheit* Scale of Temperature based on water boiling at 212°F and freezing at 32°F.

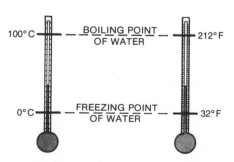

Fig.C2-16. Different Temperature Scales Measure the Same Thing.

There is a requirement for a Pilot (who may fly in different countries from time to time) to be able to convert from °F to °C and vice versa. Flight Navigation Computers have conversion scales marked on them to make it easier for the Pilot, but you should still know the mathematical relationship that exists between °C and °F. How these formulae are developed is explained in Volume 4, Chapter 30.

- Temperature in °F = $\frac{9}{5}$ x °C + 32

- Temperature in °C = $\frac{5}{9}$ x (°F – 32)

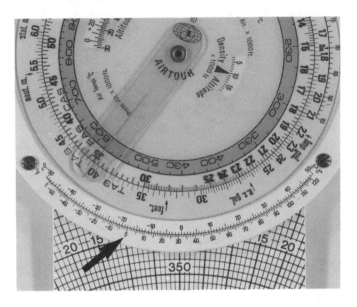

Fig.C2-17. Temperature Conversion Scale On The Airtour CRP-1.

☐ Now tackle **Exercises C2 — Heating Effects in the Atmosphere.**

C3

ATMOSPHERIC PRESSURE

The molecules that make up the air move at high speed in random directions and bounce off any surface that they encounter. The force which they exert on a unit area of that surface is called the **Atmospheric Pressure**.

Because of the fewer air molecules at the higher levels and the less weight of molecules pressing down from above, atmospheric pressure decreases with height. An aeroplane flying at altitude, or a town located in a mountainous area, will therefore experience a lower pressure than at sea level.

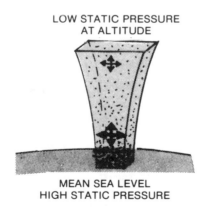

LOW STATIC PRESSURE
AT ALTITUDE

MEAN SEA LEVEL
HIGH STATIC PRESSURE

Fig.C3-1. Atmospheric Pressure Decreases with Height.

Atmospheric Pressure can be measured by:

- **a Mercury Barometer**, where atmospheric pressure at sea level can support a column of approximately 26 inches of mercury by pushing it into a partial vacuum; or

- an **Aneroid Barometer**, where a flexible metal chamber that is partially evacuated is compressed by the atmospheric pressure. The aneroid is used in aircraft altimeters to measure the atmospheric pressure and equate variations in air pressure to changes in altitude.

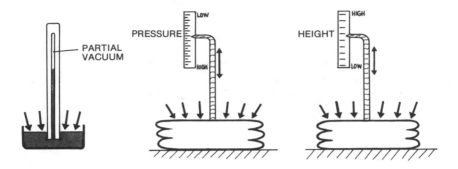

Fig.C3-2. The Mercury Barometer, the Aneroid Barometer and the Altimeter.

In the United Kingdom the unit of pressure used in aviation is the **millibar** (abbrevated **mb**). This is gradually being changed throughout the World to an equivalent unit known as the **hectoPascal**, abbreviated **hPa**, however for the forseeable future **millibars are to be used in the UK**. At sea level on a *standard day,* the atmospheric pressure is 1013·2 mb (or hPa).

As height above sea level is gained in the lower levels of the atmosphere, the pressure drops by approximately 1 mb per 30 ft. An altimeter that reads 0 ft at sea level is calibrated to read 30 ft when the pressure has dropped by 1 mb, 300 ft when it has dropped 10 mb, and 1000 ft when it has dropped 33 mb, and so on.

Altimetry is covered in more detail in other parts of this series – (Aviation Law earlier in this Volume, Navigation (Volume 3) and in Chapter 25 of Volume 4).

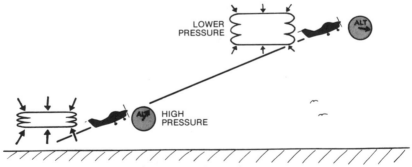

Fig.C3-3. The Altimeter Equates a Pressure Drop with an Increase in Height.

The atmospheric pressure at a particular place is continually varying. These variations may be:

- irregular, due to pressure systems which are passing, intensifying or weakening; and
- regular, due to the daily heating and cooling effects of the Sun – known as the **semi-diurnal variation of pressure**, since it has a 12 hour (½ day) cycle with maximum pressures occurring at about 10 am and 10 pm, and pressures some 2 or 3 mb less occurring in between.

THE PRESSURE GRADIENT.

Readings of atmospheric pressure are taken at many locations on a regular basis and, because these locations are at various altitudes, reduced to a sea level value for comparison purposes.

Places that are experiencing the same calculated sea level pressures are then joined with lines on maps. These lines are known as **isobars**. For reasons of clarity on meteorological charts, the isobars are usually spaced at 2 mb intervals or greater. (Isobars on the Weather Maps published in daily newspapers, which cover a large area, are spaced at 8 mb intervals.)

The isobars often form patterns on the weather map that are very meaningful – some isobars surrounding areas of high pressure, others surrounding areas of low pressure, and others being straight.

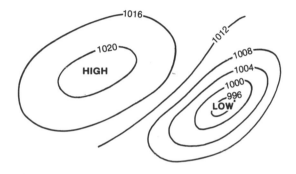

Fig.C3-4. Isobars Join Places of Equal Sea Level Pressure.

The variation of pressure with horizontal distance is called the **Pressure Gradient**, which occurs at right-angles to the isobars. If the isobars are very close together rapid changes in pressure occur and the Pressure Gradient is said to be *'steep'* or *'strong';* if they are widely spaced, the pressure changes are more gradual and so the Pressure Gradient is *'flat'* or *'weak'.*

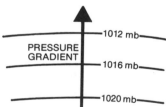

Fig.C3-5. Pressure Gradient.

There is a natural tendency for air to flow from areas of high pressure to areas of low pressure. This increases with the steepness of the Pressure Gradient. As we shall see in the chapter on *'Wind'*, the final air flow is not directly from High to Low, but is somewhat modified as a result of the Earth's rotation.

REGIONAL QNH.

Flights cruising with QNH set in the altimeter subscale should reset the QNH, as advised, to the **current Regional QNH** (also known as *Regional Pressure Setting),* and also when entering a new *'Region'.* If the QNH is **not** revised, then if flying towards an area of low pressure, the aeroplane will gradually descend.

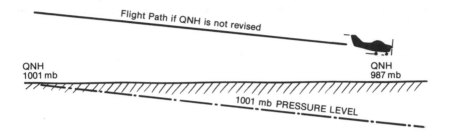

Fig. C3-6. Reset Altimeter to the Current Regional QNH, when Cruising.

This situation could be dangerous, since the altimeter will be indicating the height above the pressure level in the subscale, and this will be higher than the aeroplane's actual height above sea level, i.e. the altimeter will over-read unless the subscale is reset to the lower QNH.

Conversely, flying towards an area of high pressure the situation is reversed. The altimeter will under-read, the aeroplane being at a higher altitude than that indicated, unless the subscale is periodically reset to the higher QNH.

☐ **Exercises C3 — Atmospheric Pressure.**

C4

THE INTERNATIONAL STANDARD ATMOSPHERE (THE ISA)

To act as a measuring stick against which to compare the actual atmosphere existing at any place or time, an **International Standard Atmosphere** has been defined. It is commonly known as the **'ISA'** (pronounced *'eye-sah'*) or the ICAO Standard Atmosphere (ICAO being the International Civil Aviation Organisation, which is a 'wing' of the United Nations).

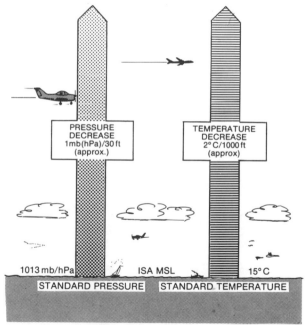

Fig.C4-1. The International Standard Atmosphere (the ISA).

The International Standard Atmosphere is based on **mean sea level** values of:
- pressure 1013·2 mb(hPa);
- temperature +15°C;
- density 1225 gm/cubic metre;
each of which decreases as height is gained.

The temperature falls at a rate of 2°C/1000 ft until the Tropopause is reached at about 36 500 ft AMSL, above which the temperature is assumed to remain constant at –57°C. (In precise terms, the temperature lapse rate is 1·98°C/1000 ft and remains constant at -56·5°C).

The pressure falls at about 1 mb(hPa) per 30 ft gained in the lower levels of the atmosphere (up to about 5000 ft).

IN REALITY, THE ATMOSPHERE DIFFERS FROM THE ISA.

The actual atmosphere can differ from the ISA in many ways. Sea level pressure varies from day to day, indeed from hour to hour, and the temperature also fluctuates between wide extremes at all levels.

The variation of ambient pressure throughout the atmosphere – both horizontally and vertically – is of great significance to Pilots as it affects the operation of the altimeter. This is considered elsewhere in this series.

☐ **Exercises C4 — The International Standard Atmosphere.**

C5

WIND

WHAT IS 'WIND'?

The term *'wind'* refers to the flow of air over the Earth's surface. This flow is almost completely horizontal, with only about 1/1000th of the total flow being vertical.

Despite being only a small proportion of the overall flow of air in the atmosphere, vertical airflow is extremely important to weather and to aviation, since it leads to the formation of cumuliform clouds and thunderstorms. Some vertical winds are so strong, in fact, that they are a hazard to aviation and can destroy aeroplanes. In general, however, the term *'wind'* is used in reference to the horizontal flow of air.

HOW WIND IS DESCRIBED.

Both the direction and strength of a wind are significant and are expressed thus:
- wind direction is the direction **from which the wind is blowing** and is expressed in ° (degrees) measured clockwise from North;
- wind strength is expressed in knots (abbreviated kt).

Direction and strength together describe the **'wind velocity'**, which is usually written in the form 270/35, i.e. a wind blowing from 270° at a strength of 35 knots.

Fig.C5-1. Examples of Wind Velocity.

Meteorologists relate Wind Direction to **True North** and so all winds that appear on forecasts are expressed in °T, i.e. 340/12 on a forecast or meteorological observation means a wind strength of 12 knots from a direction of 340°T.

Runways, however, are described in terms of their **magnetic direction**, so that when an aeroplane is lined up on the runway ready for take-off, its magnetic compass and the runway direction should agree, at least approximately.

The wind direction relative to the runway direction is extremely important when taking-off and landing. For this reason, winds passed to the Pilot by the tower have direction expressed in **degrees magnetic**. This is also the case for the recorded messages on the Automatic Terminal Information Service (ATIS) that a Pilot can listen to on his radio at some airfields.

'VEERING' AND 'BACKING'.

A wind whose direction is changing in a clockwise direction is called a **veering** wind. For example, following a change from 150/25 to 220/30, the wind is said to have veered.

A wind whose direction is changing in an anticlockwise direction is called a **backing** wind. A change from 100/15 to 030/12 is an example of a wind that has backed.

Fig.C5-2. A 'Veering Wind'   and   a 'Backing Wind'.

WHAT CAUSES A WIND TO BLOW?

A change in velocity (speed and/or direction) is called acceleration. Acceleration is caused by a force (or forces) being exerted on an object, be it an aeroplane, a car or a parcel of air.

The combined effect of all the forces acting on a body is known as the net (or resultant) force, and determines the acceleration of the body. If all of the forces acting on a parcel of air balance each other so that the resultant force is zero, then the parcel of air will not accelerate, but will continue to move in a straight line at a constant speed (or stay still). A steady wind velocity is known as **balanced flow**.

THE PRESSURE GRADIENT FORCE.

In the atmosphere the force that is usually responsible for starting a parcel of air moving is the **Pressure Gradient Force**. This acts to move air from areas of **High** pressure to areas of **Low** pressure.

Places on the Earth where air pressure is the same are joined on meteorological maps with lines which are called **isobars**, so the Pressure Gradient force will act at right angles to these and in the direction from the High to the Low pressure. The stronger the Pressure Gradient (i.e. the greater the pressure difference over a given distance), the greater this force will be and, consequently, the stronger the wind will blow.

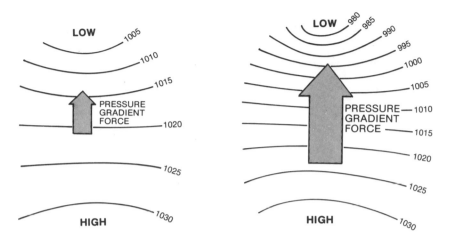

Fig.C5-3. The Pressure Gradient Force Will Start a Parcel of Air Moving.

If the Pressure Gradient force was the only force acting on a parcel of air, it would continue to accelerate towards the Low pressure, getting faster and faster, and eventually the High and Low pressure areas would disappear because of this transfer of air.

We know that this, in fact, does not occur, so there must be some other force that acts on the parcel of air to prevent it rushing from the High pressure area into the Low pressure area. This other force is due to the rotation of the Earth and is known as the 'Coriolis' force.

THE CORIOLIS FORCE.

The Coriolis force acts on a **moving** parcel of air. It is not a 'real' force, but an 'apparent' force resulting from the passage of the air over the rotating Earth.

Imagine a parcel of air that is stationary over Point A on the Equator. It is in fact moving with Point A as the Earth rotates on its axis from West to East. Now, suppose that a Pressure Gradient exists with a High pressure at A and a Low pressure at Point B, directly North of A. The parcel of air at A starts moving towards B, but still with its motion towards the East due to the Earth's rotation.

The further North one goes away from the Equator, the less is this easterly motion of the Earth and so the Earth will lag behind the easterly motion of the parcel of air. Point B will only have moved to B', but the parcel of air will have moved to A''. In other words, to an observer standing on the Earth's surface the parcel of air will **appear** to turn to the right. This effect is due to the 'Coriolis' force.

If the parcel of air was being accelerated in a southerly direction from a High pressure area in the Northern Hemisphere towards a Low near the Equator, the Earth's rotation towards the East would 'get away from it' and so the air flow would appear to turn right also – A having moved to A', but the airflow having only reached B'' to the West.

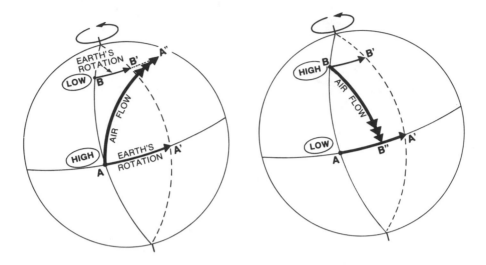

Fig.C5-4. The Coriolis Force Acts Towards the Right in the Northern Hemisphere.

The faster the airflow, the greater the Coriolis effect – if there is no air flow, then there is no Coriolis effect. The Coriolis effect is also greater in regions away from the Equator and towards the Poles, where changes in latitude cause more significant changes in the speed at which each point is moving towards the East.

In the Northern Hemisphere, the Coriolis force deflects the wind to the **right;** in the Southern Hemisphere, the situation is reversed and it deflects the wind to the left.

THE GEOSTROPHIC WIND.

The two forces acting on a moving airstream are:

- the Pressure Gradient force;
  and
- the Coriolis force.

The Pressure Gradient force gets the air moving and the Coriolis effect turns it to the right. This curving of the airflow over the Earth's surface will continue until the Pressure Gradient force is balanced by the Coriolis force, resulting in a wind flow that is steady and blowing in a direction **parallel to the isobars**. This **balanced flow** is called the **Geostrophic Wind**.

The **Geostrophic Wind** is important to a Weather Forecaster because it flows in a **direction** parallel to the isobars with the low pressure to its left, and at a strength directly proportional to the spacing of the isobars (i.e. proportional to the Pressure Gradient). The closeness of the isobars on a chart enables a reasonable forecast of the wind strength to be made.

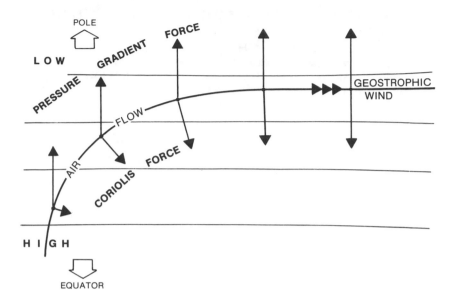

Fig.C5-5. Balanced Flow Will Occur Parallel to the Isobars – the Geostrophic Wind.

BUYS BALLOT'S LAW.

Buys Ballot was a Hollander who noticed that:

> *"If you stand with your back to the wind in the Northern Hemisphere, the low pressure will be on your left".*

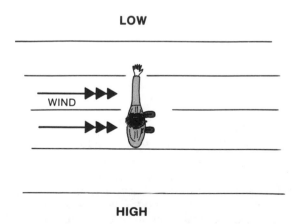

Fig.C5-6. If You stand With Your back to the Wind in the Northern Hemisphere, the LOW Pressure Will Be On Your LEFT – Buys Ballot's Law.

FLYING FROM HIGH TO LOW — STARBOARD (RIGHT) DRIFT — BEWARE BELOW.

If an aeroplane in the Northern Hemisphere is experiencing starboard (right) drift, the wind is from the left and therefore, according to Buys Ballot's Law, the aeroplane is flying towards an area of lower pressure. Low pressure often has poor weather associated with it, such as low cloud, rain and poor visibility.

FLYING FROM LOW TO HIGH — PORT (LEFT) DRIFT.

If an aeroplane in the Northern Hemisphere is experiencing left (port) drift, the wind is from the right and therefore, according to Buys Ballot's Law, the aeroplane is flying towards an area of higher pressure. High pressure often indicates a more stable atmosphere and generally better weather (although fog may occur). Conversely, with right drift the aeroplane is flying towards an area of lower pressure (and, unless the Pilot periodically resets the lower Regional QNHs, the altimeter will over-read, which is not a healthy situation – see Chapter C3).

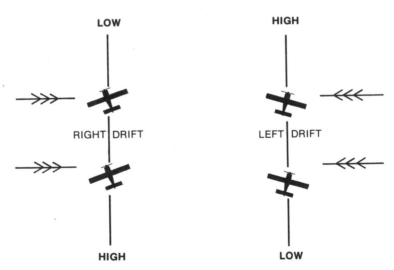

Fig.C5-7. Right (Starboard) Drift –
Low Pressure Area Ahead.

Fig.C5-8. Port (Left) Drift –
High Pressure Area Ahead.

THE 'GRADIENT WIND' BLOWS AROUND CURVED ISOBARS.

Isobars (the lines joining places of equal pressure) are usually curved. For the wind to flow parallel to these isobars, it must be accelerated, in the sense that its direction is changing. In the same manner as a stone when being swung on a string is pulled into the turn by a force, a curving air flow must have a resultant (or net) force acting on it to pull it into the turn.

For a wind that is blowing (anticlockwise) around a LOW in the Northern Hemisphere, the net force results from the Pressure Gradient force being greater than the Coriolis force, thereby pulling the air flow in towards the LOW.

For a wind that is blowing (clockwise) around a HIGH the net force results from the Coriolis force being greater than the Pressure Gradient force. Since the Coriolis force increases with wind speed, it follows that wind speed around a HIGH will be greater than wind speed around a LOW with similarly spaced isobars.

In the Northern Hemisphere, the result is a wind flowing parallel to the isobars, clockwise around a HIGH (known as *'anticyclonic motion'*) and anticlockwise around a LOW (known as *'cyclonic motion'*). Balanced wind flow around curved isobars is called the **Gradient Wind**.

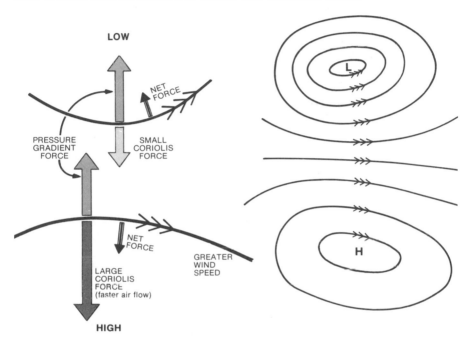

Fig. C5-9. Wind Flows Clockwise Around a HIGH and Anticlockwise Around a LOW in the Northern Hemisphere.

THE SURFACE WIND.

The surface wind is very important to pilots because of the effect it has on take-offs and landings. *'Surface wind'* is measured at 10 metres (30 ft) above level and open ground, i.e. where windsocks and other wind indicators are generally placed.

Wind is usually less strong near the surface than at higher levels. The gradient wind at height that flows parallel to the curved isobars is slowed down by the friction that exists between the lower layers of the airflow and the Earth's surface. The Coriolis effect will be less due to the lower wind speed, and so the wind will *back* in direction. The rougher the surface is, the greater the slowing down. Friction forces will be least over oceans and flat desert areas, and greatest over hilly or city areas with many obstructions.

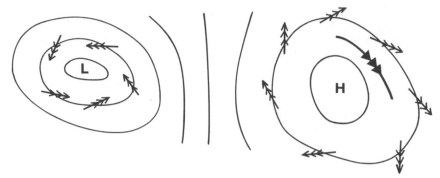

Fig.C5-10. Friction Causes the Surface Wind to Weaken in Strength and Back in Direction.

A reduced wind speed results in a reduced Coriolis force (since it depends upon speed). Therefore the Pressure Gradient force will have a more pronounced effect in the lower levels, causing the wind to flow in towards the Low Pressure Area and out towards the High Pressure Area rather than flow parallel to the isobars. In other words, **the Surface Wind tends to 'back' compared to the Gradient Wind**.

Over oceans, the surface wind may slow to about two-thirds of the Gradient Wind strength and the backing may only be about 10°, but over land surfaces it may slow to only one-third of the Gradient Wind strength and be some 30° back from the gradient flow parallel to the isobars.

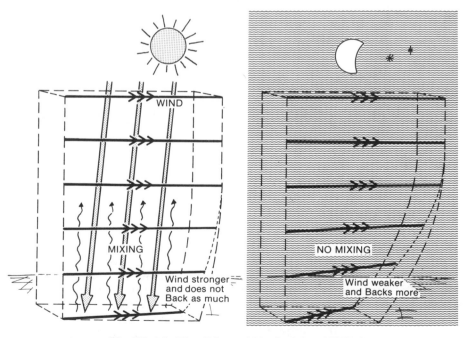

Fig.C5-11. The Diurnal Variation of Wind.

Frictional forces due to the Earth's surface decrease rapidly with height and are almost negligible above 2000 ft above ground level (AGL). The turbulence due to wind flow over rough ground also fades out at about the same height above the surface.

The Diurnal (i.e. Daily) Variation in the Surface Wind.

During the day, heating of the Earth's surface by the rays of the Sun, and the consequent heating of the air in contact with it, will cause vertical motion in the lower levels of the atmosphere. This promotes mixing of the various layers of air and consequently the effect of the Gradient Wind at altitude will be brought closer to the Earth's surface.

The Surface Wind by day will resemble the Gradient Wind more closely than the Surface Wind by night, i.e. the *'Day Surface Wind'* will be seen as a stronger wind that has veered compared to the *'Night Surface Wind'*.

During the night, mixing of the layers will decrease. The Gradient Wind will continue to blow at altitude, but its effects will not be mixed with the air flow at the surface to such an extent as during the day. The Night Wind at surface level will drop in strength and the Coriolis effect will weaken, i.e. **compared to the Day Wind, the Night Wind will drop in strength and back in direction.**

LOCALISED FRICTION EFFECTS.

The Surface Wind may bear no resemblance to the Gradient Wind at 2000 ft AGL and above if it has to blow over and around obstacles such as hills, trees, buildings, etc. The wind will form turbulent eddies, the size of which will depend upon both the size of the obstructions and the wind strength.

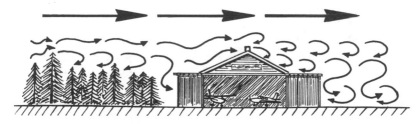

Fig. C5-12. Friction and Obstacles Affect the Surface Wind.

FLIGHT IN TURBULENCE.

Some degree of turbulence is almost always present in the atmosphere and Pilots quickly become accustomed to its minor versions. Moderate or severe turbulence, however, is uncomfortable and can even overstress the aeroplane.

Vertical gusts will increase the angle of attack, causing an increase in the Lift generated at that particular airspeed and therefore an increased Load Factor. Of course, if the angle of attack is increased beyond the critical angle, the wing will stall and this can occur at a speed well above the published 1g stalling speed.

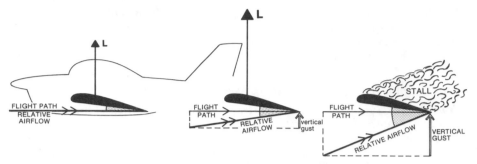

Fig. C5-13. Vertical Gusts Increase Angle of Attack and Will Increase the Load Factor and/or Stall the Wing.

Load Factor (or g-force) is a measure of the stress on the aeroplane and each category of aeroplane is built to take only certain Load Factors. It is important that these Load Factors are not exceeded. One means of achieving this is to fly the aeroplane at *'turbulence penetration speed'* which is usually slower by some 10–20% than normal cruise speed, but not so slow as to allow the aeroplane to stall, remembering that in turbulence the aeroplane may stall at a speed higher than that published.

When encountering turbulence:

- fasten seat belts;
- hold the attitude for the desired flight phase (i.e. climb, cruise, descent), using whatever aileron movements are needed to retain lateral control, but being fairly gentle on the elevator to avoid over-stressing the airframe structurally through large changes in angle of attack and Lift produced;
- the Air Speed Indicator will probably be fluctuating so will be less useful than normally. Aim to have the airspeed fluctuate around the selected turbulence penetration speed, which may require reduced power. Use power to maintain speed.

It is of course better to avoid turbulence, and to some extent this is possible:

- avoid flying underneath, in or near thunderstorms where airflows can be enormous;
- avoid flying under large cumulus clouds because of the large updrafts that cause them;
- avoid flying in the lee of hills when strong winds are blowing, since they will tumble over the ridges and possibly be quite turbulent as well as flowing down into valleys at a rate which your aeroplane may not be able to outclimb;
- avoid flying at a low level over rough ground when strong winds are blowing.

WINDSHEAR.

Windshear is the variation of wind speed and/or direction from place to place. It affects the flight path and airspeed of an aeroplane and can be a hazard to aviation. Flight considerations involving Windshear are covered in Volume 4, (Chapter 36) of this series.

Windshear is generally present to some extent as an aeroplane approaches the ground for a landing, because of the different speed and direction of the surface wind compared to the wind at altitude. Low level windshear can be quite marked at night or in the early morning when there is little mixing of the lower layers, for instance when a temperature inversion exists.

Windshear can also be expected when a Sea Breeze or a Land Breeze is blowing, or when in the vicinity of a Thunderstorm. Cumulonimbus clouds have enormous updrafts and downdrafts associated with them, and the effects can be felt up to 10 or 20 nm away from the actual cloud. **Windshear and turbulence associated with a Thunderstorm can destroy an aeroplane.**

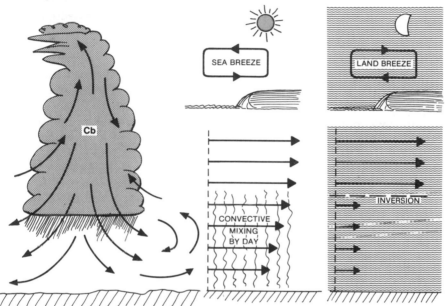

Fig.C5-14. Windshear is a Change of Wind Speed and/or Direction Between Various Places.

WIND ASSOCIATED WITH MOUNTAINS.

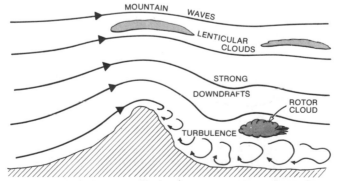

Fig.C5-15. Avoid Flying Near Mountains in Strong Winds.

Wind that flows over a mountain and down the lee side can be a hazard to aviation, not only because it may be turbulent, but also because the aeroplane will have to *'climb'* into it even to maintain altitude. For this reason, an aeroplane should maintain a vertical clearance of several thousand feet above mountainous areas in strong wind conditions.

There may also be local wind effects, such as the Katabatic Wind that flows down cool slopes at night and in the morning, and also Valley Winds.

Large mountains or mountain ranges cause an effect on the wind that may extend well above ground level, resulting in **Mountain Waves**, possibly with associated lenticular clouds. The up-currents and down-currents associated with mountain waves can be quite strong, and can extend for 30 or 40 nm downwind of the mountains. Rotor areas may form beneath the crests of the nearer lee waves, and are often characterised by a Roll Cloud. There may be severe turbulence in the rotor zone.

WIND IN THE TROPICS.

In tropical areas, Pressure Gradients are generally fairly weak and so will not cause the air to flow at high speeds. Local effects, such as Land and Sea Breezes, may have a stronger influence than the Pressure Gradient.

The Coriolis force that causes the air to flow parallel to the isobars is very weak in the tropics since the distance from the Earth's axis remains fairly constant. The Pressure Gradient force, even though relatively weak, will dominate and the air will tend to flow more from the High pressure areas to the Low pressure areas than parallel to the isobars.

Instead of using isobars (which join places of equal pressure) on tropical weather charts, it is more common to use:
- **streamlines** to indicate wind direction, which will be **outdrafts** from high pressure areas and **indrafts** to low pressure areas;
  in combination with
- **isotachs**, which are dotted lines joining places of equal wind strength.

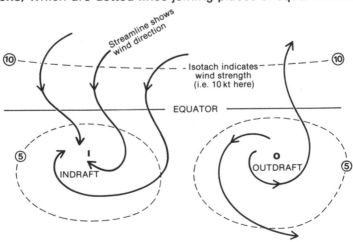

Fig.C5-16. Streamline/Isotach Analysis Chart.

☐ Now you should be able to breeze through **Exercises C5 — Wind.**

C6

CLOUD

A cloud is a visible aggregate of minute particles of water and/or ice in the free air. The effect of cloud on aviation, particularly visual flight, makes them an important topic in training to become a Pilot. The presence of low *'Stratus'* clouds, for example, can cause a flight to divert or even turn back without reaching the destination.

Large build-ups of cloud can develop in *'unstable'* atmospheric conditions into the highly significant hazards to flight that we call thunderstorms – known in meteorological terms as *'Cumulonimbus'*.

Unfortunately, the classification of cloud types and of individual clouds is not straightforward, because clouds may take on numerous different forms, many of which continually change. It is important to have an understanding of cloud classification because the meteorological forecasts and reports use this system to give a picture of the weather for the Pilot.

The four main groups of clouds are:
- **cirriform** (or fibrous);
- **cumuliform** (or heaped);
- **stratiform** (or layered); and
- **nimbus** (or rain-bearing).

Clouds are further divided according to the level of their bases Above Mean Sea Level, resulting in ten basic types.

HIGH LEVEL CLOUDS.

High level clouds have a base above 20 000 ft and look quite fine and spidery because they are distant from the observer. As they are in a quite cold region of the atmosphere they are composed of ice crystals rather than water particles.

(1) Cirrus (Ci): detached clouds in the form of white delicate filaments, white patches or narrow bands. These clouds have a fibrous or silky appearance.

(2) Cirrocumulus (Cc): a thin, white patch, sheet or layer of cloud without shading, composed of very small elements in the form of grain or ripples, joined together or separate, and more or less regularly arranged. Most of the elements have an apparent width of less than 1° of arc (approximately the width of the little finger at arm's length). 'Cirrus' indicates *high* and 'cumulus' indicates *lumpy* or *heaped*.

(3) Cirrostratus (Cs): a transparent whitish veil of fibrous or smooth appearance, totally or partly covering the sky and generally producing a *halo* phenomenon (a luminous white ring around the sun or moon with a faint red fringe on the inside). 'Cirrus' indicates *high* and 'stratus' indicates *sheet*.

MIDDLE LEVEL CLOUD.

Middle level cloud has a base above about 6500 ft AMSL.

(4) Altocumulus (Ac): a layer of patches of cloud composed of laminae or rather flattened globular masses, rolls, etc., the smallest elements having a width of between 1° and 5° of arc (the width of three fingers at arm's length). They are arranged in groups or lines or waves which may be joined to form a continuous layer or appear in broken patches and shaded either white or grey. Coronae (one or more coloured rings around the Sun or Moon) are characteristic of this cloud. In an unstable atmosphere, the vertical development of *Ac* may be sufficient to produce precipitation in the form of *'Virga'* (rain that does not reach the ground) or slight showers. 'Alto' means *middle level* and 'cumulus' means *heaped*.

(5) Altostratus (As): a greyish or bluish cloud sheet of fibrous or uniform appearance totally or partly covering the sky and having parts thin enough to reveal the sun at least vaguely as though through ground glass. Precipitation in the form of rain or snow can occur with As. 'Stratus' means *layer* and so Altostratus is *middle level layer cloud.*

LOW LEVEL CLOUD.

Low cloud has a base below about 6500 ft AMSL.

(6) Nimbostratus (Ns): a dark grey cloud layer generally covering the whole sky and thick enough throughout to hide the Sun or Moon. The base appears diffuse due to more or less continuously falling rain or snow. At times *Ns* may be confused with *As* since it is like thick Altostratus, but its darker grey colour and lack of a distinct lower surface distinguish it as *Ns*. It may be middle or low level cloud. 'Nimbus' means *rain-bearing* and 'stratus' means *layer*.

(7) Stratocumulus (Sc): a grey or whitish patch or sheet of cloud which has dark parts composed of rounded masses or rolls which may be joined or show breaks between the thicker areas. Most of the rounded masses have an apparent width of more than 5° of arc (the width of three fingers at arm's length). The associated weather, if any, is very light rain, drizzle or snow. 'Stratus' means *layer* and 'cumulus' means *heaped*.

(8) Stratus (St): a generally grey cloud layer with a fairly uniform base, which may give precipitation in the form of drizzle. When the Sun is visible through the cloud, its outline is clearly discernible. 'Stratus' means *layer*.

(9) Cumulus (Cu): detached clouds, generally dense and with sharp outlines, developing vertically in the form of rising mounds, domes or towers, of which the upper part often resembles a cauliflower. The sunlit parts of these clouds are mostly brilliant white. Their base is relatively dark since sunlight may not reach it and nearly horizontal. Precipitation in the form of rain or snow showers may occur with large Cumulus. 'Cumulus' means *heaped*.

(10) Cumulonimbus (Cb): a heavy and dense cloud with considerable vertical extent in the form of a mountain or huge tower. At least part of its upper portion is usually fibrous or striated, often appearing as an anvil or vast plume. The base of the cloud appears dark and stormy. Low ragged clouds are frequently observed below the base and generally other varieties of low cloud, such as *Cu* and *Sc*, are joined to or in close proximity to the *Cb*.

Lightning, thunder and hail are characteristic of this type of cloud, while associated weather may be moderate to heavy showers of rain, snow or hail. 'Cumulo' means *heaped* and 'nimbus' means *rain-bearing*.

Noting any precipitation can help in recognising the particular type of cloud. Showers (which start and stop suddenly and may be followed by a clear sky) fall only from convective clouds such as Cumulus and Cumulonimbus.

PRECIPITATION.

Intermittent or continuous precipitation (which usually starts and finishes gradually, perhaps over a long period) is usually associated with stratiform cloud, e.g. drizzle from Stratus and Stratocumulus, heavy continuous rain or snow from Nimbostratus, rain from Altostratus. Showers are associated with cumuliform clouds.

The above are the ten main cloud classifications, but there are certain variations that you may see mentioned, such as:

- **stratus fractus and cumulus fractus** – stratus or cumulus, as appropriate, observed as shreds or fragments below the base of nimbostratus or altostratus;

- **castellanus** – a number of small, cumiliform clouds sharing a common base and indicating the growth of middle level clouds in an unstable atmosphere;

- **lenticularis** – lens-shaped clouds formed in standing waves over mountains caused by strong winds aloft and often associated with cumiliform cloud.

Before continuing with the remainder of the material in this chapter, we recommend that you study the colour plates of the main forms of cloud.

MOISTURE IN THE ATMOSPHERE

Cloud, of course, is formed from water vapour which is contained in the atmosphere. It is taken up into the atmosphere by evaporation from the oceans and other bodies where water is present.

THE THREE STATES OF WATER.

Water in its vapour state is not visible, but when the water vapour condenses out to form water droplets we see it as cloud, fog, mist, rain or dew. Frozen water is also visible as cloud (high level), snow, hail, ice or frost. Water therefore exists in three states – gas (vapour), liquid (water) and solid (ice).

Under certain conditions water can change from one state to the other, absorbing heat energy if it moves to a higher energy state (from ice to water to vapour) and giving-off heat energy if it moves to a lower energy state (vapour to water to ice). This heat energy is known as **latent heat** and is a vital part of any change of state.

The three states of water, the names of the various transfer processes and the absorption or giving-off of latent heat are shown in the diagram below.

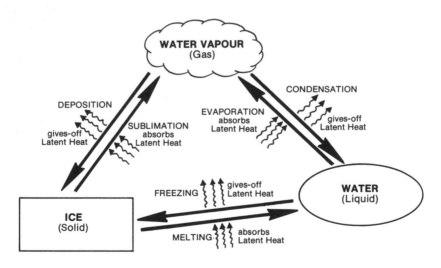

Fig.C6-13. The Three States of Water.

HUMIDITY.

The **amount of water vapour** present in the air is called **humidity,** but the actual amount is not as important as whether the air can support that water vapour or not.

*Fig.C6-1.
Filaments of
Cirrus (Ci).*

*Fig.C6-2.
Cirrostratus (Cs).*

*Fig.C6-3.
Altostratus (As),
thickening towards
horizon; Cu fractus
below.*

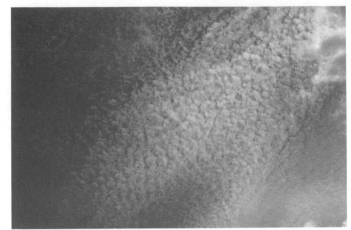

Fig.C6-4.
Altocumulus (Ac).

Fig.C6-5.
Nimbostratus (Ns).

Fig.C6-6.
Stratocumulus (Sc).

*Fig.C6-7.
Stratus (St);
terrain (and TV
mast!) in cloud.*

*Fig.C6-8.
Cumulus (Cu).*

*Fig.C6-9.
Large Cumulus
build-up;
(showers and poor
visibility below).*

*Fig.C6-10.
Mature
Cumulonimbus (Cb);
(avoid Cb clouds,
with or without
anvil).*

*Fig.C6-11.
Ac Castellanus
formation.*

*Fig.C6-12.
Lenticular
Altocumulus.*

RELATIVE HUMIDITY.

When a parcel of air is supporting as much **water vapour** as it can, it is said to be **'saturated'** and have a **'Relative Humidity of 100%'**. If it is supporting less than its full capacity of water vapour, it is said to be unsaturated and its Relative Humidity will be less than 100%. Air supporting only a third of the water vapour that it could has a Relative Humidity of 33%. There are of course many degrees of saturation ranging from 0% to 100%. In cloud and fog it is 100%, whereas over a desert it may be 20%.

Relative Humidity is defined as the ratio of water vapour actually in the parcel of air relative to what it can hold (i.e. when it is saturated) at a particular temperature and pressure.

$$RH = \frac{\text{mass of water vapour}}{\text{mass of water vapour at saturation}} \times \frac{100}{1} \%$$

How much water a particular parcel of air can support is dependent upon the air temperature – warm air being able to support more than cool air. If the temperature falls, the amount of water vapour that the air can support decreases and so the Relative Humidity will increase. In other words, even though no moisture has been added, the Relative Humidity of a parcel of air will increase as its temperature drops.

DEWPOINT TEMPERATURE.

Dewpoint is the temperature at which a parcel of air becomes saturated if it cools (at constant pressure), i.e. the temperature at which it is no longer able to support all of the water vapour that it contains; the more moisture in the air, the higher its dewpoint temperature.

A parcel of air that has a temperature higher than its Dewpoint will be unsaturated, i.e. its Relative Humidity is **less** than 100%. The closer the actual temperature is to the Dewpoint, the closer the air is to being saturated.

At its Dewpoint, the air will be fully saturated (RH = 100%) and if it becomes cooler than its Dewpoint, then the excess water vapour will condense out as visible water droplets (or, if it is cool enough, as ice). This process can be seen both when moist air cools at night to form fog, dew or frost, and as air rises and cools, the water vapour condensing out into the small water droplets that form clouds. If the air is unable to support these water droplets (for example, if they become too large and heavy), then they fall as precipitation (rain, hail or snow).

ADIABATIC PROCESSES.

An adiabatic process is one in which heat is neither added to nor removed from the system. The expansion and compression of gases are adiabatic processes where, although heat is neither added nor removed, the temperature of the system may change, e.g. placing your finger over the outlet of a bicycle pump will illustrate that compressing air increases its temperature.

Conversely, air that is compressed and stored at room temperature will feel cool if released to the atmosphere and allowed to expand. Reducing pressure will lower the temperature.

THE FORMATION OF CLOUD

A very common adiabatic process that involves the expansion of a gas and its cooling is when a parcel of air rises in the atmosphere. This can be initiated by the heating of the parcel of air, causing it to expand and become less dense than the surrounding air, hence it will rise. A parcel of air can also be forced aloft as it blows over a mountain range.

Unsaturated air will cool adiabatically at about 3°C/1000 ft as it rises. This is known as the **Dry Adiabatic Lapse Rate (DALR)**.

Cooler air can support less water vapour, so, as the parcel of air rises and cools, its Relative Humidity will increase. At the height where its temperature is reduced to the dewpoint temperature (i.e. Relative Humidity reaches 100%), water will start to condense out and form cloud.

Above this height the now-saturated air will continue to cool as it rises but, because latent heat will be given-off as the water vapour condenses into the lower energy liquid state, the cooling will not be as great. The rate at which saturated air cools as it rises is known as the **Saturated Adiabatic Lapse Rate (SALR)** and may be assumed to have a value of approximately half the DALR, i.e. 1·5°C/1000 ft.

The Type of Cloud Which Forms Depends Upon the Atmospheric Environment.

The nature and extent of any cloud which forms depends upon the nature of the surrounding atmosphere through which the parcel of air is ascending. As long as the parcel of air is warmer than its surroundings, it will continue to rise. An atmosphere in which a parcel of air, when given vertical movement, continues to move away from its original level is called **'unstable'**. Cumiliform clouds (i.e. heaped) may form to a high level in such an atmospheric situation; the more moisture in the air, the higher its dewpoint temperature.

If the surrounding atmosphere is warmer than the parcel of air, it will stop rising because its density will be greater than the surroundings. An atmosphere in which air tends to remain at the one level is called a **'stable'** atmosphere.

The rate of temperature change in the surrounding atmosphere is called the **Environmental Lapse Rate (ELR)** and its relationship to DALR and SALR is a main factor in determining the levels of the bases and tops of the clouds that form.

The International Standard Atmosphere (ISA), which is simply a theoretical *'measuring stick'* against which the actual atmosphere at any time or place can be compared, assumes an ELR of 2°C/1000 ft. The actual ELR in a real atmosphere, however, may differ greatly from this.

CLOUD FORMED BY CONVECTION DUE TO HEATING.

Suppose that a parcel of air overlying a large ploughed field is heated to +17°C, whereas the air in the surrounding environment is only 12°C. The heated parcel of air will start to rise, due to its lower density, and cool at the Dry Adiabatic Lapse Rate of 3°C/1000 ft.

If the Environmental Lapse Rate happens to be 1°C/1000 ft, then the environmental air through which the heated parcel is rising will cool at only 1°C/1000 ft.

Suppose that the moisture content of the parcel of air is such that the dewpoint temperature is 11°C. By 2000 ft AGL the rising parcel of air will have reached this and so water will start to condense out and form cloud. At 2000 ft AGL, the environmental air will have cooled to 10°C, so the parcel of air will continue rising since it is still warmer (11°).

As the parcel of air continues to rise above the level at which cloud first forms, latent heat will be given-off as more and more vapour condenses into liquid water. This reduces the rate at which the rising air cools to the **'Saturated Adiabatic Lapse Rate'** of 1·5°C/1000 ft.

In this example, at this new rate of cooling the parcel of air will have cooled to the same temperature as the surrounding environment (8°C) at a height of 4000 ft AGL and so will cease rising. A Cumulus cloud, base 2000 ft and tops 4000 ft, has been formed.

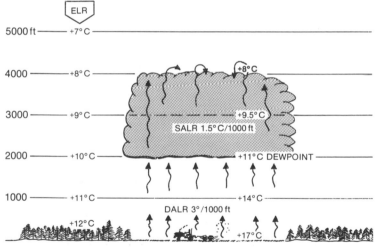

Fig.C6-14. The Formation of a Cumulus Cloud.

CLOUD FORMED BY OROGRAPHIC UPLIFT.

Air flowing over mountains rises and cools adiabatically. If it cools to below its **dewpoint temperature**, then the water vapour will condense out and cloud will form.

Descending on the other side of the mountains, however, the air flow will warm adiabatically and, once its temperature exceeds the dewpoint for that parcel of air, the water vapour will no longer condense out. The liquid water drops will now start to vaporise, and the cloud will cease to exist below this level.

A cloud that forms as a *'cap'* over the top of a mountain is known as **Lenticular** cloud. It will remain more or less stationary whilst the air flows through it.

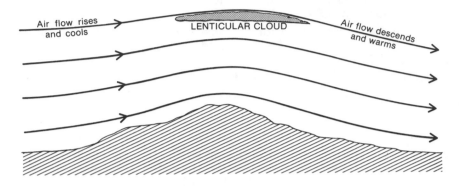

Fig.C6-15. Lenticular Cloud as a Cap Over a Mountain.

Sometimes, when an air stream flows over a mountain range and there is a stable layer of air above, **Standing Waves** occur. This is a wavy pattern as the air flow settles back into a more steady flow and, if the air is moist, **Lenticular clouds** may form in the crest of the lee waves, and a **Rotor** or **Roll cloud** may form at a low level.

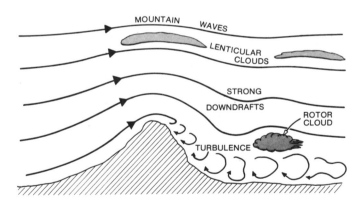

Fig.C6-16. Mountain Waves.

The level at which the cloud base forms depends upon the moisture content of the parcel of air and its dewpoint temperature. The cloud base may be below the mountain tops or well above them depending upon the situation. Once having started to form, the cloud may sit low over the mountain as stratiform cloud (if the air is stable), or (if the air is unstable) the cloud will be cumiliform and may rise to high levels.

For interesting reading regarding *'Flight Over And In The Vicinity Of High Ground'*, refer to Aeronautical Information Circular (AIC) 79/1984 (Pink 66).

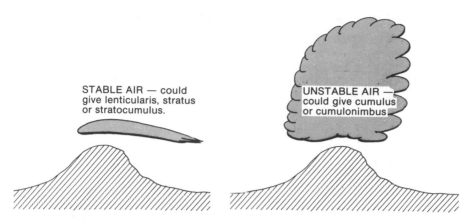

Fig.C6-17. Orographic Uplift Can Lead to Cloud Formation.

THE FOEHN WIND EFFECT.

If the air rising up a mountain range is moist enough to have a high dewpoint temperature and is cooled down to it before reaching the top of the mountain, then cloud will form on the windward side. If any precipitation occurs, moisture will be removed from the airflow and, as it descends on the lee side of the mountain, it will therefore be drier. The dewpoint temperature will be less and so the cloud base will be higher on the lee side of the mountain.

As the dry air beneath the cloud descends, it will warm at the Dry Adiabatic Lapse Rate of 3°C/1000 ft, which is at a greater rate than the rising air cooled inside the cloud (Saturated Adiabatic Lapse Rate: 1·5°C/1000 ft). The result is a warmer and drier wind on the lee side of the mountains. This very noticeable effect is seen in many parts of the world, for example the **'Foehn'** (pronounced *'fern'*) wind in Switzerland and Southern Germany, from which this effect gets its name.

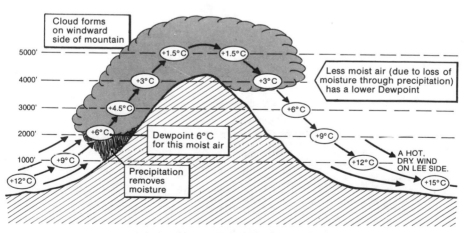

Fig.C6-18. The Foehn Wind Effect.

CLOUD FORMED BY TURBULENCE AND MIXING.

As air flows over the surface of the Earth, frictional effects cause variations in local wind strength and direction. Eddies are set up which cause the lower levels of air to mix – the stronger the wind and the rougher the Earth's surface, the larger the eddies and the stronger the mixing.

The air in the rising currents will cool and, if the turbulence extends to a sufficient height, it may cool to the dewpoint temperature, water vapour will condense out to form liquid water droplets and cloud will form.

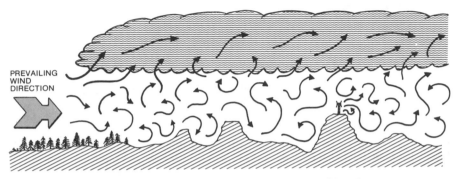

Fig.C6-19. Formation of Turbulence Cloud.

The descending air currents in the turbulent layer will warm and, if the air's dewpoint temperature is exceeded, the liquid water droplets that make up the cloud will return to the water vapour state. The air will dry out and cloud will not exist below this level.

With turbulent mixing, stratiform cloud may form over quite a large area, possibly with an undulating base. It may be continuous Stratus or broken Stratocumulus.

CLOUD CAN BE FORMED BY THE WIDESPREAD ASCENT OF AN AIR MASS.

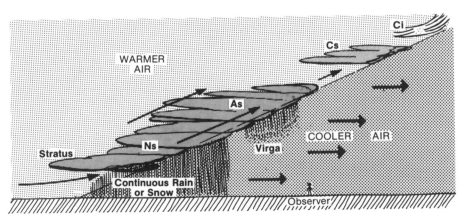

Fig.C6-20. Cloud Formation due to Widespread Ascent.

When two large masses of air of differing temperatures meet, the warmer and less dense air will flow over (or be undercut by) the cooler air. As the warmer air mass is forced aloft it will cool and, if the dewpoint temperature is reached, cloud will form. The boundary layer between two air masses is called a **'Front'**. Weather associated with frontal activity is considered in Chapter C8.

PRECIPITATION ASSOCIATED WITH CLOUD.

Precipitation refers to falling water that finally reaches the ground, including:
- rain consisting of liquid water drops;
- drizzle consisting of fine water droplets;
- snow consisting of branched and star-shaped ice crystals;
- hail consisting of small balls of ice;
- freezing rain or drizzle which freezes on contact with a cold surface (which may be the ground or an aircraft in flight).

Continuous rain or snow is often associated with Nimbostratus and Altostratus clouds and intermittent rain or snow with Altostratus or Stratocumulus. Rain or snow showers are associated with cumiliform clouds such as Cumulonimbus, Cumulus and Altocumulus, extremely heavy showers and/or hail coming from Cumulonimbus.

Fine drizzle or snow is associated with Stratus and Stratocumulus.

It is possible to use precipitation as a means of identifying the cloud type – showers generally falling from cumuliform clouds and non-showery precipitation from stratiform clouds, mainly Altostratus and Nimbostratus.

Fig.C6-21. Showers Fall from Cumuliform Clouds.

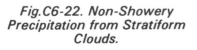

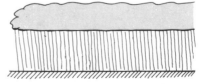

Fig.C6-22. Non-Showery Precipitation from Stratiform Clouds.

Rain that falls from the base of clouds but evaporates before reaching the ground (hence is not really precipitation) is called **Virga**. It can, of course, affect aeroplanes that fly through it.

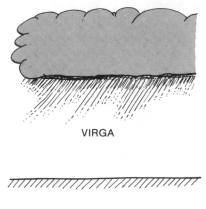

VIRGA

Fig.C6-23. Virga.

☐ Now complete **Exercises C6 — Cloud.**

C7

THUNDERSTORMS

Thunderstorms generate spectacular weather which may be accompanied by thunder, lightning, heavy rain showers and sometimes hail, squalls and tornadoes. Thunderstorms are associated with Cumulonimbus clouds and there may be several Thunderstorm *'cells'* within the one cloud. They constitute a severe hazard to the aviator, especially in light aircraft.

Associated with Thunderstorms is lightning, which is a discharge of static electricity that has been built up in the cloud. The air along the path that the lightning follows experiences intense heating. This causes it to expand violently, and it is this expansion which produces the familiar *clap* of thunder.

Three conditions are necessary for a Thunderstorm to develop:

- **deep instability** in the atmosphere, so that once the air starts to rise it will continue rising (for example, a steep lapse rate with warm air in the lower levels and cold air in the upper levels);

- a **high moisture** content;

- a **trigger action** (or catalyst) to start the air rising, from:
  - a front forcing the air aloft;

    - a mountain forcing the air aloft;

    - strong heating of the air in contact with the Earth's surface; or

    - heating of the lower layers of a polar air mass as it moves to lower latitudes, (i.e. towards the Equator).

THE LIFE CYCLE OF A THUNDERSTORM.

1. The Cumulus Stage.

As the moist air rises, it is cooled until its dewpoint temperature is reached. Then the water vapour starts to condense out as liquid droplets and cloud forms. Latent heat is given-off in the condensation process and so the rising air cools at a lesser rate. At this early *cumulus stage* in the formation of a Thunderstorm, there are strong, warm updrafts over a diameter of one or two miles, with no significant downdrafts.

Air is drawn horizontally into the cell at all levels and causes the updraft to become stronger with height. The temperature inside the cloud is higher than the outside environment and the cloud continues to build to greater and greater heights. This often occurs at such a rate that an aeroplane cannot out-climb the growing cloud.

The strong, warm updrafts carry the water droplets higher and higher, to levels often well above the freezing level, where they may freeze or continue to exist as liquid water in a supercooled state. The liquid droplets will coalesce to form larger and larger drops.

The Cumulus Stage typically lasts 10 to 20 minutes.

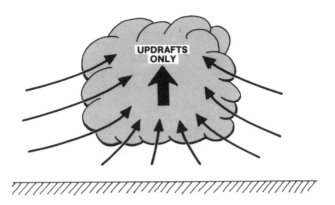

Fig.C7-1. The Cumulus Stage in the Development of a Thunderstorm.

2. The Mature Stage.

The water drops eventually become too large and heavy to be supported by the updrafts (even though the updrafts may be in excess of 5000 ft/min) and so start to fall. As they fall in great numbers inside the cloud, they drag air along with them causing **downdrafts**. Often the first lightning flashes and the first rain from the cloud base will occur at this stage.

The descending air warms adiabatically, but the very cold drops of water slow down the rate at which this occurs, resulting in very cool downdrafts in contrast to the warm updrafts. Heavy rain or hail may fall from the base of the cloud, generally being heaviest for the first 5 minutes.

The top of the cloud in this mature stage may reach as far as the Tropopause, being some 20000 ft in temperate latitudes and 50000 ft in the tropics. The cloud may have the typical shape of a Cumulonimbus, with the top spreading out in an **'anvil'** shape in the direction of the upper winds. The passage of an aeroplane through the Windshear of these violent updrafts and downdrafts, (which are very close to each other), can result in structural failure.

The rapidly changing direction from which the airflow strikes the wings could also result in a stall, so **flying into a mature Cumulonimbus cloud would be a very foolhardy thing to do.**

As the cold downdrafts flow out of the base of the cloud (at a great rate) they change direction and begin to flow horizontally as the ground is approached. **Strong Windshear will occur. This has caused the demise of many aeroplanes.** The outflowing cold air will undercut the inflowing warmer air and, like a *mini cold front,* a gusty wind and a sudden drop in temperature may precede the actual storm.

A **roll cloud** may also develop at the base of the main cloud where the cold downdrafts and warm updrafts pass.

The Mature Stage typically lasts from 20 to 40 minutes.

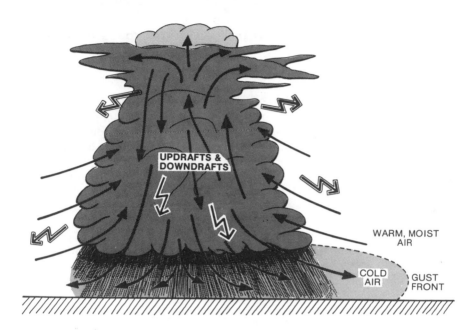

Fig.C7-2. The Mature Stage.

3. The Dissipating Stage.

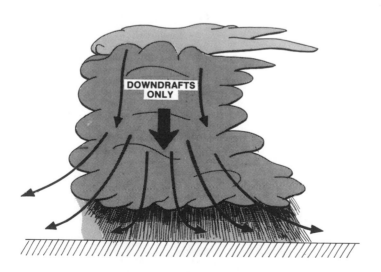

Fig.C7-3. The Dissipating Stage.

The cold downdrafts gradually cause the warm updrafts to weaken and so reduce the supply of warm, moist air to the upper levels of the cloud. The cold downdrafts continue (since they are colder than the environment surrounding the cloud) and spread out over the whole cloud, which starts to collapse from above.

Eventually the temperature inside the cloud warms to reach that of the environment and what was once a towering Cumulonimbus may collapse into a stratiform cloud.

THUNDERSTORMS ARE A HAZARD TO AVIATION.

The dangers to aviation from a Thunderstorm do not exist just inside or under the cloud, but for quite some distance around it. **Thunderstorms are best avoided by at least 10 nm** and, **in severe situations, by 20 nm or more.** Most jet transports and advanced aeroplanes are equipped with Weather Radar to enable their Pilots to do this. The visual Pilot without Weather Radar has to use his eyes and common sense.

Some obvious dangers to aeroplanes from Thunderstorms include:
• severe Windshear (causing flight path deviations and handling problems, loss of airspeed and possibly structural damage);
• severe turbulence (causing loss of control and structural damage);
• severe icing (possibly the very dangerous clear ice formed from large supercooled water drops striking a sub-zero surface);
• damage from hail (to the airframe and cockpit windows);
• reduced visibility;
• damage from lightning strikes, including electrical damage;
• interference to radio communications and radio navigation instruments.

Avoid Thunderstorms by at least ten nautical miles (10 nm) and, in severe situations, by 20 nm or more.

□ Now complete **Exercises C7 — Thunderstorms.**

C8

AIR MASSES AND FRONTAL WEATHER

AIR MASSES

An Air Mass is a large parcel of air with fairly consistent properties (such as temperature and moisture content) throughout. It is usual to classify an air mass according to:

- its **origin**;
- its **path** over the Earth's surface; and
- whether the air is **diverging** or **converging**.

THE ORIGIN OF AN AIR MASS.

'**Maritime air**' flowing over an ocean will absorb moisture and tend to become saturated in its lower levels; '**continental air**' flowing over a land mass will remain reasonably dry since little water is available for evaporation.

THE TRACK OF AN AIR MASS ACROSS THE EARTH'S SURFACE.

'**Polar air**' flowing towards the lower latitudes will be warmed from below and so become unstable. Conversely, '**tropical air**' flowing to higher latitudes will be cooled from below and so become more stable.

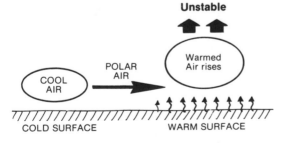

Fig.C8-1. Polar Air Warms and Becomes Unstable.

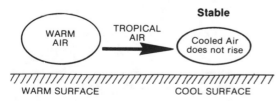

Fig.C8-2. Tropical Air Cools and Becomes Stable.

171

DIVERGENCE OR CONVERGENCE.

An Air Mass influenced by the **divergence** of air flowing out of a HIGH pressure system at the Earth's surface will slowly sink (known as *'subsidence'*) and become warmer, drier and more stable. An Air Mass influenced by **convergence** as air flows into a LOW pressure system at the surface will be forced to rise slowly, becoming cooler, moister and less stable.

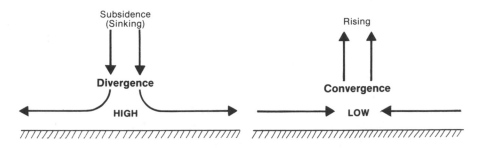

Fig.C8-3. Subsiding Air, Resulting from Divergence, is Stable.

Fig.C8-4. Rising Air, Resulting from Convergence, is Unstable.

TYPES OF AIR MASS THAT AFFECT THE UK.

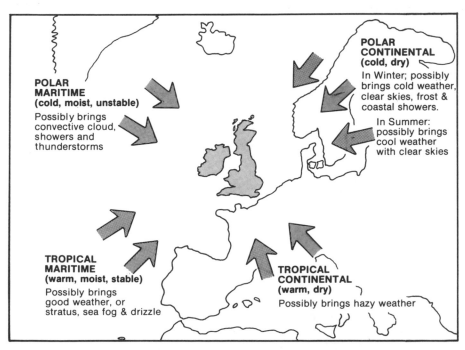

Fig.C8-5. Air Masses that Affect the United Kingdom.

FRONTAL WEATHER

Air Masses have different characteristics, depending upon their origin and the type of surface over which they have been passing. Because of these differences there is usually a distinct division between adjacent air masses. These divisions are known as **'Fronts'**, and there are two basic types – **Cold Fronts** and **Warm Fronts**. *'Frontal Activity'* describes the interaction between the air masses, as one mass replaces the other.

THE WARM FRONT.

If two air masses meet so that the warmer air replaces the cooler air at the surface, a **Warm Front** is said to exist. The boundary at the Earth's surface between the two air masses is represented on a weather chart as a line with semi-circles pointed in the direction of movement.

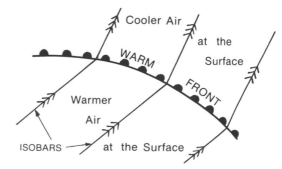

Fig.C8-6. Depiction of a WARM FRONT on a Weather Chart.

The slope formed in a Warm Front as the warm air slides up over the cold air is fairly shallow and so the cloud that forms in the (usually quite stable) rising warm air is likely to be stratiform. In a Warm Front the frontal air at altitude is actually well ahead of the line as depicted on the weather chart. The Cirrus could be some 600 nm ahead of the surface front, and rain could be falling up to approximately 200 nm ahead of it. The slope of the warm front is typically 1 in 150, much flatter than a cold front, and has been exaggerated in the diagram.

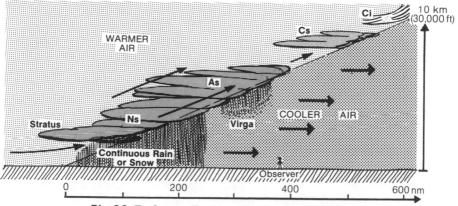

Fig.C8-7. Cross-Section of a WARM FRONT.

The Warm Front As Seen By An Observer On The Ground.

As a Warm Front gradually passes, an observer on the ground may first see high Cirrus cloud, which will slowly be followed by a lowering base of Cirrostratus, Altostratus and Nimbostratus. Fig.C6-3 shows an example.

Rain may be falling from the Altostratus and possibly evaporating before it reaches the ground, i.e. Virga, and from the Nimbostratus. The rain from the Nimbostratus may be continuous until the Warm Front passes and may, due to its evaporation, cause fog. Also, the visibility may be quite poor.

The **atmospheric pressure** usually will fall continuously as the Warm Front approaches and, as it passes, either stop falling or fall at a lower rate. The **air temperature** will rise as the warm air moves in over the surface. The warm air will hold more moisture than the cold air, and the Dewpoint Temperature in the warmer air will be higher.

In the Northern Hemisphere, the **wind direction** will **veer** as the Warm Front passes (and **back** in the Southern Hemisphere). Behind the Warm Front, and after it passes, there is likely to be Stratus. Visibility may still be poor. Weather associated with a Warm Front may extend over several hundred miles.

The general characteristics of a Warm Front are:
● lowering stratiform cloud;
● increasing rain, with the possibility of poor visibility and fog;
● a falling pressure that slows down or stops;
● a wind that veers; and
● a temperature that rises.

The Warm Front As Seen By A Pilot.

What a Pilot sees, and in which order he sees it, will depend upon the direction of flight. He may see a gradually lowering cloud base if he is in the cold sector underneath the warm air and flying towards the Warm Front, and steady rain may be falling.

If the aeroplane is at sub-zero temperatures, the rain may freeze and form ice on the wings, thereby decreasing their aerodynamic qualities. The cloud may be as low as ground level (i.e. hill fog) and sometimes the lower layers of stratiform cloud conceal Cumulonimbus and Thunderstorm activity.

Visibility may be quite poor.

There will be a wind change either side of the front and a change of heading may be required to maintain track.

THE COLD FRONT.

If a cooler air mass undercuts a mass of warm air and displaces it at the surface, a Cold Front is said to occur. The slope between the two air masses in a Cold Front is generally quite steep (typically 1 in 50) and the frontal weather may occupy a band of only 30 to 50 nautical miles.

The boundary between the two air masses at the surface is shown on weather charts as a line with barbs pointing in the direction of travel of the front. The Cold Front moves quite rapidly, with the cooler frontal air at altitude lagging behind that at the surface.

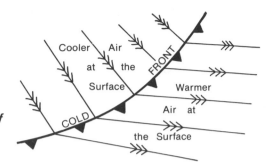

Fig.C8-8. Depiction of a COLD FRONT on a Weather Chart.

The air that is forced to rise with the passage of a Cold Front is unstable and so the cloud that is formed is cumiliform in nature, e.g. Cumulus and Cumulonimbus. **Severe weather hazardous to aviation,** such as thunderstorm activity, squall lines, severe turbulence and windshear, may accompany the passage of a Cold Front.

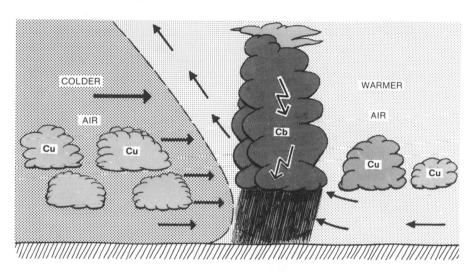

Fig.C8-9. Cross-Section of a COLD FRONT.

The Passage Of A COLD FRONT As Seen By An Observer On The Ground.

The atmospheric pressure will fall as a Cold Front approaches and the change in weather with its passage may be quite pronounced. There may be Cumulus and possibly Cumulonimbus cloud with heavy rain showers, thunderstorm activity and squalls, with a sudden drop in temperature and change in wind direction as the front passes (**veering** in the Northern Hemisphere, **backing** in the Southern Hemisphere).

The cooler air mass will contain less moisture than the warm air, and so the dewpoint temperature after the Cold Front has passed will be lower. Once the Cold Front has passed, the pressure may rise rapidly.

The general characteristics of a Cold Front are:
● cumiliform cloud – Cumulus, Cumulonimbus;
● a sudden drop in temperature, and a lower dewpoint temperature;
● a veering of the wind direction; and
● a falling pressure that rises once the front is past.

The COLD FRONT As Seen By A Pilot.

Flying through a Cold Front may require diversions to avoid weather. There may be thunderstorm activity, violent winds (both horizontal and vertical) from Cumulonimbus clouds, squall lines, windshear, heavy showers of rain or hail, and severe turbulence. Icing could be a problem. Visibility away from the showers and the cloud may be quite good, but it is still a good idea for a Pilot to consider avoiding the strong weather activity that accompanies many Cold Fronts.

THE OCCLUDED FRONT.

Because Cold Fronts usually travel much faster than Warm Fronts it often happens that a Cold Front overtakes a Warm Front, creating an *'Occlusion'* (or *Occluded Front*). This may happen in the final stages of a frontal depression (which is discussed shortly). Three air masses are involved and their vertical passage, one to the other, will depend upon their relative temperatures. The Occluded Front is depicted by a line with alternating barbs and semi-circles pointing in the direction of motion of the front.

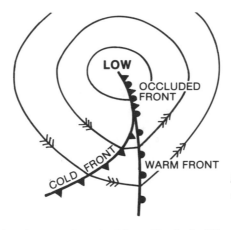

Fig.C8-10. Depiction of an OCCLUDED FRONT on a Weather Map.

The cloud that is associated with an Occluded Front will depend upon what cloud is associated with the individual Cold and Warm Fronts. It is not unusual to have cumiliform cloud (Cu, Cb) from the Cold Front as well as stratiform cloud from the Warm Front. Sometimes the stratiform cloud can conceal thunderstorm activity. Severe weather can occur in the early stages of an Occlusion as unstable air is forced upwards, but this period is often short.

Flight through an Occluded Front may involve encountering intense weather, as both a Cold Front and a Warm Front are involved with a warm air mass being squeezed up between them. The wind direction will be different either side of the front.

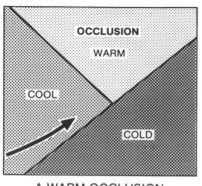

A WARM OCCLUSION

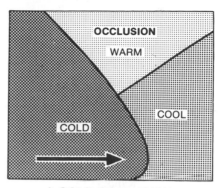

A COLD OCCLUSION

Fig.C8-11. Cross-Sections of OCCLUDED FRONTS.

ATLANTIC WEATHER — February 16

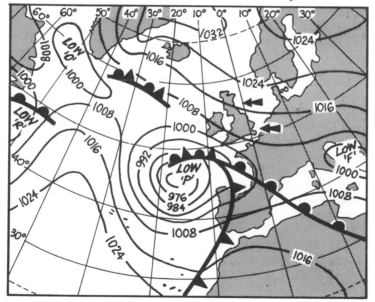

Lows 'P' and 'F' will move east and slowly fill as Low 'R' tracks north-east and deepens. Low 'O' will lose its identity.

*Fig.C8-12. A Weather Map
Showing COLD, WARM and
OCCLUDED FRONTS.*

DEPRESSIONS —
AREAS OF LOW PRESSURE

A Depression or LOW is a region of low pressure at the surface, the pressure gradually rising as you move away from its centre. A LOW is depicted on a weather chart by a series of concentric isobars joining places of equal sea level pressure, with the lowest pressure in the centre.

In the Northern Hemisphere, winds circulate anticlockwise around a LOW. Flying towards a LOW, an aeroplane will experience right (starboard) drift.

Depressions generally are more intense than HIGHs, being spread over a smaller area and with a stronger Pressure Gradient (change of pressure with distance). The more intense the Depression, the 'deeper' it is said to be. LOWs move faster across the face of the Earth than HIGHs and do not last as long.

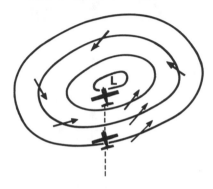

Fig.C8-13. A DEPRESSION or LOW PRESSURE SYSTEM.

Because the pressure at the surface in the centre of a Depression is lower than in the surrounding areas, there will be an inflow of air, known as **'Convergence'.** The air above the Depression will rise and flow outwards.

The three-dimensional pattern of airflow near a Depression is:
- convergence (inflow) in the lower layers;
- rising air above; and
- divergence (outflow) in the upper layers.

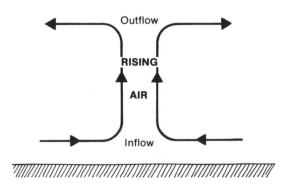

Fig.C8-14. The Three Dimensional Flow of Air Near A LOW.

The Depression at the surface may in fact be caused by the divergence aloft removing air faster than it can be replaced by convergence at the surface.

WEATHER ASSOCIATED WITH A DEPRESSION.

In a depression, the rising air will be cooling and so cloud will tend to form. Instability in the rising air may lead to quite large vertical development of cumiliform cloud accompanied by rain showers. Visibility may be good (except in the showers), since the vertical motion will tend to carry away all the particles suspended in the air.

TROUGHS OF LOW PRESSURE.

A V-shaped extension of isobars from a region of Low Pressure is called a **'Trough'**. Air will flow into it (i.e. convergence will occur) and rise. If the air is unstable, weather similar to that in a Depression or a Cold Front will occur, e.g. cumiliform cloud, possibly with cumulonimbus and thunderstorm activity.

The Trough may in fact be associated with a front. Less prominent Troughs, possibly more U-shaped than V-shaped, will generally have less severe weather.

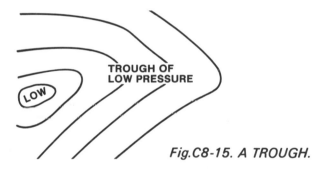

Fig.C8-15. A TROUGH.

THE WAVE OR FRONTAL DEPRESSION.

The boundary between two air masses moving (relative to one another) side by side is often distorted by the warmer air bulging into the Cold Air Mass, with the bulge moving along like a wave. This is known as a **'Frontal Wave'**. The leading edge of the bulge of warm air is a Warm Front and its rear edge is a Cold Front.

The pressure near the tip of the wave falls sharply and so a Depression forms, along with a Warm Front, a Cold Front, and possibly an Occlusion. It is usual for the Cold Front to move faster across the surface than the Warm Front.

Fig.C8-16. The FRONTAL DEPRESSION.

THE CYCLONE OR TROPICAL REVOLVING STORM.

The tropical revolving storm can be violent and destructive. Fortunately they do not occur in the UK, but rather over warm tropical oceans at about 10–20° latitude during certain periods of the year.

Occasionally, weak troughs in these areas develop into intense depressions. Air converges in the lower levels and flows into the depression and then rises, the warm, moist air forming large Cumulus and Cumulonimbus clouds. The very deep depression may be only quite small (200–300 nm in diameter) compared to the typical depression in temperate latitudes, but its central pressure can be extremely low.

Winds can exceed 100 kt, with heavy showers and thunderstorm activity becoming increasingly frequent as the centre of the storm approaches.

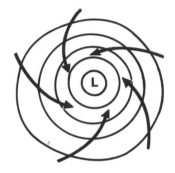

Fig.C8-17. A TROPICAL REVOLVING STORM or CYCLONE.

The **'Eye'** of a Tropical Revolving Storm is often only some 10 nm in diameter, with light winds and broken cloud. It is occupied by very warm subsiding air, one reason for the extremely low pressure. Once the eye has passed, a very strong wind from the opposite direction will occur.

In the Northern Hemisphere, pronounced starboard (right) drift due to a strong wind from the left will mean that the eye of the storm is ahead (and vice versa in the Southern Hemisphere).

Cyclones are best avoided by all aircraft.

ANTICYCLONES —
AREAS OF HIGH PRESSURE

An Anticyclone, or HIGH, is an area of high pressure at the surface surrounded by roughly concentric isobars. HIGHs are generally greater in extent than LOWs, but with a weaker Pressure Gradient and slower moving, although they are more persistent and last longer.

In the Northern Hemisphere, the wind circulates clockwise around the centre of a HIGH. Flying towards a HIGH an aircraft will experience Left (Port) drift.

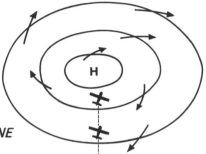

Fig.C8-18. The ANTICYCLONE or HIGH.

The **three-dimensional flow** of air associated with an Anticyclone is:
- an outflow of air from the high pressure area in the lower layers (i.e. divergence);
- the slow subsidence of air over a wide area from above; and
- an inflow of air in the upper layers (i.e. convergence).

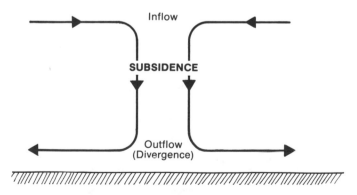

Fig.C8-19. The Three Dimensional Flow of Air Near a HIGH.

The high pressure area at the surface originates when the convergence in the upper layers adds air faster than the divergence in the lower layers removes it.

WEATHER ASSOCIATED WITH A HIGH.

The subsiding air in a High pressure system will be warming as it descends and so cloud will tend to disperse as the dewpoint temperature is exceeded and the relative humidity decreases. Subsiding air is very stable.

It is possible that the subsiding air may warm sufficiently to create an inversion, with the upper air warming to a temperature higher than that of the lower air, and possibly causing stratiform cloud to form (Stratocumulus, Stratus) and/or trapping smoke, haze and dust beneath it. This can happen in the UK winter, leading to rather gloomy days with poor flight visibility. In summer, heating by the Sun may disperse the cloud, leading to a fine but hazy day.

If the sky remains clear at night, greater cooling of the Earth's surface by radiation heat loss may lead to the formation of Fog. If the High Pressure is situated entirely over land, the weather may be dry and cloudless, but with any air flowing in from the sea, extensive stratiform cloud in the lower levels can occur.

A RIDGE OF HIGH PRESSURE.

Isobars which extend out from a HIGH in a U-shape indicate a ridge of High Pressure (like a ridge extending from a mountain). Weather conditions associated with a Ridge are, in general, similar to the weather found with Anticyclones.

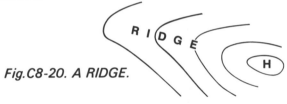

Fig.C8-20. A RIDGE.

A COL.

The area of almost constant pressure (and therefore indicated by a few very widely-spaced isobars) that exists between two HIGHs and two LOWs is called a **'Col'.** It is like a *'saddle'* on a mountain ridge.

Light winds are often associated with Cols, with fog a possibility in winter and high temperatures in summer possibly leading to showers or thunderstorms.

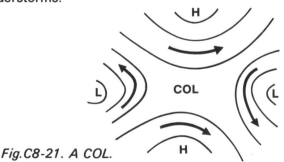

Fig.C8-21. A COL.

☐ **Exercises C8 — Air Masses and Frontal Weather.**

C9

ICING

THE FORMATION OF ICE.

If the temperature is less than 0°C, which is the freezing point of water, then ice may form, either:
- directly from water vapour (sublimation, causing hoar frost); or
- from water droplets (freezing, causing rime ice and/or clear ice).

ICING CAN BE HAZARDOUS TO AVIATION.

Ice accretion on an aeroplane or within the engine induction system can significantly reduce flight safety by causing:

- **adverse aerodynamic effects** – ice accretion on the **airframe** can modify the airflow pattern around aerofoils (wings, propeller blades, etc.), leading to a serious loss of Lift and an increase in Drag;

- **a loss of engine power, or even complete stoppage,** if ice blocks the air intake (in sub-zero temperatures) or **carburettor ice** forms (in moist air up to +**25°C**);

- **a Weight increase** and a **change in the position of the Centre of Gravity** of the aeroplane, as well as unbalancing of the various control surfaces and the propeller, perhaps causing severe vibration and/or control difficulties;

- **blocking of the pitot tube and/or static vent,** producing errors in the pressure instruments (Air Speed Indicator, Altimeter, Vertical Speed Indicator);

- **degradation in radio communications** (if ice forms on the aerials).

SUPERCOOLED WATER DROPS.

Liquid water drops can exist in the atmosphere at temperatures well below the normal freezing point of water (0°C), possibly at –20°C or even lower. This is known as being **'supercooled'**, and such drops will freeze on contact with a surface – the skin of an aeroplane, or the propeller blades, for example.

CLEAR ICE.

Once the freezing process actually begins, a large water drop with a temperature **between 0°C and –20°C** will not freeze instantaneously. The freezing process could be triggered by the drop striking a cold aircraft surface, where it will start to freeze. Because latent heat is released in this process, the rate of freezing will reduce, and the remaining liquid water will spread back and coalesce with water from other partially frozen water drops, before freezing on the cold airframe or propeller surfaces. The result is a sheet of solid, clear, glazed ice with very little air enclosed.

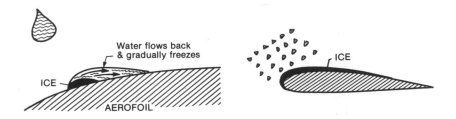

Fig.C9-1. Clear Ice Formed From Large, Supercooled Water Drops.

The surface of Clear Ice is smooth, usually with undulations and lumps. **Clear Ice can alter the aerodynamic shape of aerofoils quite dramatically and reduce or destroy their effectiveness.** Along with the increased weight, this creates a hazard to safety. Clear Ice is very tenacious but, if it does break off, it could be in large chunks capable of doing damage.

RIME ICE.

Rime ice occurs when small, supercooled liquid water droplets freeze on contact with a surface whose temperature is sub-zero. Because the drops are small, the amount of water remaining after the initial freezing is insufficient to coalesce into a continuous sheet before freezing. The result is a mixture of tiny ice particles and trapped air, giving a rough, opaque, crystalline deposit that is fairly brittle.

Rime Ice often forms on leading edges and can affect the aerodynamic qualities of an aerofoil or the airflow into the engine intake. It does cause a significant increase in weight.

CLOUDY OR MIXED ICE.

It is common for the drops of water in falling rain to be of many sizes and often, if ice forms, it will be a mixture of Clear Ice (from large drops) and Rime Ice (from small drops), resulting in cloudy or mixed ice.

HOAR FROST.

Hoar Frost occurs when moist air comes in contact with a sub-zero surface, the water vapour, rather than condensing to form liquid water, sublimating directly to ice in the form of Hoar Frost. This is a white crystalline coating that can usually be brushed off.

Hoar Frost will form in clear air when the aeroplane is parked in sub-zero temperatures or when the aeroplane flies from sub-zero temperatures into warmer moist air – for example, on descent, or when climbing in an inversion. Although hoar frost is not as dangerous as clear ice, it can obscure vision through a cockpit window, and possibly affect the lifting characteristics of the wings.

ICE ACCRETION ON THE AIRFRAME, AND CLOUD TYPE.

Ice adhering to the airframe is a very important consideration for instrument-rated Pilots who may be flying in cloud; it is also an important consideration for visual Pilots who may be flying in rain or drizzle which freezes on a cold aeroplane. Carburettor ice, which is discussed shortly, can of course occur without the presence of cloud or precipitation.

Cumulus-type cloud nearly always consists predominantly of liquid water droplets down to about –20°C, below which either liquid drops or ice crystals may predominate. Newly formed parts of the cloud will tend to contain more liquid drops than in mature parts. The risk of airframe icing is severe in cumiliform cloud in the range 0 to –20°C, moderate to severe in the range –20° to –40°C, with the chance of airframe icing below –40°C being only small. Since there is a lot of vertical motion in convective clouds, the composition of the clouds may vary considerably at the one level, and the risk of icing may exist throughout a wide altitude band in (and under) the cloud. If significant icing does occur, it may be necessary to descend into warmer air.

Stratiform cloud usually consists entirely or predominantly of liquid water drops down to about –15°C, with the risk of airframe icing. If significant icing is a possibility, it may be advisable to fly at a lower level where the temperature is above 0°C, or at a higher level where the temperature is less than –15°C. In certain conditions, such as stratiform cloud associated with an active front or with orographic uplift, the risk of icing is increased at temperatures lower than usual; continuous upward motion of air generally means a greater retention of liquid water in the cloud.

Raindrops and drizzle from any sort of cloud will freeze if they meet an aeroplane whose surface is below 0°C, with a severe risk of clear ice forming the bigger the water droplets are. A Pilot needs to be cautious when flying in rain at freezing temperatures. This could occur for instance with an aeroplane flying in the cool sector underlying the warmer air of a Warm Front from which rain could be falling.

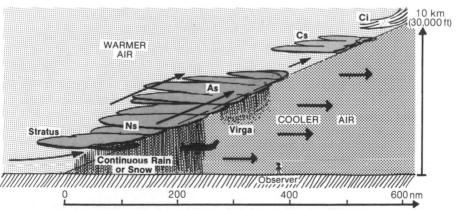

Fig.C9-2. Danger Area Beneath a Warm Front.

Cirrus clouds are usually composed of ice crystals, and the risk of airframe icing is therefore only slight.

CARBURETTOR ICING.

Ice can form in the carburettor and induction system in **moist air** with Outside Air Temperatures as high as +**25°C** (or even higher). It will disturb or prevent the flow of air and fuel into the engine, causing it to lose power, run roughly and perhaps even stop.

Cooling occurs when the induction air expands as it passes through the venturi in the carburettor (adiabatic cooling), and occurs also as the fuel vaporises (absorbing the latent heat of vaporisation). This can easily reduce what was initially quite warm air to a temperature well below zero and, if the air is **moist**, ice will form.

Throttle icing is more likely to occur at lower power settings when the partially-closed butterfly creates a greater venturi cooling effect, compared with high power settings when the butterfly is more open and the venturi effect is less.

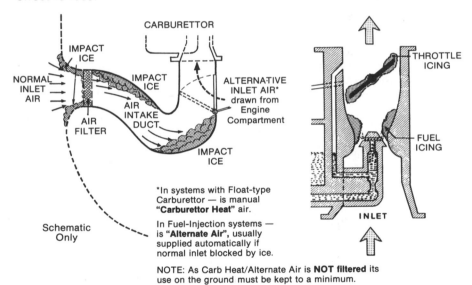

Fig.C9-3. Carburettor Ice.

All aeroplanes whose engines have carburettors are fitted with a Carburettor Heat Control that can direct hot air from around the engine to be taken into the carburettor, instead of the ambient air. Being hot, it should be able to melt the ice and prevent further ice from forming. The correct method of using the Carburettor Heat control for your aeroplane will be found in the Pilot's Operating Handbook, and its use is also covered in Volume 1 of this series.

Remember that carburettor ice can form on a warm day in moist air!

ICING OF THE PITOT-STATIC SYSTEM.

This can affect the readings of the pressure-operated Flight Instruments (i.e. the Air Speed Indicator, the Altimeter, and the VSI). Please refer to Volume 4, Chapter 25 – *'Pressure Instruments'*.

WARNING!

Ice of any type on the airframe or propeller, or in the carburettor and induction system, deserves the Pilot's immediate attention and removal. Wings which are contaminated by ice prior to take-off will lengthen the take-off run because of the higher speed needed to fly – a dangerous situation!

An ice-laden aeroplane may even be incapable of flight. Ice or frost on the leading edge and upper forward area of the wings (where the majority of the Lift is generated) is especially dangerous.

Most training aeroplanes are not fitted with airframe de-icers (removal) or anti-icers (preventative), so Pilots of these aeroplanes should avoid flying in icing conditions (i.e. in rain or moist air at any time the airframe is likely to be at sub-zero temperatures). If a pitot heater is fitted, use it to avoid ice forming over the pitot tube and depriving you of airspeed information.

☐ **Exercises C9 — Icing.**

C10

VISIBILITY

To the non instrument-rated Pilot flight visibility is one of the most important aspects of weather. He or she needs a natural horizon as a guide to the attitude of the aeroplane in both pitch and bank, as well as having sufficient slant visibility to see the ground for navigational purposes.

Meteorological visibility is defined as the greatest horizontal distance at which a specified object can be seen in daylight conditions. It is a measure of how transparent the atmosphere is to the human eye.

VISIBILITY CAN BE REDUCED BY PARTICLES SUSPENDED IN THE AIR.

On a perfectly clear day visibility can exceed 100 nm, however this is rarely the case since there are always some particles suspended in the air to prevent all of the light from a distant object reaching the observer.

Particles that restrict visibility include:
- minute particles of smoke so small that even very light winds can support them:
  - dust or oil causing haze;
  - liquid water or ice producing mist, fog or cloud;
- larger particles of sand, dust or sea spray which require stronger winds and turbulence for the air to hold them in suspension;
- precipitation (rain, snow, hail), the worst visibility being associated with very heavy rain or with large numbers of small particles, e.g. thick drizzle or heavy, fine snow.

VISIBILITY FOR A PILOT.

The most important visibility to the visual Pilot is that from the aeroplane to the ground, i.e. **slant or oblique visibility.** This may be quite different to the horizontal visibility – for example, when a layer of particles is suspended in the air, such as Stratus, Fog, or Smog that is held beneath a *Temperature Inversion.*

A common situation is when a Ground Fog occurs. To an observer on the ground, horizontal visibility might be reduced to just a few hundred metres, yet vertical visibility might be unlimited with a blue sky quite visible above.

To a Pilot flying overhead the aerodrome, the runway might be clearly visible and the horizontal visibility ahead unlimited, yet, once he has positioned the aeroplane on final approach, the runway might be impossible to see. This is because his line of sight must now penetrate a much greater thickness of Fog.

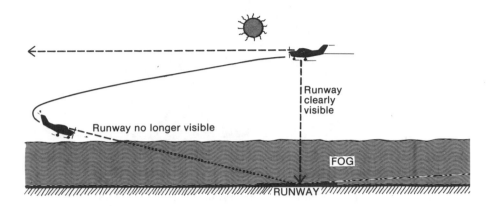

Fig.C10-1. Slant Visibility May Be Severely Reduced by Fog, Smog or Stratus.

MIST AND FOG.

Mist and Fog occur when small water droplets are suspended in the air, thereby reducing visibility. The difference between Mist and Fog is only one of degree – **'Mist'** existing if the visibility exceeds 1 km, **'Fog'** existing if it falls below 1 km.

It is usual for Mist to precede Fog at a place and to follow Fog as it disperses, unless of course an already formed Fog is blown in across an area – for example a Fog blown in off the sea.

The condensation process that causes Mist/Fog is usually associated with cooling of the air by an underlying cold surface (causing Radiation Fog or Advection Fog) or by the interaction of two air masses (Frontal Fog). In Fog, the relative humidity is 100%; in Mist, the relative humidity is slightly less than this.

RADIATION FOG.

Conditions suitable for the formation of Radiation Fog are:
- **a cloudless night**, allowing the earth to lose heat by radiation to the atmosphere and thereby cool, also causing the air in contact with it to lose heat;
- **moist air** (i.e. a high relative humidity) that only requires a little cooling to reach the dewpoint temperature; and
- **light winds** (5–7 knots) to mix the lower levels of air with very light turbulence, thereby thickening the Mist/Fog layer.

These conditions are commonly found with an anticyclone (HIGH pressure system).

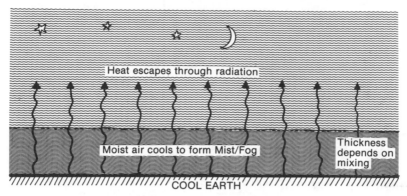

Fig.C10-2. Radiation Fog.

Air is a very poor conductor of heat, so that if the wind is absolutely calm, only the very thin layer of air an inch or two thick actually in contact with the surface will lose heat to it. This will cause Dew or Frost to form on the surface itself, instead of Fog forming above it. **Dew** will form at temperatures above zero and **Frost** will form at sub-zero temperatures.

If the wind is stronger than about 7 knots, the extra turbulence may cause too much mixing and, instead of Fog right down to the ground, a layer of Stratus may form above the surface.

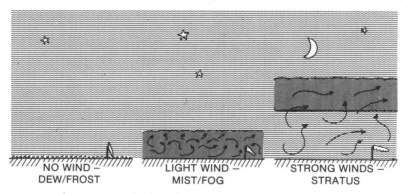

Fig.C10-3. Wind Strength Will Affect the Formation of Dew/Frost, Mist/Fog or Stratus Cloud.

The temperature of the Sea remains fairly constant throughout the year, unlike that of the Land which warms and cools quite quickly on a diurnal (daily) basis. Radiation Fog is therefore much more likely to form over Land than over the Sea.

The Dispersal of Radiation Fog Depends Upon Heating Of The Air.

As the Earth's surface begins to warm up again some time after sunrise, the air in contact with it will also warm, causing the Fog to gradually dissipate. In the UK spring it is common for this to occur by early or mid morning. Possibly the Fog may rise to form a low layer of Stratus before the sky fully clears.

If the Fog that has formed overnight is thick, however, it may act as a blanket, shutting out the Sun and impeding the heating of the Earth's surface after the sun has risen. As a consequence, the air in which the Fog exists will not be warmed from below and the Fog may last throughout the day. This is sometimes experienced in the UK during autumn.

ADVECTION FOG.

A warm, moist air mass flowing across a significantly colder surface will be cooled from below. If its temperature is reduced to the dew-point temperature, then Fog will form. Since the term **'advection'** means heat transfer by the horizontal flow of air, Fog formed in this manner is known as 'Advection Fog', and can occur quite suddenly, day or night, if the right conditions exist.

Light to moderate winds will encourage mixing in the lower levels to give a thicker layer of Fog, but stronger winds may cause Stratus rather than Fog. Advection Fog can persist in much stronger winds than Radiation Fog.

A warm, moist maritime air flow over a cold land surface can lead to Advection Fog over land.

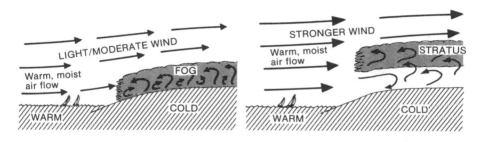

Fig.C10-4. Fog or Stratus Caused By Advection.

FOG AT SEA AND ALONG COASTAL AREAS.

Sea Fog is Advection Fog, and it may be caused by:
- tropical maritime air moving towards the Pole over a colder ocean or meeting a colder air mass; or by
- an air flow off a warm land surface moving over a cooler sea, which can occur in the UK summer, affecting aerodromes in coastal areas.

FRONTAL FOG.

This type of fog forms from the interaction of two air masses in one of two ways:
- as cloud that extends down to the surface during the passage of the front (forming mainly over hills and consequently called **'Hill Fog'**); or
- as air becomes saturated by the evaporation from rain that has fallen.

These conditions may develop in the cold air ahead of a Warm Front (or an Occluded Front), the pre-frontal Fog possibly being very widespread.

191

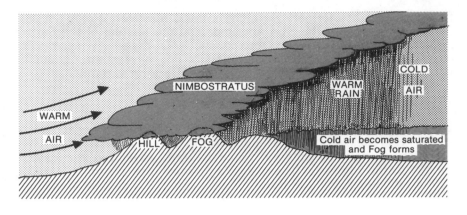

Fig.C10-5. Fog Associated with a Warm Front.

SMOG CAN FORM BENEATH AN INVERSION AND SEVERELY REDUCE VISIBILITY.

An inversion occurs when the air temperature increases with height (rather than the usual decrease), and this can act as a blanket, stopping vertical convection currents. Air that starts to rise meets warmer air and so will stop rising.

Particles suspended in these lower layers will be trapped there and so a rather dirty layer will form, particularly in industrial areas. These small particles may act as **'condensation particles'** and encourage the formation of Fog as well, the combination of smoke and fog being known as **'Smog'**.

Similar effects can be seen in rural areas if there is a lot of pollen, dust or other matter in the air.

Inversions can occur by cooling of the air in contact with the Earth's surface overnight, or by subsidence associated with a HIGH as descending air warms.

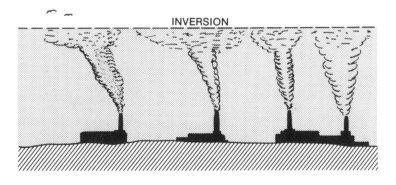

Fig.C10-6. Inversions Can Lead to Reduced Visibility.

PRECIPITATION CAN REDUCE VISIBILITY.

Rain or snow will of course reduce the distance that a Pilot can see, as well as possibly obscuring the horizon. Poor visibility in the whole area may occur in mist, fog, smog, stratus, drizzle or rain. Unstable air may cause cumuliform clouds to form with poor visibility in the showers falling from them, but good visibility otherwise.

Heavy rain may collect on the windscreen, especially if the aeroplane is flying fast, and cause optical distortions. If freezing occurs on the windscreen, either as ice or frost, vision may also be impaired.

SAND AND DUST STORMS CAN REDUCE VISIBILITY.

Strong winds can raise dust or sand from the surface and, in some parts of the world, visibility may be reduced to just a few metres.

SEA SPRAY CAN REDUCE VISIBILITY.

Sea spray often evaporates after being blown into the atmosphere, leaving behind small salt particles that can act as condensation nucleii. The salt particles attract water and can cause condensation at relative humidities as low as 70%, restricting visibility much sooner than would otherwise be the case. Haze produced by sea salt often has a whitish appearance.

VISIBILITY IN FORECASTS AND REPORTS.

Visibility is given to the Pilot in kilometres or, if it is very poor, in metres. A Forecast that contains the term **'8000 05HZ'** can be interpreted, using a Decode Table, as 'Visibility 8000 metres in Haze'. (The **'05'** before the **HZ** is not significant to a Pilot.) If visibility is 10 km or more (i.e. in excess of 9999 metres), it will be written as **'9999'**; a visibility of 4 km or 4000 metres will be written as **'4000'**; a visibility of less than 100 metres will be written as **'0000'**.

For instrument-rated Pilots attempting to operate on runways in very poor visibility, the Runway Visual Range, known as the RVR, may be quoted in metres, possibly followed by the runway designator. For instance, **'R0300/25'** on a Meteorological Observation means 'a Runway Visual Range of 300 metres on Runway 25'. It is the visibility in the direction along the runway that is important to the Pilot, and not the general visibility around the aerodrome which may be quite different.

THE POSITION OF THE SUN CAN REDUCE VISIBILITY.

Flying *'down-sun'* where the Pilot can see the sunlit side of objects, visibility may be much greater than when flying into the Sun. As well as reducing the visibility, flying into the Sun may cause glare. If landing into the Sun is necessary, consideration should be given to altering the time of arrival.

Remember that the onset of darkness is earlier on the ground than at altitude and, even though visibility up high might be good, flying low in the circuit area and approaching to land on a darkening field may cause problems.

☐ **Exercises C10 — Visibility.**

C11

WEATHER FORECASTS AND REPORTS

Since weather conditions vary from place to place and from time to time, it is good airmanship (commonsense) for a Pilot to be aware of the weather that he is likely to encounter. He can do this by his own observations to a limited extent, and by consideration of the information available to him from the Meteorological Office. This information will include temperatures, winds, pressure patterns, the cloud base and extent, and the possibility of fog, icing, thunderstorms or other phenomena.

The primary method of pre-flight meteorological briefing for aircrew in the UK is to obtain appropriate Area Forecasts and Aerodrome Forecasts or Reports by **self-briefing,** using either:
- facilities, information and documentation routinely available or displayed in **Aerodrome Briefing Areas; or**
- the **Public Telephone Network** to ring:
    - the 'AIRMET Telephone Recording Service' to obtain a regional Area Forecast; and
    - a Meteorological Office to obtain Aerodrome Forecasts (TAFs) or Reports (METARs).

Self-briefing is available at all times and does not require prior notification by the Pilot. For Pilots using the Public Telephone Network, telephone numbers are listed on the AIRMET AREAS chart that follows. The recorded message may be listened to for as long as a Pilot wishes, but it is requested that calls to a Meteorological Office, which will involve Meteorological Personnel, be kept reasonably brief. These calls will be made to obtain TAFs and/or METARS (which should normally be limited by the Pilot to four, i.e. departure aerodrome, destination aerodrome, and two alternates), or to seek clarification of the Area Forecast(s) already obtained.

At some time in the future, the CAA will provide an automated telephone service for TAFs and METARs for aerodromes in the forecast area, however this service is not yet available.

Where necessary, the personal advice of a Forecaster or the supply of additional meteorological information can be obtained from the designated forecast office for the departure aerodrome (listed in UK AIP MET 1-1, and in Pooley's *Pilots Information Guide).*

A **Forecast** is a prediction (or prognosis) of what the weather is likely to be, the common aviation forecasts being:
- **Area Forecasts; and**
- **Aerodrome Forecasts (TAFs or TRENDs);**
    OR
- **Special Forecasts.**

A Report is an observation of what the weather actually is (or was) at a specific time, the common Aviation Weather Reports being:

- Aerodrome Weather Reports (**METAR**s on a routine basis, **SPECI**s when special conditions exist);
- Automatic Terminal Information Service (**ATIS**);
- In-flight Weather Reports (obtainable in recorded form on **VOLMET** and ATIS, and by radio communication with an Air Traffic Service Unit, although this is the least preferred method since it occupies a communications frequency).

Significant weather that may affect the safety of flight operations may be advised in the form of a **SIGMET**. The criteria for raising a SIGMET include active thunderstorms, tropical revolving storms, a severe line squall, heavy hail, severe turbulence, severe airframe icing, marked mountain waves, widespread dust or sandstorm.

As a means of improving the meteorological information service to Pilots, it is common to attach to an Aerodrome Report (i.e. an observation of actual weather) a forecast **trend** of what the weather tendency over the following two hours is expected to be. This is a much shorter period than the duration of a normal Aerodrome Forecast (9 hours) and therefore should be more accurate.

A **TREND** is commonly referred to as a **Landing Forecast**.

METEOROLOGICAL FORECASTS

AREA FORECASTS.

The type of receiving equipment at your aerodrome Briefing Office determines in which form your Area Forecast will be. Forecast Offices issue Area Forecasts on a routine basis:

(a) via facsimile*, in the form of two graphic low level Weather Charts, issued four times daily, which show: (1) general weather below 15,000 ft, and (2) spot winds and air temperatures to 24,000 ft; and;

(b) via the Aeronautical Fixed Telecommunications Network (AFTN), telex and public telephone networks. These take the form of text messages following the 'AIRMET' regional system described below.

NOTE: To 'decode' Weather Forecasts and Reports it is necessary to know the meaning of various **Symbols and Abbreviations.** These are included in a later part of this chapter. They can also be found in the UK AIP MET section. The Met Office *LAPFORM 216,* available from Forecast Offices, contains decode information for the facsimile-networks charts.

Details of the UK Low Level Weather Chart are contained in the AIP MET – see last page of AIP MET inclusions reprinted at the end of the chapter.

* Two facsimile networks known as *CAMFAX* and *DOCFAX* distribute weather information to suitably equipped Briefing Offices. The advantage of facsimile is the ability to transmit graphic charts as well as text. See AIP MET 1-1 list of aerodromes and their equipment.

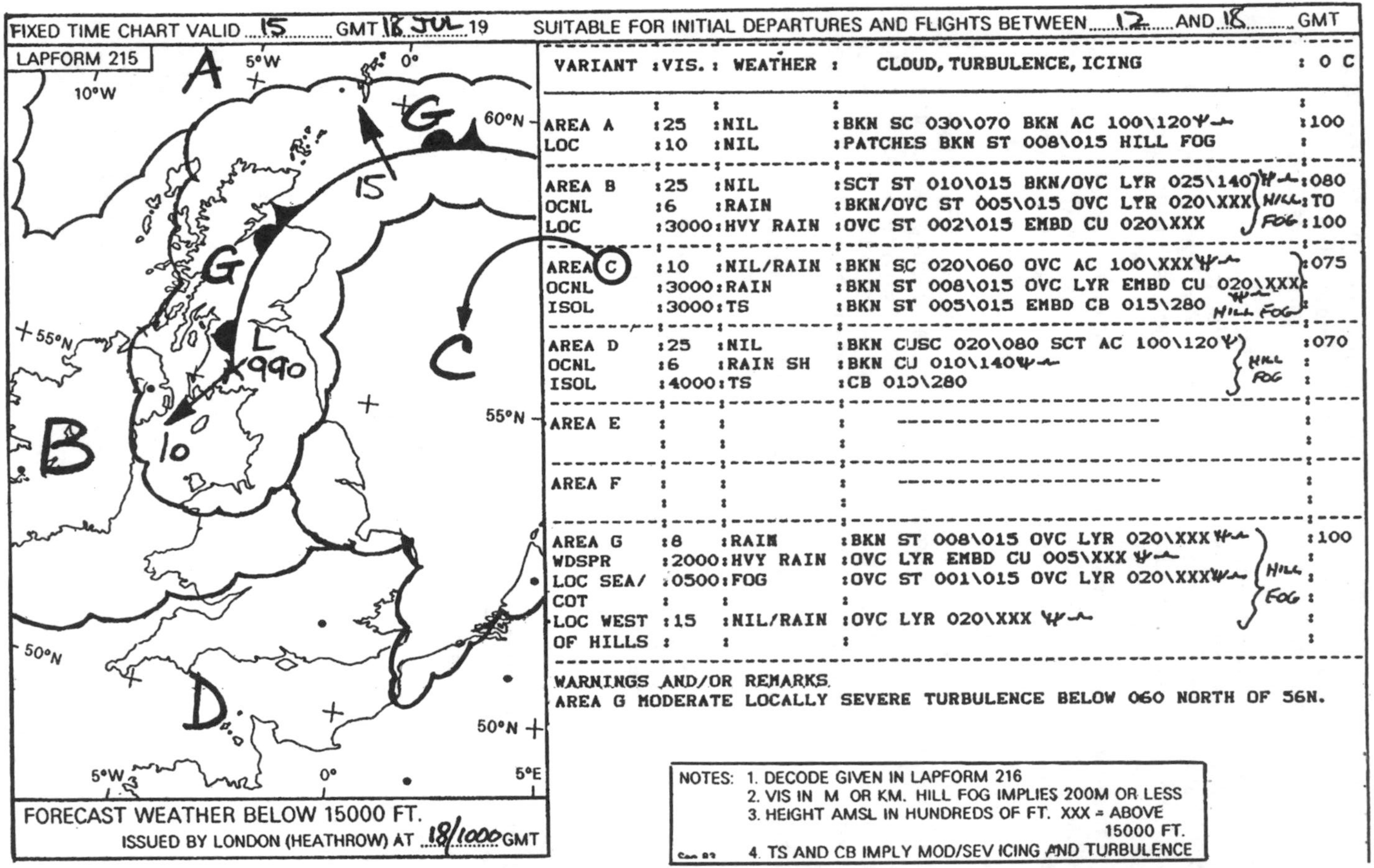

Fig.C11-1. Reduced Example of a UK Area Forecast sent out via Facsimile Networks (DOCFAX or CAMFAX): (Note that 'Areas' mentioned are different to 'AIRMET' Areas system.)

196

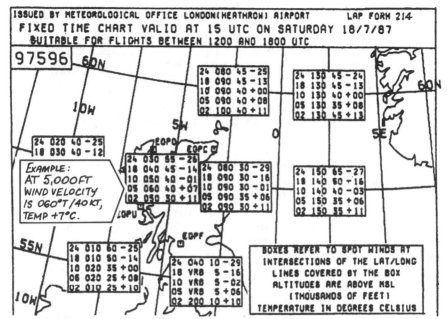

Fig.C11-2. Top Portion of a sample UK Low Level Spot Wind chart (reduced).

The 'AIRMET' Service.

The *AIRMET* weather forecast service comprises low level Area Forecasts grouped into three Regions covering the UK and near continent. The forecasts are in plain language (text or spoken form), with vertical coverage from the surface (ground or sea level) to 15,000ft AMSL, and winds and air temperatures to 18,000 ft AMSL. They are available:

- in spoken form at dictation speed via the **Public Telephone Network;** and
- in text form via the Aeronautical Fixed Telecommunications Network (AFTN), or by Telex (and available in **Aerodrome Briefing Areas**).

The three AIRMET Regions are:

- Southern England;
- Northern England and Wales; and
- Scotland and Northern Ireland.

To facilitate dissemination of more localised weather in the AIRMET Forecasts, each AIRMET Region is subdivided into 'Areas'. See AIRMET AREAS map – *Fig.C11-5.*

AIRMET Forecasts are issued four times daily at the times shown below, and amended as necessary between those times to account for significant weather changes. Each forecast will include a brief outlook to the end of the subsequent forecast period to give a preview of subsequent weather conditions. The information for a particular Period of Validity will become available:

- in text form – 1 hour before the commencement of the period;
- by telephone – at the commencement of the period (i.e. 1 hour is allowed for recording the information).

6.4.3 Forecasts are issued four times daily at the times shown below and amended as necessary (MET 3-9 Table K) between those times:

Available on AFTN and telex by	Available on telephone by*	Period of Validity	Includes Forecast Outlook to
0500	0600	0600–1400	2000
1100	1200	1200–2000	0200
1700	1800**	1800–0200	0800
2300	2300**	0001–0800	1400

These times will be one hour earlier than shown during the Summer period (GEN 1-18).

Fig.C11-3. Excerpt from AIP-MET – Times of AIRMET Forecasts.

Perhaps **the easiest way to understand the weather service is to use it** – by visiting an aerodrome Briefing Office to obtain the information in text form, and/or by using the Public Telephone Network. Try ringing the listed telephone numbers and writing down the AIRMET information.

A 'Pilot's Proforma', published in UK AIP MET 2-7 *(see Fig. C11-6)*, although not essential, will simplify this task. The length of each forecast will vary according to the complexity of the weather situation, and may at times exceed six minutes. The format is designed to enable telephone users to determine early in the broadcast if conditions are suitable for VFR operations or not. If conditions are not suitable for the intended flight, the telephone call can be curtailed and only minimal cost incurred.

```
PART 1 OF 2 PARTS
AVIATION FORECAST-SOUTHERN ENGLAND
ALL ALTITUDES ABOVE MSL-ALL TIMES UTC
VALID JULY 170500 TO 171300
METEOROLOGICAL SITUATION:
LOW PRESSURE SW APPROACHES MOVING SLOWLY EAST. MOIST UNSTABLE
AIRMASS AFFECTS REGION.
WEATHER:
SCT SH SOME HEAVY. SH MERGING AT TIMES TO GIVE AREAS OF MOD.OR
HEAVY RAIN. ISOL TS MAINLY IN W. LOW STRATUS IN TS, HEAVY SH AND
RAIN, WITH HILL FOG.
WARNINGS:
ISOL TS. MOD OR SEV TURB IN AND NEAR LARGE CU AND CB.
WINDS:
2000FT:
AREAS 1 TO 13 VRB/08 PS10
5000FT:
AREAS 1 AND 4 TO 7 VRB/08 PS05
AREAS 2,3,8,9 AND 11 TO 13 220/10 GRADUALLY VEERING 260/15 PS06
AREA 10 160/25 PS12
10000FT:
AREAS 1,4 TO 7 AND 9 150/15 MS03
AREAS 2,3,8 AND 11 TO 13 250/15 MS03
AREA 10 180/25 PS02
18000FT:
AREAS 1 TO 5 VARIABLE MAINLY 260/15 MS 20
AREAS 6 TO 11 180/30 MS 17
AREAS 12 AND 13 260/30 MS19
CLOUD:
SCT OR BKN CU BASE 2000FT TOP 10000 FT ISOL TOP 15000FT.
ISOL LARGE CU OR CB BASE 1000 FT TOP 24,000FT. OCNL BKN LYR 8000FT
TO 15000FT AND ABOVE. PATCHES ST BASE 500FT TOP 1500FT COVERING
HIGH GROUND.
SURFACE VISIBILITY:
25KM, 6KM IN SH OR RAIN. 3000M HEAVY SH OR RAIN OR TS. 200M HILL
FOG.
ZERO DEG C. ISOTHERM:
7000FT BUT AREA 10 11,000FT.
AIRFRAME ICING:
MOD. OR SEV IN LYR CLOUD AND LARGE CU AND CB.
OUTLOOK TO 171900 SIMILAR
```

Fig.C11-4. AIRMET Area Forecast (Southern England Region) sample (reduced) as sent out on AFTN and Telex networks.

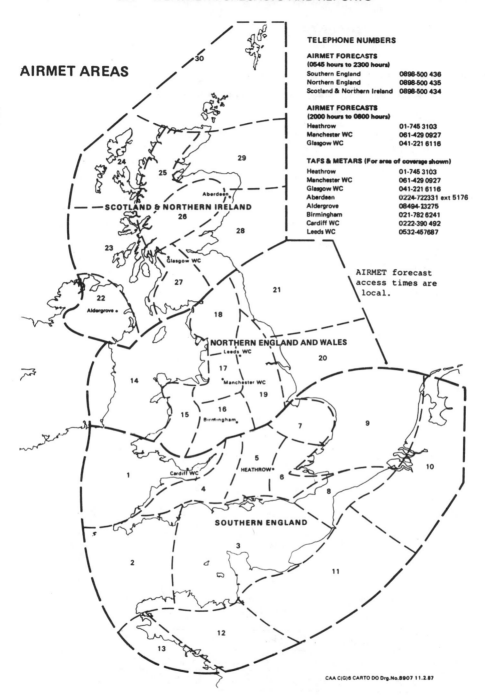

AIRMET AREAS

TELEPHONE NUMBERS

AIRMET FORECASTS
(0545 hours to 2300 hours)
Southern England	0898-500 436
Northern England	0898-500 435
Scotland & Northern Ireland	0898-500 434

AIRMET FORECASTS
(2000 hours to 0600 hours)
Heathrow	01-745 3103
Manchester WC	061-429 0927
Glasgow WC	041-221 6116

TAFS & METARS (For area of coverage shown)
Heathrow	01-745 3103
Manchester WC	061-429 0927
Glasgow WC	041-221 6116
Aberdeen	0224-722331 ext 5176
Aldergrove	08494-13275
Birmingham	021-782 6241
Cardiff WC	0222-390 492
Leeds WC	0532-457687

AIRMET forecast
access times are
local.

CAA C(G)6 CARTO DO Drg.No.8907 11.2.87

Fig.C11-5. AIRMET Regions and Areas Map (reduced).

199

Civil Aviation Authority

AIRMET

PILOTS PROFORMA

NOTES: 1 Forecast area coverage and telephone numbers are shown on the map on the reverse.

2 All altitudes are above Mean Sea Level, all times are UTC.

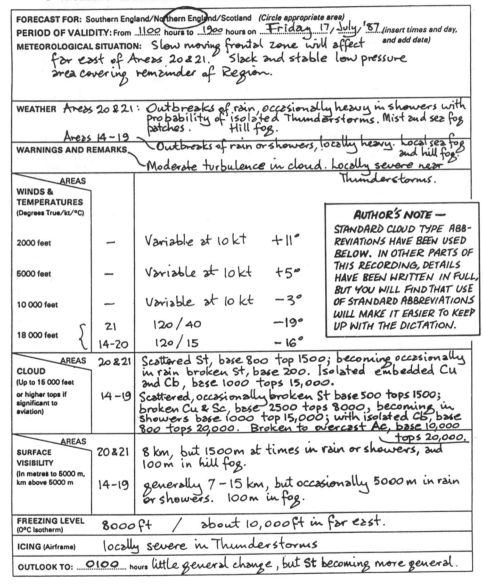

FORECAST FOR: Southern England/Northern England/Scotland *(Circle appropriate area)*

PERIOD OF VALIDITY: From ...1100... hours to ...1900... hours on *Friday 17/July/'87* *(insert times and day, and add date)*

METEOROLOGICAL SITUATION: Slow moving frontal zone will affect far east of Areas 20 & 21. Slack and stable low pressure area covering remainder of Region.

WEATHER Areas 20 & 21 : Outbreaks of rain, occasionally heavy in showers with probability of isolated Thunderstorms. Mist and sea fog patches.   Hill fog.

Areas 14 - 19 :

WARNINGS AND REMARKS Outbreaks of rain or showers, locally heavy. Local sea fog and hill fog.

Moderate turbulence in cloud. Locally severe near Thunderstorms.

AREAS WINDS & TEMPERATURES (Degrees True/kt/°C)			
2000 feet	—	Variable at 10 kt	+11°
5000 feet	—	Variable at 10 kt	+5°
10 000 feet	—	Variable at 10 kt	−3°
18 000 feet { 21	120 / 40		−19°
14-20	120 / 15		−16°

> **AUTHOR'S NOTE —**
> STANDARD CLOUD TYPE ABB-REVIATIONS HAVE BEEN USED BELOW. IN OTHER PARTS OF THIS RECORDING, DETAILS HAVE BEEN WRITTEN IN FULL, BUT YOU WILL FIND THAT USE OF STANDARD ABBREVIATIONS WILL MAKE IT EASIER TO KEEP UP WITH THE DICTATION.

AREAS CLOUD (Up to 15 000 feet or higher tops if significant to aviation)		
20 & 21	Scattered St, base 800 top 1500; becoming occasionally in rain broken St, base 200. Isolated embedded Cu and Cb, base 1000 tops 15,000.	
14 - 19	Scattered, occasionally broken St base 500 tops 1500; broken Cu & Sc, base 2500 tops 8000, becoming in showers base 1000 top 15,000; with isolated Cb, base 800 tops 20,000. Broken to overcast Ac, base 10,000 tops 20,000.	

AREAS SURFACE VISIBILITY (In metres to 5000 m, km above 5000 m)	
20 & 21	8 km, but 1500m at times in rain or showers, and 100m in hill fog.
14-19	generally 7 – 15 km, but occasionally 5000 m in rain or showers. 100m in fog.

FREEZING LEVEL (0°C Isotherm)	8000 ft / about 10,000 ft in far east.
ICING (Airframe)	locally severe in Thunderstorms
OUTLOOK TO: ...0100... hours	little general change, but St becoming more general.

Fig.C11-6. Example of an AIRMET regional Area Forecast (reduced), taken down using Telephone Service, onto Proforma.

SPECIAL FORECASTS.

For flights over long routes the Pilot can request a Forecast Office to prepare a Special Forecast specifically for his flight. This takes time and so **at least** 2 hours notice is required (4 hours if the route distance exceeds 500 nm).

Special Forecasts are issued via facsimile, AFTN or telex, however if your departure aerodrome is not so equipped you can phone the Forecast Office for a dictation. Special Forecasts can also include Aerodrome Forecasts for the departure, destination and up to three alternates.

NOTE: As Special Forecasts only cover that portion of the route which is outside the area of coverage of UK Area Forecasts, an appropriate UK Area Forecast must also be obtained. For further information consult AIP MET.

AERODROME FORECASTS (TAFs).

TAFs are available in the ICAO format for aerodromes where observations are taken. TAFs are usually issued for a 9 hour period and may be preceded on a print-out by *'TAF'*, or by *'FC'* or *'FT'* (Forecast), followed by *'UK'* to represent the country; for instance *'FCUK'*. The standard ICAO TAF decode is included at the end of this chapter and can be found in the UK AIP MET 2-2. The four-figure ICAO location identifiers for UK aerodromes are listed in UK AIP COM 1-1 and *Pooley's Flight Guide*.

Examples of TAFs:

TAF EGPD 0716 13012 4000 6ST004

This decodes to read:
>   **Location:** Aberdeen (Dyce)
>   **Period of validity:** 0700–1600 UTC
>   **Surface wind:** 130°T/12 kt
>   **Visibility:** 4000 metres
>   **Weather:** nil
>   **Cloud:** 6 OKTAS Stratus base 400 ft AGL
>   **Significant variations:** nil.

EGNX 1019 20016 8000 05HZ 5ST010 6SC025 6AC100 TEMPO 1012 5000 58RA 7ST005 PROB20 TEMPO 1216 9999

This decodes to read:
>   **Location:** Tees-Side
>   **Period of validity:** 1000–1900 UTC
>   **Surface wind:** 200°T/16 kt
>   **Visibility:** 8000 metres
>   **Weather:** Haze
>   **Cloud:**   5 OKTAS Stratus 1000 ft AGL;
>   6 OKTAS Stratocumulus 2500 ft AGL;
>   6 OKTAS Altocumulus 10000 ft AGL;
>   **Significant variations:** for periods of less than 60 minutes (TEMPO) between 1000 and 1200 UTC visibility will be reduced to 5000 metres in rain with 7 OKTAS Stratus base 500 ft AGL; 20% probability for periods of less than 60 minutes (TEMPO) between 1200 and 1600 UTC visibility will be in excess of 10 km.

EGSS 1019 18013 9999 5CU022 TEMPO 1012 5000 5SC015

This decodes to read:
Location: London (Stansted)
Period of validity: 1000–1900 UTC
Surface wind: 180°T/13 kt
Visibility: in excess of 10 km
Weather: nil
Cloud: 5 oktas Cumulus 2200 ft AGL (Cloud base in TAFs is Above Ground Level and not AMSL)
Significant variations: for periods of less than 60 minutes (TEMPO) between 1000 and 1200 UTC, visibility will be reduced to 5000 metres and cloud will be 5 OKTAS Stratocumulus base 1500 ft AGL.

PRESTEL WEATHER INFORMATION SERVICE.

Selected Area and Aerodrome Forecasts, intended primarily for General Aviation users, are provided on a 24 hour basis on PRESTEL (teletext for domestic television receivers). Details of this service can be obtained from the Meteorological Office, or on PRESTEL Key *20971#.

METEOROLOGICAL REPORTS

METARs are ROUTINE AERODROME REPORTS.

Routine weather observations are taken at many aerodromes on the hour and half hour and issued on a routine basis, usually preceded by *METAR* or *SA* (Surface Actual). A code almost identical to that used for TAFs is used with some variations:

- the time of observation is specified in a METAR as a four figure group of hours and minutes past the hour (whereas TAFs have a four figure group, the first two representing the hour of commencement of the validity period and the final two, the hour at which it ends);

- two temperatures are given; e.g. 09/07 where 09 is the actual temperature and 07 is the dewpoint temperature, the difference between them acting as a guide of the possibility of mist/fog that will occur when the temperature and the dewpoint coincide.

Examples:

EGPE 0750 08009 4500 58RA 2ST003 4ST005 4ST005 7ST007 09/08 1006

This METAR (actual aerodrome meteorological observation) decodes as:

Location: Inverness (Dalcross)
Time of report: 0750 UTC
Surface wind: 080°T/9 kt
Visibility: 4500 metres
Weather: rain
Cloud: 2 OKTAs Stratus base 300; 4 OKTAs Stratus base 500; 7 OKTAs Stratus base 700 ft AGL
Temperature: +9°C
Dewpoint: +8°C (i.e. if the temperature falls to this, mist or fog will form)
QNH: 1006 mb

Trends (or Landing Forecasts).

Trend forecasts are added to the end of METARs to forecast the weather changes expected to occur in the **two hours** immediately after the time of the report. If no significant change is expected, the observation will be followed by NOSIG.

Example of a Trend (or Landing Forecast):

METAR EGBO 0940 25015/28 4000 80RASH 6SC035 11/08 1002 NOSIG

> **Halfpenny Green**
> 0940 UTC
> 250°T/15 kt gusting to 28 kt
> 4000 metres visibility
> Rain showers
> 6 OKTAs 3500 ft AGL
> Temperature 11°C
> Dewpoint 8°C
> QNH 1002 mb
> **No significant change expected in the two hours to 1140 UTC.**

VHF IN-FLIGHT WEATHER REPORTS.

Weather information may be obtained at any time by radio from the Flight Information Service (FIS) or Air Traffic Control (ATC), who will also initiate a broadcast of any hazardous or significant weather that may be relevant to aircraft in the area (e.g. severe turbulence, thunderstorm activity, icing conditions, fog, etc.).

Weather reports and trends for selected aerodromes are broadcast continuously on discrete VHF frequencies. This service is called **VOLMET**.

The **VOLMET** broadcast for each aerodrome is updated each hour and half-hour and includes:
- the actual weather report;
- landing forecast;
- SIGMET (significant weather, if any); and
- the forecast trend for the two hours following the time of the report.

Information is also obtainable from the Automatic Terminal Information Service (ATIS), which is a tape-recorded message of the current aerodrome information and is broadcast on appropriate VOR or discrete frequencies to off-load the ATC communications frequencies.

Some aerodromes have both an arrivals and a departure ATIS. One variation on the ATIS is that the wind direction is given in °Magnetic to allow the Pilot to relate it to the runway direction (which is in °M) more easily, and this also applies to winds passed to the Pilot by the Tower.

IMPORTANT POINTS TO NOTE.
- The cloud base in a TAF (Aerodrome Forecast) or a Trend Forecast (both of which refer to a particular aerodrome), is given **Above Aerodrome Level** (AAL); whereas,
- Area Forecasts give the cloud base **Above Mean Sea Level** (AMSL), i.e. as altitudes.

TAFs and Trend Forecasts, then, provide the Pilot with an immediate appreciation of the cloud ceiling at a particular aerodrome. *'AAL'* is, in fact, the height above the highest point in the landing area.

Over large areas of countryside, however, with mountains, valleys, plateaus and coastlines, a constant reference for the cloud height is needed and of course the only satisfactory one is MSL. To determine the expected level of the cloud base above the ground from the information in an Area Forecast you need to know the ground elevation, which can be determined from a suitable aeronautical chart.

SYMBOLS AND ABBREVIATIONS

SYMBOLS ON UK LOW LEVEL WEATHER CHARTS.

Facsimile-network Area Forecasts and Special Forecasts will contain symbols and abbreviations from the following standard sets.

1   SYMBOLS FOR SIGNIFICANT WEATHER, TROPOPAUSE AND PRESSURE SYSTEMS

Symbol	Meaning	Symbol	Meaning
R	Thunderstorm	,	Drizzle
6	Tropical cyclone	" "	Rain
ͮ	Severe line squall	*	Snow
△	Hail	▽	Shower
⌒	Moderate turbulence	S	Severe sand or dust haze
⌁	Severe turbulence	S	Widespread sandstorm or duststorm
CAT	Clear air turbulence	∞	Widespread haze
●	Marked mountain waves	=	Widespread mist
ⱱ	Light aircraft icing	≡	Widespread fog
ⱱ	Moderate aircraft icing	≢	Freezing fog
ⱱ	Severe aircraft icing	⌢	Widespread smoke
⌒	Freezing precipitation		

440 Tropopause altitude (FL440)

 H / 400 'High' centre and tropopause altitude (FL400)

 340 / L 'Low' centre and tropopause altitude (FL340)

∿ Boundary of area of significant weather.

—— —— Boundary of area of clear air turbulence. The CAT area may be marked by a numeral inside a square and a legend describing the numbered CAT area may be entered in a margin.

— — — — Altitude of the 0°C isotherm in flight levels.

Fig.C11-7. Symbols for Significant Weather on Met Charts.

NOTES: Altitudes between which phenomena are expected are indicated by flight levels, top over base. 'XXX' means the phenomenon is expected to continue above and/or below the verticle coverage of the chart. Phenomena of relatively lesser significance, for example light aircraft icing or drizzle, are not usually shown on charts even when the phenomenon is expected. The thunderstorm symbol implies hail, moderate or severe icing and/or turbulence.

2   FRONTS AND CONVERGENCE ZONES

▲▲	Cold front at the surface	⌒▲⌒▲	Occluded front above the surface
△△	Cold front above the surface	⌒●⌒●	Quasi-stationary front at the surface
●●	Warm front at the surface	⌄▽⌄▽	Quasi-stationary front above the surface
⌒⌒	Warm front above the surface	⌵⌵	Convergence line
▲●▲●	Occluded front at the surface	Ⅲ Ⅱ	Inter-tropical convergence zone

Fig.C11-8. Symbols for Fronts and Convergence Zones on Met Charts.

NOTE: An arrow with associated figures indicates the direction and speed of movement of the front in knots.

CLOUD ABBREVIATIONS.

Cloud Types are abbreviated according to the standard set of abbreviations:

CI	= Cirrus	NS	= Nimbostratus
CC	= Cirrocumulus	SC	= Stratocumulus
CS	= Cirrostratus	ST	= Stratus
AC	= Altocumulus	CU	= Cumulus
AS	= Altostratus	CB*	= Cumulonimbus

* CB implies hail, moderate or severe icing and/or turbulence LYR = Layer or layered (instead of the cloud type).

Altitudes are indicated in flight levels, top over base.

For example $\frac{220}{30}$ is base 3000 ft, tops at 22,000 ft.

The amount of **Cloud Coverage** is often given in *eighths* of the sky covered or *OKTAs*. *4 OKTAs* means that half of the sky is covered by the cloud mentioned, whereas *8 OKTAs* means complete coverage.

In Met Forecasts, the amount of cloud coverage can be indicated by:
- **SKC** – 0 OKTAs (SKy Clear);
- **SCT** – 1–4 OKTAs (SCaTtered);
- **BKN** – 5–7 OKTAs (BroKeN);
- **OVC** – 8 OKTAs (OVerCast).

Visual navigation with reference to the ground or water is difficult above more than 4 OKTAs cloud (half the sky covered). If BKN or OVC (or two lots of SCT) appear on the Area Forecast, you should compare the forecast cloud base with the elevation of the en route terrain and consider carefully whether or not safe navigation to your destination is possible beneath the cloud.

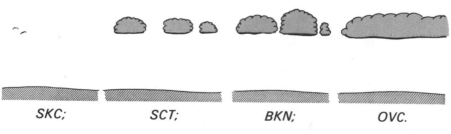

| SKC; | SCT; | BKN; | OVC. |

Fig.C11-9.

Think about how much of the ground you would actually see if you were navigating en route above 4 OKTAs of cloud predicted in an Area Forecast. For example: 4CU035 (4 OKTAs of CUmulus at 3500 ft AMSL).

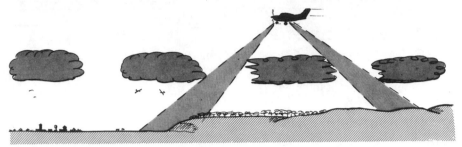

Fig.C11-10. 4CU035 Severely Restricts the Pilot's View of the Ground.

THUNDERSTORMS.

Thunderstorms (TS), which are best avoided by aircraft, are associated with Cumulonimbus (CB) clouds. The amount of CB cloud in an area is indicated by:

- **ISOL** – ISOLATED – for individual CB's;
- **OCNL** – OCCASIONAL – for well-separated CB's;
- **FRQ** – FREQUENT – for CB's with little or no separation.
- **EMBD** – EMBEDDED – thunderstorm clouds contained in layers of other clouds.

| *ISOL CB;* | *OCNL CB;* | *FRQ CB.* |

Fig.C11-11.

CAUTION: TS and CB each imply hail, moderate or severe icing and/or turbulence.

WEATHER ABBREVIATIONS.

DZ	= drizzle	COT	= at the coast	SH	= showers
LOC	= locally	WDSPR	= widespread	FZ	= freezing
TS	= thunderstorm	ISOL	= isolated	OCC	= occasionally
CAT	= Clear Air Turbulence	LYR	= layered	FRQ	= frequent

CAVOK.

The term **CAVOK** is used frequently and you should know its definition. CAVOK means that the following conditions occur simultaneously:
- visibility 10 km or more;
- no cloud below 5000 ft AAL or below the highest minimum sector altitude, whichever is the higher, and no Cumulonimbus;
- no precipitation reaching the ground, thunderstorm, shallow fog or low drifting snow.

IMPORTANT: Do not fall into the trap (as some VFR pilots have), of thinking that CAVOK means sky clear – **CAVOK does not necessarily mean blue skies.** With CAVOK you could have complete cloud coverage above 5000 ft, and any **non** IMC or Instrument-Rated Pilot cruising along at, for example, FL90 might have trouble getting down through this layer of cloud.

Also, there is a complication with the term CAVOK which can affect a non IMC-rated or IFR-rated Pilot. The criteria regarding **changes in cloud amount and base** for amending the TAF apply only when there are significant changes below 1500 ft AAL. This could mean that a Forecast specifying CAVOK may not be amended until the base falls below 1500 ft. Perhaps the safest interpretation of CAVOK, even though it specifically refers to no cloud below 5000 ft AAL, is to assume that it really means that the cloud base should not fall below 1500 ft for the period of the forecast.

VARIOUS TIME INTERVALS IN FORECASTS.

Whilst the Cumulonimbus cloud that a thunderstorm is associated with may exist for many hours, its passage through the immediate vicinity of the aerodrome may take only a brief period, say less than 60 minutes, or an even shorter time. During these *temporary* or *intermittent* periods the weather in the vicinity of the aerodrome might quite different when compared against the background of the prevailing weather.

In such a situation, the Aerodrome and Landing Forecasts would state the general conditions existing at the aerodrome (i.e. the **prevailing conditions**), and **any temporary changes** to the conditions would be indicated by:

- **TEMPO –** temporary variation lasting less than one hour or, if recurring, lasting in total less than half the TREND (or TAF, see MET 3-4) period; that is, changes take place sufficiently infrequently for the prevailing conditions to remain those forecast for the period.

- **INTER –** intermittent variations, more frequent than TEMPO; conditions fluctuate almost constantly.

Example:

TAF EGBS 2008 12010 9999 50DZ 2ST010 5CU020 INTER 2023 5000 5ST010

We interpret this to mean:
- the Aerodrome Forecast (TAF) is for SHOBDON;
- for the period 2000 to 0800 UTC.

Prevailing Conditions:
- wind velocity 120°T/10 knots;
- visibility in excess of 10 nm (indicated by 9999);
- Drizzle;
- 2 OKTAs of Stratus at 1000 ft AGL;
- 5 OKTAs CUmulus at 2000 ft AGL;

with frequent, brief occurrences (INTER):
- between 2000 and 2300 UTC;
- of visibility reduced to 5000 metres; and
- 5 OKTAs STratus at 1000 ft AGL*.

NOTE: **'INTER'** and **'TEMPO'** can relate to improvements as well as deteriorations in wind, visibility, weather or cloud.

  * In other words, intermittent deteriorations in the Shobdon weather for short periods during the three hours from 2000 to 2300 UTC; conditions as specified.

'GRADU' and 'RAPID'.

These expressions are used to indicate more lasting changes in the prevailing weather itself, whereas *'TEMPO'* and *'INTER'* are used to indicate temporary or intermittent variations from the prevailing weather.

Once the GRADU or RAPID changes are completed, there is new prevailing weather. Once TEMPO or INTER events are finished, however, the original prevailing weather re-asserts itself.

- **GRADU** – gradual change at approximately constant rate throughout the period or during a specified part thereof.

- **RAPID** – changing over less than half an hour.

Example.

TAF EGDL 0716 08008 9999 6ST008 GRADU 1012 9999 6SC020 GRADU 1315 CAVOK

We interpret this Aerodrome Forecast (TAF) for Lyneham aerodrome to mean:
- valid from 0700 UTC to 1600 UTC; and
Initial Prevailing Weather:
- wind from 080T at 8 knots;
- visibility in excess of 10 km;
- 6 OKTAs stratus at 800 ft AGL; plus:

A Gradual Change commencing around 1000 UTC and completed by around 1200 UTC, to give the New Prevailing Conditions of:
- visibility in excess of 10 km;
- 6 OKTAs stratocumulus at 2000 ft AGL.
(and this should be the weather at 1200 hours lasting until the next forecast change); plus:
Another Gradual Change forecast to commence at 1300 UTC and end at 1500 UTC, at which time the Prevailing Weather is forecast to remain as:
- CAVOK.

Example.

TAF EGBN 0716 33018/35 3600 65XXRA 6ST010 6SC020 8AS070 MOD TURB BLW 6000 FT RAPID 1314 16015 9999 WX NIL 6SC020 3AC100

Aerodrome Forecast (TAF) for Nottingham, valid from 0700 to 1600 UTC.

Initial Prevailing Weather:
- a gusty wind of 18 to 35 knots from the North-West (330T);
- visibility reduced to 3600 metres in rain;
- cloud is:
    - 6 OKTAs Stratus at 1000 ft AGL;
    - 6 OKTAs Stratocumulus at 2000 ft AGL;
    - 8 OKTAs Altostratus at 7000 ft AGL;
- moderate turbulence below 6000 ft AGL; plus:

A Rapid Change lasting less than 30 minutes is forecast to occur at some time in the period between 1300 and 1400 UTC, after which the Prevailing Weather is forecast to be:
- a southerly wind of 15 knots (from 160T);
- visibility in excess of 10 kilometres;
- an improvement to nil significant weather;
- cloud:
    - 6 OKTAs Stratocumulus at 2000 ft AGL,
    - 3 OKTAs Altocumulus at 10000 ft AGL.

In other words, the Forecaster is expecting quite an improvement in the weather.

Other terms that appear include:
- NOSIG – no significant change;
- TEND – changing, but none of the other change groups applies (TEND = tendency);
- WX NIL – the end of Thunderstorms or freezing precipitation, regardless of any other weather phenomenon that might be expected.

PROBABILITY.

Sometimes the Forecaster is uncertain of whether conditions will occur and, if he assesses the probability of them occurring as 50% or less, he may preface them with a 'PROBability' percentage.

Example. If the following was included in an Aerodrome Forecast (TAF):

PROB 40 TEMPO 1012 1000 97XXTS 7ST005 6CB040

– it means that the Forecaster has placed **a 40% probability factor** of periods of less than 60 minutes duration (TEMPO) between the hours of 1000 and 1200 UTC, with:
- 1000 metres visibility;
- heavy thunderstorms;
- 7 OKTAs of stratus at 500 ft AGL;
- 6 OKTAs of cumulonimbus at 4000 ft AGL.

NOTE: Code numbers such as *97*XXTS, *50*DZ, describe the nature of the following weather. Their significance will be explained to you by the Met Briefing Officer, or you can determine their meaning from the *'decoding card'*.

WHAT DO YOU DO WHEN THE FORECAST PREDICTS POOR WEATHER?

Whilst most of the time in your cross-country navigational flights you will be flying in reasonably good weather conditions, occasionally you may encounter conditions at the Met Briefing (either forecast or actual) that are not so good. Then you are faced with a **difficult decision** – does the flight commence and if so under what conditions?

Like most things in flying, it is not the every-day situation that tests us, but rather the unusual situations that have a habit of occurring from time to time. **Making sound operational decisions is what flying is all about.**

The following pages are reprinted from the Aeronautical Information Publication (AIP) for your interest and information.

MET 3-2 (2 Jul 87)   **UK AIP**

TABLE I

ACTUAL AND FORECAST WEATHER DECODE

Actuals

Report Type	Location Identifier	Time	Wind	Visibility	RVR	Weather	Cloud	Cloud	Temp/ Dewpoint	QNH	Trend
METAR	EGKK	0420	12005	0800	R1400	44FG	4ST001	8SC015	00/M01	1002	NOSIG

Report Type

METAR   Aviation routine weather report.
SPECI   Aviation selected special weather report.
COR   Correction; sometimes CCA, CCB etc.
RTD   Retard (late entry); sometimes RRA, RRB etc.
AMD   Amendment; sometimes AAA, AAB etc.

Location Identifier
ICAO four-letter code (for UK aerodromes see COM 1-1).

Time
UTC
The report type and time of observation do not always appear in the places shown. In the bulletin heading the METAR form is indicated by SA and the SPECI form by SP, followed by two letters to represent the country, for example SAUK, followed by the time of observation.

Wind
Wind direction in degrees True (three digits), followed by the windspeed in knots (two digits, exceptionally three). Calm winds are indicated by 00000, variable wind directions by the abbreviation VRB followed by the speed. A further two or three digits preceded by a diagonal gives the maximum gust speed in knots when it exceeds the mean speed by 10 kt or more.

Visibility
Horizontal surface visibility in metres. 9999 indicates a visibility of 10 km or more; 0000 a visibility of less than 100 metres.

RVR
Preceded by R, then the RVR in metres. When the RVR is greater than the maximum reportable value, the RVR is reported as 'P' followed by the maximum reportable value. When the RVR is less than the minimum reportable value, the RVR is reported as 'MM' followed by the minimum reportable value. RVR is only reported when the surface visibility is 1 500 metres or less except when IRVR is available and the indicated value is equal to or less than the maximum reportable value. For multi-site RVR/IRVR systems, the value given is that for the Touchdown Zone (TDZ). If RVR is assessed on two or more runways simultaneously, the RVR for each runway is given, each value being followed by a diagonal and the runway designator.

Weather

A two digit number precedes these weather code letters to define the weather more precisely for meteorological purposes:

FU	smoke		FC	funnel cloud (tornado or waterspout)
HZ	dust haze		DZ	drizzle
SA	duststorm, sandstorm, rising dust or sand		RA	rain
PO	dust devils		SN	snow
BR	mist		GR	hail
FG	fog		SG	snow grains
TS	thunderstorms		PE	ice pellets
SQ	squall		SH	showers.

Additionally:

MI	shallow	XX	heavy	BL	blowing	FZ	freezing
RE	recent (within the last hour but now ceased)	DR	low drifting	BC	patches		

Cloud

A single digit showing oktas (eighths) of cloud cover, followed by:

CI	cirrus	NS	nimbostratus
CC	cirrocumulus	SC	stratocumulus
CS	cirrostratus	ST	stratus
AS	altostratus	CU	cumulus
AC	altocumulus	CB	cumulonimbus

followed by height of cloud above aerodrome in hundreds of feet.

Reporting of layers or masses of clouds is made as follows:

First group;	lowest cloud of any amount (1 okta or more)
Second group;	the next higher cloud of 3 oktas or more
Third group;	the next higher cloud of 5 oktas or more
Fourth group;	cumulonimbus cloud if not already reported in the first three groups.

Sky obscured is coded as '9//' followed by the vertical visibility in hundreds of feet. A further three diagonals in place of the vertical visibility means it is indeterminate.

CAVOK

The visibility, RVR, weather and cloud groups are replaced by CAVOK when the following conditions exist:

(a)   visibility is 10 km or more

(b)   no cloud below 5 000 ft or below the highest Minimum Sector Altitude, whichever is the greater, and no cumulonimbus

(c)   no precipitation reaching the ground, thunderstorm, shallow fog or low drifting snow.

Air Temperature/Dewpoint

Degrees Celsius, M indicates a negative value.

QNH

Rounded down to next whole millibar.

continued

Trend
Landing Forecast of conditions during the two hours after the observation time.

NOSIG	no significant change	INTER	intermittent variations, more frequent than TEMPO; conditions fluctuate almost constantly
GRADU	gradual change at approximately constant rate throughout the period or during a specified part thereof	RAPID	changing over less than half an hour
TEMPO	temporary variation lasting less than one hour or, if recurring, lasting in total less than half the TREND (or TAF, see MET 3-4) period; that is, changes take place sufficiently infrequently for the prevailing conditions to remain those forecast for the period	TEND	changing, but none of the other change groups applies.

Followed (except for NOSIG) by the forecast weather changes in the METAR code. The weather change can be preceded by the time of the significant change or of the beginning of the period during which the change is expected to take place, expressed as four digits and the letters HR. SKC means sky clear, WX NIL means the end of thunderstorms or freezing precipitation, regardless of any other weather phenomenon that might be expected.

Plain language supplementary information can be added to the end of the METAR, as can an additional eight figure Runway State Group, the decode of which is shown at the end of this decode section.

Forecasts
Many of the METAR groups are also used in Aerodrome Forecasts, significant differences being shown below:

Report Type	Location Identifier	Validity Times	Wind	Visibility	Cloud	Probability	Variant	Validity Times	Visibility	Weather	Cloud
TAF	EGLL	1322	13010	9999	5CU025	PROB20	INTER	1619	4000	81XXSH	7CB012

Report Type
TAF   Aerodrome Forecast

The report does not always appear in the place shown. In the bulletin heading, the TAF form is indicated by FC or FT, followed by two letters to indicate the country. FC forecasts are valid for periods of less than 12 hours, FT forecasts for periods of 12 to 24 hours. The validity times can also appear in the heading instead of the place shown.

Validity Times
First two digits are whole hours of time of commencement of forecast, the second two digits are the time of ending of the forecast in whole hours.

Probability
Probability of occurrence as a percentage (never more than 50%).

Variant Validity Times
Two pairs of digits denoting the hours of validity of the sub-period.

Weather
WX NIL means the cessation of weather conditions forecast in the main part of the TAF.

TABLE J

METEOROLOGICAL ABBREVIATIONS USED IN SIGMETS, SPECIAL FORECASTS ETC

Note: The following abbreviations are those that have not already been described under Chart Symbology or the Actual and Forecast Weather Decode.

AAL	above aerodome level		LAN	inland or overland
ACT	active		LSQ	line squall
ADJ	adjacent		LTD	limited
AGL	above ground level		LV	light and variable (wind)
AIREP	Air Report		M	metres
AMD	amend or amended		MAR	at or over sea
AMSL	above mean sea level		MAX	maximum
			MB	millibars
BLO	below clouds		MNM	minimum
BLW	below (other than clouds)		MOD	moderate
BTL	between layers		MON	above or over mountains
BTN	between (other than layers)		MOV	move or moving or movement
			MPS	metres per second
C	degrees Celsius		MS	minus
CBR	cloud base recorder (ceilometer)		MSL	mean sea level
CC	counter clockwise		MT	mountain
CFO	Central Forecast Office (Bracknell)		MTW	mountain waves
CIT	near or over large towns		MX	mixed clear and rime ice
CLA	clear ice			
CLD	cloud		NC	no change or not changing
CNS	continuous (for cloud, vertically)		NM	nautical miles
CUF	cumuliform			
CW	clockwise		OBS	observed or observation
			OBSC	obscure or obscured or obscuring
DECR	decrease		OPA	rime ice
DEG	degrees		OTP	on top
DENEB	fog dispersal operations			
DIF	diffuse		PS	plus
DP	dewpoint		PSN	position
DTRT	deteriorate or deteriorating		PROV	provisional
DUC	dense upper cloud			
			QFA	meteorological forecast
EXP	expect or expected or expecting			
EXTD	extend or extending		RAG	ragged
			RWY	runway
FA	area forecast (ARFOR)			
FBL	light (icing etc)		SEV	severe
FCST	forecast		SFC	surface
FLUC	fluctuating or fluctuation or fluctuated		SFLOC	synoptic report of the location of sources of atmospherics
FM	from			
FOQNH	forecast Regional QNH		SIGWX	significant weather
FPM	feet per minute		SLW	slow
FR	route forecast (ROFOR)		SPOT	spot wind
FT	feet		STF	stratiform
FU	upper wind and temperature forecast (WINTEM)		STNR	stationary
			T	temperature
GND	ground		TC	tropical cyclone
			TCU	towering cumulus
HGT	height or height above		TDO	tornado
HPA	Hectopascals		TIL	until (time)
HURCN	hurricane		TIP	until past (place)
			TURB	turbulence
IAO	in and out of clouds		TYPH	typhoon
ICE	icing			
IMPR	improve or improving		UA	Air Report (AIREP)
IMT	immediate or immediately		VAL	in valleys
INC	in cloud		VER	vertical
INCR	increase		VERVIS	vertical visibility
INTSF	intensify or intensifying		VIS	visibility
INTST	intensity		VRB	variable
IR	ice on runway		VSP	vertical speed
			WKN	weaken or weakening
JTST	Jetstream		WRNG	warning
			WS	SIGMET or windshear
KM(H)	kilometres (per hour)		WTSPT	waterspout
KT	knots		WX	weather
			XS	atmospherics

AVIATION METEOROLOGY

4 WEATHER ABBREVIATIONS

DZ	=	drizzle	COT	=	at the coast	SH	=	showers
LOC	=	locally	WDSPR	=	widespread	FZ	=	freezing
TS	=	thunderstorm						

5 WIND SYMBOLS

5.1 Wind/Temperature Chart

Wind 300°(T) 30kt, temperature −36°C at arrow head.

Wind 090°(T), 60kt, temperature −56°C at arrow head.

Wind 240°(T) 15kt, temperature +2°C at arrow head.

5.2 Significant Weather/Tropopause/Maximum Wind Chart

Maximum wind 270°(T); 110kt at FL380

6 UK LOW LEVEL WEATHER CHART

6.1 The chart covers flight conditions from the surface to 15 000 feet and comprises three sections: a forecast chart, a tabular forecast, and relevant warnings and/or remarks. The forecast chart and tabular sections relate to the fixed time shown in the chart heading.

6.2 Forecast chart

6.2.1 The surface position of pressure centres is shown by 'X' for a low centre and 'O' for a high centre, together with the letter L or H respectively, and the central pressure in millibars. The direction and speed of movement (in knots) of centres and fronts is given. Movement of less than 5 knots is shown as 'SLOW'.

6.2.2 Weather areas are enclosed by continuous scalloped lines. Each area is allotted a distinguishing letter that refers to an entry in the tabular section.

6.3 Tabular section

6.3.1 The top line for each area gives the main expected conditions under the headings VIS (visibility), WEATHER, CLOUD, TURBULENCE, ICING and 0°C. If significant differences from the main conditions are likely within that area at the Fixed Time, these are given on subsequent lines after an explanatory remark in the VARIANT column.

6.3.2 Surface visibility is expressed in metres using four figures up to 5 000 M, and in whole kilometres using one or two figures for 6km or more.

6.3.3 Weather if any is given in plain language or by using a combination of abbreviations.

6.3.4 Cloud amount and type, with altitude of base and top is given. All altitudes are expressed in hundreds of feet AMSL. 'XXX' is normally used for tops in excess of 15 000 feet but an altitude is always specified for CB tops. The expected occurence of turbulence is indicated using the standard symbols alongside the associated cloud type. Icing, where applicable, will be indicated using the standard symbols alongside the associated cloud data and will normally cover the altitude from the main level of the 0°C isotherm to the cloud top. When additional layers with sub zero temperatures occur below the main 0°C level the altitude of the bottom and top layer will be shown in the 0°C section with any amplifying information in the remarks section. The words 'HILL FOG' imply cloud covering hills, with a consequent visibility of 200 metres or less. 'TS' and 'CB' each imply hail, moderate or severe icing and/or turbulence.

6.3.5 The main level (highest altitude) in hundreds of feet AMSL of the zero degree Celsius isotherm over the area given. The altitude of any layers where the temperature is lower than 0°C which occur below the main level will also be given. Any amplifying details may be given in the warning and/or remarks section.

6.3.6 Single numerical values given for any element represent the most probable mean in a range of values covering approximately ± 25%.

6.4 Warnings and/or remarks

6.4.1 Significant changes with time (for example CB developing, fog dispersing) expected during the period stated in the top right hand corner of the chart are given.

6.4.2 Warnings are given to supplement the forecast information given in the tabular section (for example surface gales, low level turbulence).

7 UK LOW LEVEL SPOT WIND CHART

The boxes refer to spot winds at the interception of the latitude/longitude lines covered by the box. Altitudes are in thousands of feet above mean sea level. Temperature is in degrees Celsius.

☐ Now, finally, complete **Exercises C11 — Weather Forecasts and Reports.**

Part (D)

EXERCISES
for Vols 2, 3 & 4

ABOUT THE EXERCISES

These Exercises form a vital part of the course.

We suggest that you take a blank piece of paper and jot your answer down, with the number of the question beside it. This leaves your textbook unmarked and suitable for later revisions. The answers are to be found at the end of each section; (see previous page Index for page numbers).

Some questions involve **multiple-choice answers.** Whilst these are not a good learning aid (continually reading incorrect statements is confusing), many of the exams you will do in the course of obtaining your licence and ratings will use this method of questioning. Here is an example:

8. In the signals area of an aerodrome, a white 'T' means:
   (a) landing direction is parallel with the shaft towards the cross-arm.
   (b) land on hard surfaces only.
   (c) land and taxi on hard surfaces only.
   (d) do not land.

A good technique in answering multi-choice questions is, prior to reading through the selection, think in your own mind what the answer might be. Then read the four choices, and quite often you will find the answer you already have in mind is amongst them. If not, then proceed to eliminate the incorrect statements. In the example above, the correct statement is **(a)**, so just record **'8.(a)'** for later reference to the correct answers, prior to moving on to the next chapter in the text.

Many other exercises contain **alternative answers.** These are shown in brackets, with an oblique stroke dividing the choices. Here is an example:

18. In general, an aeroplane (may/should not) land on a runway that is not clear of other aircraft.

Having diligently read through Chapter A1 on *Rules of the Air,* you already know the answer is **'should not'**.

Where an exercise requires you to think of the missing word(s) or numeral(s) in a statement, there is a series of dots (corresponding to the size of the missing word(s), etc, to assist you). For example:

24. The left wing navigation light is coloured ... .

NOTE: Exercises containing a number of parts are shown as (1), (2), (3) etc., to distinguish them from multi-choice questions.

Prior to sitting for the examination in the particular subject, you should be getting almost total success in these exercises.

So, now it is into it!

EXERCISES
on
AVIATION LAW

EXERCISES A1 — RULES OF THE AIR.

1. The UK Rules of the Air apply to all UK-registered aircraft:
   (a) wherever they may be.
   (b) only when in UK airspace.
   (c) only when in UK airspace and near offshore installations.

2. The UK Rules of the Air apply to (all/only UK-registered) aircraft in UK airspace and in the neighbourhood of offshore installations.

3. If two aircraft are approaching head-on, each must turn ....

4. When on converging courses, the 'give way to the .... rule' applies.

5. If two aircraft are well-separated but on converging courses, the aircraft with right-of-way (should/need not) maintain course and speed.

6. An aircraft which is obliged to give way to another aircraft must avoid passing ...... or .... or ...., unless passing well clear of it.

7. Another aircraft is approaching at the same level with a constant relative bearing of 30° right of the nose. A collision risk (exists/does not exist).

8. A flying machine (must/need not) give way to a glider and (must/need not) give way to another flying machine towing a glider.

9. A glider (has/does not have) right-of-way over a flying machine and (has/does not have) right-of-way over a balloon.

10. An aeroplane being overtaken (has/does not have) right-of-way.

11. When overtaking another aeroplane flying in the same direction at the same level, keep clear by turning ....

12. When overtaking another aeroplane flying in the same direction at the same level, keep the other aeroplane on the .... .

13. If two aircraft in flight are well-separated but on a collision course, the aircraft with the other on its left should:
    (a) give way by turning right.
    (b) give way by turning left.
    (c) maintain its course and speed.
    (d) climb.

14. If two aircraft in flight are well-separated but on a collision course, the aircraft with the other on its right should:
    (a) give way by turning right.
    (b) give way by turning left.
    (c) maintain its course and speed.
    (d) climb.

15. When flying in the vicinity of an aerodrome a Pilot (should/need not) conform with the traffic pattern, otherwise keep well clear.

16. The turns in most aerodrome traffic patterns are to the (left/right).

17. A landing aircraft (has/does not have) right-of-way over an aeroplane taxiing for take-off.

18. In general, an aeroplane (may/should not) land on a runway that is not clear of other aircraft.

19. When approaching to land on an aerodrome at which take-off and landing operations are not confined to a runway (i.e. it is an *'all-over field'*), you should land to the (left/right) of another aircraft that has just landed.

20. When approaching to land on an all-over field, you should keep another aircraft that has just landed on your (left/right).

21. After landing on an all-over field, an aeroplane should turn (left/right).

22. When following a line feature, keep to the (right/left) of it.

23. When following a line feature, keep it on your (left/right).

24. The left wing navigation light is coloured ..... .

25. The right wing navigation light is coloured ....

26. The red navigation light is visible from straight ahead through an arc of ...°.

27. The tail navigation light is coloured ..... and is visible from behind and in an arc ....° either side.

28. Night is defined (for the Rules of the Air) as ... minutes after sunset until ... minutes before sunrise.

29. At night you see the red navigation light of an aeroplane whose range is decreasing out to your left. A risk of collision (does/does not) exist.

30. At night you see the red navigation light of an aeroplane whose range is decreasing out to your right. A risk of collision (does/does not) exist.

31. At night you see the green navigation light of an aeroplane whose range is decreasing on a relative bearing of 030° (i.e. 30° to the right of your nose). A risk of collision (does/does not) exist.

32. At night you see two navigation lights of an aircraft whose range is decreasing, the green on your left and the red on your right. The situation is:
    (a) a risk of collision exists and you should turn right.
    (b) a risk of collision exists and you should immediately turn left.
    (c) no risk of collision exists.
    (d) you should turn right and overtake the aeroplane ahead.

33. At night you see the white navigation lights of an aircraft about 3 nm ahead whose range is decreasing. The situation is:
    (a) a risk of collision with the aeroplane ahead exists and you should turn right to overtake it.
    (b) a risk of collision exists and you should immediately turn left.
    (c) no risk of collision exists.

34. If a navigation light fails in flight at night, you should advise ATC. If for some reason radio contact is not made, then you should:
    (a) continue with the flight as planned.
    (b) land as soon as it is possible at a suitable aerodrome.
    (c) fire a distress flare.
    (d) switch the other navigation lights *OFF*.

35. An aircraft must not fly closer than .... ft to any person, vessel, vehicle or structure.

36. An aeroplane flying over a congested area such as a town (should/need not) fly at a height that would enable it to land clear if the engine failed.

37. Aerobatics are not permitted (below 5000 ft AMSL/in controlled airspace/over a congested area such as a city, town or settlement).

38. Aerobatics within controlled airspace (must/need not) have specific approval from the controlling authority.

39. In general, the minimum height over a congested area is ..... ft above the highest fixed object within ..... ft.

40. In general, the minimum height over a large open-air gathering is ..... ft.

41. The responsibility for an aeroplane maintaining sufficient height to glide clear of a congested area in the event of an engine failure lies with:
(a) the Pilot-in-Command.
(b) Air Traffic Control.

42. When simulated instrument flying is taking place, the aeroplane (must/need not) have dual flying controls and, in the second control seat, a (safety pilot/unqualified observer) must be seated.

EXERCISES A2 — AERODROMES.

1. Is prior permission required to use a military aerodrome under normal operating conditions?

2. Is prior permission required to use an unlicensed aerodrome under normal operating conditions?

3. Is permission required to use a civil aerodrome with an Ordinary Licence under normal operating conditions?

4. A civil aircraft may land at an aerodrome not listed in the UK AIP in an E........ in flight or by obtaining p.... p......... from the aerodrome operator.

5. Is a runway considered to be part of the manoeuvring area of an aerodrome?

6. Is a taxiway considered to be part of the manoeuvring area of an aerodrome?

7. Is an apron or maintenance area considered to be part of the manoeuvring area of an aerodrome?

8. Identification beacons at military aerodromes flash a (one/two/three) morse code identification group every 12 seconds in the colour ....

9. Identification beacons, when in use at civil aerodromes, flash a (one/two/three) morse code identification group every 12 seconds in the colour ....

10. Aerodrome beacons give an alternating flash signal using the colours .... and ...., or white and white.

11. When two aircraft are approaching head-on or nearly so when taxying, each must turn ..... .

12. Overtake when taxying by turning to the ..... and passing so that the other aircraft is on your ..... .

13. When taxying, give way to the .... .

14. A landing aeroplane has right-of-way over a taxying aeroplane. (True/False)?

15. Which has right of way -— a taxying aeroplane or an aeroplane under tow by a tractor.

16. In the signals area of an aerodrome, a white 'T' means:
    (a) landing direction is parallel with the shaft towards the cross-arm.
    (b) land on hard surfaces only.
    (c) land and taxi on hard surfaces only.
    (d) do not land.

17. In the signals area of an aerodrome, a white dumb-bell means:
    (a) landing direction is parallel with the shaft towards the cross-arm.
    (b) land on hard surfaces only.
    (c) land and taxi on hard surfaces only.
    (d) do not land.

18. (i) In the signals area of an aerodrome, a red square with a single yellow diagonal stripe means:
    (a) do not land.
    (b) take special care when landing because of the poor state of the manoeuvring area.
    (c) gliders are operating.
    (d) helicopters are operating.

18. (ii) The addition of black stripes to each circular portion of a white dumb-bell at right angles to the shaft means that aeroplanes should take-off or land on (a runway/any surface be it hard or soft), and that movement on the ground (is/is not) confined to hard surfaces.

19. In the signals area of an aerodrome, a red square with a diagonal yellow cross means:
    (a) do not land.
    (b) take special care when landing because of the poor state of the manoeuvring area.
    (c) gliders are operating.
    (d) helicopters are operating.

20. A red and yellow striped arrow bent through 90° around the edge of the signals area and pointing in a clockwise direction means that:
    (a) landing direction is parallel with the shaft towards the cross-arm.
    (b) a large obstacle is out to the right.
    (c) land and taxi on hard surfaces only.
    (d) right circuits are in force.

21. An aerodrome marked as 'PPR' means that:
    (a) Private Pilots only should use the aerodrome.
    (b) prior permission is required to use the aerodrome.
    (c) its identifying code is 'PPR'.
    (d) it is unserviceable.

22. Aerodromes not listed in the AGA section of the UK Aeronautical Information Publication may be used:
    (a) at any time.
    (b) only if prior permission has been obtained or in an emergency.
    (c) only in an emergency.
    (d) never.

23. Permission (should/need not) be obtained from ATC to fly in an Aerodrome Traffic Zone.

24. The dimensions of an Aerodrome Traffic Zone surrounding an airfield whose longest runway is 1230 metres are: ... nm radius from the mid-point of the longest runway, up to a height of .... ft Above Aerodrome Level.

25. Is an apron or maintenance area considered to be part of the manoeuvring area of an aerodrome?

26. An aeroplane is flying at 3000 ft Above Mean Sea Level directly overhead an aerodrome which has an elevation of 1263 ft AMSL. Is the aeroplane within the Aerodrome Traffic Zone?

27. A long white strip with two short strips across it, i.e. a double white cross, means ....

28. An unfit section of taxiway or runway is indicated by two ...... crosses.

29. A square yellow board with a black 'C' indicates the building where a Pilot can report to ATC or other aerodrome authority. (True/False)?

30. When dropping a tow rope at an aerodrome the Pilot (should/need not) fly in a direction appropriate for landing and drop the tow rope in the area designated by a (yellow/red/white/yellow and red) cross, or as directed by ATC or the person in charge.

31. At an aerodrome where the circuit is variable, a .... flag indicates that a left-hand circuit is in operation, and a ...... flag indicates that a right hand circuit is in force.

32. A continuous red light directed from the Tower to an aeroplane taxying means ....

33. A flashing green light directed from the Tower to an aeroplane taxying means ....

34. A flashing green light directed from the Tower to an aeroplane in flight means ....

35. A continuous green light directed from the Tower to an aeroplane in flight means ....

36. Red flashes directed to an aeroplane in flight mean ....

37. A continuous red light directed to an aeroplane in flight means ....

38. A red flare or red pyrotechnic light directed to an aeroplane in flight means ....

39. To indicate that he is compelled to land a Pilot should:
    (a) switch his landing and/or navigation lights *ON* and *OFF*.
    (b) take no special action.

40. To indicate that he is compelled to land and is in need of immediate assistance a Pilot should:
    (a) switch his landing and/or navigation lights *ON* and *OFF*.
    (b) take no special action.
    (c) fire a red flare.

41. The marshaller's hands held vertically above his head means ....

42. The marshalling signal of both arms repeatedly crossed above the head means:
    (a) turn right.
    (b) turn left.
    (c) move ahead.
    (d) stop.

43. The marshalling signal of both arms repeatedly and rapidly crossed above the head means ....

44. The marshalling signal of both arms moving upward and back means:
    (a) turn right.
    (b) turn left.
    (c) move ahead.
    (d) stop.

45. The marshaller's right arm down (i.e. on your left) and his left arm repeatedly moving upward and backward means:
    (a) turn left.
    (b) turn right.
    (c) stop.
    (d) increase power.

46. The marshaller's arms placed down towards the ground palms down, and then moved slightly up and down several times means:
    (a) stop.
    (b) stop the engine.
    (c) slow down.
    (d) increase speed.

EXERCISES A3 — ALTIMETER SETTING PROCEDURES.

1. As height is gained, atmospheric pressure (increases/decreases/stays the same).

2. Atmospheric pressure at a given place (changes/does not change) from time to time.

3. The altimeter subscale (is/is not) used to set the pressure datum from which the height will be measured.

4. To measure the vertical distance Above Mean Sea Level (AMSL) the altimeter subscale should be set to (QNH/QFE/1013).

5. To measure the vertical distance Above Aerodrome Level (AAL) the altimeter subscale should be set to (QNH/QFE/1013).

6. To measure the Pressure Altitude when flying at a Flight Level the altimeter subscale should be set to (QNH/QFE/1013).

7. A Pressure Altitude of 3500 ft is Flight Level ..... .

8. A Pressure Altitude of 24 500 ft is FL.... .

9. The altitude below which aeroplanes cruise with QNH set in the altimeter subscale is called the ....

10. The level above which aeroplanes cruise with 1013 set in the altitmeter subscale is called the ....

11. Choose the cruising level carefully to ensure that there is adequate separation from .... and other ....

12. For take-off and landing the altimeter subscale may be set to either the Aerodrome .... or the Aerodrome .... .

13. When cruising below 3000 ft AMSL the altimeter subscale should be set to the ....

14. If the QNH is not periodically adjusted as the aeroplane flies towards an area of lower pressure, the aeroplane will:
    (a) gradually climb.
    (b) gradually descend.
    (c) maintain the same height AMSL.

15. Flying beneath a Terminal Control Area (TMA) the Pilot should set:
    (a) Regional QNH.
    (b) Aerodrome QNH.
    (c) 1013.
    (d) Aerodrome QFE.

16. Penetrating a Military Aerodrome Traffic Zone (MATZ) the Pilot will be asked to set:
    (a) Regional QNH.
    (b) Aerodrome QNH.
    (c) 1013.
    (d) Aerodrome QFE.

17. Explain what is meant by 'Clutch QFE'.

18. With Aerodrome QNH set the altimeter should read:
    (a) zero when the aeroplane is on the ground.
    (b) aerodrome elevation when the aeroplane is parked.
    (c) aerodrome elevation when the aeroplane is parked at the highest point on the landing area.
    (d) zero when the aeroplane is parked at the highest point on the landing area.

19. With Aerodrome QFE set the altimeter should read:
    (a) zero when the aeroplane is on the ground.
    (b) aerodrome elevation when the aeroplane is parked.
    (c) aerodrome elevation when the aeroplane is parked at the highest point on the landing area.
    (d) zero when the aeroplane is parked at the highest point on the landing area.

20. The Quadrantal rule for aeroplanes flying under the Instrument Flight Rules and cruising above the Transition Level is based on (magnetic/true) track.

21. An IFR aeroplane on a track of 040°M to satisfy the Quadrantal Rule should cruise at:
    (a) FL50.
    (b) FL55.
    (c) FL60.
    (d) FL65.

22. An IFR aeroplane on a track of 090°M to satisfy the Quadrantal Rule should cruise at:
    (a) FL50.
    (b) FL55.
    (c) FL60.
    (d) FL65.

23. An IFR aeroplane flying with a heading of 085°M in a strong wind blowing from the north experiences 8° right drift. To satisfy the Quadrantal Rule it should cruise at:
    (a) FL50.
    (b) FL55.
    (c) FL60.
    (d) FL65.

24. An aeroplane has a true track of 265°T in an area where the Magnetic Variation is 7°W and therefore is a magnetic track of (265 + 7 =) 272°M. To satisfy the Quadrantal Rule, it should cruise at:
    (a) FL35.
    (b) FL40.
    (c) FL45.
    (d) FL50.

25. Convert FL50 to an Altitude if the QNH is 980 mb(hPa).

26. Convert FL50 to an Altitude if the QNH is 1033 mb(hPa).

27. When an aircraft is descending to below the Transition Level, before commencing approach for a landing at a civil aerodrome, ATC will pass (Aerodrome QNH/Aerodrome QFE/Regional QNH).

28. In the UK it is usual to make a visual approach using an altimeter setting of either Aerodrome ..... to indicate height above the runway, or Aerodrome ... to indicate height above mean sea level.

EXERCISES A4 — AIRSPACE.

1. The basic division of airspace in the UK is into the ...... and .... Flight Information Regions, abbreviated ...s.

2. FIRs in the UK extend upwards to a limit of .. ... feet, Flight Level ... .

3. The airspace above the FIRs is known as .... , and abbreviated as ... which stands for .... Region.

4. Airspace is 'categorised' as either Un..........., or C......... .

5. Uncontrolled airspace around certain aerodromes that require special rules because of heavy traffic or airline traffic and is regulated to some extent by ATC is called ....

6. A Special Rules Area (SRA) is one of the two types of Special Rules Airspace and extends upwards from a specified altitude or flight level. The other type of Special Rules Airspace is called a .... abbreviated ... , and extends upwards from ....

7. A well-used route in Uncontrolled Airspace, between specified locations, in which a traffic separation service is available to all participating aircraft is called an ...., abbreviated ... . Such a route is deemed to be .. nm wide.

8. The term ATZ is an abbreviation for ....

9. Describe the dimensions of an ATZ.

10. An aircraft fitted with radio, entering or leaving an ATZ, must transmit .... and ...... to the appropriate Air Traffic Service Unit.

11. The term MATZ is an abbreviation for ....

12. Describe the dimensions of a MATZ with one stub.

13. A MATZ (is/is not) regulated airspace.

14. A MATZ (does/does not) contain an ATZ.

15. When transitting a MATZ, a pilot will be requested to set .... in the altimeter subscale.

16. An area around certain aerodromes from ground level to a specified altitude within which an Air Traffic Control service is provided to all flights is called:
    (a) a Control Zone.
    (b) a Terminal Control Area.
    (c) a Special Rules Area.

17. A Control Zone is abbreviated as ... and extends from .... to a specified altitude or flight level.

18. A control area in the form of a corridor between major aerodromes is called an ....

19. A Control Area established at the confluence of Airways in the vicinity of major Aerodromes is called a .... and is commonly abbreviated to .... .

20. The dimensions of an Airway are ... nm either side of a straight line joining certain places and (has/does not have) specified vertical limits.

21. As an Airway approaches a TMA, its lower level (may/will not) descend.

22. A Private Pilot without an Instrument Rating (may/may not) enter an Airway.

23. State the only two exceptions under which a basic PPL holder (i.e. no IMC or Instrument Rating) may enter **Rule 21 Controlled Airspace**.

24. Even without a 'Special VFR Clearance' issued by the appropriate ATC unit, a basic PPL holder may enter certain **Non Rule 21 Airspace** in accordance with the Visual Flight Rules provided he remains .. ..

25. A Special VFR Clearance will only be issued for flight into certain:
    (a) Airways.
    (b) CTRs.
    (c) TMAs.
    (d) CTAs.

26. The holder of a basic PPL (may/may not) fly at right-angles across the base of an Airway, the lower limit of which is specified as a Flight Level (FL).

27. A Pilot with an Instrument Rating, even in an aeroplane not fully-equipped for IFR flight, (may/may not) cross an Airway by penetrating it, provided the conditions are VMC by day, he has a filed a Flight Plan and obtained an ATC crossing clearance.

28. An area in which flight is prohibited is called a .... Area.

29. An area in which flight is restricted according to certain conditions is called a .... Area.

30. Airspace in which activities dangerous to flight may occur within scheduled hours are known as ...... Areas and are shown on some aeronautical charts with a solid ... outline.

31. Airspace in which activities dangerous to flight may occur as advised by NOTAM are known as ...... Areas and are shown on some aeronautical charts with a .... outline.

32. A section of airspace designated as D703/15 is a .... Area located between Latitudes .... and .... extending from the surface to an altitude of .... ft AMSL.

33. An airspace designated as D505A/1-4.5 is a .... Area located between Latitudes .... and .... extending from ...... to ....

34. Known permanent obstructions ..... (AGL/AMSL) or higher are published in the UK AIP and shown on aeronautical charts.

35. Permanent obstructions over ..... are lit.

36. Known hang-gliding sites are depicted on aeronautical charts. Thermalling hang-gliders may be at heights up to (the cloud base or the base of controlled airspace whichever is the lower/the cloudbase or 5000 ft whichever is the lower/5000 ft).

37. Parascenders may be at heights up to ....

38. Launch cables for parascenders may be carried up to .... ft (AMSL/AGL).

39. Winch-launched gliders may carry the cable up to a height of ...... ft (AGL/AMSL) or more before releasing it.

40. Pilots should avoid flying at less than ..... ft AGL over areas where birds are known (or likely) to concentrate.

41. Military low flying occurs in many parts of the UK at heights up to .... ft AGL, but with the greatest concentration between ..... and ...... ft AGL, a height band that Civil Pilots are strongly recommended to avoid when possible.

42. Aircraft towing targets for military practice may trail up to ...... ft of cable and fly at up to ..... ft AMSL. The areas in which target-towing trials may occur (are/are not) listed in the UK AIP.

43. Royal Flights are conducted, where possible, within existing controlled airspace but, if this is not possible, temporary controlled airspace known as a .... Airway is established along the route. Details (are/are not) promulgated by NOTAM.

44. Free-fall parachuting may occur at heights up to ..... .

EXERCISES A5 — AIR TRAFFIC SERVICES.

1. ATC is the abbreviation for ....

2. ATC at an aerodrome may be shared between .... and ....

3. Information is usually passed from ATC to aicraft in-flight by means of radio, but, for non-radio flights or in the case of radio failure, may also be passed by .... or .... signals from the Control Tower and by .... signals in the aerodrome signals area.

4. AFIS is the abbreviation for ....

5. ATC provides control. AFIS (does/does not) provide control.

6. A/G radio (does/does not) provide control at an aerodrome.

7. 'Southampton Approach' refers to (ATC/AFIS/'A/G').

8. 'Binbrook Tower' refers to (ATC/AFIS/'A/G').

9. 'Newtownards Radio' refers to (ATC/AFIS/'A/G').

10. 'Rochester Information' refers to (ATC/AFIS/'A/G').

11. When departing on a flight, a Pilot will normally '.... out' with ATC.

12. A Pilot is **advised** to submit a flight plan if intending to fly over sparsely populated or mountainous areas or more than ... nm from the coast.

13. A Flight Plan (must/need not) be submitted for a night training flight.

14. A flight plan (must/may/need not) be submitted for a flight during which it is intended to use the Air Traffic Advisory Service on an Advisory Route.

15. A flight plan (must/may/need not) be submitted for a flight to or from the UK which will cross a UK FIR boundary.

16. A flight plan (must/may/should not/need not but should) be submitted for a flight more than ten miles from the coast or over sparsely populated or mountainous areas.

17. Flight Plans should normally be submitted to ATC at least ...... minutes before requesting a taxi or start-up clearance.

18. Due to poor weather or some other cause, a flight for which a flight plan has been submitted diverts and lands at an aerodrome other than the destination specified. The ATSU at the planned destination must be told within ...... minutes of the Estimated Time of arrival there.

19. A request for a special forecast for a flight of 623 nm, proceeding outside the area of coverage of UK area forecasts, should be made at least .... hours prior to flight.

20. The AIRMET area forecast system for the UK (is/is not) available via the AFTN and teleprinter networks.

21. The *AIRMET* weather forecast service (is/is not) available via the public telephone network.

22. The simplification of formalities for international air transport is called F........ .

EXERCISES A6 — VISUAL FLIGHT RULES.

1. The minimum conditions for VFR flight in Controlled Airspace for a Private Pilot (without an IMC Rating or Instrument Rating) are:
   - a flight visibility of .. nm;
   - a horizontal distance from cloud of ....;
   - a vertical distance from cloud of ....

2. The minimum conditions for VFR flight above 3000 ft in Uncontrolled Airspace for a Private Pilot (without an IMC Rating or Instrument Rating) are:
   - a flight visibility of .. nm;
   - a horizontal distance from cloud of ....;
   - a vertical distance from cloud of ....

3. The minimum conditions for VFR flight at 160 knots below 3000 ft in Uncontrolled Airspace for a Private Pilot (without an IMC Rating or Instrument Rating) are:
   - a flight visibility of .. nm;
   - a horizontal distance from cloud of ....;
   - a vertical distance from cloud of ....

4. VFR flight (may/may not) occur on Airways, which are notified for IFR flight only.

5. The minimum flight visibility required for VFR flight at 120kt below 3000 ft in Uncontrolled Airspace is ... nm, but for a Private Pilot (without an IMC Rating or Instrument Rating) this is increased to ... nm without passengers and ... nm with passengers.

6. There is no flight under the Visual Flight Rules (VFR) at night. (True/False)?

7. When outside Controlled Airspace, the Pilot is subject to ATC Clearances only when in:
   - ....; and
   - ....

8. 'SVFR' stands for ....

9 To enter a Control Zone in weather conditions below VFR, the VFR Pilot requires .... Clearance.

10. An SVFR clearance through a Control Zone (is/is not) a concession granted by ATC.

11. SVFR flight (is/is not) permitted in an Airway.

12. An SVFR clearance at a low level (absolves/does not absolve) the Pilot from the 1500 ft low flying rule over congested areas provided he can still land clear in the event of an engine failure.

13. A Flight Plan (is/is not) required for an SVFR flight.

14. The responsibility for maintaining adequate flight visiblity and distance from cloud on a Special VFR clearance rests with (ATC/the Pilot).

15. The minimum flight visibility generally required for an SVFR flight in a control zone is:
    (a) 5 nm.
    (b) 10 nm;
    (c) 3 nm;
    (d) 1.5 nm.

16. The usual minimum flight visibility for an SVFR clearance may be relaxed at some aerodromes in control zones where there are entry/exit lanes specified in the UK AIP as allowing flight in Instrument Meteorological Conditions without full IFR procedures being followed. (True/False)?

17. What is the ANO definition of 'Night'.

EXERCISES A7 — INSTRUMENT FLIGHT RULES.

1. 'IFR' stands for ....

2. In general, an IFR flight must not fly at less than ..... ft above the highest obstacle within ... nm.

3. The above requirements for an IFR flight are reduced during take-off and landing, and when flying:
   - at ...... ft AMSL or below; and
   - (clear/not within 1 nm) of cloud; and
   - (within/not within) sight of the surface.

4. A Pilot flying under the Instrument Flight Rules outside controlled airspace should have 1013 set on the altimeter subscale and fly at a Flight Level according to the Quadrantal Rule:
    (a) at all heights.
    (b) above 3000 ft amsl.
    (c) above the Transition Altitude.
    (d) above 3000 ft amsl or the Transition Altitude, whichever is the higher.
    (e) above 5000 ft amsl.

5. When following the Quadrantal Rule, the Pilot of an aeroplane on a Magnetic Track of 140°M should cruise at Flight Level (70/75/80/85) with (1013/QNH) set on the altimeter subscale.

EXERCISES A8 — DISTRESS, URGENCY, SAFETY AND WARNING SIGNALS.

1. Distress, Urgency or 'Lost' calls can be made on the frequency in use or on the emergency service frequency ...... MegaHertz.

2. Repeated switching on and off of the aircraft landing lights is:
    (a) an 'urgency' signal.
    (b) a 'distress' signal.
    (c) a 'warning' signal.
    (d) of no significance.

3. A succession of pyrotechnic single reds fired at short intervals is:
    (a) an 'urgency' signal.
    (b) a 'distress' signal.
    (c) a 'warning' signal.
    (d) of no significance.

4. A red parachute flare is:
   (a) an 'urgency' signal.
   (b) a 'distress' signal.
   (c) a 'warning' signal.
   (d) of no significance.

5. A pilot should, on seeing a series of projectiles fired from the ground at intervals of ten seconds, each showing on bursting red and green pyrotechnics, check if he is about to enter, or is already in, and active Danger Area, Restricted Area, or Prohibited Area, and if so take immediate action.
   (a) to avoid the area, or leave it by the shortest route without changing level.
   (b) to land as soon as possible.
   (c) to climb.

6. 'MAYDAY' is:
   (a) an 'urgency' signal.
   (b) a 'distress' signal.
   (c) a 'warning' signal.
   (d) of no significance.

7. 'PAN PAN' is:
   (a) an 'urgency' signal.
   (b) a 'distress' signal.
   (c) a 'warning' signal.
   (d) of no significance.

8. The emergency service VHF radio communication frequency 121.5 MHz should be used only for:
   (a) urgency calls.
   (b) distress calls.
   (c) requests for assistance.
   (d) all of the above.

EXERCISES A9 — SEARCH AND RESCUE.

1. 'SAR' stands for: ....

2. The emergency service VHF frequency is .... MHz and is generally reserved for ...., ... and .... calls

3. A constant SAR watch over your flight is better achieved when flying in a remote part of Scotland by filing a .... with ATC.

4. Pilots are advised to file a flight plan for SAR purposes when flying over water and more than .. nm from the coast.

5. Pilots (may/may not) file a flight plan for any flight.

6. The Pilot of an aircraft not fitted with a radio is advised to file a ....

7. If an aircraft is expected at an aerodrome, the Pilot must inform the ATCU or other Authority at that aerodrome of:
   (a) any change in destination.
   (b) any estimated delay of 45 minutes or more.
   (c) any estimated delay in excess of 1 hour.
   (d) any estimated delay of 3 hours or more.

8. If a Pilot lands at an aerodrome other than the intended destination, or decides en route not to land at the originally intended destination, he must ensure that the Air Traffic Service Unit at the intended destination is informed within .... minutes of his planned Estimated Time of Arrival there in order to avoid unnecessary action by the Alterting Services.

9. If an aeroplane fails to arrive at the planned destination, Search and Rescue action will commence ..... minutes after the Estimated Time of its Arrival.

EXERCISES A10 — ACCIDENT INVESTIGATION.

1. A notifiable accident in or over the UK should be reported by the Pilot (or Operator) to:
   - the .... Accident Investigation Branch by the quickest possible means; and
   - the local ....

2. If a person is seriously injured in a taxying collision, should an 'accident' be notified?

3. If a person is seriously injured whilst the aeroplane is undergoing maintenance in a hangar, should an 'accident' be notified?

4. If a fuelling truck runs into an unoccupied parked aeroplane, should an accident be notified?

5. If a fuelling truck runs into parked aeroplane which has just been boarded prior to flight, should an accident be notified?

6. If the engine fails in flight and a safe forced landing on a nearby aerodrome is achieved, should an accident be notified?

7. If the engine fails in flight and a forced landing is achieved in which no person is injured, but one wing is severely damaged, should an accident be notified?

8. If the engine fails in flight and a safe forced landing is achieved in an inaccessible area, should an accident be notified?

9. If the propeller slipstream blows stones back causing a large window to break, but no person is seriously injured, should an accident be notified?

EXERCISES A11 — AVIATION DOCUMENTS.

1. Official information regarding *'The Rules of the Air and Air Traffic Services'* is found in the ... section of the UK ....

2. 'NOTAM' stands for .... to ....

3. Urgent NOTAMs are given Class (One/Two) distribution, which is by ....

4. Non-urgent information is often distributed to Pilots as an .... Circular, and those directly associated with air safety are printed on .... paper.

The following questions are based on AICs, which you should read thoroughly.

5. A Pilot should not fly for at least ... hours after taking small amounts of alcohol, and proportionally longer if larger amounts are consumed.

6. A light aeroplane taking-off behind a heavy aeroplane, but departing from an intermediate part of the same runway should allow ... minutes for the dispersal of wake turbulence.

7. A light aeroplane taking-off behind a heavy aeroplane and using the full length of the same runway should allow ... minutes for the dispersal of wake turbulence.

8. A light aircraft following a heavy aircraft on final approach to land should stay well behind by a distance of at least .... nm and a time of .... min.

9. Can a Pilot fly if taking tranquillizers?

10. If a Pilot wears full-lens spectacles for reading only, are they likely to be suitable for flying?

11. Is a small amount of frost, ice, snow or any other contamination on the upper leading edge of a wing dangerous?

12. A 10% increase in aircraft weight will increase the take-off distance to 50 ft by approximately ... %, and the landing distance from 50 ft by ...%.

13. A tailwind component equal to 10% of the lift-off speed will increase the take-off distance to 50 ft by .... %.

14. Soft ground or snow may increase the take-off distance to 50 ft by ... % or more.

15. AVGAS filler points should be painted ..... to avoid confusion with turbine fuel filler points.

16. AVTUR filler points should be painted ..... to avoid confusion with gasoline filler points.

17. Is 'JET A-1' a turbine fuel or gasoline?

18. Take-off, Climb and Landing Performance of Light Aeroplanes is discussed in AIC ..... .

19. 'ANO' stands for ....

20. The ANO is sub-divided into P.... which consist of A....... numbered consecutively from the beginning of the ANO.

EXERCISES A12 — REGISTRATION AND AIRWORTHINESS.

1. Are aeroplanes and gliders required to be registered?

2. Notification in writing to the CAA regarding any change in ownership or part-ownership, or the destruction or permanent withdrawal from use of an aircraft (is/is not) required by the Air Navigation Order.

3. A Certificate of Airworthiness in the UK usually lasts for ... years.

4. For an aeroplane to tow a glider, its CofA must be endorsed to this effect. (True/False)?

5. Unserviceable items should be recorded after flight in the ....

6. Should the operator of an aeroplane maintain an Engine Logbook?

7. That part of the Certificate of Airworthiness which approves certain weight limitations is known as the ....

8. Operating outside the conditions specified in the CofA may, apart from making the Pilot liable for imprisonment or a fine, invalidate ...., ... and .... on the aircraft and its equipment.

9. For how long should an aircraft, engine or propeller logbook be preserved after the particular aircraft, engine or propeller has been destroyed or permanently withdrawn from use.

10. A Weight Schedule prepared by the operator of an aeroplane should be preserved until (0/6/12/18/36) months after the next official weighting.

EXERCISES A13 — OPERATION OF AIRCRAFT.

1. Should a loaded firearm be carried on an aeroplane?

2. Should a drunk person be carried in an aeroplane?

3. Following the consumption of even just a small amount of alcohol the CAA advises that a Pilot should not fly for at least .... hrs. If excessive amounts of alcohol have been consumed a person's ability to fly (may/will not) be significantly impaired for much longer periods.

4. Is an appropriate radiotelephony operator's licence required by a qualified Private Pilot to operate the radio in a radio-equipped aircraft?

5. A series of red and green stars directed at an aeroplane in flight means ....

6. Can flying training in an aeroplane occur at any landing area?

7. The Commander of an Aircraft is required by the ANO to produce his licence and personal flying logbook if so required by an authorised person for up to (1 month/1 year/2 years/3 years/5 years) from the date of the last entry.

8. Unless specified by NOTAM a captive balloon or kite will not be moored within a distance of .... from an aerodrome and be not more than a height above ground level of ....' .

9. Flying training for the purpose of obtaining a licence may occur at which of the following:
   (a) Aerodromes licensed for the purpose by the CAA.
   (b) A Government Aerodrome notified for the purpose.
   (c) A CAA-operated Aerodrome notified for the purpose.
   (d) Any landing area.

10. AVGAS fuelling equipment is usually marked .... .

11. Is the requirement to carry full documentation waived for an aerial work flight that will remain in UK airspace and the intent is to take-off and land at the same aerodrome.

12. Is the requirement to carry full documentation waived for an aerial work flight that will remain in UK airspace and the intent is to take-off and land at different aerodromes?

13. Is the requirement to carry full documentation waived for an aerial work flight that will take-off and land at the same aerodrome in the UK, but will enter foreign airspace during the flight?

14. Planned parachuting is only permitted with the written permission of the (aircraft owner/aircraft operator/CAA), and then only in such a manner as to not damage people or property, and in an aircraft whose (Certificate of Airworthiness/Maintenance Release to Service/Certificate of Registration) contains a provision that it may be so used.

15. If an aeroplane is expected at an aerodrome the Commander must inform the authorities at the aerodrome as soon as possible if the destination is changed or if arrival will be delayed by ..... minutes or more. This is to avoid any unnecessary *'overdue action'* being taken.

16. When a Pilot considers that the safety of his aircraft has been endangered by the proximity of another aircraft, this is known as an ...., and he should:
   (a) wait until he lands before reporting the incident to the authorities.
   (b) report the incident immediately by Radio to the ATSU with which he is in contact, and within 7 days confirm the incident on the appropriate CAA form.

EXERCISES A14 — THE PRIVATE PILOT LICENCE.

1. The minimum age for the granting of a Private Pilot Licence is ... years.

2. The period of validity of a Private Pilot Licence, provided the medical and flight test or experience requirements are met, is:
   (a) 3 years.
   (b) 5 years.
   (c) for life.

3. The privileges of a Private Pilot Licence may only be exercised if certain medical, flight test or recency requirements are met. A Certificate of Experience or a Certificate of Test remains valid for .... months.

4. A Private Pilot (without an IMC or Instrument Rating) may fly in cloud. (True/False)?

5. A Private Pilot (without an IMC or Instrument Rating) when flying alone outside controlled airspace may fly in a minimum flight visibility of ... nm.

6. A Private Pilot (without an IMC or Instrument Rating) may only carry a passenger at night if he has a Night Rating and has within the last six months carried out .... night take-offs and landings.

7. The additional licence required by a PPL holder to operate a radio equipped aircraft is known as the .... Licence, abbreviated .... . This licence (is/is not) also required for a Student Pilot to train in a radio-equipped aircraft.

8. A Private Pilot (without an IMC or Instrument Rating) requires a minimum flight visibility of .. nm when flying on a Special VFR Clearance in a control zone.

9. Does a Private Pilot require a group (D) rating to fly a microlight aircraft?

10. Is a Pilot required by the ANO to record details of each flight in his logbook?

11. Is a Pilot required by the ANO to record the details of every flight simulator session in his logbook? If not, are there any particular flight simulator sessions that must be recorded in his logbook?

12. If a Pilot is medically unfit to act as flight crew, the CAA must be advised in writing (as soon as possible/within 7 days/within 20 days/within 90 days) in the case of injury or pregnancy, and in the case of illness (as soon as possible/within 7 days/within 20 days/within 90 days/as soon as 20 days has elapsed).

ANSWERS –
Aviation Law

ANSWERS A1 —
RULES OF THE AIR.

1. (a).
2. all.
3. right.
4. right.
5. should.
6. over, under or crossing ahead.
7. exists.
8. must, must.
9. has, does not have.
10. has.
11. right.
12. left.
13. (c).
14. (a).
15. should.
16. left.
17. has.
18. should not.
19. right.
20. left.
21. left.
22. right.
23. left.
24. red.
25. green.
26. 110°.
27. white, 70°.
28. 30, 30.
29. does not.
30. does.
31. does not.
32. (a).
33. (a).
34. (b).
35. 500 ft.
36. should.
37. over a congested area such as a city, town or settlement.
38. must.
39. 1500 ft, 2000 ft.
40. 3000 ft.
41. (a).
42. must, safety pilot.

ANSWERS A2 —
AERODROMES.

1. yes.
2. yes.
3. yes.

4. Emergency, prior permission.
5. yes.
6. yes.
7. no.
8. two, red.
9. two, green.
10. green and white, or white and white.
11. right.
12. turn left and keep the other aircraft on your right.
13. right.
14. True.
15. The aeroplane under tow.
16. (a).
17. (c).
18. (i). (b).
    (ii). take-off or land on a runway, but taxying is not confined to hard surfaces.
19. (a)
20. (d).
21. (b).
22. (b).
23. should.
24. 2 nm, 2000 ft AAL.
25. no.
26. yes.
27. gliding is taking place at the aerodrome.
28. white.
29. True.
30. should, yellow cross.
31. Red flag for left hand, Green flag for right hand.
32. stop.
33. clear to move on the manoeuvring area and apron.
34. return to the aerodrome and wait for permission to land.
35. you may land.
36. do not land; aerodrome not available for landing.
37. give way to other aircraft and continue circling.
38. do not land; wait for permission.
39. (a).
40. (c).
41. park in this bay.
42. (d).
43. stop urgently.
44. (c).

AIRLIFE PUBLISHING LTD.
101 LONGDEN ROAD
SHREWSBURY
SHROPSHIRE SY3 9BR

45. (a).
46. (c).

ANSWERS A3 – ALTIMETER SETTING PROCEDURES.

1. decreases.
2. changes.
3. is.
4. QNH.
5. QFE.
6. 1013.
7. FL35.
8. FL245.
9. Transition Altitude.
10. Transition Level.
11. terrain and other traffic.
12. Aerodrome QNH or QFE.
13. Regional QNH, also known as the Regional Pressure Setting.
14. (b).
15. (b).
16. (d).
17. the QFE of the aerodrome with the highest elevation in a combined MATZ.
18. (c).
19. (d).
20. magnetic track.
21. (a).
22. (b).
23. (b).
24. (c).
25. 4000 ft.
26. 5600 ft.
27. Aerodrome QNH.
28. Aerodrome QFE, Aerodrome QNH.

ANSWERS A4 – AIRSPACE.

1. London and Scottish, FIRs.
2. 24 500 feet, FL245.
3. Upper Airspace, UIR, Upper Information Region.
4. Uncontrolled or Controlled.
5. Special Rules Airspace.
6. Special Rules Zone, SRZ, ground level.
7. Advisory Route, ADR, 10 nm wide.
8. Aerodrome Traffic Zone.
9. *see our notes.*
10. position and height.
11. Military Aerodrome Traffic Zone.
12. *see our notes.*

13. is not.
14. does.
15. Aerodrome QFE.
16. (a).
17. CTR, ground level.
18. Airway.
19. Terminal Control Area, TMA.
20. 5 nm, has.
21. may.
22. may not.
23. • Those *Rule 21 CTRs* in which provision is made for VFR flights in Access Lanes;
    • Under the conditions specified in a *Special VFR Clearance* issued by the appropriate ATC unit; available in CTRs and not CTAs, TMAs or Airways.
24. in sight of the surface.
25. (b).
26. may.
27. may.
28. Prohibited Area.
29. Restricted Area.
30. Danger Areas, solid red.
31. Danger Areas, pecked red.
32. Danger Area, 57°N – 58°N, 15,000 ft AMSL.
33. Danger Area, 55°N – 56°N, 1000 – 4500 ft AMSL.
34. 300 ft AGL.
35. 500 ft AGL.
36. heights up to the cloud base, or the base of controlled airspace, whichever is the lower.
37. heights up to the cloud base or the base of controlled airspace, whichever is the lower.
38. 2000 ft AGL.
39. 1500 ft AGL.
40. 1500 ft AGL.
41. 2000 ft AGL, between 250 and 500 ft AGL.
42. 2000 ft of cable, altitude 10,000 ft AMSL, are.
43. Purple airway, are.
44. FL 150.

ANSWERS A5 – AIR TRAFFIC SERVICES.

1. Air Traffic Control.
2. Aerodrome Control and Approach Control.
3. lamp or pyrotechnic signals, ground signals.
4. Aerodrome Flight Information Service.

5. does not.
6. does not.
7. ATC.
8. ATC.
9. A/G (Air/Ground).
10. AFIS.
11. 'Book Out'.
12. ten (10) nm.
13. need not.
14. must.
15. must.
16. need not but should.
17. thirty (30) minutes.
18. 30 minutes.
19. four (4).
20. is.
21. is.
22. Facilitation.

ANSWERS A6 —
VISUAL FLIGHT RULES.
1. 5 nm, 1 nm, 1000 ft.
2. 5 nm, 1 nm, 1000 ft.
3. 3 nm, 1 nm, 1000 ft.
4. may not.
5. 1 nm, 1.5 nm, 3 nm.
6. True.
7. an Aerodrome Traffic Zone; in Special Rules Airspace.
8. Special VFR.
9. a Special VFR Clearance.
10. is.
11. is not.
12. absolves.
13. is not.
14. the Pilot.
15. (a).
16. True.
17. the time between 30 minutes after sunset and 30 minutes before sunrise, as measured at surface level.

ANSWERS A7 —
INSTRUMENT FLIGHT RULES.
1. Instrument Flight Rules.
2. 1000 ft within 5 nm.
3. 3000 ft AMSL, clear of cloud and in sight of the surface.
4. (d).
5. FL 75, 1013.

ANSWERS A8 —
DISTRESS, URGENCY, SAFETY AND WARNING SIGNALS.
1. 121.5 MHz.

2. (a).
3. (b).
4. (b).
5. (a).
6. (b).
7. (a).
8. (d).

ANSWERS A9 —
SEARCH AND RESCUE.
1. Search And Rescue.
2. 121.5 MHz, MAYDAY (distress), PAN PAN (urgency) or requests for assistance (e.g. 'lost').
3. Flight Plan.
4. 10 nm.
5. may.
6. Flight Plan.
7. (a) and (b).
8. 30 minutes.
9. 30 minutes.

ANSWERS A10 —
ACCIDENT INVESTIGATION.
1. Department of Transport Accident Investigation Branch, local Police Authority.
2. yes.
3. no.
4. no.
5. yes.
6. no.
7. yes.
8. yes.
9. no.

ANSWERS A11 —
AVIATION DOCUMENTS.
1. RAC section of the UK Aeronautical Information Publication.
2. Notice to Airmen.
3. Class One, by teleprinter.
4. Aeronautical Information Circular, pink.
5. 8 hours.
6. 3 minutes.
7. 2 minutes.
8. 8 nm, 4 min.
9. no.
10. no.
11. yes.
12. 20%, 10%.
13. 20%.
14. 25% or more.
15. red.

16. black.
17. turbine fuel.
18. AIC 52/1985 (Pink 76).
19. Air Navigation Order.
20. Parts, Articles.

ANSWERS A12 — REGISTRATION AND AIRWORTHINESS.

1. aeroplanes yes, gliders no.
2. is.
3. 3 years.
4. True
5. Technical Log.
6. yes.
7. Aircraft Weight Schedule.
8. Insurance policies, warranties and guarantees.
9. two years.
10. six months.

ANSWERS A13 — OPERATION OF AIRCRAFT.

1. no.
2. no.
3. 8 hours, may be impaired.
4. yes.
5. it is approaching, or is in, an active Danger Area, Restricted Area, or Prohibited Area.
6. yes, except when the training is for the purpose of qualifying for a pilot's licence, aircraft rating or night rating.

7. 2 years.
8. 5 km, 60 metres.
9. (a), (b) & (c).
10. red.
11. yes.
12. no.
13. no.
14. CAA, Certificate of Airworthiness.
15. 45 mins.
16. Airmiss, (b).

ANSWERS A14 — THE PRIVATE PILOT LICENCE.

1. 17 years.
2. (c)
3. 13 months.
4. False
5. 1.5 nm.
6. five (5).
7. Flight Radiotelephony Operator's Licence, FRTO, is not.
8. 5 nm.
9. yes.
10. yes.
11. no; yes – particulars of flight simulator tests.
12. injury and pregnancy: as soon as possible; illness: as soon as 20 days has elapsed.

EXERCISES
on
AEROMEDICINE
& SAFETY

EXERCISES B1 — ARE YOU FIT TO FLY?

1. Can a cold cause you discomfort whilst flying?

2. Having consumed a small amount of alcohol, you should not fly for at least .... hours.

3. If you are on medication, the effect of which you are unsure, then you (may/should not) fly.

4. A faulty exhaust system may be dangerous because of the possibility of .... poisoning.

5. Carbon monoxide in an aircraft cabin is:
   (a) easily recognisable because of its peculiar odour.
   (b) easily recognisable because of its peculiar colour.
   (c) difficult to recognise because it is odourless and colourless.

EXERCISES B2 — IN-FLIGHT MEDICAL FACTORS.

1. The amount of oxygen available (increases/decreases/remains the same) as altitude is gained.

2. The lack of oxygen can affect a Pilot dramatically and this is known as ..... .

3. Cigarette smoke from a passenger (will/will not) affect the amount of oxygen in the Pilot's blood.

4. Hyperventilation can lead to (a shortage/an excess) of oxygen.

5. The body suffering from low temperatures is called ....

6. In an unpressurised aeroplane, at high altitudes the amount of oxygen that diffuses across the lung membranes and into the blood is:
   (a) decreased because of the low partial pressure of oxygen.
   (b) decreased because of the lower temperatures.
   (c) unchanged to that at sea level.

7. The percentage content of oxygen in the air (does/does not) decrease significantly as altitude is gained.

8. At higher altitudes where air density is less, each breath by the Pilot in an unpressurised aeroplane will contain (more/less/approximately the same number) of oxygen molecules compared to a breath at sea level.

9. At higher altitudes in an unpressurised aeroplane, (fewer/more/the same number of) oxygen molecules will diffuse across the lung membranes, enter the blood, and be transported around the body to generate energy, compared to at sea level.

EXERCISES B3 — SAFETY AND CARE OF PASSENGERS.

1. Passengers (should/should not) be briefed before they approach the aeroplane.

2. Cigarette smoking (is/is not) permitted on the apron, especially near an aeroplane that is being refuelled.

3. The propeller when it is stationary (should/should not) be regarded as dangerous.

4. Cabin ventilation (is/is not) important for passenger comfort.

5. In a ditching, life-jackets should be inflated (before/after) evacuation.

6. Is it safe to use a BCF (Halon) fire extinguisher in the cockpit and, if so, what precautions should be taken?

7. Does a BCF (Halon) fire extinguisher leave any residue that requires the cockpit, instruments, etc., to be cleaned after its use?

8. Could the use of a Dry Chemical fire extinguisher restrict visibility in the cockpit?

9. Is the use of a Dry Chemical fire extinguisher more likely to cause breathing difficulties than the use of a BCF (Halon) fire extinguisher?

10. Does a Dry Chemical fire extinguisher leave any residue that requires the cockpit, instruments, etc., to be cleaned after its use?

11. Is Carbon Dioxide suitable for fighting an electrical fire?

12. Is Carbon Dioxide suitable for fighting an engine fire on start-up, once the engine has been shut down?

13. Is Carbon Dioxide likely to cause breathing difficulties?

14. What is the reason for not holding the nozzle of a CO_2 fire extinguisher whilst it is discharging extinguishant?

15. Is it recommended to use a Carbon Dioxide fire extinguisher in a confined space such as an enclosed cockpit?

16. Is a Water Fire Extinguisher suitable for fighting an electrical fire?

17. Is a Water Fire Extinguisher suitable for fighting a fluid fire (e.g. fuel)?

18. Is a Water Fire Extinguisher suitable for fighting a smouldering fabric fire?

19. When combatting a fire, the extinguishant (should/should not) be directed at the base of the fire.

EXERCISES B4 — FIRST AID.

1. List five actions to take in the case of a passenger feeling airsick.

2. List four items to take in managing a person who has fainted.

3. In the event of a medical emergency in-flight the safety of the flight (does/does not) take precedence over the individual.

4. An unconscious passenger, evacuated from an aircraft after an accident, should be placed in the .... position, to aid blood supply to the brain and any vomit to escape without blocking the ....

5. List the various indications of head injury.

6. Mild head injuries (should/need not) be treated seriously.

7. In the case of a head injury, the Pilot may decide to place the patient in the 'Coma Position' and ensure that .... is unobstructed by the tongue or dentures.

8. Prolonged bleeding can lead to ..... and even ....., consequently it is important to control bleeding as quickly as possible, even before other injuries.

9. Profuse bleeding may be reduced by .... the sides of a wound, applying a ...., or hand pressure to block the blood flow.

10. To manage internal bleeding the patient should be ...... absolutely, elevating the legs comfortably and .... tight clothing.

11. List the points to follow in managing a fracture.

12. In managing a burn, the clothing in the affected area should be cut away unless it is ..... to the skin.

13. Shock is progressive and may take some hours to become obvious. The pulse may be very .... and ..... .

14. In considering the safety and care of passengers and crew, it is good airmanship for the operator to provide a ...., although not required by law in non-public transport aircraft.

15. A guide to contents suitable for a First Aid Kit can be found in the ... . Order, Schedule 5, Scale B.

ANSWERS –
Aeromedicine & Safety

ANSWERS B1 —
ARE YOU FIT TO FLY?
1. yes.
2. 8 hours.
3. should not.
4. carbon monoxide.
5. (c).

ANSWERS B2 —
IN-FLIGHT MEDICAL
FACTORS.
1. decreases.
2. hypoxia.
3. will.
4. an excess.
5. hypothermia.
6. (a).
7. does not.
8. less.
9. fewer.

ANSWERS B3 —
SAFETY AND CARE OF
PASSENGERS.
1. should.
2. is not.
3. should.
4. is.
5. after.
6. yes, ventilate the cabin after its use.
7. no.

8. yes.
9. yes.
10. yes.
11. yes.
12. yes.
13. yes.
14. the nozzle will become very cold and could cause skin to freeze to it.
15. no.
16. no.
17. no.
18. yes.
19. should.

ANSWERS B4 —
FIRST AID.
1. *refer to the text.*
2. *refer to the text.*
3. does.
4. coma, breathing passages.
5. *refer to the text.*
6. should.
7. breathing.
8. shock, death.
9. pressing together, constrictive bandage.
10. rested, loosening.
11. *refer to the text.*
12. stuck.
13. weak and rapid.
14. First Aid Kit.
15. Air Navigation Order.

EXERCISES
on
AVIATION METEOROLOGY

EXERCISES C1 — THE ATMOSPHERE.

1. The atmosphere extends further into space above the (Equator/Poles).

2. The region of the atmosphere closest to the Earth and in which 'weather' occurs is called the ....

3. The second layer of the atmosphere is called the .... and the boundary between it and the Troposphere is called the ....

4. The main gases that form the atmosphere are ....

5. Most of the water vapour in the atmosphere is contained in the:
   (a) Tropopause.
   (b) Troposphere.
   (c) Stratosphere.

6. Air Density generally (increases/decreases/stays the same) as altitude is gained.

7. At sea level, air density is approximately:
   (a) 1225 grammes per cubic metre.
   (b) 1013 mb(hPa).
   (c) 29·6 inches of mercury.

8. Temperature generally (increases/decreases/stays the same) as altitude is gained.

9. There is marked vertical movement of air in the Troposphere. (True/False)?

10. A body of air over an ocean is referred to as:
    (a) maritime air.
    (b) continental air.
    (c) polar air.
    (d) oceanic air.

11. An air mass that passes over an ocean is likely to be (more/less) moist than an air mass that passes over a continent.

EXERCISES C2 — HEATING EFFECTS IN THE ATMOSPHERE.

1. The air surrounding the Earth is mainly:
   (a) heated directly by the Sun.
   (b) heated from below by the Earth's surface.

2. Heating is greatest in the:
   (a) tropics.
   (b) temperate zones.
   (c) polar regions.

3. Hot air (rises/sinks).

4. Cool air (rises/sinks).

5. Terrestrial radiation is:
   (a) the direct heating of the Earth by the Sun.
   (b) the re-radiation of heat from the Earth.

6. Solar heating of the Earth occurs:
   (a) only by day.
   (b) continually.

7. The sea heats (more/less) rapidly than land.

8. The sea cools (more/less) rapidly than land.

9. Generally the sea is (warmer/cooler) by day than the land.

10. Generally the sea is (warmer/cooler) by night than the land.

11. Water has a (higher/lower) specific heat than land.

12. Cloud coverage (reduces/increases/does not affect) the heating of the Earth's surface.

13. Cloud coverage (reduces/increases/does not affect) the cooling of the Earth's surface by the terrestrial re-radiation of heat.

14. The transfer of heat as electromagnetic waves is called the process of ....

15. The transfer of heat from body to body is called the process of ....

16. The transfer of heat by the horizontal motion of an air mass is called ....

17. The transfer of heat by the vertical motion of an air mass is called ....

18. A Sea Breeze blows (offshore/onshore) during the late afternoon.

19. The Land Breeze blows (offshore/onshore) at dawn.

20. The wind that flows down mountain slopes at night due to cooling is called a ...... wind.

21. The wind that flows up mountain slopes by day caused by heating is called an ...... wind.

22. If the air at the Earth's surface is cooler than that above, a .... is said to exist.

23. Convert 10°C to °F.

24. Convert –15°C to °F.

25. Convert 41°F to °C.

26. An inversion means that the temperature (increases/decreases/stays constant) as height increases.

EXERCISES C3 — ATMOSPHERIC PRESSURE.

1. Atmospheric pressure (increases/decreases/stays the same) as height is gained.

2. Pressure drops by about ... mb per 30 ft gain in height in the lower levels of the atmosphere.

3. The daily heating and cooling effects cause the .... variation of pressure.

4. A line on a map joining places of equal sea level pressures is called:
   (a) an Isobar.
   (b) an Isopress.
   (c) a pressure gradient.
   (d) an equi-pressure line.

5. The variation of pressure with horizontal distance is called the ....

6. There is a natural tendency for air to flow from areas of ...... pressure to areas of ... pressure.

7. An aeroplane, flying so that the altimeter indicates 2500 ft with the current Regional QNH set in the subscale, is flying towards an area of Low pressure. If the Pilot fails to revise the subscale setting as the QNH changes, then the aeroplane will:
   (a) gradually descend.
   (b) gradually climb.
   (c) maintain 2500 ft AMSL.

8. Unless the Pilot periodically resets the lower Regional QNH as an aeroplane flies towards an area of low pressure, the altimeter will (over/under)-read, and the aeroplane will be (lower/higher) than what the altimeter indicates.

EXERCISES C4 — THE INTERNATIONAL STANDARD ATMOSPHERE.

1. 'ISA' stands for the International ....-

2. Temperature at sea level in the ISA is ..... .

3. Pressure at sea level in the ISA is ..... .

4. Density at sea level in the ISA is ..... .

5. Temperature in the ISA decreases by ...°C for each 1000 ft gained in the lower levels of the atmosphere.

6. The actual rate of decrease of temperature with altitude is called the ....

7. Above approximately 36,000 ft in the theoretical International Standard Atmosphere, the temperature ceases to fall and remains constant at approximately (0°C/+57°C/–57°C/+57°F/–57°F).

EXERCISES C5 — WIND.

1. The horizontal flow of air is called .... .

2. Meteorologists relate wind direction to (True/Magnetic) North, and so all winds that appear on Meteorological Forecasts or Observations are in (°T/°M).

3. Runways are described in terms of their (True/Magnetic) direction, and so any winds passed to the Pilot by the Tower for the purpose of taking-off or landing are in (°T/°M).

4. 280/34 on a Meteorological Forecast or Observation means a wind of strength of .... blowing from a direction of ...... °T.

5. A wind of 270/25 is passed to the Pilot of an aeroplane on approach to land by the Tower. The wind direction is expressed (°M/°T) and its strength is 25 (knots/mph/kph/metres per second).

6. A wind whose direction has changed in a clockwise direction has ....

7. A wind whose direction has changed in an anticlockwise direction has ....

8. A wind changing from 280/12 to 340/18 has (veered/backed).

9. The force that causes a parcel of air to start moving from an area of high pressure to an area of low pressure is called the .... force.

10. The apparent force that causes the curving direction change of the wind is called the .... force.

11. The Coriolis force is caused by the ...... of the Earth and is greatest near the (poles/equator/temperature zones).

12. The faster the airflow, the (greater/lesser) the Coriolis effect.

13. In the Northern Hemisphere, the Coriolis force curves the airflow to the (right/left).

14. If the Pressure Gradient force is balanced by the Coriolis force so that the wind blows parallel to the isobars, then this wind is called the .... wind.

15. The Geostrophic Wind has the low pressure area on its (left/right) in the Northern Hemisphere.

16. State Buys Ballot's Law for the Northern Hemisphere.

17. If an aircraft (in the Northern Hemisphere) is experiencing right drift (i.e. the wind is from the left), it is flying towards a region of (high/low) pressure.

18. If the aeroplane is experiencing left drift (i.e. the wind is from the right), it is flying towards a region of (high/low) pressure.

19. In the Northern Hemisphere, when flying at a constant indicated altitude towards an area of low pressure, an aeroplane will experience (left/right/no) drift and, unless the subscale is periodically reset, the altimeter will read (too high/too low/correctly.

20. For the wind to blow anticlockwise around a low pressure system, the Pressure Gradient force will (exceed/be less than) the Coriolis force.

21. For the wind to blow clockwise around a high pressure system, the Pressure Gradient force will (exceed/be less than) the Coriolis force.

22. The wind that flows around curved isobars is called the:
    (a) Curved Wind.
    (b) Geostrophic Wind.
    (c) Gradient Wind.
    (d) isobaric wind.

23. Surface wind is measured at .... metres above ground level.

24. Compared to the wind at altitude, the surface wind is (increased/decreased) in strength by the effects of ....

25. Compared to the gradient wind at altitude, the surface wind will (back/veer).

26. The backing of the surface wind is more pronounced over (land/sea).

27. The surface wind resembles the gradient wind at altitude more closely by (day/night).

28. There is (more/less) vertical motion in the atmosphere by day than by night.

29. The surface wind by day is generally (stronger/weaker) than the surface wind by night.

30. Flight at low level in strong winds is likely to be (more/less) turbulent over the land than over the sea.

31. If the wind at altitude is 240/35, the most likely wind on the ground is:
    (a) 270/20.
    (b) 270/40.
    (c) 220/40.
    (d) 220/20.

32. Strong air flows associated with a Cumulonimbus cloud will occur (within/in the vicinity of) the cloud.

33. If the surface wind is 330/20, the wind at 2000 ft is likely to be:
    (a) 350/30.
    (b) 310/30.
    (c) 350/15.

34. The variation of wind speed and/or direction from place to place is called ....

35. Low level windshear (is possible/will never occur) when an aeroplane flies through an inversion layer.

36. A strong wind flow over a mountain range will cause strong downcurrents and turbulence on the (windward/lee) side of the mountains.

37. Lenticular (lentil shaped) clouds may form well above the mountains as a result of strong winds causing m.......... w..... or s.......... w....... .

38. Strong westerly winds across a north-south mountain range may cause strong and possibly hazardous downdrafts to the (north/south/east/west) of the mountain range.

39. The ability of an aeroplane to climb is degraded when flying up valleys towards high ground in a strong (headwind/tailwind).

40. A good indication that Mountain Waves are present is the formation of (Stratus/Cumulus/Lenticular) clouds.

41. When a strong wind flows over a mountain range, there may be strong downdrafts on the (windward/lee) side, which an aeroplane may not be able to outclimb.

42. The effect of mountain waves may sometimes be felt as far as (1/5/20/40) nm downwind from the mountains that cause them.

EXERCISES C6 — CLOUD.

1. Name the four main families of clouds.

2. 'Lumpy' or 'heaped' clouds belong to the ..... family.

3. An extensive layer of cloud belongs to the ...... family.

4. Dense, white clouds resembling a *'cauliflower'*, and from which showers are falling, are called .... clouds.

5. A heavy, dense cloud with associated thunder and lightning is a .... cloud.

6. A rain-bearing cloud may have the word (stratus/nimbus/cumulus/cirrus) associated with its name.

7. As water vapour condenses to form liquid water, it (absorbs/gives-off) latent heat.

8. The amount of water vapour carried in a parcel of air is called ....

9. Warm air can hold (more/less/the same amount of) water vapour compared to cold air.

10. The greater the amount of water vapour in a parcel of air, the (higher/lower) its Dewpoint Temperature.

11. As a parcel of air cools, its ability to hold water vapour (increases/decreases/remains unaltered).

12. If a parcel of air cools to the particular temperature where it is carrying the maximum amount of water vapour that it can, then it is said to be ....

13. The percentage of water vapour in the air compared to what it is capable of carrying at that temperature is called its ....

14. When a parcel of air is saturated, its relative humidity is:
    (a) 100%.
    (b) 0.

15. As a parcel of air cools, its relative humidity (increases/decreases/stays the same).

16. The temperature at which a cooling parcel of air reaches saturation is called its:
    (a) saturation temperature.
    (b) dewpoint temperature.
    (c) moisture temperature.
    (d) cooling temperature.

17. As air temperature cools to the Dewpoint Temperature, the Relative Humidity:
    (a) falls.
    (b) remains constant.
    (c) rises.
    (d) rises to 100%.

18. The closer the actual air temperature is to the Dewpoint Temperature, the (higher/lower) the Relative Humidity, and the (closer to/further from) saturation is the parcel of air.

19. If the air continues to be cooled below the temperature at which it reaches saturation (i.e. below its dewpoint temperature), then the water vapour will ....

20. As air expands, it (warms/cools).

21. A process in which heat is neither added nor subtracted is called an .... process.

22. As a parcel of air rises and cools, its relative humidity (increases/decreases/stays the same).

23. Is cumulus cloud formed by an adiabatic process as air rises?

24. Unsaturated (or 'dry') air cools adiabatically as it rises by about ....°C/1000 ft gain in height. This is known as the .... Lapse Rate.

25. After the air is cooled to its dewpoint, the water vapour starts to condense into liquid water and so a .... is formed.

26. As water vapour condenses into liquid water it (absorbs/gives off) latent heat, which (increases/decreases) the rate at which saturated air cools as it rises.

27. The Saturated Adiabatic Lapse Rate is approximately (one half/one third/the same as) the Dry Adiabatic Lapse Rate. The SALR is approximately ......°C/1000 ft.

28. The rate of change of temperature in the surrounding air that is not rising is called the ....

29. The level at which the cloud base forms depends upon:
    (a) the moisture content of the cloud and its dewpoint temperature.
    (b) the temperature of the environment.

30. If the moisture content of a parcel of air is such that its Dewpoint Temperature is +7°C, at what height above the ground is its base likely to form if the surface air temperature is +16°C?

31. If the moisture content of a parcel of air is such that its Dewpoint Temperature is +7°C, at what height above the ground is its base likely to form if the surface air temperature is +19°C?

32. If the moisture content of a parcel of air is such that its Dewpoint Temperature is +7°C, at what height above the ground is its base likely to form if the surface air temperature is +22°C?

33. If the moisture content of a parcel of air is such that its Dewpoint Temperature is +13°C, at what height above the ground is its base likely to form if the surface air temperature is +22°C?

34. Cloud formed by turbulence and mixing is known as .... cloud.

35. Cloud formed by a mountain range causing the uplift of air is called .... cloud.

36. Orographic uplift of unstable air is more likely to cause the formation of (stratiform/cumuliform) cloud.

37. Orographic uplift of stable air is more likely to cause the formation of (stratiform/cumuliform) cloud.

38. If moist air flows up and over a mountain range, forming cloud and causing rain, the wind on the lee side of the mountain range will be (warmer/cooler/the same temperature) and (drier/wetter/the same humidity). This is called the .... Wind Effect.

39. As air flows up a mountain range its temperature will fall at about:
    (1) ....°C/1000 ft when it is unsaturated; and
    (2) ....°C/1000 ft once it has cooled sufficiently to become saturated.

40. Precipitation consisting of water drops is called ....

41. Precipitation consisting of small balls of ice is called .... .

42. Precipitation consisting of branched and star-shaped ice crystals is called .... .

43. Showers generally fall from (cumuliform/stratiform) clouds.

44. Drizzle generally falls from (cumuliform/stratiform) clouds.

45. Rain which falls from the base of clouds but which evaporates before reaching the ground is called ..... .

46. The cloud associated with standing waves (or mountain waves) is known as .... cloud.

EXERCISES C7 — THUNDERSTORMS.

1. List three conditions necessary for a thunderstorm to develop.

2. List the three stages of a thunderstorm's life cycle.

3. Specify three types of 'trigger actions' that can lead to the formation of a thunderstorm in unstable, moist air.

4. At what stage in the life of a typical thunderstorm are there strong warm updrafts over a diameter of 1 or 2 nm with no significant downdrafts?

5. The temperature in a forming Cumulonimbus cloud is (higher than/lower than/the same as) the outside environment.

6. The beginning of what stage in the life of a typical thunderstorm is signalled by the first lightning flashes and the first rain from the cloud base?

7. In the mature stage of a typical thunderstorm there (will be/will not be) both strong updrafts and downdrafts inside the cloud, and there will be very strong (warm/cool) downdrafts flowing from the base of the cloud.

8. If the top of a Cumulonimbus cloud spreads out, it is referred to as an ..... , and is a sign that the cloud is well-developed.

9. There are only updrafts inside a Cumulonimbus cloud. (True/False)?

10. A thundercloud is a hazard to aviation:
    (a) only within the cloud.
    (b) only within and directly under the cloud.
    (c) within about 10 nm.

11. List four of the hazards to aviation caused by thunderstorms.

EXERCISES C8 — AIR MASSES AND FRONTAL WEATHER.

1. An air mass that has passed over an ocean is referred to as .... air.

2. An air mass that has passed over a large land mass is referred to as ..... air.

3. As cool air travels across warm land it absorbs heat and becomes (stable/unstable).

4. Warm air moving across a cooler surface will lose heat and become more (stable/unstable).

5. Tropical air moving North over the oceans until it reaches the UK will be (stable/unstable) and (dry/moist).

6. The slow sinking of an upper air mass is called ....

7. The slow rising of a large air mass is associated with (convergence/divergence) at the Earth's surface.

8. Convergence at the Earth's surface is associated with a (HIGH/LOW) pressure system.

9. Divergence at the Earth's surface is associated with a (HIGH/LOW).

10. Subsiding air becomes (warmer/cooler), (moister/drier) and more (stable/unstable).

11. Subsidence is associated with (stability/instability).

12. Convergence is associated with (stability/instability).

13. A LOW pressure system is associated with (stability/instability).

14. Warm air displacing cold air at the surface is called a ....

15. As a Warm Front approaches, the cloud base (lowers/rises).

16. The general cloud associated with a Warm Front is (stratiform/cumuliform).

17. If an aeroplane takes-off at an aerodrome prior to the passage of a warm front, it will be in the (warm/cold) air mass.

18. In a Warm Front, the warm air at altitude (precedes/follows) the passage of the front at the surface.

19. The slope of a typical Warm Front is 1 in (10/50/150/1000).

20. As a Warm Front approaches, the first sign could be high level (Cirrus/Stratus/Cumulonimbus) cloud about (20/200/600/2000) nm ahead of the surface front.

21. Rain associated with a Warm Front may fall:
    (a) only after the surface front has passed.
    (b) only in a narrow band some 10 nm wide near the surface front.
    (c) up to several hundred miles ahead of the surface front.

22. List the five general characteristics of a Warm Front.

23. Cold air displacing warm air at the surface is called a ....

24. Cloud associated with a Cold Front is of the (cumuliform/stratiform) type.

25. The change in weather with the passage of a Cold Front (may/will not) be quite sudden.

26. Precipitation associated with a Cold Front is most likely to be (drizzle/showers).

27. As a Cold Front passes, the wind will (veer/back).

28. As a Cold Front passes, the air temperature will (rise/fall), and the Dewpoint Temperature will (rise/fall).

29. Visibility following the passage of a Cold Front is likely to be:
    (a) poor in continuous drizzle
    (b) excellent in all directions
    (c) good, except in showers

30. The slope of a typical Cold Front is 1 in (10/50/150/1000).

31. As a Cold Front passes, the temperature will (rise/fall).

32. As a Warm Front passes, the wind will (veer/back).

33. As a Warm Front passes, the temperature will (rise/fall).

34. As a Warm Front passes, the air temperature will (rise/fall), and the Dewpoint Temperature will (rise/fall).

35. A wind of 20 knots from the West does not allow you to take-off on the North-South runway at Sleap in your particular aeroplane because the maximum crosswind limit is exceeded. If a Cold Front passes, it is likely that you will be able to take-off into the (North/South).

36. Rain is more likely to precede the passage of a Warm Front than a Cold Front. (True/False)?

37. The general visibility away from the clouds and showers associated with a Cold Front will be (better/poorer) than the general visibility associated with a Warm Front.

38. If a Cold Front overtakes a Warm Front, the result is an .... Front.

39. There (may/will never) be intense weather associated with an Occluded Front.

40. Flying towards an area where the cloud base is lowering to within 1000 ft of the terrain, ice starts to form on the wings. Your best course of action is to:
    (a) climb, even though it means entering cloud.
    (b) descend into warmer air, but continue on.
    (c) maintain track and level.
    (d) turn back.

41. In the Northern Hemisphere, wind flows ....wise around a LOW.

42. Flying towards a LOW an aeroplane will experience ..... drift.

43. In the Northern Hemisphere, wind flows ....wise around a HIGH.

44. Flying towards a HIGH in the Northern Hemisphere, an aeroplane will experience ..... drift.

45. (Convergence/divergence) at the surface is associated with a LOW.

46. (Rising/sinking) air is associated with a LOW.

47. A V-shaped extension of low pressure is called a ....

48. A Cold Front usually moves (faster/slower) than a Warm Front.

49. HIGHs generally have a (weaker/stronger) pressure gradient than LOWs.

50. (Convergence/divergence) at the surface is associated with a HIGH.

51. (Rising/subsiding) air is associated with HIGH pressure systems.

52. Subsiding air is very (stable/unstable).

53. Another name for the HIGH is the ....

54. A U-shaped extension of isobars surrounding a HIGH is called a ....

55. An area of almost constant pressure located between two HIGHs and two LOWs is called a ... .

56. If the wind veers and rain/drizzle that has been falling steadily for many hours gradually ceases, then it is possible that a (warm/cold) front has passed.

57. If an aeroplane is experiencing right (starboard) drift in the Northern Hemisphere and the Pilot fails to periodically revise the Regional QNH set in the altimeter subscale, then the aeroplane will gradually (climb/descend).

EXERCISES C9 — ICING.

1. Water may freeze when the temperature is less than ..... °C.

2. Ice that forms on the wings, fuselage, propeller, etc, is known as ..... ice.

3. Ice that forms in the carburettor is known as .... ice, which (can/cannot) form if the outside air temperature is as high as +25°C.

4. The most dangerous form of airframe icing is:
   (a) clear ice.
   (b) hoar frost.
   (c) dry ice.
   (d) rime ice.

5. Airframe icing (may/will not) be more severe at an air temperature of –3°C than at –40°C.

6. Sometimes water exists as liquid even though its temperature is less than the freezing point of water. Such droplets are said to be ....

7. Large supercooled water drops striking a cold airframe are likely to form:
   (a) clear ice.
   (b) hoar frost.
   (c) dry ice.
   (d) rime ice.

8. Very small supercooled water droplets striking a cold airframe are likely to form:
   (a) clear ice.
   (b) hoar frost.
   (c) dry ice.
   (d) rime ice.

9. For carburettor ice to form, the outside air must be:
   (a) below freezing.
   (b) moist.
   (c) dry.
   (d) cold and moist.

10. Frost or ice on the leading edge of a wing (is/is not) dangerous.

11. Ice of any type should be cleared off the aeroplane before flight. (True/False)?

12. If ice forms over the static vent of an aeroplane and blocks it during the climb, the Altimeter will read:
    (a) zero.
    (b) a constant altitude.
    (c) correctly.

13. If ice forms over the static vent of an aeroplane and blocks it during the climb, the Vertical Speed Indicator will read:
    (a) zero.
    (b) a constant altitude.
    (c) correctly.

14. If ice forms over the static vent of an aeroplane and blocks it during the climb, the Air Speed Indicator will read:
    (a) zero.
    (b) too fast.
    (c) too slow.
    (c) correctly.

15. Carburettor ice is most likely to form if the air temperature and dewpoint temperature are respectively:
    (a) –10°C and –20°C.
    (b) +12°C and +10°C.
    (c) +12°C and 0°C.
    (d) 0°C and –6°C.

16. Throttle icing is more likely at (high/low) power settings.

17. When flying in the cold sector underlying the warmer air in a Warm Front there is:
    (a) no possibility of airframe ice forming.
    (b) no possibility of airframe ice forming if the temperature of the rain falling out of the warm sector is above 0°C.
    (c) a possibility of clear ice forming in rain.
    (d) rarely any rain.

EXERCISES C10 — VISIBILITY.

1. When approaching to land, (slant/vertical/horizontal) visibility is most important to a Pilot.

2. Small liquid droplets suspended in the air that reduce the visibility to less than 1 km is called ....

3. Small liquid droplets suspended in the air that reduce the visibility to say 1.5 km is called ....

4. Terrestrial re-radiation causes the surface of the Earth to cool at night. It, in turn, cools the air in contact with it and .... fog may form.

5. List three requirements for radiation fog to form.

6. If a warm, moist air mass flows over a cold surface, it will cool. If it cools to its dewpoint, then fog will form. This is known as .... fog.

7. A warm maritime airflow over land may give rise to .... fog.

8. Fog formed by the interaction of two air masses is called .... fog.

9. If the air temperature increases with height, then an .... exists.

10. It is more likely that an inversion will exist at (dawn/dusk).

11. If Radiation Fog forms on a clear night with light winds, an increase in wind strength from 5 kt to 18 kt:
    (a) will change the Radiation Fog to Advection Fog.
    (b) may cause the fog to lift and become low Stratus.
    (c) will have no effect.

12. An early morning fog over the sea lasts all day. As the land heats up, the Sea Fog:
    (a) may drift in over the land.
    (b) will always disperse.
    (c) will always remain over the sea.

13. Visibility will be (greater/poorer) when flying into the sun than when flying *'down-sun'*.

14. On a cool and cloudless night with no wind, and the air in contact with the surface cooled to its dewpoint temperature (say +5°C), which of the following is most likely to form?
    (a) Dew.
    (b) Frost.
    (c) Mist.
    (d) Fog.
    (e) Stratus.

15. On a cool and cloudless night with no wind, and the air in contact with the surface cooled to its dewpoint temperature (say –5°C), which of the following is most likely to form?
    (a) Dew.
    (b) Frost.
    (c) Mist.
    (d) Fog.
    (e) Stratus.

16. On a cool and cloudless night with a light wind, and the very moist air in contact with the surface cooled to its dewpoint temperature (say +7°C), which of the following is most likely to form?
    (a) Dew.
    (b) Frost.
    (c) Mist.
    (d) Fog.
    (e) Stratus.

17. If warm maritime air flows over a cold land surface, it may form:
    (a) Radiation Fog.
    (b) Frontal Fog.
    (c) Advection Fog.
    (d) Hail.

18. Radiation Fog is most likely to form:
    (a) over a cool sea by night.
    (b) over a warm sea by night.
    (c) over land on cool, clear nights.
    (d) over land during the afternoon.

19. Advection Fog is most likely to form:
    (a) over a cool sea by night.
    (b) over a warm sea by night.
    (c) over land on cool, clear nights.
    (d) over land during the afternoon.
    (e) at any time, day or night, when the conditions are right.

20. Is Radiation Fog formed as moist air loses heat to a cold land surface the result of an adiabatic process?

21. Is Advection Fog formed as warm moist air moves over a cold land mass the result of an adiabatic process?

22. When flying beneath an inversion, visibility is likely to be poor because of
    (a) mist, fog or smog.
    (b) showers from cumulus clouds.

23. The figures '9999' in a Meteorological Forecast or Report mean ....

24. The visibility group '6000' in a Meteorological Forecast or Report means .... .

25. The visibility group 'R0400/35' in a Meteorological Forecast or Report means .... .

EXERCISES C11 — WEATHER FORECASTS AND REPORTS.

1. The primary method of obtaining Meteorological Information in the UK prior to flight (is/is not) by self-briefing using information in the aerodrome briefing area or by using the telephone recorded-message service.

2. A weather forecast is:
   (a) a prediction.
   (b) an observation.

3. A weather report is:
   (a) a prediction.
   (b) an observation.

4. The forecast of expected weather at an aerodrome is called an .... and it has the code name ... .

5. A routine aerodrome report has the code name M....... .

6. Significant weather that may affect a flight may be advised in the form of a ....

7. List four of the types of significant weather phenomena which may affect the safety of flight operations and that could be passed by the Flight Information Service to the Pilot in the form of a SIGMET.

8. At aerodromes with suitable communications facilities such as AFTN or Telex, Area Forecasts plus Aerodrome Forecasts (TAFs) and/or Aerodrome Reports (METARs) (are/are not) available in text form.

9. AIRMET is available:
   (a) through the post.
   (b) by radio.
   (c) via the public telephone network.
   (d) from aerodrome Briefing Offices connected to AFTN or Telex.

10. There (is/is not) a standard form or *'Proforma'* on which to note down the appropriate AIRMET information, when utilising the AIRMET telephone recording service.

11. The service where weather Reports and Trends for a number of selected aerodromes are broadcast continuously on discrete VHF frequencies is called (METAR/TAF VOLMET/SIGMET/Area Forecast).

12. Weather information for certain aerodromes is available in recorded form on the VOLMET service:
    (a) through the post.
    (b) by radio.
    (c) via the public telephone network.
    (d) from ATC prior to flight.

13. A Forecast for a particular aerodrome, usually issued for a 9 hour period, is called a (METAR/TAF/VOLMET/SIGMET/Area Forecast).

14. A Report of weather at a particular aerodrome is called a (METAR/TAF VOLMET/SIGMET/Area Forecast).

15. A visibility term in a TAF or a METAR of '4000' means a visibility of .....

16. The term 'NOSIG' appended to a METAR means .... expected for a period of ..... hours after the time of observation.

17. The cloud term '7SCO35' in a TAF or METAR means .. oktas of ...... cloud with a base of ..... ft (AMSL/AAL).

18. Decode the following TAF for GUERNSEY:
EGJB 1221 23015 9999 6SC025

19. Decode the following TAF for WICK:
EGPC 1221 24015/25 6000 4CU035 INTER 5000 RASH 6CU020

20. In TAFs and METARs, the cloud base is given as the height above:
(a) the aerodrome.
(b) mean sea level.
(c) the highest ground within 10 nm of the aerodrome.

21. In a TAF, '9999' means ....

22. What is meant by CAVOK?

23. What is meant by INTER?

24. What is meant by TEMPO?

25. What is meant by GRADU?

26. What is meant by RAPID?

27. What is meant by PROB?

28. If the weather forecast for a particular aerodrome included the term *'GRADU'*, you (would/would not) expect a permanent change to the weather to become established during the forecast period.

29. In a TAF, the time group '1220' means ....?

30. In a METAR, the time group '1220' means ....?

31. A METAR finishes off '1014 NOSIG'. What does the 1014 signify?

32. What is meant by the letters 'XX'?

33. What is meant by the letters 'RASH'?

34. What is meant by the letters 'XXRASH'?

35. According to the Decode Table, the two-digit numbers that precede weather code letters in TAFs and METARs, such as in '45FG' or '80RASH', (are/are not) used to define the weather more precisely for meteorological purposes and (must/need not) be memorised by Pilots.

36. A temperature group '11/08' in a METAR means ......

37. A temperature group '03/M01' in a METAR means ....

38. The term 'SAUK' means a UK (TAF/METAR).

39. The term 'FCUK' means a UK (TAF/METAR).

40. The term 'TAFAMD' means .... .

41. What does the following symbol mean? ↖

42. What does the following symbol mean? ⱳ

43. What does the following symbol mean? △

44. What does the following symbol mean?   =

45. What does the following symbol mean?   ≡

46. What does the following symbol mean?   **CAT**

47. What does the following symbol mean?   ⌒

48. What does the following symbol mean?   ⌐ 200/40

49. What is meant by the letters 'COT'?

50. What is meant by the letters 'FZ'?

51. What is meant by the letters 'LYR'?

52. What is meant by the symbol: ▲▲ ?

Read Table D 'Meteorological Charts – Symbology' and test yourself on its content.

ANSWERS –
Aviation Meteorology

ANSWERS C1 —
THE ATMOSPHERE.
1. Equator.
2. Troposhere.
3. Stratosphere, Tropopause.
4. oxygen, nitrogen, water vapour.
5. (b).
6. decreases.
7. (a).
8. decreases.
9. True.
10. (a).
11. more.

ANSWERS C2 —
HEATING EFFECTS.
1. (b).
2. (a).
3. rises.
4. sinks.
5. (b).
6. (a).
7. less.
8. less.
9. cooler.
10. warmer.
11. higher.
12. reduces.
13. reduces.
14. radiation.
15. conduction.
16. advection.
17. convection.
18. onshore.
19. offshore.
20. Katabatic.
21. Anabatic.
22. temperature inversion.
23. 50°F.
24. 5°F.
25. 5°C.
26. increases.

ANSWERS C3 —
ATMOSPHERIC PRESSURE.
1. decreases.
2. 1 mb(hPa) per 30 ft.
3. semi-diurnal.
4. (a).
5. Pressure Gradient.
6. areas of High pressure to areas of Low pressure.
7. (a).
8. over-read, lower.

ANSWERS C4 —
THE ISA.
1. International Standard Atmosphere.
2. +15°C.
3. 1013·2 mb(hPa).
4. 1,225 grammes per cubic metre.
5. 2°C.
6. temperature lapse rate.
7. –57°C.

ANSWERS C5 —
WIND.
1. wind.
2. True North, °T.
3. Magnetic, °M.
4. 34 kt from 280°T.
5. °M, 25 knots.
6. veered.
7. backed.
8. veered.
9. Pressure Gradient force.
10. Coriolis force.
11. rotation, poles.
12. greater.
13. right.
14. Geostrophic Wind.
15. left.
16. *refer to the text*.
17. low.
18. high.
19. right drift, altimeter will read too high.
20. exceed.
21. be less than.
22. (c).
23. 10 metres.
24. decreased, friction.
25. back.
26. land.
27. day.
28. more.
29. stronger.

30. more.
31. (d).
32. in the vicinity of (and perhaps up to 10 nm distance from) the actual cloud.
33. (a).
34. windshear.
35. is possible.
36. lee.
37. mountain waves, standing waves.
38. east.
39. headwind.
40. lenticular.
41. lee.
42. 40 nm.

ANSWERS C6 — CLOUD.

1. cirriform, cumuliform, stratiform and nimbus.
2. cumuliform.
3. stratiform.
4. Cumulus.
5. Cumulonimbus.
6. nimbus.
7. gives off.
8. humidity.
9. more.
10. higher.
11. decreases.
12. saturated.
13. relative humidity.
14. (a).
15. increases.
16. (b).
17. (d).
18. higher, closer to.
19. condense out as liquid water.
20. cools.
21. adiabatic.
22. increases.
23. yes.
24. 3°C/1000 ft, Dry Adiabatic Lapse Rate.
25. cloud.
26. gives off, decreases.
27. one half, 1·5°C/1000 ft.
28. Environmental Lapse Rate.
29. (a).
30. 3000 ft AGL.
31. 4000 ft AGL.
32. 5000 ft AGL.
33. 3000 ft AGL.
34. turbulence cloud.
35. orographic cloud.
36. cumuliform.

37. stratiform.
38. warmer, drier, foehn wind effect.
39. 3°C/1000 ft unsaturated, 1·5°C/1000 ft saturated.
40. rain.
41. hail.
42. snow.
43. cumuliform.
44. stratiform.
45. Virga.
46. lenticular.

ANSWERS C7 — THUNDERSTORMS.

1. instability, moisture and a trigger action.
2. the cumulus stage, the mature stage, the dissipating stage.
3. *refer to the text.*
4. the early cumulus stage.
5. higher than.
6. the mature stage.
7. will be, cool downdrafts.
8. anvil.
9. False.
10. (c).
11. *refer to the text.*

ANSWERS C8 — AIR MASSES & FRONTAL WEATHER.

1. maritime.
2. continental.
3. unstable.
4. stable.
5. stable and moist.
6. subsidence.
7. convergence.
8. LOW.
9. HIGH.
10. warmer, drier and more stable.
11. stability.
12. instability.
13. instability.
14. Warm Front.
15. lowers.
16. stratiform.
17. cold.
18. precedes.
19. 1 in 150.
20. cirrus, 600 nm.
21. (c).
22. *refer to the text.*
23. Cold Front.
24. cumuliform.
25. may.

26. showers.
27. veer.
28. fall, fall.
29. (c).
30. 1 in 50.
31. fall.
32. veer.
33. rise.
34. rise, rise.
35. North.
36. True.
37. better.
38. Occluded Front.
39. may.
40. (d).
41. anticlockwise.
42. right (starboard).
43. clockwise.
44. left (port).
45. convergence.
46. rising.
47. trough.
48. faster.
49. weaker.
50. divergence.
51. subsiding.
52. stable.
53. anti-cyclone.
54. ridge.
55. col.
56. warm.
57. descend.

ANSWERS C9 — ICING.

1. 0°C.
2. airframe ice.
3. carburettor, can.
4. (a).
5. may.
6. supercooled.
7. (a).
8. (d).
9. (b).
10. is.
11. True.
12. (b).
13. (a).
14. (c).
15. (b).
16. low.
17. (c).

ANSWERS C10 — VISIBILITY.

1. slant.

2. fog.
3. mist.
4. radiation fog.
5. cloudless night, moist air, light winds.
6. advection fog.
7. advection fog.
8. frontal fog.
9. inversion.
10. dawn.
11. (b).
12. (a).
13. poorer.
14. (a).
15. (b).
16. (d) or (c).
17. (c).
18. (c).
19. (e).
20. No, since there is a transfer of heat from the air mass to the land.
21. No, since there is a transfer of heat from the air mass to the land.
22. (a).
23. visibility of 10 km or greater.
24. visibility of 6000 metres (6 km).
25. Runway Visual Range of 400 metres on Runway 35.

ANSWERS C11 — WEATHER FORECASTS AND REPORTS.

1. is.
2. (a).
3. (b).
4. Aerodrome Forecast, TAF.
5. METAR.
6. SIGMET.
7. Active thunderstorms, tropical revolving storms, a severe line squall, heavy hail, severe turbulence, severe airframe icing, marked mountain waves, widespread dust or sandstorm.
8. are.
9. (c) and (d).
10. is.
11. VOLMET.
12. (b).
13. TAF.
14. METAR.
15. 4000 metres.
16. no significant change, 2 hours.
17. 7 OKTAs of Stratocumulus at 3500 ft AAL.

18. from 1200–2100 UTC wind 230°/15 kt, visibility in excess of 10 km, 6 OKTAs Stratocumulus base 2500 AAL.
19. 1200–2100 UTC, wind 240°/15–25 kt, visibility 6000 metres, 4 OKTAs Cumulus base 3500 AAL, intermittently visibility 5000 metres in rain showers and cloud 6 OKTAs Cumulus base 2000 ft AAL.
20. (a).
21. visibility in excess of 10 km.
22 – 27. *refer to the text*.
28. would.
29. from 1200 to 2000 UTC.
30. at time 1220 UTC.
31. QNH 1014 mb.
32. heavy.
33. rain showers.
34. heavy rain showers.
35. are, need not.
36. observed air temperature +11°C; dewpoint temperature +8°C.
37. observed air temperature +3°C; dewpoint temperature -1°C.
38. METAR.
39. TAF.
40. Amended Aerodrome Forecast.
41. Thunderstorm.
42. severe aircraft icing.
43. Hail.
44. Widespread Mist.
45. Widespread Fog.
46. Clear Air Turbulence.
47. Freezing Precipitation.
48. Severe turbulence from 4000 ft to 20,000 ft AMSL.
49. at the coast.
50. freezing.
51. layer.
52. Cold Front at the surface.

EXERCISES
on
AIR NAVIGATION

EXERCISES 1 — THE PILOT/NAVIGATOR.

1. Since **time is of vital importance** to a Pilot/Navigator, you must ensure that you have an accurate and serviceable w.... or c.... .

2. The basis of a confident cross-country flight and navigational exercise is s.... prep....... .

3. The length of the shortest line joining two points around the surface of the Earth is called the d....... between them.

4. For most navigational purposes, distance is stated in n....... m.... .

5. One nautical mile travelled over the ground or water is sometimes referred to as a g..... n....... m... .

6. One nautical mile travelled through an air mass is called an a.. n....... m... .

7. The abbreviation for a nautical mile is . . .

8. The abbreviation for a ground nautical mile is ... .

9. The abbreviation for an air nautical mile is ... .

10. The usual navigation unit for Air Speed is the ...., which is 1 .... per hour.

11. The accepted unit of length for shorter distances such as runway length is the m.... .

12. The accepted unit for altitude, elevation of aerodromes, etc, is the .... .

13. A circle on the Earth's surface, whose centre is the centre of the Earth, is called a G.... C..... .

14. A circle may be divided into ... degrees and each one of these degrees may be further subdivided into .. minutes.

15. Great Circles on the Earth's surface, passing through the North and South Geographic Poles, are known as meridians of l........ .

16. Position on the surface of the Earth is specified by reference to a graticule in terms of la...... and lo....... .

17. Parallels of latitude (do/do not) run parallel to the Equator and to each other.

18. 1 minute of arc of a Great Circle on the Earth's surface has a length of ... nautical mile.

19. Whilst the usual navigational unit for distance between places on Earth is the nautical mile, shorter distances are referred to by different units, for instance distance from cloud in the Visual Flight Rules is specified in f..., and runway length is referred to in m..... .

20. 1 nautical mile = ... metres.

21. As a simple method of expressing direction we divide a full circle into 360 degrees and number them from 000 through 090, 180, 270 to 360 in a c....wise direction.

22. If OOO (and 360 of course) are aligned with North, then 090 is .... .

23. If 360 is aligned with North, then 180 is ..... .

24. If OOO is aligned with North, then 270 is .... .

25. The speed of the aeroplane relative to the air mass is called its T... A.. S...., which is abbreviated as ... .

26. To completely specify the motion of an aeroplane relative to an air mass we need to specify two things – its H...... and its T... A.. S.... .

27. The *Heading – True Air Speed* vector is symbolised by a s.....-headed arrow.

28. The movement of an air mass relative to the ground is called w... .

29. The wind direction, by convention, is the direction that the wind blows f... .

30. A northerly wind blows (from/towards) the North.

31. A westerly wind blows (from/towards) the West.

32. The passage of an aeroplane over the ground is called its T.... .

33. The speed of an aeroplane relative to the ground is called its G..... S....

34. The direction in which an aeroplane points is called its ....

35. The direction of travel over the ground is called an aeroplane's ..... .

36. The aeroplane is blown from its Heading to its Track by the .... effect.

37. The angle between the direction an aeroplane is pointing (i.e. its Heading) and the direction in which it is travelling over the ground (i.e. its Track) is called the ..... angle.

38. Label the shaded angle shown in Fig.1.

39. Is this drift left (port) or right (starboard)?

40. Sometimes the actual drift experienced in-flight differs to that expected and the aeroplane makes good a Track (i.e. TMG) different to the desired track. The difference between desired track and TMG is called the ....

41. Label the shaded angle in the Fig.2.

42. Is this track error left (port) or right (starboard)?

43. In Fig.3, label the vectors A and B and the angle D with their appropriate navigational terms.

44. Which statement best fits the situation in Fig.3?
    (a) TAS exceeds GS.
    (b) GS exceeds TAS.
    (c) Drift is left (port).
    (d) The wind is easterly.

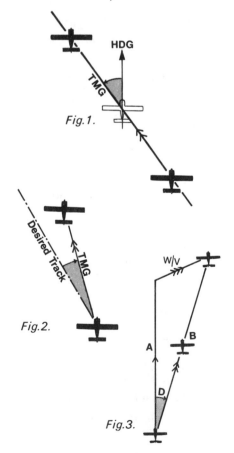

Fig.1.

Fig.2.

Fig.3.

EXERCISES 2 — SPEED.

Speed-1.

1. The rate of progress of an aeroplane through an air mass is called its T... A.. S.... .

2. The speed of an aeroplane relative to the ground is called its G..... S.... .

3. The reason that there may be a difference between TAS and GS is due to the effect of .... .

4. The cockpit instrument used to measure Air Speed is called an ... . Indicator and its abbreviation is ... .

5. The speed that a Pilot reads on the Air Speed Indicator is called the .... Air Speed and its abbreviation is ... .

6. Performance of the aeroplane depends upon its (Indicated/True) Air Speed.

7. Navigation and Flight Planning depend upon (Indicated/True) Air Speed.

8. The Air Speed Indicator is usually graduated in ..... .

9. If the Pilot corrects the Indicated Air Speed that he reads on his Air Speed Indicator for errors such as the instrument error and position error peculiar to that particular ASI, then he ends up with the R......... Air Speed, which is also known as the C........ Air Speed.

10. Errors in modern Air Speed Indicators are generally not significant and we can usually assume that the I........ and R......... (or C...........) Air Speeds are the same value.

11. The speed that a Pilot reads on his ASI is called the:
    (a) IAS.   (b) RAS or CAS.   (c) TAS.   (d) GS.

Exercises 2 — Speed-2.

1. Air density (Rho) will normally (increase/decrease) with altitude.

2. The air density is affected by both t.......... and p...... .

3. Air Speed Indicators are calibrated to read correctly only under I............ Standard Atmosphere M... S.. L.... conditions.

4. At high altitudes the True Air Speed will be (greater than/less than) the air speed indicated on the ASI in the cockpit.

NOTE: For the following questions, you may assume that the Instrument and Position Error for the Air Speed Indicator is zero, and therefore Rectified Air Speed is equal to the Indicated Air Speed. *IAS* may be taken to mean *RAS* (or *CAS)*.

5. At 5000 ft density altitude, your TAS will exceed the Indicated Air Speed by about .. %.

6. An IAS of 100 kt at density altitude 5000 ft will give you a TAS ... kt.

7. A RAS of 200 kt at density altitude 5000 ft will give you a TAS ... kt.

8. A RAS of 120 kt at density altitude 5000 ft will give you TAS ... kt.

9. At 10,000 ft density altitude, your TAS will exceed the IAS by about ..%.

10. At density altitude 10,000 ft, RAS = 100 kt, your TAS will be ... kt.

11. At density altitude 10,000 ft, RAS = 200 kt, your TAS will be ... kt.

12. At density altitude 10,000 ft, RAS = 120 kt, your TAS will be ... kt.

Exercises 2 — Speed-3.

1. Complete the following table:

Pressure Alt	Temperature	RAS	TAS
3000 ft	+2°C	134 kt	
3000 ft	+6°C	134 kt	
3000 ft	–10°C	134 kt	
5000 ft	–10°C	134 kt	
5000 ft	+10°C	134 kt	

NOTE: If you are given a question where altitude is stated, but not QNH, then you may assume *altitude* to mean *pressure altitude*. The difference in answers for TAS, neglecting the effect of QNHs other than 1013 mb, is generally not operationally significant.

2. If you are cruising at pressure altitude 6500 ft with an Indicated Air Speed of 162 kt, Outside Air Temperature minus 5°C, your True Air Speed is:
   (a) 162.   (b) 176.   (c) 180.   (d) 194.

3. You are flying at FL50 (pressure altitude 5000 ft). Outside Air Temperature (OAT) is ISA+5. IAS(RAS) is 98 kt. Determine the TAS.

4. You are a vigilant passenger in the cockpit of a Cessna 421 that is flying at FL140, ISA+10. The speed indicated on the aircraft's Air Speed Indicator is 154 kt. What is its TAS?

5. At altitude 8500 ft AMSL on QNH 999 mb and temperature ISA–5, what Rectified Air Speed is required to achieve a True Air Speed of 150 kt?

6. At altitude 8500 on QNH 1030 mb, OAT is –8°C, what RAS is required to achieve TAS 150 kt?

EXERCISES 3 — DIRECTION.

1. The standard for measuring direction is to start at North and proceed in a clockwise direction for ... degrees until you are back at North again.

2. The direction 090 degrees clockwise from North is called .... .

3. The direction 180 degrees clockwise from North is called ..... .

4. The direction 270 degrees clockwise from North is called .... .

5. The Earth rotates on its axis and the two points where this axis meets the Earth's surface are called the physical N.... Pole and the physical S.... Pole. They are also referred to as T... N.... and T... S.... .

6. Any 'straight' line drawn on the Earth's surface between the two physical poles (e.g. longitude meridians) will run in a true N....-S.... direction.

7. Near the Earth's true physical poles are areas from where the Earth's magnetic field emanates. These two points are called the N.... M....... P... and the S.... M....... P... .

8. A bar magnet, like that in a simple magnetic compass, will align itself approximately with M....... N.... and M....... S.... .

9. The angular difference from True to Magnetic North is called V........ .

10. If Magnetic North lies to the East of True North, then Variation is .... .

11. If Magnetic North lies to the West of True North, then Magnetic Variation is said to be .... .

12. Lines drawn on a chart joining places of identical Magnetic Variation are called I........ .

13. Variation East, Magnetic .....; Variation West, Magnetic .... .

14. Complete the table:

HDG(T)	Variation	HDG(M)
090°T	7°W	
273°T	7°W	
359°T	7°W	
005°T	7°W	
156°T	5°W	
	5°W	270°M
	5°E	082°M
	4°W	003°M

15. Due to local magnetic fields in the aircraft, the magnetic compass may not point directly towards Magnetic North but rather towards C...... North.

16. The degree to which the magnetic compass is deviated from Magnetic North by these local magnetic fields is called ....

17. The angular difference between a magnetic heading and a compass heading is called c...... d........ .

18. Given the following Deviation Card, fill in the blank spaces in the table:

FOR	STEER	HDG(T)	Varn.	HDG(M)	HDG(C)
N(360)	003	012°T	8°W	020°M	
E(090)	087	270°T	8°W	278°M	
S(180)	181	189°T	8°W		
W(270)	272	285°T	7°W		
		100°T		106°M	
			7°W		280°C

19. To achieve a True Heading of 330°T in an area where the Magnetic Variation is 7°W, what Compass Heading must be steered if the Deviation is 2°W?

20. If the aircraft is headed 097°C and experiences 8° starboard (right) drift, calculate its True Track, given Deviation 1°W on that heading, and Variation 5°W.

21. If the aircraft is headed 358°C and experiences 4° starboard drift, calculate its True Track, given Deviation 2°E on that heading, and Variation 7°W.

22. If the aircraft is headed 358°C and experiences 5° port (left) drift, calculate its True Track, given Deviation 2°E on that heading, and Variation 6°W.

23. Storing your transistor radio and a spare set of headphones near the magnetic compass (is/is not) a good practice.

24. If you are taking-off on R/W 34, your compass (provided you are not turning or accelerating) should read about:
    (a) 034.   (b) 340.   (c) 000.   (d) 160.

25. Acceleration errors in the direct reading magnetic compass are greatest on a heading of:
    (a) North.   (b) South.   (c) East.   (d) West
    (e) North and South.   (f) East and West.

26. Turning errors in the direct reading magnetic compass are greatest on a heading of:
    (a) North.   (b) South.   (c) East.   (d) West.
    (e) North and South.   (f) East and West.

27. When accelerating on a heading of due East in the UK, the magnetic compass will indicate:
    (a) a turn to the left (i.e. towards North).
    (b) a turn to the right (i.e. towards South).
    (c) correctly.

28. When accelerating on a heading of due West in the UK, the magnetic compass will indicate:
    (a) a turn to the left (i.e. towards South).
    (b) a turn to the right (i.e. towards North).
    (c) correctly.

29. When accelerating on a heading of due North in the UK, the magnetic compass will indicate:
    (a) a turn to the left.
    (b) a turn to the right.
    (c) correctly.

30. When accelerating on a heading of due South in the UK, the magnetic compass will indicate:
    (a) a turn to the left.
    (b) a turn to the right.
    (c) correctly.

31. After having accelerated on a heading of 090°C and settled down to a new steady cruising speed, the magnetic compass will have:
    (a) read correctly throughout the acceleration.
    (b) initially indicated a false heading change towards North, before gradually returning to a correct reading of 090°C.
    (c) initially indicated a false heading change towards South, before gradually returning to a correct reading of 090°C.
    (d) initially indicated a false heading change towards North, and will continue to indicate incorrectly even after the speed settles down.

32. When turning through North in the UK, the Pilot should:
    (a) undershoot the desired heading.
    (b) overshoot the desired heading.
    (c) stop the turn immediately the compass indicates the desired heading.

33. When turning through North in the UK, the magnetic compass will:
    (a) indicate correctly throughout.
    (b) under-indicate the amount of turn, requiring the Pilot to stop the turn before the desired heading is indicated.
    (c) over-indicate the amount of turn, requiring the Pilot to stop the turn after the desired heading has been indicated.

34. When turning through South in the UK, the Pilot should:
    (a) undershoot the desired heading.
    (b) overshoot the desired heading.
    (c) stop the turn immediately the compass indicates the desired heading.

35. When turning through East in the UK, the magnetic compass will:
    (a) indicate correctly.
    (b) over-indicate the amount of turn, requiring the Pilot to stop the turn before the desired heading is indicated.
    (c) under-indicate the amount of turn, requiring the Pilot to stop the turn after the desired heading has been indicated.

36. When turning onto an easterly heading in the UK, the Pilot should:
    (a) undershoot the desired heading.
    (b) overshoot the desired heading.
    (c) stop the turn when the compass indicates East.

37. When turning through West in the UK, the magnetic compass will:
    (a) indicate correctly.
    (b) over-indicate the amount of turn, requiring the Pilot to stop the turn before the desired heading is indicated.
    (c) under-indicate the amount of turn, requiring the Pilot to stop the turn after the desired heading has been indicated.

38. When turning onto a westerly heading in the UK, the Pilot should:
    (a) undershoot the desired heading.
    (b) overshoot the desired heading.
    (c) stop the turn when the compass indicates West.

39. When turning through North in the UK, the direct reading magnetic compass will:
    (a) indicate correctly throughout the turn.
    (b) show an exaggerated turn when turning either left or right.
    (c) show an exaggerated turn when turning left, but under-indicate a right turn.
    (d) show an exaggerated turn when turning right, but under-indicate a left turn.
    (e) under-indicate turns both left and right.

40. When turning through South in the UK, the direct reading magnetic compass will:
    (a) indicate correctly throughout the turn.
    (b) show an exaggerated turn when turning either left or right.
    (c) show an exaggerated turn when turning left, but under-indicate a right turn.
    (d) show an exaggerated turn when turning right, but under-indicate a left turn.
    (e) under-indicate turns both left and right.

41. When turning through East in the UK, the direct reading magnetic compass will:
    (a) indicate correctly.
    (b) show an exaggerated turn when turning either left or right.

    (c) show an exaggerated turn when turning left, but under-indicate a right turn.

    (d) show an exaggerated turn when turning right, but under-indicate a left turn.

    (e) under-indicate turns both left and right.

42. When turning through West in the UK, the direct reading magnetic compass will:

    (a) indicate correctly.

    (b) show an exaggerated turn when turning either left or right.

    (c) show an exaggerated turn when turning left, but under-indicate a right turn.

    (d) show an exaggerated turn when turning right, but under-indicate a left turn.

    (e) under-indicate turns both left and right.

43. Turning from North-East to North-West by the shortest way, a magnetic compass will:

    (a) indicate correctly.

    (b) over-indicate the number of degrees turned.

    (c) under-indicate the number of degrees turned.

44. The gyroscopic Direction Indicator should be aligned with the magnetic compass (once per flight/every 10 or 15 minutes).

45. You (should/should not) align the DI with the compass when the aeroplane is turning.

46. Once aligned with the compass, the DI is (easier/harder) than the magnetic compass to use for turning onto a new heading, because the DI is not subject to turning and acceleration errors like the magnetic compass.

47. The direction of an object related to the nose of the aeroplane is called the r.......
b...... of the object from the aeroplane.

48. If a radio mast bears 60 degrees to the right of the nose of the aircraft, then its relative bearing is ... REL.

49. If a small township bears 80 degrees to the left of the nose of the aircraft, then its relative bearing is ... REL.

50. If a hill bears 50 degrees to the right of the aircraft's nose, then its relative bearing is ... REL and, if the aircraft's HDG is 035M, then the magnetic bearing of the hill from the aircraft is ... M.

51. In what direction would someone on the hill look to see the aeroplane?

EXERCISES 4 — WIND-SIDE OF THE NAVIGATION COMPUTER.

Wind-Side-1.

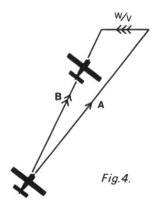

Fig.4.

1. Label the sides marked A and B in the diagram (Fig.4).

2. The wind blows an aeroplane from its .... to its ..... .

3. At the Flight Planning stage, we measure the direction on our chart of the d...... t..... .

4. Using the forecast wind velocity given in knots and °True, and knowing the True Air Speed that we can expect from our aeroplane at the selected altitude, we can calculate H...... and G..... S.... .

5. Calculate the True Heading and Ground Speed for TAS 98 kt, W/V 280°T/35 and Track 340°T.

6. Calculate the True Heading and Ground Speed for TAS 98 kt, W/V 280°T/35 and Track 251°T.

7. Calculate the True Heading and Ground Speed for TAS 98 kt, W/V 280°T/35 and Track 100°T.

8. Calculate the True Heading and Ground Speed for TAS 98 kt, W/V 280°T/35 and Track 072°T.

9. If you wish to maintain a Ground Speed of 120 kt on track, calculate the True Heading and TAS required if W/V is 280°T/35 and Track 072°T.

10. If you wish to maintain a Ground Speed of 80 kt on track, calculate the True Heading and TAS required if W/V is 090°T/20 and Track 180°T.

11. Complete the following table, doing your computer manipulations using °True on the computer to find True Heading and Ground Speed, then convert the True Heading to a Magnetic Heading. (This is the same procedure you will use when completing a flight log form prior to flight.)

TAS	Track(T)	W/V(T)	HDG(T)	Varn.	HDG(M)	GS
120	085°T	055°T/36		7°W		
120	055°T	055°T/36		7°W		
140	120°T	350°T/30		6°W		
140	300°T	350°T/30		6°W		

12. If you wish to maintain a Ground Speed of 120 kt on track, calculate the True Heading and TAS required if W/V is 280°T/35 and Track 072°T.

13. If you wish to maintain a Ground Speed of 80 kt on track, calculate the True Heading and TAS required if W/V is 090°T/20 and Track 180°T. What Rectified Air Speed (CAS, or IAS if the Air Speed Indicator is perfect) would this require at pressure altitude 5000 ft and temperature +12°C?

14. To achieve a Track of 300°T, calculate the Magnetic Heading and Ground Speed if you plan to cruise at FL100 (pressure altitude 10,000 ft), where the forecast wind velocity and temperature is 280°T/25 and +6°C, at an Indicated Air Speed of 100 kt. Variation is 6°W.

15. Some Flying Instructors prefer to convert to °Magnetic as early as possible, and then do all of the working that follows in °M, i.e. the track, heading and wind direction set up on the computer are **all** in Magnetic (rather than **all** in True) If this is the case, then you would perform the calculations in the following manner. Note that you end up with the same answers for HDG(M) and GS as in the previous question. Complete the table:

TAS	Track(T)	Varn.	TR(M)	W/V(T)	W/V(M)	HDG(M)	GS
120	085°T	7°W		055°T/36			
120	055°T	7°W		055°T/36			
140	120°T	6°W		350°T/30			
140	300°T	6°W		350°T/30			

Exercises 4 — Wind-Side-2.

1. You are flying at TAS 125 kt on HDG 280°T. From two position fixes you calculate your TMG and GS to be 286°T and 144 kt. Calculate the wind velocity.

2. Calculate the W/V if Heading is 290°T, TAS 110 kt, GS 95 kt and drift 5° port (left).

3. Calculate the W/V if Heading is 356°T, TAS 100 kt, GS 93 kt and Track Made Good 010°T?

4. Calculate the W/V if Heading is 070°T, TAS 96 kt, GS 108 kt and drift 7° starboard.

Exercises 4 — Wind-Side-3.

1. Complete the following table where you are given HDG/TAS and W/V, and have to find TR/GS.

TAS	W/V(T)	HDG(T)	TR(T)	GS
120	055°T/36	076°T		
140	350°T/30	110°T		
140	350°T/30	310°T		
120	055°T/36	104°T		
120	055°T/36	014°T		
120	055°T/36	055°T		

2. You are flying over featureless terrain at TAS 157 kt on a HDG 346°M. The forecast wind is 315°T/30. What is your Dead Reckoning True TR and GS? Variation is 7°W.

Exercises 4 — Wind-Side-4.

1. The Tower passes you a surface wind of 050°M/30.
   What are the headwind and crosswind components on Runway 34?

2. If your aircraft has a crosswind limitation of 15 kt, could you take-off on RWY 34 under these circumstances?

3. Would RWY 03 or RWY 21 be suitable under the circumstances of Question 2?

EXERCISES 5 — CALCULATOR-SIDE OF THE NAVIGATION COMPUTER.

Calculator-1.

1. At a GS of 147 kt, how far will you travel in 11 minutes?

2. At a GS of 183 kt, how far will you travel in 17 minutes?

3. At a GS of 120 kt, how far will you travel in 10 minutes?

Exercises 5 — Calculator-2.

1. If we cover 23 nm over the ground in 9 minutes, what is our GS?

2. If we cover 17 nm over the ground in 11 minutes, what is our GS?

3. If we cover 18 nm over the ground in 6 minutes, what is out GS?

4. If we cover 9 nm over the ground in 3 minutes, what is our GS?

5. If we travel 20 nm over the ground in 8 minutes, what is our GS and what is the Estimated Time Interval (ETI) to fly a further 30 nm in the same direction, assuming no change in GS?

6. If we cover 22 gnm in 10 minutes, what is our GS and how long will it take us to reach the next checkpoint which is still 73 nm further on in the same direction?

7. If we cover 25 nm in 12 minutes, how long will it take us to cover 31 nm in the same direction?

8. At a GS of 137 kt, how long will it take you to travel 27 nm?

9. At a GS of 153 kt, how long will it take you to travel 33 nm?

10. The distance from **Alfa** to **Bravo** is 107 nm. 10 minutes after leaving **Alfa** the aeroplane has travelled 16 nm towards **Bravo**. How much longer until it reaches **Bravo** if the same GS is maintained?

11. The distance from **Bournemouth** to **Cardiff** is 68 nm. If an aeroplane departs **Bournemouth** at time 1230 UTC (previously called GMT), and passes over the disused aerodrome at **Henstridge**, 23 nm en route, at time 1242 UTC, what is the Estimated Time of Arrival (ETA) overhead **Cardiff** if the same Ground Speed is maintained?

12. The distance from **Edinburgh** to **Prestwick** is 50 nm. If an aeroplane departs **Edinburgh** at time 0807 UTC and passes over the railway line at **Motherwell**, 22 nm from **Edinburgh**, at time 0816 UTC, what is the Estimated Time of Arrival (ETA) overhead **Prestwick** if the same TAS is maintained and the W/V does not change?

Exercises 5 — Calculator-3.

1. If you burn fuel at the rate of 32 litres/hour, how much will you burn in 25 minutes?

2. If you burn fuel at the rate of 28 litres/hour, what fuel will you burn in 8 minutes?

3. If you burn 15 litres of fuel in 34 minutes, what is your rate of fuel consumption?

4. If you burn 5 US gallons of fuel in 40 minutes, what is your rate of fuel consumption?

5. If you burn 12 litres of fuel in 24 minutes, what is your rate of fuel consumption, and how long would it take to burn 17 litres?

6. If full tanks is 48 USG of usable fuel and the average consumption rate is 8 USG/hr, calculate the safe endurance for flight if you wish to retain 1 hour's fuel as reserve.

7. If full tanks is 26 USG of usable fuel and the average consumption rate is 5·5 USG/hr, calculate the safe endurance for flight if you wish to retain 1 hour's fuel as reserve.

8. If full tanks is 36 USG of usable fuel and the average consumption rate is 7·5 USG/hr, calculate the safe endurance for flight if you wish to retain 45 minutes fuel as reserve.

9. What total fuel is required if GS is 120 kt, distance 300 nm, average fuel consumption 7·3 USG/hr and you wish to carry 1 hours fuel as reserve? If you refuelled to a whole number of gallons, how much fuel would you carry?

10. What total fuel is required if GS is 98 kt, distance 130 nm, average fuel consumption 6·5 USG/hr and you wish to carry 1 hours fuel as reserve? If you refuelled to a whole number of gallons, how much fuel would you carry?

11. If there is 27 USG on board and the average fuel consumption is 6·8 USG/hr, how far can you fly at a GS of 93 kt and still have 1 hour's reserve remaining in the tanks?

12. If there is 27 USG on board and the average fuel consumption is 6·8 USG/hr, how far can you fly at a GS of 93 kt and still have 6 USG reserve remaining in the tanks?

Exercises 5 — Calculator-4.

1. If you are off-track by 3 nm after travelling 20 nm, how far off-track will you be after travelling a total of 60 nm?

2. If you are off-track by 6 nm after travelling 30 nm, how far off-track will you be after having travelled a total of 45 nm, and a total of 60 nm?

3. If you are 2 nm off-track after 15 nm, what distance will you be off-track after travelling a total of 60 nm and what is your track error in degrees?

4. If you are 4 nm off-track after 20 nm, what distance off-track will you be after a total of 60 nm, and what is the Track Error (TE) in degrees?

Exercises 5 — Calculator-5.

1. Convert a temperature of +38°C to degrees F.

2. Convert +32°F to C.

3. Convert +20°C to F.

Exercises 5 — Calculator-6.

1. Convert 100 nm to statute miles and kilometres.

2. Convert 55 nm to kilometres.

3. Convert 1000 km to nm.

4. Convert 50 kt to km/hr (or kph), metres/hour, metres/min and metres/second.

Exercises 5 — Calculator-7.

1. An older Pilot refers to a particular runway as being 1300 ft long. How long is this in metres?

2. A runway 1213 metres long is how long in feet?

3. A visibility of 500 metres is how many feet?

4. A continental European topographical chart shows an obstruction with an elevation of 100 metres. How high is this in feet?

5. A French topographical chart shows an obstruction with an elevation of 375 metres. How high is this in feet? At what altitude in ft AMSL would you fly to clear it by 1000 ft?

Exercises 5 — Calculator-8.

1. Convert 60 lb to kg.
2. Convert 631 lb to kg.
3. Convert 80 kg to lb.
4. Convert 845 kg to lb.
5. Convert 5700 kg to lb.

Exercises 5 — Calculator-9.

1. The Specific Gravity of 100 octane or greater AVGAS is .... .
2. 1 Imperial Gallon of AVGAS weighs .... lb.
3. 1 litre of AVGAS will weigh .... kg.
4. 10 litres of AVGAS will weigh ... kg.
5. 50 litres of AVGAS will weigh .... kg.
6. 1 Imperial Gallon = ... U.S. gallons.
7. 5 Imperial Gallons = ... USG.
8. 10 Imperial Gallons = ... USG = ... litres.
9. 10 USG = ... litres.
10. 1 USG = ... litres.
11. Your fuel gauges are graduated in USG. You wish to fuel up from 27 USG to 45 USG. How many litres of AVGAS would you order from the fuel agent?
12. To refuel from 16 USG to 45 USG you should order .... litres.
13. If your fuel gauges initially read 12 USG and the refueller has added 86 litres, what should your gauges read approximately?
14. What is the weight in kg of 100 litres of AVGAS?
15. What is the weight in kg of 53 litres of AVGAS?
16. 30 USG of AVGAS = ... litres = ... kg.
17. 37 USG of AVGAS = ... litres = ... kg.

Assuming a SG of 0·71 for your fuel:

18. Convert 44 USG to kg.
19. Convert 27 USG to litres.
20. Convert 27 USG to kg.
21. Convert 91 USG to kg and litres.
22. Convert 48 USG to UK Imperial Gallons and calculate its weight given that, in this case, 1 Imperial Gallon of fuel weighs 7 lb.

EXERCISES 6 — VERTICAL NAVIGATION.

Vertical Nav-1.

1. The vertical distance of a point Above Mean Sea Level (AMSL) is called its a........ .

2. The standard unit for altitude in the UK is the ....

3. The Altimeter provides the Pilot with an (exact/approximate) altitude.

4. A Pilot needs to know the altitude of the aeroplane for t...... clearance, t...... separation, and to calculate the aeroplane's p.......... capabilities.

5. Air Pressure (decreases/increases) with an increase in height.

6. The altimeter is a p.......-sensitive instrument.

7. The International Civil Aviation Organisation (ICAO) Standard Atmosphere is abbreviated to read ... .

8. The ISA is a theoretical standard atmosphere and is used as a m........ s..... .

9. Standard Mean Sea Level pressure in the ISA is ...... millibars/hectoPascals.

10. Standard Mean Sea Level temperature in the ISA is ...°C.

11. From ground level up to a pressure altitude of about 36,000 ft, the temperature in the ISA is assumed to fall at ..°C/1000 ft.

12. The main purpose of the International Standard Atmosphere is to c........ a......... .

13. The p....... a....... of a point is the height in the ISA above the 1013·2 mb pressure level at which the pressure equals that of the point under consideration.

14. As altitude increases, air pressure will ....

15. Up to about 5000 ft AMSL, atmospheric pressure drops approximately 1 mb for each .. ft increase in altitude.

16. If the MSL pressure is 1013 mb, what is the pressure at 30 ft AMSL?

17. If the MSL pressure is 1013 mb, what is the pressure at 60 ft AMSL?

18. If the MSL pressure is 1013 mb, what is the pressure at 3000 ft AMSL?

19. If the MSL pressure is 1013 mb, at what pressure altitude would you expect the pressure to be 990 mb?

20. If the MSL pressure is 1013 mb, at what pressure altitude would you expect to find a pressure of 900 mb?

Exercises 6 — Vertical Nav-2.

1. The standard Mean Sea Level temperature in the International Standard Atmosphere (the ISA) is ...°C.

2. What is the ISA temperature at 1000 ft pressure altitude?

3. What is the ISA temperature at 5000 ft pressure altitude?

4. What is the ISA temperature at 10,000 ft pressure altitude?

5. Calculate the ISA values of temperature and pressure for a pressure altitude of 3000 ft.

6. Calculate the ISA values of temperature and pressure for a pressure altitude of 600 ft.

7. Calculate the ISA values of temperature and pressure for a pressure altitude of –600 ft.

8. What is the pressure altitude of the 970 mb pressure surface?

9. What is the pressure altitude of the 1010 mb pressure surface?

10. What is the pressure altitude of the 1020 mb pressure surface?

Exercises 6 — Vertical Nav-3.

1. With 1013 mb set on the altimeter subscale, the altimeter will read height above the ...... mb pressure level, which we call 'pressure altitude' or 'pressure height'.

2. The ISA MSL pressure is defined as 1013·2 mb(hPa). Does this mean the actual MSL pressure existing at all times in a real atmosphere is 1013·2 mb?

3. Does Mean Sea Level pressure at a particular place vary from day to day?

4. The approximate value of the actual Mean Sea Level pressure in millibars is called Q.. .

5. Altitude is the height of an aeroplane (Above Mean Sea Level/above the 1013·2 mb pressure level).

6. To measure altitude, we should set (QNH/1013·2) on the altimeter's subscale.

7. If you are taxying at an aerodrome, and QNH is set on the altimeter subscale, then the altimeter should indicate (aerodrome elevation AMSL/ pressure altitude/zero).

8. If you wind an extra 20 mb (say from 1013 to 1033 mb) onto the subscale, you would also wind the altimeter's pointer on to indicate .. ft higher, even though the actual height of the aeroplane has not changed.

9. QNH is M... S.. L.... pressure in millibars.

10. You enter your aeroplane which has been parked overnight at an aerodrome (elevation 1545 ft). The altimeter reads 1635 ft with 1011 mb set on the subscale. You wind the knob until 1545 ft is indicated. What appears in the subscale and what is the current QNH?

11. The elevation of an aerodrome is 386 ft AMSL. With QNH set on the subscale and the aeroplane on the runway, the altimeter should read approximately ... ft.

12. An aerodrome has an elevation of 1334 ft AMSL. On the ground with QNH set, the altimeter should read ....ft. Flying a circuit 1000 ft above the aerodrome level, the altimeter should read .... ft.

    Departing the circuit area in a north-easterly direction where the highest terrain is 3669 ft AMSL, to clear it by a minimum of 1000 ft your altimeter, with QNH set, should indicate at least .... ft.

Exercises 6 — Vertical Nav-4.

1. With QFE set on the subscale, the altimeter will measure height above the ... pressure datum, which is usually chosen to be the level of the a..... .

2. To simplify circuit procedures for a student flying at an aerodrome of elevation 1334 ft, the Instructor may set the altimeter on the ground so that it reads 0 ft. The setting on the subscale would be referred to as Q.., and flying around the circuit the altimeter would indicate the height (Above Aerodrome Level/Above Mean Sea Level).

Exercises 6 — Vertical Nav-5.

1. The UK is divided into a number of ASRs, A........ S...... R........ .

2. Aircraft cruising at 3000 ft AMSL should have R.......... QNH set on the altimeter subscale.

3. For take-off and landing, the Pilot may set either Aerodrome .... or Aerodrome ... on the altimeter subscale.

4. When cruising below the Transition Altitude, the Pilot should update the .... when crossing ASR boundaries or when it is amended by ATC.

5. For approach and landing, a Pilot may set either Aerodrome ... or ... .

6. When flying beneath a Terminal Control Area (TMA) or beneath Special Rules Airspace (SRA), the Pilot may have to set (1013 mb/QNH of a nearby aerodrome beneath the TMA or SRA).

7. When flying through a Military Aerodrome Traffic Zone (MATZ), the Pilot may have to set (1013/Aerodrome QFE) and then, after having left the MATZ, return to .... QNH.

8. Transition Altitude in the UK is usually ...... ft AMSL.

9. Transition Level in the UK is usually FL.. .

10. If the Pilot intends cruising at FL55, then he should set ..... mb on the altimeter subscale as the aeroplane climbs through (Transition Altitude/5000 ft/ Transition Level).

11. If the QNH is 1013, Transition Altitude is ..... ft AMSL, and Transition Level is FL35, which will be .... ft AMSL. Do this by calculation and also by using the chart.

12. If the QNH is 1003, Transition Altitude is ..... ft AMSL, and Transition Level is FL35, which will be .... ft AMSL.

13. If the QNH is 1023, Transition Altitude is ..... ft AMSL, and Transition Level is FL35, which will be .... ft AMSL.

14. If the Manchester TMA in the area where you are flying extends from 2500 ft ALT to FL245, and the QNH is 1006, what is the maximum altitude at which you can fly and not penetrate controlled airspace? (Note: the lower level of controlled airspace is still outside controlled airspace.)

15. If the Daventry CTA in the area where you are flying extends from FL45 to FL245, and the QNH is 1006, what is the maximum altitude at which you can fly and not penetrate controlled airspace?

16. If the Daventry CTA in the area where you are flying extends from FL45 to FL245, and the QNH is 1018, what is the maximum altitude at which you can fly and not penetrate controlled airspace?

Exercises 6 — Vertical Nav-6.

1. The highest obstacle within 5 nm of track is 1536 ft AMSL, and within 10 nm of track is 1642 ft AMSL. What Minimum Safe Altitude would you nominate to achieve a safety clearance of:
   (1) 1000 ft within 5 nm of track.
   (2) 1500 ft within 5 nm of track.
   (3) 10% plus 1500 ft within 5 nm of track.
   (4) 1000 ft within 10 nm of track.
   (5) 1500 ft within 10 nm of track.
   (6) 10% plus 1500 ft within 10 nm of track.

Exercises 6 — Vertical Nav-7.

1. For each deviation from ISA of degree Celsius, the density altitude increases by ... ft.

2. An aerodrome has elevation 1334 ft, Outside Air Temperature (OAT) 0°C, QNH 1013. What is its pressure altitude and density altitude?

EXERCISES 7 — TIME.

Time-1.

Express the following dates and times as a six-figure date/time group:

1. November 29th, 1015 am.

2. July 19th, 3.17 pm.

3. April 1st, 5 pm.

4. Express the dates and times above as an eight-figure date/time group.

Exercises 7 — Time-2.

Convert the following time intervals to arc units:

1. 1 hour

2. 3 hours

3. 10 hours

4. 9 hours 30 minutes

Convert the following arcs to time:

5. 150 degrees.

6. 135 degrees

7. 120 degrees

Exercises 7 — Time-3.

1. Cardiff is 3° of longitude West of London. How much earlier or later will noon occur at Cardiff compared to noon at London?

2. Norwich is 1° of longitude East of London. How much earlier or later will noon occur in Norwich compared to noon in London?

3. Portsmouth is at 01°W longitude. Plymouth is at 04°W longitude. Which place is behind in Local Mean Time, and by how much?

Convert the following times from LMT to UTC:

4. 151345 LMT at 03°W.

5. 251732 LMT at 01°E.

6. 090840 LMT at 02°30'W.

Convert the following times from UTC to LMT:

7. 191000 UTC at longitude 04°W.

8. 271234 UTC at longitude 150°E.

9. 270434 UTC at 03°45'W.

Exercises 7 — Time-4.

1. Travelling eastwards across the date line from Hong Kong to Hawaii, you would expect to (lose/gain) 1 day.

2. British Standard Time is based on the .... meridian of longitude.

3. West German Time (MEZ) is based on the 15°E meridian of longitude, so is ... hour (ahead of/behind) UTC.

4. You depart Nottingham at 1018 UTC for a 3 hour 15 minute flight to Hamburg. The ETA at Hamburg is ..... UTC, ... MEZ.

5. You depart Hamburg at 1540 MEZ for the 3 hour 30 minutes return flight to Nottingham. The ETA at Nottingham is ..... UTC.

Exercises 7 — Time-5.

1. Night, for the purposes of Air Navigation in the United Kingdom, commences at S..... plus .. mins, at surface level.

2. Sunrise and sunset times (are/are not) available from ATS units and Met Forecast offices.

3. The official source of sunrise and sunset times is the A.. A....., (a publication not required by a Pilot).

4. High ground to the West of an aerodrome will cause the (earlier/later) onset of darkness.

5. Cloud cover will cause the (earlier/later) onset of darkness.

6. Heavy smog would cause the (earlier/later) onset of darkness.

7. Sunrise and sunset times vary with the l....... and the d... .

8. British Summer Time (BST) applies from .... to ....

9. For British Summer Time, UK clocks are (advanced/retarded) by ... hour(s) from UTC.

10. Convert 1400 British Summer Time on July 28th to UTC.

11. Convert 1023 UTC on September 30th to British Summer Time.

EXERCISES 8 — THE EARTH.

1. The plane of a Great Circle on the Earth (passes/does not pass) through the centre of the Earth.

2. The centre of a Great Circle drawn on the Earth's surface (is/is not) the centre of the Earth.

3. The plane of a Small Circle drawn on the surface of the Earth (passes/does not pass) through the centre of the Earth.

4. The reference plane from which we measure **Latitude** is the plane of the E......, from which we measure angular distance in degrees North or South.

5. The Equator is Latitude 0, and (is/is not) a Great Circle.

6. A **Parallel Of Latitude** joins all points of the same latitude and is a (Small/Great) Circle (except for the equator).

7. The circumference around a parallel of latitude becomes smaller the closer the particular parallel is to the (pole/equator).

8. Parallels of latitude (are/are not) parallel to the equator and to each other.

9. The basic reference for **Longitude** is the P.... Meridian that passes through the Gr....... Observatory just outside London.

10. Meridians of Longitude all pass through the North and South Geographic Poles and are (Small/Great) Circles.

11. **Longitude** is angular position E... or W... of the Prime Meridian.

12. The length of one minute of arc of a Great Circle on the Earth's surface is .. nm.

13. 1 minute of latitude (is/is not) 1 nm in length.

14. 1 degree of latitude is .. nm.

15. 1 nm = ... metres.

16. It (is/is not) important for the map-maker to use a projection that preserves angular relationships when making aeronautical charts.

17. **'Scale'** is the ratio of c.... length to e.... distance.

18. A large scale map can show (more/less) detail than a small scale map.

19. What Earth distance is represented by a chart length of 8 inches on a 1:250 000 chart?

20. What Earth distance is represented by a chart length of 8 inches on a 1:500 000 chart?

21. What Earth distance is represented by a chart length of 4·3 inches on a 1:500 000 chart?

22. 8 inches on a 1:500 000 chart represents approximately 55 nm. How many kilometres does 8 inches represent on a 1:250 000 chart?

23. 8 inches on a 1:500 000 chart represents approximately 55 nm. How many statute miles does 8 inches represent on a 1:250 000 chart?

24. 3 inches on a chart represents approximately 10·3 nm. Is the scale of the chart 1:250 000, 1:500 000, or 1:1 000 000?

EXERCISES 9 — AERONAUTICAL CHARTS.

1. The most commonly used charts for visual air navigation in the UK are the:
   (a) 1:500 000 ICAO series.
   (b) CAA 1:250 000 UK Topographical Air Charts.
   (c) 1:1 000 000 ONC series.

2. The CAA 1:250 000 Topographical series (does/does not) show aeronautical information regarding Controlled or Special Rules Airspace whose base (i.e. lower limit) is below 3000 ft AMSL.

3. Water features (i.e. hydrographic features) are generally depicted in the colour ....

4. Contour lines join places of:
   (a) equal Magnetic Variation.
   (b) equal height Above Mean Sea Level.
   (c) equal Latitude.

5. Spot elevations (the greatest height in the immediate vicinity) are indicated on aeronautical charts used in the UK by:
   (a) a small arrow with the elevation stated.
   (b) a small black dot with the elevation stated beside it in feet.
   (c) a small black dot with the elevation stated beside it in metres.

6. If a spot height on an aeronautical chart is found to be in error, it can be amended by N...... .

7. Mount Snowdon has its elevation shown on the 1:500 000 chart in large print against a white background surrounded by a black border. Why?

8. A Restricted Area shown on a French aeronautical chart has a lower limit of 2500 metres AMSL. What is this in feet?

9. Convert 3300 metres to feet.

10. Convert 5000 ft to metres.

Refer now to your copy of the **1:500 000 ICAO Chart, Sheet No 2171AB**, for **Northern England and Northern Ireland.**

11. Military Aerodrome Traffic Zones (MATZ) extend from the surface to:
    (a) 3000 ft Above Mean Sea Level.
    (b) 3000 ft Above Aerodrome Level.
    (c) 5000 ft Above Mean Sea Level.
    (d) 5000 ft Above Aerodrome Level.

12. Military aerodromes are portrayed in:
    (a) blue.
    (b) magenta.
    (c) black.

13. What is the Magnetic Variation at York (approximately 54°N, 01°W)?

14. What is the Magnetic Variation (correct to the nearest 1°) at Liverpool (approximately 53°26′N, 02°58′W)?

15. **Aerodrome A** is located at (54°14′N, 00°58′W). What aerodrome is it?

16. What is the elevation of Aerodrome A?

17. The position of **Aerodrome B** is (53°47′N, 00°11′W). What aerodrome is it?

18. What is the elevation of Aerodrome B?

19. What is the distance in nm from Aerodrome A to Aerodrome B?

20. What is the true Rhumb Line track from A to B (accurate to +/–1°)?

21. What is the true Rhumb Line track from B to A?

22. What is the mean Magnetic Variation for the flight between A and B (to the nearest whole degree)?

23. What is the height of the highest obstruction within 10 nm of Aerodrome A, both AGL and AMSL, and what is its true bearing and distance from the aerodrome? Describe the obstruction.

24. Aerodrome A is in the Vale of York AIAA. What does 'AIAA' mean and what are its vertical limits in this case?

25. What additional aerial activity occurs at Aerodrome A?

26. What do the letters 'ASR' represent?

27. What Altimeter Setting Region(s) does the track between A and B lie within?

28. What does the magenta circle centred on (54°11′N, 00°25′W) signify?

29. What radio frequency should be used to contact London Flight Information Service en route between A and B?

30. What radio frequency (or frequencies) should be used to contact the Lower Airspace Radar Service en route between A and B?

31. What is the highest obstacle within 10 nm of the two aerodromes and the track between A and B?

32. If you wanted to clear all obstacles within 10 nm of the track between A and B by at least 1000 ft, at what minimum altitude would you fly?

33. What is the highest obstacle within 10 nm of the track between A and B, if you do not consider the high ground behind you when departing Aerodrome A?

34. If you wanted to clear all obstacles within 10 nm of the track between A and B by at least 1000 ft, neglecting high obstacles behind Aerodrome A, at what minimum altitude would you fly?

35. What Controlled Airspace exists between A and B?

36. What Controlled Airspace exists in the vicinity of Aerodrome B and between what levels?

37. Just North of Aerodrome B is an egg-shaped area specially marked. What is it, and what precautions are advised even if you operate outside this area?

38. Some aerodrome names are underlined, such as **Bridlington.** What does this signify?

39. Some aerodrome names are printed in blue. What does this signify?

40. South of Liverpool are two small aerodromes, **Hawarden** and **Wrexham/Borras.** Would a flight between these two aerodromes at 2000 ft AMSL pass through Controlled Airspace?

41. What is the base of the Controlled Airspace above **Hawarden?**

42. What is the base of the Controlled Airspace above **Wrexham/Borras?**

43. Describe the airspace that you would pass through on a flight from **Wrexham/Borras** direct to **Newton** (52°58'N, 00°59'W) at FL55.

44. The village of **Grassington** lies at (54°04'N, 02°00'W). According to the relief shown on the chart using colours, what is the maximum possible elevation of Grassington?

45. Just south-east of **Macclesfield**, which lies in the Manchester Control Zone, is Danger Area 314. What are its vertical limits, and which NATSU can pass you information on it?

46. Interpret the information printed on the chart within 5 nm of **Bridlington** aerodrome (54°08'N, 00°14'W).

47. Around the boundary of the Manchester Control Zone, the letter 'E' is shown in various places. What does it signify?

48. Part of the Daventry CTA, East of Manchester Control Zone, has vertical limits of FL45–FL245. By flying at its lower limit, you will not penetrate the CTA. What is the maximum altitude (in ft AMSL) at which you can fly without penetrating the CTA if the QNH is:
(1) 1013?   (2) 1004?   (3) 1024?

49. Aeronautical charts are amended from time to time by manuscript amendments made available to Pilots as a N.... .

50. Lines of equal magnetic variation are called I........ .

51. The 7°W isogonal joins all places on the chart that experience a magnetic v........ of .... and is depicted by a dashed ....-coloured line.

52. Places of zero variation where True North and Magnetic North are the same direction are joined by the A..... line.

53. The bearing of the Rhumb Line and Great Circle tracks will be the same at the m..-m....... .

54. True direction is measured against (True/Magnetic) North.

55. Meridians of longitude run (True/Magnetic) North and South.

56. To convert from a true direction that you have measured on a chart to a magnetic direction for use when flying on a magnetic compass, you would need to apply M....... V......... .

57. Variation West, Magnetic ..... !

58. Distance on a chart can be measured against the graduated s.... l... shown on the chart somewhere, usually at the bottom.

59. Distance on any chart can be measured against the lat..... s.... down the side of that particular chart, because 1 minute of latitude = .. nautical mile(s).

EXERCISES 10 — INTRODUCTION TO FLIGHT PLANNING.

1. Whilst planning a cross-country flight, you should study m........... forecasts for weather conditions, and N.......s for other operational considerations.

2. It is recommended that, for a cross-country flight, the cloud ceiling be at least .... ft above all obstacles en route or within a reasonable distance either side of the planned route (say 5 nm or 10 nm).

3. For a flight Outside Regulated Airspace flown by a Private Pilot under the Visual Flight Rules in an aeroplane that cruises at or less than 140 kt:
   • the aeroplane (must/need not) remain clear of cloud;
   • the aeroplane (must/need not) remain in sight of the surface;
   • flight visibility must be at least ... nm if passengers are carried;
   • flight visibility must be at least ... nm without passengers.

4. VFR flight should occur only by day. (True/False)?

5. Flight time to the destination, where Night commences at 1917 UTC, is 53 minutes. What is the latest Estimated Time of Departure if you wish to arrive at least 30 minutes before Night commences?

6. Flight time to the destination, where Night commences at 1917 UTC, is 53 minutes. The weather conditions at the destination are not all that good, so you carry sufficient fuel for a 23 minute flight to an alternate aerodrome where Night commences at 1915 UTC. What is the latest Estimated Time of Departure if you wish to arrive at least 30 minutes before Night time?

EXERCISES 11 — PRE-FLIGHT BRIEFING.

1. A Pilot (should/need not) obtain a meteorological forecast, if available, before embarking upon a cross-country flight.

2. AIRMET information providing Area Forecasts is available via:
   (a) aerodrome Briefing Offices using AFTN or Telex.
   (b) the public telephone network.
   (c) the postal service.

3. The relevant contact telephone numbers for the "AIRMET Telephone Recording Service" can be found on the "AIRMET AREAS" chart published in the UK AIP MET 2-8 (True/False).

4. The cloud base on an Area Forecast is given as height:
   (a) Above Mean Sea Level.
   (b) Above Aerodrome Level.

5. The cloud base on an Aerodrome Forecast is given as height:
   (a) Above Mean Sea Level.
   (b) Above Aerodrome Level.

6. Define CAVOK.

7. A period of weather phenomena expected to last less than 30 minutes may be described as ..... .

8. A period expected to last for less than 60 minutes may be expressed as ..... .

9. A lasting change in the prevailing weather that is expected to occur gradually over a period of hours may be described in a TAF as ..... .

10. A lasting change in the prevailing weather that is expected to occur in a period less than 30 minutes may be described in a TAF as ..... .

11. The TAF for Cardiff reads as follows:
    TAF EGFF 1221 20010 9999 7SC020
    GRADU 1416 9999 4SC025
    TEMPO 1720 5000 51DZ 5ST010

    (1) Is the visibility good throughout the whole period? If not, discuss it.
    (2) What cloud conditions can you expect at 1630 UTC?
    (3) Is this cloud base in the TAF AGL or AMSL?
    (4) Do you foresee any problems landing at Cardiff at 1 pm British Standard Time?
    (5) Do you foresee any problems landing at Cardiff at 6 pm British Standard Time?

12. As well as a meteorological briefing you should have an operational briefing and study the appropriate N..... .

13. Interpret the following NOTAM:
    AC D511 0830—1930 til 30 APR, 0830—2030 01 til 31 MAY, 2500 ft, Active.

14. Interpret the following NOTAM:
    RF 119 29 APR   RAF Linton-on-Ouse 1215 to Heathrow 1325.

15. You are considering a flight to the Isle of **Eday** (5911N, 0246W) in the Orkneys. (Refer to UK AIP AGA 3-1 or *Pooley's Flight Guide.*)
    (1) What is the Landing Distance Available at Eday?
    (2) What surface is the runway?
    (3) Is Prior Permission Required and, if so, how can it be obtained?

EXERCISES 12 — ROUTE SELECTION AND CHART PREPARATION.

1. The shortest distance between two points on the Earth's surface is the Great Circle track which, on most aeronautical charts including the ICAO 1:500 000 series, is a straight line. (True/False)?

2. If possible, it is advisable to avoid areas of high or rugged terrain, as well as areas where aerial activity such as parachuting and glider towing is concentrated, even if this involves a route slightly longer than the direct track. (True/False)?

3. To assist in the estimation of distance it is a good idea to have d....... markings along track; .. nm markings being very suitable.

4. The estimation of angles (such as track error or closing angle) on your aeronautical chart is aided by ruling in t.... g..... on the chart.

5. It is best to fold your chart so that you fly ('up'/'down') the chart.

6. A note is made on the 1:500 000 chart that it may become obsolete after approximately ...... months.

EXERCISES 13 — FLIGHT LOG.

1. Complete a Flight Log for a flight:
   from: **Elstree** (51°39'N, 00°19'W);
      to: overhead **Ipswich** aerodrome (52°02'N, 01°11'E);
         overhead **Cambridge** aerodrome (52°12'N, 00°11'E);
      to **Elstree** for a landing.
   - Calculate the Safety Altitude on a clearance of 1500 ft above all obstacles within 10 nm of track.
   - Cruise at 3000 ft if possible, where conditions are 090°/25 kt, +12°C.
   - Cruise at IAS 120 kt, consumption 8 USG/hr. Fixed Reserve is to be 60 minutes, with a total of 22 USG on board.

2. Complete a series of Flight Logs for the following flights:
   (1) from **Leeds** to **Newcastle,** via **Harrogate** and **Scotch Corner,** carrying **Tees-side** as an alternate;
   (2) from **Newcastle** to **Tees-side,** via VRP **Sedgefield,** carrying **Newcastle** as the alternate;
   (3) from **Tees-side** to **Leeds,** via **Scotch Corner** and **Harrogate,** carrying **Sherburn** (south-east of Leeds) as the alternate.

   The wind is 300°T/20 kt, and you can plan on a TAS 90 kt with a fuel consumption of 24 litres/hour. Fixed reserve should be 45 minutes.

3. Complete a Flight Log for a flight:
   from: **Gloucester/Cheltenham** (Staverton) (51°54'N, 02°10'W);
      to: overhead **Desborough** (52°25'N, 00°50'W);
         overhead **Cranfield** aerodrome (52°04'N, 00°37'W); thence
         from Cranfield to overhead **Oxford** (Kidlington) aerodrome (51°51'N, 01°19'W) **via** the **Beckley** TV mast several miles south-east of the aerodrome; and thence from Oxford to **Staverton** for a landing.

   - Calculate Safety Altitudes on the basis of the highest obstacle within 5 nm of track, plus 10%, plus 1500 ft.
   - Cruise at 3000 ft on the first leg, then at appropriate Flight Levels for the rest.
   - The wind is 250°/20 kt at 3000 ft, and 260°T/25 kt at 4000 ft and above.
   - Temperatures are: +12°C at 3000 ft, +10°C at 4000 ft.
   - Cruising speed is RAS 90 kt.
   - Fuel consumption is at 8·5 USG/hr; Fixed Reserve is to be 60 minutes at cruise rate; Fuel on Board is 40 USG.

4. You are planning a flight of 82 minutes duration with 12 USG of flight fuel required. Cruise rate is 8·8 US gph. Taxi allowance is 1 USG. Total Fuel Capacity is 38 USG (usable). Fixed Reserve is 45 minutes.
   (1) What is the minimum required fuel to nearest US gal?
   (2) What endurance does this give you?
   (3) If you carry full tanks, what endurance will you have?
   (4) If you carry 30 USG, what endurance will you have?
   (5) Is 19 USG sufficient for the flight?

5. Repeat the above calculations for an aerodrome that is 40 minutes flight time away.

6. Your aeroplane can carry 36 USG (usable) and has a fuel consumption of 6·5 US gph. Show the fuel calculations for a flight of 120 minutes duration if you carry full tanks.

7. Repeat the above calculation for a flight of 65 minutes.

8. You are planning a flight of 53 minutes duration with a flight fuel of 7 USG required. Cruise rate is 8 US gph. Taxi allowance is 1 USG.
   (1) What is the minimum fuel that you require?
   (2) What endurance does this give you?
   (3) If you carry 30 USG what does your endurance become?

9. Repeat the above calculation if you decide to carry fuel for an alternate that is 20 minutes flight time away.

10. Repeat the above calculation if you change your alternate aerodrome to one that is 35 minutes away from your destination.

EXERCISES 14 — THE FLIGHT PLAN.

1. Complete a Flight Plan form for a private VFR flight with a Pilot and two passengers in a Cessna 172, registered as G-BCDE, from **Cardiff** (EGFF) to **Humberside** (EGNJ), carrying **Sturgate** (EGCS) as an alternate, and tracking via **Daventry** (DTY) and **Gamston** (GAM).

   Departure is expected to be at 1120 UTC, flight time 2 hours 30 minutes, and endurance 3 hours 45 minutes.

   The aeroplane has Standard Radio Equipment, a Transponder with 4096 codes (Type A), no Survival Equipment, but does carry an Emergency Locator Beacon-Aircraft. The aeroplane is coloured blue and white, and the Pilot's name is B. McInnes.

EXERCISES 15 — EN ROUTE NAVIGATION TECHNIQUES.
En Route Nav Techniques-1.

1. The angle between the HDG and the TMG is called ..... .

2. The angle between the desired track and the Track Made Good is called the ....

3. A known position of an aeroplane at a given time is called a f.. or a p....... .

4. A fix is symbolised by a small ....

5. A DR (dead reckoning) position is symbolised by a small ....

6. Normal en route visual navigation should consist of flying accurate H....... and identifying I........ .

7. You cross a small town at 0325 UTC followed by a railway junction some 27 nm further on at 0340 UTC. What is your Ground Speed?

Exercises 15 — En Route Nav Techniques-2.

1. If you are 3 nm off-track to the right in 20 nm, what is your Track Error?

2. If you are 5 nm off-track to the right in 30 nm, your TE is .... ?

3. If you are 2 nm off-track to the left in 40 nm, TE is ... ?

Exercises 15 — En Route Nav Techniques-3.

1. You are 2 nm left of track after travelling 15 nm.
   (1) What is the Track Error?
   (2) To regain track in another 15 nm, what is the Closing Angle?
   (3) To regain track in another 30 nm, what is the Closing Angle?

2. You are 4 nm right of track after travelling 20 nm. By how many degrees should you change heading to regain track in another 40 nm?

3. You are on a long flight of 249 nm across featureless terrain. After flying a steady HDG for 96 nm you find yourself 13 nm right of track. By what should you alter your HDG by to regain track:
   (1) at the destination?
   (2) 50 nm before the destination?
   (3) 20 nm before the destination?

4. At 0315 UTC you are on track, HDG 080M.
   At 0325 UTC you are 3 nm left of track after travelling 20 nm.
   By what amount should you alter HDG to to be back on track at 0335 UTC?

Exercises 15 — En Route Nav Techniques-4.

1. We obtain a fix 5 nm left of track and make a HDG correction in an attempt to return to track. 20 nm further on we find that we are now 8 nm left of track.
   (1) What is the TE?
   (2) What is the Closing Angle (CA) if we want to return to track in another 60 nm?
   (3) By how much should we alter HDG to do this?

2. You are 3 nm left of track and make a HDG change to regain track. 30 nm later you pinpoint your position as 3 nm right of track.
   (1) What is your TE?
   (2) What is the CA to regain track in another 15 nm?
   (3) If your HDG was 110°M, what will be your new HDG?

Exercises 15 — En Route Nav Techniques-5.

1. Having maintained HDG 320°M you fix your position 2 nm left of track in 15 nm and wish to regain track in another 30 nm.
   (1) What is your TE?
   (2) What is your CA?
   (3) What should you alter HDG to initially?
   (4) What should you alter HDG to upon regaining track?

2. HDG 293°M and 4 nm right of track after 34 nm.
   (1) What is the TE?
   (2) What is the CA to regain track in another 48 nm?
   (3) What HDG should you take up to regain track?
   (4) On track, what would you expect your HDG to be?

Exercises 15 — En Route Nav Techniques-6.

1. You want to descend 3500 ft at 500 fpm rate of descent. How long will that take?

2. At 300 fpm, how long will it take to descend 2700 ft?

3. To descend 4500 ft in 11 minutes, what rate of descent is required?

4. You are 18 nm from the field and have a GS on descent of 100 kt. You wish to overfly the field (elev 500 ft AMSL) at 2000 ft AGL. If you are cruising at 6000 ft, how many minutes from the field are you and what rate of descent do you require to arrive overhead the field as stated?

EXERCISES 16 — NAVIGATION IN REMOTE AREAS.

1. Navigation in remote areas requires very careful p..-f..... planning.

2. When navigating in remote areas especially, you should maintain h.......
   accurately and keep an in-flight l.. .

EXERCISES 17 — ENTRY/EXIT LANES
AND LOW LEVEL ROUTES.

1. Special Access Lane Exit/Entry points (are/are not) shown on aeronautical
   charts and identified by a capital 'E' enclosed in a box.

2. Entry/Exit Lanes are situated in close proximity to C...... Z.... .

3. Navigation in Entry/Exit Lanes and Low Level Routes should be accurate and
   we achieve this by following normal VFR procedures of flying a....... h......s and
   backing up with frequent visual f.... .

4. Prior to entering an Entry/Exit Lane you should accurately position your
   aeroplane over a l....... and check that your D.......... l........ is aligned with the
   magnetic compass to assist you in flying accurate headings.

EXERCISES — CLIMB PLANNING (Appendix 2).

1. Show the climb and cruise calculations for a Piper Warrior on a flight from a
   MSL aerodrome to a cruise altitude of 8,000 ft AMSL under ISA conditions and
   nil wind. The first check point is 70 nm away. Compare the figures with those
   obtained without a climb allowance. CRZ TAS is 108 kt at 8·8 US gph.

2. Repeat Q.1 above for a Cessna 172 with a CRZ TAS of 112 kt at 7·4 US gph.

ANSWERS –
Air Navigation

ANSWERS 1 —
THE PILOT/NAVIGATOR.
1. watch or clock.
2. sound preparation.
3. distance.
4. nautical miles.
5. ground nautical mile.
6. air nautical mile.
7. nm.
8. gnm.
9. anm.
10. 1 knot is 1 nautical mile per hour.
11. metre.
12. foot.
13. Great Circle.
14. 360 degrees, 60 minutes.
15. Longitude.
16. latitude and longitude.
17. do.
18. one.
19. feet, metres.
20. 1 nm = 1852 metres.
21. clockwise.
22. East.
23. South.
24. West.
25. True Air Speed, TAS.
26. heading and True Air Speed.
27. single-headed arrow.
28. wind.
29. from.
30. from.
31. from.
32. track.
33. ground speed.
34. heading.
35. track.
36. wind effect.
37. drift.
38. drift angle.
39. left drift.
40. track error.
41. track error.
42. right.
43. A: HDG/TAS, B: TR/GS, D: DRIFT.
44. (b) GS exceeds TAS.

ANSWERS 2 — SPEED.
Speed-1.
1. True Air Speed.
2. Ground Speed.
3. wind.
4. Air Speed Indicator, abbreviated to ASI.
5. Indicated Air Speed – IAS.
6. Indicated Air Speed.
7. True Air Speed.
8. knots.
9. Rectified Air Speed, Calibrated Air Speed.
10. Indicated Air Speed and Rectified (Calibrated) Air Speed.
11. (a) Indicated Air Speed.

Speed-2.
Note: airspeeds should be accurate to +/–1 kt.
1. decrease.
2. Temperature and Pressure.
3. International Standard Atmosphere Mean Sea Level conditions.
4. greater than.
5. 8%.
6. 108 kt.
7. 216 kt.
8. 130 kt.
9. 17%.
10. 117 kt.
11. 234 kt.
12. 139 kt.

Speed-3.
1. 141, 139, 135, 141, 146; (within +/–1 kt is acceptable).
2. (b) 176.
3. OAT = +10°C, TAS = 107 kt.
4. OAT = –3°C, TAS = 195 kt.
5. Pressure altitude is 8920 ft, say 9000 ft, where ISA = –3°C, and therefore ISA–5 = –8°C; IAS(RAS) = 131 kt.
6. Pressure altitude = 7990, say 8000 ft. OAT = –8°C; RAS = 134 kt.

ANSWERS 3 — DIRECTION.
1. 360.
2. East.
3. South.
4. West.
5. True North, True South.
6. True North-South.
7. North Magnetic Pole, South Magnetic Pole.
8. Magnetic North, Magnetic South.
9. Variation.
10. East.
11. West.
12. Isogonals
13. Varn. East, Magnetic Least, Varn. West, Magnetic Best.
14. 097M, 280M, 006M, 012M, 161M, 265T, 087T, 359T.
15. Compass North.
16. deviation.
17. compass deviation.
18. 022C, 280C, 197M and 198C, 292M and 294C, 6W and 103C, 271T and 278M.
    (Note: answers calculated using interpolation of Deviation Card between Cardinal Points.)
19. Heading is 337°M, 339°C.
20. Track is 105°C, 104°M, 099°T.
21. Track is 002°C, 004°M, 357°T.
22. Track is 353°C, 355°M, 349°T.
23. is **not**.
24. (b).
25. (f).
26. (e).
27. (a).
28. (b).
29. (c).
30. (c).
31. (b).
32. (a).
33. (b).
34. (b).
35. (a).
36. (c).
37. (a).
38. (c).
39. (e).
40. (b).
41. (a).
42. (a).
43. (c).
44. every 10 or 15 minutes.
45. should not.
46. easier.
47. relative bearing.
48. 060 REL.
49. 280 REL.
50. 050 REL and 085M.
51. 265M.

ANSWERS 4 — WIND-SIDE OF THE NAVIGATION COMPUTER.
Wind-Side-1.
1. A: HDG/TAS, B: TR/GS.
2. heading to track.
3. desired track.
4. calculate Heading and Ground Speed.
5. HDG 322°T, GS 75 kt.
6. HDG 261°T, GS 66 kt.
7. HDG 100°T, GS 133 kt.
8. HDG 062°T, GS 127 kt.
9. HDG 061°T, TAS 90 kt.
10. HDG 166°T, TAS 82 kt.
11. 077°T, 084°M, 88 kt.
    055°T, 062°M, 84 kt.
    111°T, 117°M, 157 kt.
    308°T, 314°M, 120 kt.
    (The last two tracks are reciprocals, but note that the headings are not reciprocals; this is because you must point the nose of the aeroplane into wind to allow for drift.)
12. HDG 061°T, TAS 90 kt.
13. HDG 166°T, TAS 82 kt, RAS 75 kt.
14. TAS 119 kt, HDG 296°T and 302°M, GS 95 kt.
15. 092°M, 062°M/36, 085°M, 88 kt.
    062°M, 062°M/36, 062°M, 84 kt.
    126°M, 356°M/30, 117°M, 157 kt.
    306°M, 356°M/30, 314°M, 120 kt.
    (The last two tracks are reciprocals, but note that the headings are not reciprocals; this is because you must point the nose of the aeroplane into wind to allow for drift.)

Wind Side-2.
1. 140T/24.
2. 318T/17.
3. 290T/25.
4. 300T/17.

Wind Side-3.

1.

TAS	Wind(T)	HDG(T)	TR(T)	GS
120	055/36	076°	085°	87
140	350/30	110°	120°	158
140	350/30	310°	300°	119
120	055/36	104°	120°	100
120	055/36	014°	060°	96
120	055/36	055°	055°	84

2. HDG 339°T, drift 5° right, TR 344°T, GS130 kt.

Wind Side-4.

1. headwind 11 kt, crosswind 28 kt.
2. no.
3. RWY 03 has only 10 kt of crosswind, and 28 kt of headwind and therefore is OK. RWY 21, the reciprocal runway, has a 10 kt crosswind, but has a 28 kt tailwind, therefore is unsuitable. (Note: We do not advise taking-off downwind normally, even though a 10 kt max tailwind component is specified for many aircraft. Our reasons are discussed in The Air Pilot's Manual, Volume 4, especially in the chapters on Performance and Windshear.)

ANSWERS 5 — CALCULATOR-SIDE OF THE NAVIGATION COMPUTER.

Calculator-1.

1. 27 nm
2. 52 nm
3. 20 nm

Calculator-2.

1. 153 kt.
2. 93 kt.
3. 180 kt.
4. 180 kt.
5. 150 kt, 12 minutes.
6. GS 132 kt, ETI 33 min.
7. 15 minutes.
8. 12 minutes.
9. 13 minutes.
10. 57 min.
11. GS 115 for 45 nm = ETI 23·5 min, say 24 min, therefore ETA 1306 UTC.
12. GS 147 for 28 nm = ETI 11·4 min, say 11 min, therefore ETA 0827 UTC.

Calculator-3.

1. 13·3, say 14 litres; (always round fuel figures upwards).
2. 3·7, say 4 litres.
3. 26·4, say 27 litres/hour; (notice again how we always round-up the fuel figure for safety reasons).
4. 7·5, say 8 USG/hr.
5. 30 litres/hr, 34 min
6. 40 USG of flight fuel, 300 minutes or 5 hours.
7. 20·5 USG of flight fuel, 224 minutes or 3 hours 44 min.
8. 45 min = 5·6 USG, therefore 30·4 USG of flight fuel, 243 minutes or 4 hours 3 min.
9. ETI 150 min, flight fuel 18·2 USG, reserve 7·3 USG, total fuel 25·5 USG, say 26 USG.
10. ETI 80 min, flight fuel 8·7 USG, reserve 6·5 USG, total fuel 15·2 USG, say 16 USG. (NOTE: always round fuel up, i.e. carry at least the bare minimum.)
11. Flight fuel 20·2 USG, safe flight endurance 178 min at GS 93 kt, 276 nm.
12. Flight fuel 21 USG, safe flight endurance 185 min at GS 93 kt, 287 nm.

Calculator-4.

1. 9 nm.
2. 9 nm, 12 nm.
3. 8 nm, 8 degrees.
4. 12 nm, 12 degrees.

Calculator-5.

1. +100°F.
2. 0°C.
3. +68°F.

Calculator-6.

1. 115 sm, 185 km.
2. 102 km.
3. 538 nm.
4. 92·5 km/hr, 92,500 metres/hr, 1540 metres/min, 25·7 metres/sec.

Calculator-7.

1. 395 m.
2. 3,980 ft.
3. 1,640 ft.
4. 328 ft.
5. Obstruction elevation 1,230 ft, so fly at an altitude of at least 2,230 ft. (If you think 123 ft,

then obstacle clearance 1000 ft above this is **not** guaranteed!)

Calculator-8.
1. 27·2, say 28 kg.
2. 287 kg.
3. 176 lb.
4. 1860 lb (to a reasonable accuracy).
5. 12,540 lb.

Calculator-9.
1. 0·71.
2. 7·1 lb
3. 0·71 kg.
4. 7·1 kg.
5. 35·5, say 36 kg.
6. 1 IG = 1·20 USG.
7. 5 IG = 6 USG.
8. 10 IG = 12 USG = 45·3, say 46 litres.
9. 10 USG = 37·8, say 38 litres.
10. 1 USG = 3·78, say 4 litres.
11. 18 USG = 68 litres.
12. 29 USG = 110 litres.
13. 86 litres = 22·6 USG, so the gauges should read 34·6 USG, and in this case indicating it in whole USGs, working on the conservative side we would say we had only 34 USG on board.
14. 1 litre weighs 0·71 kg, therefore 100 l = 71 kg.
15. 37·7 kg
16. 114 litres, 81 kg
17. 141 l, 100 kg
18. 118 kg.
19. 102 litres.
20. 72 kg.
21. 244 kg, 344 litres.
22. 40 IG, 280 lb.

ANSWERS 6 — VERTICAL NAVIGATION.

Vertical Nav-1.
1. altitude.
2. foot.
3. approximate.
4. terrain clearance, traffic separation, performance capabilities.
5. decreases.
6. pressure.
7. ISA.
8. measuring stick.
9. 1013·25 mb(hPa).
10. +15°C.

11. −2°C/1,000 ft.
12. calibrate altimeters.
13. pressure altitude.
14. decrease.
15. 30 ft.
16. 1012 mb.
17. 1011 mb.
18. 913 mb.
19. 690 ft.
20. 3390 ft.

Vertical Nav-2.
1. +15°C.
2. +13°C.
3. +5°C.
4. −5°C.
5. +9°C, 913 mb.
6. +14°C, 993 mb.
7. +16°C, 1033 mb.
8. 1290 ft.
9. 90 ft.
10. minus 210 ft (−210).

Vertical Nav-3.
1. 1013·2.
2. no.
3. yes.
4. QNH.
5. altitude is height AMSL.
6. QNH.
7. aerodrome elevation AMSL.
8. 600 ft.
9. Mean Sea Level.
10. 1008 mb on subscale, and QNH 1008.
11. 386 ft.
12. on ground 1334 ft, in circuit 2334 ft, for terrain clearance 4669 ft.

Vertical Nav-4.
1. QFE pressure datum, aerodrome.
2. QFE, AAL.

Vertical Nav-5.
1. Altimeter Setting Region.
2. Regional QNH.
3. Aerodrome QFE, Aerodrome QNH.
4. Regional Pressure Setting or Regional QNH.
5. QFE (normal in the UK), or QNH.
6. QNH of an aerodrome beneath the TMA or SRA.
7. Aerodrome QFE, Regional QNH.
8. 3000 ft AMSL.
9. FL35.

10. 1013 mb, Transition Altitude.
11. 3000 ft AMSL, 3500 ft AMSL.
12. 3000 ft AMSL, 3200 ft AMSL.
13. 3000 ft AMSL, 3800 ft AMSL.
14. 2500 ft AMSL.
15. 4290 ft.
16. 4650 ft.

Vertical Nav-6.
1. (1) 2536 ft.
   (2) 3036 ft.
   (3) 3190 ft.
   (4) 2642 ft.
   (5) 3142 ft.
   (6) 3307 ft.

Vertical Nav-7.
1. 120 ft.
2. pressure altitude 1334 ft, say 1500 ft where ISA = +12°C. Therefore OAT +30°C = ISA+18; 18 x 120 = 2160 ft. Therefore density altitude = 1334 + 2160 = 3494 ft, say 3500 ft.

ANSWERS 7 — TIME.

Time-1.
1. 291015.
2. 191517:
3. 011700.
4. 11291015.
   07191517.
   04011700.

Time-2.
1. 15 degrees.
2. 45 degrees.
3. 150 degrees.
4. 142·5 degrees, (i.e. 142°30′).
5. 10 hours.
6. 9 hours.
7. 8 hours.

Time-3.
1. 12 min later in Cardiff.
2. 4 min earlier in Norwich.
3. Plymouth LMT is 12 min behind Portsmouth LMT.
4. 151357 UTC.
5. 251728 UTC.
6. 090850 UTC.
7. 190944 LMT.
8. 272234 LMT.
9. 270419 LMT.

Time-4.
1. lose.
2. Prime (or Greenwich) Meridian.

3. 1 hour ahead.
4. 1333 UTC, 1433 MEZ.
5. 1810 UTC.

Time-5.
1. Sunset plus 30 mins.
2. are.
3. Air Almanac.
4. earlier.
5. earlier.
6. earlier.
7. latitude and date.
8. usually the Fourth Sunday in March to the Fourth Sunday in October, (unless otherwise specified).
9. advanced by 1 hour.
10. 1300 UTC.
11. 1123 BST.

ANSWERS 8 — THE EARTH.
1. passes.
2. is.
3. does not pass.
4. equator.
5. is.
6. Small Circle.
7. pole.
8. are parallel.
9. Prime, Greenwich.
10. meridians of longitude are all GCs.
11. East or West.
12. 1 minute of GC arc = 1 nm.
13. is.
14. 60 nm.
15. 1852 metres.
16. It is **very important** because the Pilot will relate angular relationships on the chart to angular relationships on the Earth.
17. Chart length to Earth distance.
18. more detail.
19. 27·4 nm.
20. 54·9 nm.
21. 29·5 nm.
22. 51 nm.
23. 31·7 nm.
24. 1:250 000.

ANSWERS 9 — AERONAUTICAL CHARTS.

1. (a).
2. does.
3. blue.
4. (b).
5. (b).
6. NOTAM.
7. It is the highest point on that chart.
8. 8200 ft (+/–50 ft).
9. 10,830 ft (+/–50 ft).
10. 1525 metres (+/–10 m).
11. (b).
12. (a).
13. 6°W.
14. 7°W.
15. **Wombleton**.
16. 120 ft AMSL.
17. **Sproatley**.
18. 40 ft AMSL.
19. 39 nm (+/–1 nm).
20. 133°T (+/–1°).
21. 313°T.
22. 6°W (+/–½°).
23. 1050 ft AGL, 2297 AMSL, 322°T, 10 nm.
24. Area of Intense Aerial Activity, from the surface to FL200.
25. glider launching.
26. Altimeter Setting Region.
27. Barnsley ASR.
28. A High Intensity Radio Transmission Area (HIRTA).
29. 134·7 MHz.
30. Leeming LARS on 132·4 MHz; Linton LARS on 129·15 MHz.
31. 2297 ft AMSL.
32. 3297 ft AMSL.
33. 807 ft AMSL.
34. 1807 AMSL.
35. none.
36. Airway B1, from FL75 up to FL245.
37. Weapons Range Danger Area (WRDA), advisable to make use of the Radar Service, since aircraft operating in the WRDA patterns may be **outside** the WRDA (see Note 4 on the chart).
38. Permission to fly within the ATZ and to take-off or land is required, and certain communications rules apply (see Legend Note 1).
39. Government aerodrome, ATZ exists at all times.
40. no.
41. 3000 ft AMSL.
42. 3500 ft AMSL.
43. Airway A25, Shawbury AIAA, Daventry CTA, outside controlled airspace just at the base of Daventry CTA, East Midlands SRA, then outside controlled airspace again.
44. 1000 ft AMSL.
45. 0–2900 ft AMSL, Manchester Approach 119·4 MHz (from Legend).
46. aerodrome elevation 283 ft AMSL; intense parachuting; single unlit obstruction 508 ft AMSL, 300 ft AGL; boundary of Barnsley and Humber ASRs. A/G Frequency 123·25 MHz.
47. Special Access Lane Entry/Exit.
48. (1) 5500 ft AMSL.
    (2) 5230 ft AMSL.
    (3) 5830 ft AMSL.
49. NOTAM.
50. isogonals.
51. variation 7°W, magenta.
52. agonic line.
53. mid-meridian.
54. True North.
55. True North and South.
56. Magnetic Variation.
57. best.
58. scale line.
59. latitude scale, 1 nm.

ANSWERS 10 — INTRODUCTION TO FLIGHT PLANNING.

1. Meteorological Forecasts, NOTAMs.
2. 1000 ft.
3. (1) must.
   (2) must.
   (3) 3 nm.
   (4) 1·5 nm.
4. True.
5. ETD 1754 UTC.
6. ETD 1729 UTC.

ANSWERS 11 –
PRE-FLIGHT BRIEFING.
1. should.
2. (a) and (b).
3. True.
4. (a).
5. (b).
6. visibility 10 km or greater; no cloud below 5000 ft AMSL or below the highest minimum sector altitude, whichever is the higher, and no cumulonimbus; no precipitation, thunderstorm, shallow fog or low drifting snow.
7. INTER.
8. TEMPO.
9. GRADU.
10. RAPID.
11. (1) No. Visibility is reduced to 5000 metres in drizzle for temporary periods (less than 60 minutes) between 1700–2000 UTC.
    (2) 4 Oktas of Stratocumulus at 2500 ft AGL.
    (3) AGL.
    (4) No.
    (5) Yes. Temporary periods of reduced visibility, low cloud and drizzle.

12. NOTAMs
13. In the Scottish FIR, Danger Area 511 will be active between the hours of 0830–1930 UTC until April 30th, then 0830–2030 UTC between May 1st–31st, up to 2500 ft.
14. A Royal Flight departing Linton-on-Ouse at 1215 UTC and proceeding to Heathrow, arriving at 1325 UTC, on April 29th.
15. (1) 549·m, and 366 m.
    (2) grass.
    (3) Yes. Telephone Orkney Islands Council, Kirkwall (0856) 2310.

ANSWERS 12 –
ROUTE SELECTION AND CHART PREPARATION.
1. True.
2. True.
3. 10 nm distance markings.
4. track guides.
5. fly *up* the chart.
6. 12 months.

ANSWERS 13 – COMPLETING THE FLIGHT LOG.

1.

FROM / TO	SAFETY ALT	ALT / TEMP	RAS	TAS	W/V	TR °T	DRIFT	HDG °T	VAR	HDG °M	G/S	DIST	TIME	ETA
ELSTREE														
	2420	3000 / +12	120	126	090/25	069	4°L	073	5°W	078	102	60	36	
IPSWICH														
	2272	3000 / +12	120	126	"	286	3°L	289	5°W	294	150	40	16	
CAMBRIDGE														
	2420	3000 / +12	120	126	"	208	10°S	198	5°W	203	136	38	17	
ELSTREE											TOTAL	138	69	

Consumption 8 USG/hr

	min.	USG
Destination:	69	9·2
Alternate:	–	–
Flight Fuel:	69	9·2
Reserve:	60	8·0
Taxi:	–	–
Fuel Required:	129	17·2
Margin:	36	4·8
Total Fuel:	165	22·0

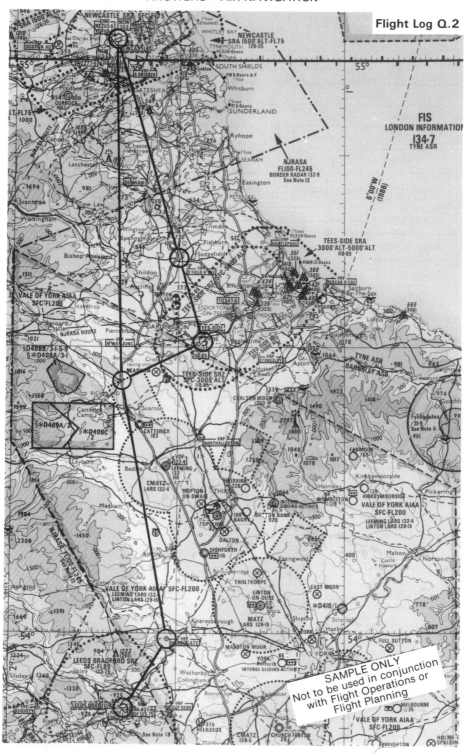

Flight Log Q.2 (cont'd)
(1)

LEEDS – NEWCASTLE

STAGE	WINDS		RUNWAY							
2000	300/20		QNH							
5000			QFE							
T.A.S.	90		WIND							

STAGE	MSA	TR (T)	HDG (T)	VAR	HDG (M)	DIST	GS	TIME	ETA	ATA
TAKE OFF									→	
SET COURSE									→	
HARROGATE	1500	034	021	6°w	027	9	90	6		
SCOTCH CORNER	1500	349	339	6°w	345	28	76	22		
NEWCASTLE ZONE BDY	2000	358	347	6°w	353	30	78	23		
NEWCASTLE	1500	358	347	6°w	353	6	78	5		
ALTERNATE TEESSIDE	(SEE	NEWCASTLE	– TEESSIDE	SHEET	TIME,	20				
LANDED									→	

LEEMING RADAR 132.4
TEESSIDE TWR 119.8
APP 118.85
NEWCASTLE TWR 119.7
APP 126.35

FUEL REQUIRED
Fuel on Board = 98 Ltr
Consumption = 24

	Time	Fuel
Route	56	23
Alternate	20	8
Reserve (45 min)	–	18
TOTAL		49

	TWR	APP	RAD	
LEEDS	120.30	123.75	121.05	**DISTRESS 121.50**

(2)

NEWCASTLE – TEESSIDE

WINDS			RUNWAY				
2000	300/20		QNH				
5000			QFE				
T.A.S.	90		WIND				

STAGE	MSA	TR (T)	HDG (T)	VAR	HDG (M)	DIST	GS	TIME	ETA	ATA
TAKE OFF									→	
SET COURSE									→	
VRP SEDGEFIELD	2000	165	174	6°w	180	25	103	15		
TEESSIDE	1500	165	174	6°w	180	8	103	5		
ALTERNATE NEWCASTLE		345	335	6°w	341	33	75	26		
LANDED									→	

NEWCASTLE TWR 119.7
APP 126.35
TEESSIDE TWR 119.8
APP 118.85

FUEL REQUIRED

Fuel on Board =
Consumption = 24

	Time	Fuel
Route	20	8
Alternate	26	11
Reserve (45 min)	–	18
TOTAL		37

	TWR	APP	RAD	
LEEDS	120.30	123.75	121.05	**DISTRESS 121.50**

Flight Log Q.2 (cont'd)

(3)

TEESSIDE — LEEDS

WINDS			RUNWAY						
2000	300/20		QNH						
5000			QFE						
T.A.S.	90		WIND						

STAGE	MSA	TR (T)	HDG (T)	VAR	HDG (M)	DIST	GS	TIME	ETA	ATA
TAKE OFF									→	
SET COURSE									→	
SCOTCH CORNER	1500	244	254	6°w	260	10	77	8		
VRP HARROGATE	1500	169	179	6°w	185	28	101	17		
LEEDS	1500	214	227	6°w	233	9	86	6		
ALTERNATE SHERBURN		108	106	6°w	112	16	109	10		
LANDED									→	

TEESSIDE TWR 119·8
APP 118·85

LEEMING RADAR 132·4

SHERBURN 122·6

FUEL REQUIRED
Fuel on Board =
Consumption = 24

	Time	Fuel
Route	31	13
Alternate	10	4
Reserve (45 min)	—	18
TOTAL		35

	TWR	APP	RAD	
LEEDS	120.30	123.75	121.05	DISTRESS 121.50

3.

FROM /TO	SAFETY ALT	ALT	RAS	TAS	W/V	TR °T	DRIFT	HDG °T	VAR	HDG °M	G/S	DIST	TIME	ETA
		TEMP												
STAVERTON		3000												
DESBOROUGH	2770	+12	90	95	250/20	056	-3	053	6°W	059	114	59	31	
CRANFIELD	2070	FL35 +11	90	96	250/20	161	+12	173	5°W	178	93	24	16	
BECKLEY	2570	FL40 +10	90	96	260/25	231	+7	238	5°W	243	73	27	22	
KIDLINGTON	2570	FL45 +10	90	97	260/25	299	-9	290	6°W	296	76	6	5	
STAVERTON	2690	FL45 +10	90	97	260/25	276	-4	272	6°W	278	72	31	26	
											TOTAL: 147		100	

Consumption **8·5 USG/hr**

	min.	USG
Destination:	100	14·2
Alternate:	–	–
Flight Fuel:	100	14·2
Reserve:	60	8·5
Taxi:	–	–
Fuel Required:	160	22·7
Margin:	124	17·3
Total Fuel:	284	40·0

4. (1) 20 USG (2) 127 min (3) 250 min (4) 195 min (5) no.
5. (1) 14 USG (2) 85 min (3) 249 min (4) 194 min (5) yes.

6.

	min.	USG
Destination:	120	13
Alternate:	–	–
Flight Fuel:	120	13
Reserve:	45	5
Taxi:	–	–
Fuel Required:	165	18
Margin:	166	18
Total Fuel:	331	36

7.

	min.	USG
Destination:	65	7
Alternate:	–	–·
Flight Fuel:	65	7
Reserve:	45	5
Taxi:	–	–
Fuel Required:	110	12
Margin:	221	24
Total Fuel:	331	36

8. (1) 14 USG (2) 98 min.
   (3) 218 min.

	min.	USG
Destination:	53	7
Alternate:	–	–
Flight Fuel:	53	7
Reserve:	45	6
Taxi:	–	1
Fuel Required:	98	14
Margin:	120	16
Total Fuel:	218	30

	min.	USG
Destination:	53	7
Alternate:	20	2·7
Flight Fuel:	73	10
Reserve:	45	6
Taxi:	–	1
Fuel Required:	118	17
Margin:	98	13
Total Fuel:	216	30

	min.	USG
Destination:	53	7
Alternate:	35	4·7
Flight Fuel:	88	12
Reserve:	45	6
Taxi:	–	1
Fuel Required:	133	19
Margin:	82	11
Total Fuel:	215	30

ANSWERS 14 — THE FLIGHT PLAN.

| FLIGHT PLAN | ATS COPY |

PRIORITY

<< ≡ FF →

ADDRESSEE(S)

<< ≡

FILING TIME

ORIGINATOR

→ <<≡

SPECIFIC IDENTIFICATION ADDRESSEE(S) AND/OR ORIGINATOR

3 MESSAGE TYPE

<< ≡ (FPL

7 AIRCRAFT IDENTIFICATION

–

8 FLIGHT RULES

–☐

TYPE OF FLIGHT

☐ <<≡

9 NUMBER

–☐

TYPE OF AIRCRAFT

–

WAKE TURBULENCE CAT.

/ ☐

10 EQUIPMENT

–☐ / <<≡

13 DEPARTURE AERODROME

–☐

TIME

<<≡

15 CRUISING SPEED

–

LEVEL

ROUTE

→

<<≡

16 DESTINATION AERODROME

–☐

TOTAL EET

HR MIN

ALTN AERODROME

→☐

2ND ALTN AERODROME

→☐ <<≡

18 OTHER INFORMATION

–

) <<≡

SUPPLEMENTARY INFORMATION (NOT TO BE TRANSMITTED IN FPL MESSAGES)

19 ENDURANCE

HR MIN

–E/

PERSONS ON BOARD

→ P/

EMERGENCY RADIO

UHF **VHF** **ELBA**

→ R/ U V E

SURVIVAL EQUIPMENT **POLAR** **DESERT** **MARITIME** **JUNGLE**

→ S / P D M J

JACKETS **LIGHT** **FLUORES** **UHF** **VHF**

→ J / L F U V

DINGHIES

NUMBER **CAPACITY** **COVER** **COLOUR**

→ D / → → C → <<≡

AIRCRAFT COLOUR AND MARKINGS

A/

REMARKS

→ N / <<≡

PILOT IN COMMAND

C/) <<≡

FILED BY

SPACE RESERVED FOR ADDITIONAL REQUIREMENTS

FLIGHT PLAN

ATS COPY

PRIORITY

ADDRESSEE(S)

<< ≡ FF →

<< ≡

FILING TIME

ORIGINATOR

→ <<≡

SPECIFIC IDENTIFICATION ADDRESSEE(S) AND/OR ORIGINATOR

3 MESSAGE TYPE

7 AIRCRAFT IDENTIFICATION

8 FLIGHT RULES

TYPE OF FLIGHT

<< ≡ (FPL   – G,B,C,D,E,   – V   G <<≡

9 NUMBER

TYPE OF AIRCRAFT

WAKE TURBULENCE CAT.

10 EQUIPMENT

–   C,1,7,2   / L   – S /C <<≡

13 DEPARTURE AERODROME

TIME

– E,G,F,F   1,1,2,0 <<≡

15 CRUISING SPEED

LEVEL

ROUTE

– N,0,1,2,0   A,0,2,5,   → DTY GAM

<< ≡

TOTAL EET

16 DESTINATION AERODROME

HR MIN

ALTN AERODROME

2ND ALTN AERODROME

– E,G,N,J   0,2,3,0   → E,G,C,S   → <<≡

18 OTHER INFORMATION

–

) <<≡

SUPPLEMENTARY INFORMATION (NOT TO BE TRANSMITTED IN FPL MESSAGES)

19 ENDURANCE

EMERGENCY RADIO

HR MIN

PERSONS ON BOARD

UHF   VHF   ELBA

–E/ 0,3,4,5   → P/ 0,0,3   → R/ ☒   ☒   E

SURVIVAL EQUIPMENT   POLAR   DESERT   MARITIME   JUNGLE   JACKETS   LIGHT   FLUORES   UHF   VHF

→ ☒ / ☒   ☒   M   ☒   → ☒ / ☒   ☒   ☒   ☒

DINGHIES

NUMBER   CAPACITY   COVER   COLOUR

→ ☒ /   →   → ☒ →   <<≡

AIRCRAFT COLOUR AND MARKINGS

A/ BLUE & WHITE

REMARKS

→ ☒ /   <<≡

PILOT IN COMMAND

C/ B. McINNES   ) <<≡

FILED BY

SPACE RESERVED FOR ADDITIONAL REQUIREMENTS

ANSWERS 15 — EN ROUTE NAVIGATION TECHNIQUES.

En Route Nav Techniques-1.
1. drift.
2. track error.
3. fix or pinpoint.
4. circle.
5. triangle.
6. flying accurate headings and identifying landmarks.
7. 108 kt.

En Route Nav Techniques-2.
1. 9 degrees right.
2. 10 degrees right.
3. 3 degrees left.

En Route Nav Techniques-3.
1. (1) 8 degrees left.
   (2) 8 degrees.
   (3) 4 degrees.
2. TE = 12°, CA = 6°, so change heading by 18 degrees left.
3. (1) 13 degrees left.
   (2) 16 degrees left.
   (3) 14 degrees left.
   (see diagrams below)
4. TE = 3 in 20 = 9° left.
   We assume that in the following 10 minutes you will travel the same distance as in the previous 10 minutes, i.e. 20 nm; therefore CA = 3 in 20 = 9°. Alter HDG by 18° to the right, i.e. to HDG 098°M.

En Route Nav Techniques-4.
1. (1) TE = 3 in 20 = 9°.
   (2) CA = 8 in 60 = 8°.
   (3) Alter HDG 17° to the right.
2. (1) TE = 6 in 30 = 12°.
   (2) CA = 3 in 15 = 12°.
   (3) Alter HDG by 24° to the left, i.e. to HDG 086°M.

En Route Nav Techniques-5.
1. (1) TE = 2 in 15 = 8°.
   (2) CA = 2 in 30 = 4°.
   (3) Alter HDG by TE + CA = 12° to the right, i.e. to HDG 332°M.
   (4) Remove the CA by turning 4° left onto HDG 328°M.
2. (1) TE = 4 in 34 = 7 in 60 = 7° (by computer).
   (2) CA = 4 in 48 = 1 in 12 = 5 in 60 = 5°.
   (3) HDG 281°M.
   (4) HDG 286°M.

En Route Nav Techniques-6.
1. 7 minutes.
2. 9 minutes.
3. 410 fpm.
4. 18 nm at GS 100 = 11 minutes to descend from 6000 to 2500 ft AMSL, i.e. 3500 ft in 11 mins = 320 ft/min.

ANSWERS 16 — NAVIGATION IN REMOTE AREAS.
1. careful pre-flight planning.
2. fly accurate headings (HDGs) and keep an in-flight log.

ANSWERS 17 — ENTRY/EXIT LANES AND LOW LEVEL ROUTES.
1. are.
2. Control Zones.
3. accurate headings (HDGs) and frequent visual fixes.
4. position yourself over a landmark, and check that the Direction Indicator is aligned with the Magnetic Compass.

En Route Nav Techniques–3: Q.3

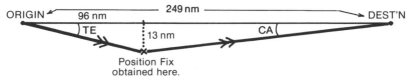

(1) Calculation to Regain TR at Destination:
  13 in 96   = TE 8°
  249 – 96 = 153
  13 in 153 = CA 5°
  To regain TR at Destination: TE 8°; CA 5°.
  ∴ Alter HDG 8° + 5° = 13° to the Left.

(2) To Regain TR 50 nm from Dest'n:

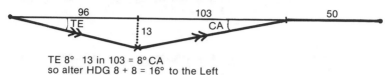

TE 8° 13 in 103 = 8° CA
so alter HDG 8 + 8 = 16° to the Left

(3) To Regain TR 20 nm from Dest'n:

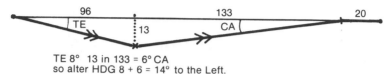

TE 8° 13 in 133 = 6° CA
so alter HDG 8 + 6 = 14° to the Left.

ANSWERS – CLIMB PLANNING

PIPER

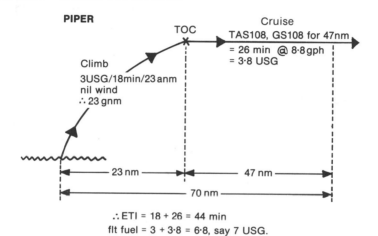

∴ ETI = 18 + 26 = 44 min
flt fuel = 3 + 3·8 = 6·8, say 7 USG.

If only CRZ was considered then,
70 nm @ GS108 = 39 min ETI @8·8 gph = 5·7, say 6 USG.

CESSNA

Climb: 17 min/3·1 USG/22 anm
nil wind
22 gnm

Cruise: TAS112, nil wind, GS112 for (70 - 22=) 48 nm
= 26 min
@7·4 gph = 3·2 USG

∴ ETI = 17 + 26 = 43 min
flt fuel = 3·1 + 3·2 = 6·3, say 7 USG

If only CRZ was considered:
70 nm @ GS 112 = 38 min ETI @ 7·4 gph = 4·7, say 5 USG

EXERCISES
on
THE AEROPLANE
— TECHNICAL

EXERCISES 1 — THE FORCES THAT ACT ON AN AEROPLANE.

1. The downwards force of attraction between the aeroplane and the Earth is called the W..... .

2. The force produced by the wings and which supports the aeroplane in flight is called the L... .

3. The force produced by the engine/propeller is called the T...... .

4. The force that resists the motion of the aeroplane through the air is called the D... .

5. In straight and level cruising flight the aeroplane is in equilibrium, with the Weight balanced by the ...., and the Drag balanced by the ....

6. The Lift force is generally much (greater/smaller) than the Drag force in flight.

EXERCISES 2 — WEIGHT.

1. The Weight of an aeroplane can be considered as a single force acting through the C..... of G...... .

2. Define the term 'wing loading'.

3. An aeroplane weighs 3,000 lb and has a wing area of 200 square feet. What is its wing loading?

EXERCISES 3 — AEROFOIL – LIFT.

1. Airflow past an aerofoil such as the wing of an aeroplane can produce a L... force.

2. The most important airflow is that nearest the surface of the aerofoil and which is called the b....... l.... .

3. A steady flow of molecules around the aerofoil where succeeding molecules follow each other is called s......... flow.

4. A disturbed flow with eddying is called t........ flow.

5. Daniel B........ showed that in a streamline flow the total energy remains constant.

6. Static Pressure in the air is exerted (in all directions/down/up).

7. Dynamic Pressure is the pressure (due to motion/due to no motion).

8. Bernoulli's Principle describes the natural effect that 'in a streamline flow, the total pressure energy remains c....... .'

9. Total Pressure Energy = S..... Pressure + D...... Pressure.

10. In streamline flow, if Dynamic Pressure increases then, for the total pressure energy to remain constant, the Static Pressure will ....

11. If the relative velocity between the airflow and the aerofoil increases, then the Dynamic Pressure, which is due to motion, will (decrease/increase).

12. If velocity increases, then Dynamic Pressure increases. For the total pressure to remain the same, the Static Pressure will ....

13. If velocity increases, Static Pressure ....

14. Increasing the curvature of the upper surface of the wing causes the airflow over it to (speed up/slow down).

15. If the velocity over the upper surface of the wing increases, then the Static Pressure will ....

16. Curvature of the wing surfaces is called C..... .

17. The line drawn half-way between the upper and lower surfaces of the wing, and which gives an indication of its curvature, is called the M... C..... L... .

18. The **Straight** line joining the Leading Edge and the Trailing Edge of an aerofoil section is called the C.... L... .

19. The length of the straight line joining the LE and the TE is the C.... .

20. The greatest distance between the upper and lower surfaces of the wing is called the T........ .

21. As the airflow accelerates across the upper surface of a well-cambered wing, the Static Pressure (increases/decreases).

22. In normal flight, the Static Pressure over the top surface of a well- cambered wing is (less than/greater than/the same as) the Static Pressure beneath the wing.

23. The difference between the Static Pressure above and below the wing generates a L... force.

24. As well as the Lift force being generated by the aerofoil, it also generates a force opposing the relative motion of the aerofoil through the air – and this force opposing motion is called .... .

25. The total force produced by an aerofoil is called the T.... R......., and which can be resolved into two components L... and D... .

26. The angle between the chord line of an aerofoil and the direction of the relative airflow well ahead of the aerofoil is called the a.... of a..... .

27. Even at zero degrees angle of attack, a wing with a well-cambered upper surface will cause the airflow to accelerate across it. The increase in velocity will cause a (decrease/increase) in Static Pressure over the upper surface resulting in the generation of a L... force.

28. If the angle of attack is increased gradually, the lifting ability of the wing (increases/decreases).

29. At a critical angle of attack known as the stalling angle the streamline airflow breaks down and becomes turbulent and the lifting ability of the wing (increases/remains good/decreases).

30. The forces acting on an aerofoil in-flight as a result of the changes in Static Pressure around it, may be considered to act through a point known as the C..... of P....... .

31. As the angle of attack is gradually increased in the normal flight range, the lifting ability of the wing increases and the Centre of Pressure (moves forwards/stays in the same place/moves rearwards) on the wing.

32. Beyond the stalling angle of attack (the critical angle when the streamline airflow breaks down and becomes turbulent), the lifting ability of the wing decreases markedly and the CP moves (forwards/rearwards/remains stationary) on the wing.

33. Name five items that the Lift force generated by an aerofoil depends on w... shape, a.... of a....., air d...... (Rho), v....... of the airflow, w... area.

34. The wing shape and the angle of attack determine the profile that the aerofoil presents to the airflow and determines the lifting a...... of the wing.

35. The 'lifting ability' of the wing is given the technical name 'C.......... of L...'.

36. The velocity of the airflow and the air density (Rho) are combined in the one expression '½ Rho V-squared' which is called the D...... P....... .

37. Write down the formula that very neatly describes the LIFT force that a wing can produce.

38. The 'CLift' of an aerofoil is determined by the wing shape and the angle of attack. The designer fixes the wing shape, but the Pilot can change the ..... of A..... .

39. As the Pilot increases the angle of attack by backwards pressure on the control column, the lifting ability (Coefficient of Lift) of the wing gradually (increases/decreases) until the critical angle of attack (the stalling angle) is reached.

40. If the Pilot increases the angle of attack so that the lifting ability (CLift) of the wing is increased, the same **Lift** force can be generated by the wing at a (higher/lower) velocity.

41. The airflow around a well-cambered wing at zero angle of attack will still have to accelerate over the upper surface – increased velocity = decreased static pressure – and so there (will/will not) be some Lift produced.

42. A symmetrical aerofoil (whose upper and lower surfaces are the same shape) at zero angle of attack will have similar airflows over both upper and lower surfaces. Therefore at zero angle of attack, the Lift generated by a symmetrical aerofoil will be (positive/zero/negative)

43. A symmetrical aerofoil moving through the air at zero degrees angle of attack:
    (a) will generate a low static pressure above the wing and a high static pressure beneath the wing.
    (b) will produce a high pressure above the wing and a low pressure beneath the wing.
    (c) will cause a similar acceleration of the airflow over both upper and lower surfaces, similar velocities of flow generating similar pressures and therefore no Lift.
    (d) will cause the air over the upper surface to travel faster than the air over the lower surface.

44. As the angle of attack of a symmetrical aerofoil is gradually increased from zero, the lifting ability (increases/decreases/stays the same).

45. Lift acts at .. degrees to the remote relative airflow.

46. The 'Coefficient of Lift' depends upon the shape of the wing chosen by the designer and the A.... of A....., which the Pilot has control over.

47. In normal flight, as the angle of attack is increased, the lifting ability of the wing known as its *'Coefficient of Lift'* (increases/decreases).

48. The **Lift** generated by an aerofoil is:
    (a) proportional to the square of the velocity of the relative airflow.
    (b) proportional to the velocity of the relative airflow.
    (c) inversely proportional to the air density.
    (d) inversely proportional to the wing surface area.

EXERCISES 4 — DRAG.

1. Drag (opposes/encourages) motion through the air.

2. Drag acts (parallel to/at 90 degrees to) the relative airflow.

3. The force used to overcome the Drag in straight and level cruising flight is the T..... produced by the engine/propeller combination.

4. If Drag can be kept low, then T..... can be kept low.

5. Total Drag is the sum total of the various Drag forces acting on the aeroplane which act (parallel to/perpendicular to) and (in the same direction as/opposite to) the direction of flight.

6. Total Drag is considered in two basic groups:
    (1) that Drag which comes about in the generation of Lift, known as I...... Drag, and
    (2) that Drag which is NOT associated with the generation of Lift, known as P....... Drag.

7. Parasite Drag consists of S... F......., F... D... and Inter....... Drag.

8. Flush rivetting and polishing the surface of an aeroplane reduce ....

9. Roughness on a surface, such as an accumulation of insects or ice-accretion, will increase S... F....... .

10. As airspeed increases, Drag due to skin friction (increases/decreases).

11. Form Drag occurs when the airflow actually sep...... from the surface of the aerofoil and becomes turb..... .

12. To reduce Form Drag, separation of the boundary layer airflow from the wing surface should be (delayed/encouraged).

13. Streamlining of shapes reduces ....

14. The additional turbulence caused by interference between various airflows around the aeroplane is called Inter....... D... .

15. As the aeroplane flies faster, Parasite Drag (increases/decreases).

16. The Drag produced as a by-product in the generation of Lift is called I...... D... .

17. For a wing to produce an upwards Lift, the static pressure on the upper surface must be (higher/lower) than on the lower surface.

18. Air flows around the wingtips from the higher pressure area on the (upper/lower) surface of the wing into the area of lower pressure. This forms Wingtip V....... .

19. The spanwise flow of air on the lower surface of the wing is (outwards to the wingtip/inwards to the wing root).

20. The spanwise flow of air on the upper wing surface is (outwards towards the tip/inwards towards the root).

21. As well as the strong wingtip vortices, where the two airflows from the upper and lower surfaces of the wing meet behind the wing, because of their different spanwise flows, they form a sheet of Trailing Edge V....... .

22. The pressure difference between the upper and lower surfaces of the wing is greatest at (high/low) angles of attack.

23. Therefore, the formation of wingtip vortices and Induced Drag is greatest at (high/low) angles of attack.

24. High angles of attack are associated with (high/low) speeds in straight and level flight.

25. Therefore, Induced Drag is greatest at high angles of attack and (high/low) airspeeds in straight and level flight.

26. Vortices that are generated at the wingtips:
    (a) cause much of the Drag at low speed;
    (b) cause much of the Drag at high speed;
    (c) cause a decrease in Drag.

27. The designer can help minimise the formation of wingtip vortices and Induced Drag by using wings of (high/low) Aspect Ratio, W...out or wingtip modification.

28. A high aspect ratio wing has a (short/long) span and a (short/long) chord.

29. A wing with *washout* has a lower angle of attack at the (wingtip/wing root).

30. Induced Drag increases at (high/low) speeds.

31. Parasite Drag increases at (high/low) speeds.

32. The Total Drag is at a minimum at (high speed/low speed/at a speed where the Parasite Drag and Induced Drag are equal).

33. At the minimum total drag speed, the propeller has only to provide minimum T..... .

34. At low speeds and high angles of attack, because of the greater .... Drag, the Thrust must be (greater/less).

35. At high speeds and low angles of attack, because of the greater .... Drag, the Thrust requirement is (greater/less).

36. To maintain a steady speed straight and level, the Thrust required is:
    (a) the same at all speeds.
    (b) greatest at normal cruise speed;
    (c) greater at a speed just above the stall than at cruise speed.

37. At high angles of attack and low airspeeds:
    (a) the induced Coefficient of Drag is high.
    (b) the induced Coefficient of Drag is low.
    (c) the parasite Coefficient of Drag is high.
    (d) all of the above are incorrect.

EXERCISES 5 — LIFT/DRAG RATIO.

1. If you require 1200 units of Lift to support the aeroplane, and the Drag is 100 units, then the L/D ratio is (10:1/12:1/120:1/5:1).

2. At high angles of attack, the Drag is high due to I...... D.... For 1200 units of Lift, the cost might be 240 units of Drag. The L/D ratio is .... .

3. At low angles of attack and high speeds, the total drag is high due to P....... Drag. If the required 1200 units of Lift is generated at a cost of 200 units, the L/D ratio is... .

4. If at say 4 degrees angle of attack where the total drag is a minimum for the particular aerofoil we are considering, the 1200 units of Lift is obtained for a cost of only 80 units Drag, then the L/D ratio is ... .

5. The angle of attack that gives the best L/D ratio is the (most/least) efficient angle of attack.

6. If you fly at the airspeed obtained at the best L/D ratio, then the required lift is obtained for the (minimum/maximum) drag.

7. Minimum Drag means (minimum/maximum) Thrust to maintain airspeed.

8. The term **'Lift/Drag'** ratio:
   (a) can be used to describe the aerodynamic efficiency of the wing.
   (b) is the ratio of the Lift produced from an aerofoil compared to the Drag produced from the aerofoil.
   (c) varies as the angle of attack of the aerofoil changes.
   (d) all the above statements are correct.

EXERCISES 6 — THRUST FROM THE PROPELLER.

1. A propeller converts engine torque into T..... .

2. A propeller is similar to a wing in that it is an Aero.... .

3. The angle that the propeller blade makes with the plane of its rotation is called the B.... A.... .

4. To ensure that it operates at an efficient angle of attack over its full length, the propeller blade is (twisted/straight).

5. The blade angle is greatest near the (hub/tip).

6. The fastest moving part of the propeller blade is near the (hub/tip).

7. The fastest moving part of the aeroplane is the P........ T.. .

8. The Total Reaction aerodynamic force on a wing is resolved into two components – Lift and Drag. The Total Reaction on the propeller blade is resolved into two components – T..... and engine torque.

9. A fixed-pitch propeller is efficient at only one set of r.. and air..... conditions.

10. For operating at high rpm and low forward airspeeds, the most efficient propeller would have a (fine/coarse) pitch.

11. For operating at very high airspeeds and low rpm, the most efficient propeller would have a (fine/coarse) pitch.

12. A *'variable-pitch'* propeller (constant speed unit) is efficient over a wide range of pow.. and airspeed conditions.

13. The slipstream effect from the propeller can cause the nose to Y.. . This is because the slipstream hits one side of the R..... more than the other.

14. When power is applied in an aeroplane fitted with a propeller that turns clockwise when viewed from behind, the aeroplane will tend to roll to the (left/right) and yaw to the (left/right).

15. As the forward speed of an aeroplane with a fixed-pitch propeller increases, what happens to the angle of attack of the propeller blades if the rpm remains constant:
    (a) angle of attack decreases as forward speed increases.
    (b) angle of attack increases as forward speed increases.
    (c) angle of attack remains unaltered as forward speed increases.
    (d) none of these.

16. If the airspeed of an aeroplane fitted with a fixed-pitch propeller is increased at constant power (say by entering a dive), the rpm will:
    (a) remain constant.
    (b) increase.
    (c) decrease.

EXERCISES 7 — STABILITY.

1. If the Centre of Pressure is aft of the Centre of Gravity, then the Lift.Weight couple will have a (nose-down/nose-up) pitching moment. Draw this.

2. If the Thrust line is lower than the Drag line, then the Thrust.Drag couple will have a (nose-up/nose-down) pitching moment. Draw this.

3. In the above situation (questions 1 and 2), if there was a sudden loss of Thrust from the engine/propeller, the nose would (pitch up/pitch down/neither).

4. If the L.W and T.D couples do not balance each other out, then there is a resultant pitching moment that will raise or lower the nose of the aircraft. A small balancing force with a long moment arm is provided by the T........ or the H......... S......... .

5. For an aeroplane to be in equilibrium in level flight:
    (a) Lift exceeds Weight, and Thrust equals Drag.
    (b) Lift equals Weight, and Thrust equals Drag.
    (c) Lift equals Drag, and Thrust exceeds Weight.
    (d) Lift, Drag, Thrust and Weight are all equal.

6. If, as is usual, the Thrust line is not aligned with the Drag line, then any power change (will/will not) cause a tendency for the nose to pitch.

7. 'Stability' is the natural ability of the aeroplane to return to its original condition after a disturbance like a gust (with/without) any action being taken on the part of the Pilot.

8. The axis that runs along the aeroplane from nose to tail is called the L........... axis, and rotation about this axis is called R...... .

9. The axis that runs 'across-ship' is called the .... axis, and rotation about this axis is called ....

10. The axis that is perpendicular or normal to the longitudinal and lateral axes is called the ...... axis, and rotation about it is called ....

11. The most important factor contributing to Longitudinal Stability is the T........ .

12. The restoring moment arm of the tailplane is greatest when the Centre of Gravity is (well forward/somewhat aft).

13. Therefore, Longitudinal Stability is greater with a (forward/aft) CG.

14. In most training aeroplanes, the Centre of Pressure is (ahead of/behind/at the same position as) the Centre of Gravity and the tailplane produces (an upward/zero/a downward) force.

15. If the aeroplane is loaded incorrectly so that the CG is forward of the allowable range, then the elevator force required to flare the aeroplane for landing will be:
    (a) the same as usual.
    (b) greater than usual.
    (c) less than usual.

16. Directional Stability is improved with a (large/small) fin or V....... Stabiliser.

17. Lateral Stability is increased if a wing has Di...... .

18. A high wing aircraft is laterally stable with a high CP and a (high/low) CG.

19. If an aircraft is displaced in roll by a gust, i.e. a wing drops, the aircraft will start to S...s... . The high keel surfaces, like the fin, will cause the nose to Y.. .

20. If an aircraft is yawed, then it will sideslip and the dihedral will cause it to R... .

21. R... and Y.. are very closely inter-related.

22. On the ground, the CG for a tricycle undercarriage aircraft (i.e. nose- wheel) must be (forward/aft) of the main wheels.

23. On the ground, the CG of a *'tail-dragger'* must be (forward, aft) of the main wheels.

24. When taxying fast and the brakes are applied heavily, a tailwheel aircraft (is/is not) more directionally stable than a nosewheel aircraft.

EXERCISES 8 — CONTROL.

1. The primary control in pitch is provided by the ....

2. Nose movement up and down is in the pitching plane. It involves angular movement of the aeroplane around its centre of gravity and its (lateral/longitudinal/normal) axis.

3. To raise the nose, the Pilot exerts backwards pressure on the control column. The elevators move so that the tail of the aeroplane goes (up/down).

4. To raise the nose and lower the tail of the aeroplane, the trailing edge of the elevator moves (up/down).

5. A stabilator is:
   (a) a balancing weight.
   (b) a vertical fin.
   (c) a fixed-tailplane and movable elevator.
   (d) a movable horizontal stabiliser.

6. When the Pilot moves the control column aft to raise the nose of the aeroplane, the leading edge of a stabilator will (rise/fall/remain stationary).

7. The primary control in roll is by the A....... .

8. Rolling is angular motion about the .... axis running through the CG.

9. For the right wing to rise, the Pilot moves the control column to the .... .

10. At normal flight speeds for the right wing to rise, the right aileron will (go down/rise).

11. For the right wing to rise, the right aileron goes down. The left aileron goes (up/down).

12. The area below the wing has (higher/lower) static pressure than the area above the wing.

13. The aileron going down (i.e. on the rising wing) goes into an area of (higher/lower) pressure and will experience (more/less) drag than the other aileron.

14. As an aeroplane is banking to the left for a left turn, the extra drag on the right aileron will tend to yaw the nose (in the direction of/away from) the turn.

15. The Aileron Drag that yaws the nose away from a turn as an aeroplane is banking is called A...... A...... Y.. .

16. Aileron Drag or Adverse Aileron Yaw can be designed out of the aeroplane by the use of D.......... A....... or by F....-type Ailerons.

17. If differential ailerons are used to counteract the effect of adverse aileron yaw, one aileron will rise by an amount (greater than/less than/the same as) the other aileron is lowered.

18. If differential ailerons are used to counteract the effect of adverse aileron yaw then, compared to the aileron on the down-going wing, the aileron on the up-going wing will be (raised/lowered) to a (greater/lesser/similar) extent.

19. The primary control in yaw is provided by the ....

20. Yawing is about the ...... axis that passes through the CG.

21. Yawing increases the speed of the outer wing causing its Lift to (increase/decrease), leading to a R... .

22. Yaw also generates a sideslip, and the dihedral on the more forward wing will cause it to (rise/fall).

23. A yaw leads to a R... .

24. Movement of the flight control surfaces is:
    (a) limited by air loads.
    (b) limited by mechanical stops.
    (c) not limited.

25. Increased airflow over control surfaces (increases/decreases) their effectiveness.

26. At high airspeeds the control surfaces are (more/less) effective than at low airspeeds.

27. Slipstream from the propeller over the rudder and elevators (increases/decreases) their effectiveness.

28. At low speeds near the stalling angle, high Thrust from the propeller sends a slipstream over the (elevator/rudder/ailerons).

29. An aeroplane designer may use 'aerodynamic balance', such as the balance tab, horn balance or inset hinge, to reduce the control pressures required of a Pilot. (True/False)?

30. Aerodynamic balance designed to assist a Pilot in deflecting a flight control surface may be:
    (a) a trim tab.
    (b) an anti-balance tab.
    (c) a mass placed forward of the hinge line.
    (d) a balance tab or some part of the surface placed ahead of the hinge line.

31. If a Pilot is exerting a steady backwards pressure on the control column, then he can remove this steady load by using the elevator T... T.., which may be controlled by a small wheel in the cockpit known as the T... Wh... .

32. The pressure that a Pilot feels through the controls is determined by the hinge moment of the control surface. The pressure distribution around the control surface can be altered to reduce the hinge moment by the use of T... T... .

33. Trim tabs are very effective. A small movement of a trim tab can have a (large/small) effect because of its moment arm to the control hinge.

34. Once a simple elevator trim tab has been set by the Pilot to remove any steady pressure on the control column, the tab position (will/will not) remain fixed relative to the elevator when the Pilot moves the control column fore and aft.

35. The correct method of using an elevator trim in an aircraft is to:
    (a) change the attitude with the elevator and/or the power with the throttle, allow the aeroplane to settle down, and then use the trim to remove steady control column pressure.
    (b) change the attitude with the trim.
    (c) change attitude, power and trim simultaneously.

36. Ailerons on some light aircraft have a fixed trim tab in the form of a metal strip that (may/must not) be adjusted on the ground following a test flight so that (lateral/longitudinal) level flight is more easily achieved.

37. An anti-balance tab may be designed into a flight control surface to:
    (a) provide 'feel' to the Pilot and prevent excessive control movements.
    (b) prevent control surface flutter.
    (c) reduce the balancing moment required from the taiplane.
    (d) aerodynamically assist the Pilot in moving the flight control surface.

38. If the stabilator is moved in the pre-flight external inspection, then the anti-balance tab should:
    (a) move in the same direction.
    (b) move in the opposite direction.
    (c) not move.

39. If the elevator is moved in the pre-flight external inspection, then the balance tab should:
    (a) move in the same direction.
    (b) move in the opposite direction.
    (c) not move.

40. A mass balance is used to:
    (a) stop flutter of the control surface when the aeroplane is parked.
    (b) prevent control surface flutter in flight.
    (c) keep the control surface flared in flight.
    (d) relieve control pressures on the Pilot.

EXERCISES 9 — FLAPS.

1. Flaps can (increase/decrease) the lifting capability, or C$_{Lift}$, of a wing.

2. If flaps increase the lifting ability of a wing, then the required Lift can be generated at a (higher/lower) airspeed.

3. The extension of flap (lowers/raises) the stalling speed.

4. The approach speed with flap extended may be (lower/higher) than the approach speed for a flapless landing.

5. Trailing edge flaps not only increase Lift – flaps also increase D... .

6. In the early stages of their extension, such as at the take-off flap settings, the flaps may be thought of as L... flaps. At their full extension, such as on approach to land, they may be thought of as D... flaps.

7. The percentage increase in Drag usually exceeds that in Lift when the flaps are extended, therefore the Lift/Drag ratio is (less/more).

8. The extension of flaps on a glide approach allows a (steeper/flatter) approach flight path or approach angle.

9. With flaps extended, the nose attitude of the aeroplane is (lower/higher).

10. Cruising with flaps extended may be achieved at a (higher/lower) airspeed, than when clean.

11. Cruising with flap extended, such as in a low speed *precautionary search* to inspect a possible landing field, allows the Pilot (better/worse) visibility of the ground because of the (higher/lower) nose attitude.

12. Extending the flaps to an appropriate take-off setting (shortens/lengthens) the ground run.

13. Extending full flap for landing allows for (faster/slower) approach speeds and a (longer/shorter) landing run.

14. Wing flaps at the recommended take-off setting:
    (a) increase lifting ability for a small penalty in Drag.
    (b) increase lifting ability for a large penalty in Drag.
    (c) significantly increase Drag for a small decrease in lifting ability.
    (d) will not affect Lift or Drag.

15. Wing flaps set to the recommended landing setting:
    (a) increase lifting ability for a small increase in Drag.
    (b) cause a large Drag increase and a small increase in lifting ability.
    (c) significantly increase Drag for a small decrease in lifting ability.
    (d) will not affect Lift or Drag.

16. Extending the wing flaps will (increase/decrease/not alter) the stalling speed.

17. Slats installed on the leading edge of a wing will (delay/ promote/prevent/not affect) the stall.

18. Slots increase the angle of attack at which a wing stalls by delaying the separation and break up of the smooth airflow over the upper surface of the wing. (True/False)?

EXERCISES 10 — STRAIGHT AND LEVEL.

1. In steady straight and level flight, the aeroplane (is/is not) in equilibrium.

2. In steady straight and level flight, the four main forces acting on the aeroplane are ...., ..., ... and ....

3. In steady straight and level flight, the Lift force is (equal/not equal) to the Weight.

4. In steady straight and level flight, the Thrust from the engine/propeller is (equal/not equal) to the Drag.

5. The four main forces acting on an aeroplane in-flight are balanced by an aerodynamic force generated by the:
    (a) propeller.
    (b) horizontal stabiliser.
    (c) flaps.
    (d) fin.

6. Write down the formula that makes it easy for us to remember the important factors influencing the production of **Lift** by an aerofoil.

7. If V represents the True Air Speed, then '½ Rho V-squared' represents the I....... A.. S.... .

8. The Coefficient of Lift (C~Lift~) represents the shape of the aerofoil and the A.... o. A...... .

9. The Lift produced by a wing can be altered by the Pilot changing the A.... o. A..... or by changing the I....... A.. S... . If you want the Lift generated to remain the same, then as one increases, the other must be made to (decrease/increase).

10. If Indicated Air Speed is increased, then for the same Lift to be generated in straight and level flight, the angle of attack must be (increased/reduced).

11. If Indicated Air Speed is decreased, then for the aeroplane to remain in straight and level flight, the angle of attack must be (increased/reduced).

12. Low IASs are associated with (high/low) angles of attack.

13. High IASs are associated with (low/high) angles of attack.

14. Straight and level flight at a high speed is associated with a (high/low) nose attitude.

15. Straight and level flight at a low airspeed is associated with a (high/low) nose attitude.

16. In steady straight and level flight, the Weight is balanced by the ..... .

17. If the Weight decreases, then, for straight and level flight to continue, the Lift must ....

18. The Lift generated can be decreased by flying at the same angle of attack but a (higher/lower) Indicated Air Speed.

19. The Lift generated can be lowered by flying at the same airspeed, but a (higher/lower) angle of attack.

20. In steady straight and level flight, the Drag is balanced by the T..... .

21. For steady straight and level flight to be maintained, a large Drag needs to be balanced by a large ..... .

22. At very high speed for your aircraft, say well in excess of the normal cruise speed, the Drag is (high/low).

23. At very low speeds, say just above the stalling speed, the Drag is also very (high/low).

24. Straight and level flight at very high speeds requires (high/low) power.

25. Steady straight and level flight at very low speeds (say just above the stalling speed) requires (high/low) power.

26. To generate the same Lift in straight and level flight at a higher altitude fly at the same I....... A.. S.... .

27. At the same IAS, but at different altitudes, the A.... o. A..... will be the same.

28. The Indicated Air Speed is associated with the Dynamic Pressure '½ Rho V-squared', where *'Rho'* is the air density and *V* is the Velocity or True Air Speed. If Indicated Air Speed remains the same as air density (Rho) decreases, say with a gain in altitude, then the Velocity or True Air Speed must (increase/stay the same/decrease).

29. In climbing at the same IAS as shown on the cockpit Air Speed Indicator, the TAS will be gradually (increasing/decreasing).

EXERCISES 11 — CLIMBING.

1. In straight and level flight at a steady speed, the Thrust is equal to the Drag. For a steady climb, Thrust must (exceed/equal/be less than) Drag.

2. In a steady climb, the Thrust not only helps overcome the Drag, but also part of the ...... of the aeroplane.

3. The angle of climb that the aeroplane is capable of depends upon the 'excess thrust', i.e. the amount of Thrust over and above that required to balance the D... .

4. The angle of climb of the same aeroplane with the Pilot and three passengers will be (greater/less) than the angle of climb when only the Pilot is on board.

5. Rate of Climb is expressed in (feet per minute/mph/knots/litres).

6. An aeroplane that climbs 350 ft in one minute has a RoC of (20/100/700/350) fpm.

7. An aeroplane that climbs 700 ft in 2 minutes has a RoC of (50/260/350/700) fpm.

8. An aeroplane that climbs 200 ft in ½ minute should climb ... ft in 1 minute.

9. An aeroplane that climbs 250 ft in 30 seconds has a rate of climb of ..... fpm.

10. To climb 500 ft in 1 minute, your rate of climb needs to be .... fpm.

11. To climb 1200 ft in 2 minutes, your RoC needs to be ... fpm.

12. Rate of Climb is shown in the cockpit on the V....... S.... I........ .

13. Rate of Climb depends upon the 'excess power', i.e. the power in excess of that required to overcome the .....

14. The altitude at which the climb performance of an aeroplane falls close to zero is called its ....

15. Climb performance at sea level is (better/worse) than climb performance at high altitudes.

16. Climb performance on a hot day is (better/worse) than climb performance on a cold day.

17. If the aeroplane has a rate of climb of 500 fpm, it will climb 500 ft in 1 minute. How much will it climb in 1 minute if there is a head wind?

18. An aeroplane will reach a given altitude in the minimum **Time** if it climbs at the (best gradient or angle climb speed/the best rate of climb speed/the cruise-climb speed).

19. An aeroplane will clear obstacles by a greater margin at (the best gradient – best angle speed/the best rate of climb speed/the cruise-climb speed).

20. The aeroplane will travel furthest horizontally over the ground at the (best gradient climb speed/best rate climb speed/cruise-climb speed).

21. If the aeroplane is climbing in a headwind following take-off, will its climb angle **relative to the ground** and obstacles on the ground be steeper than if there was no wind?

22. Would an aeroplane taking-off in a tailwind have less clearance over obstacles in the climb-out than if a headwind were present?

23. Which statement correctly describes an aeroplane in a steady climb?
    (a) Lift is equal to Weight, and Thrust is equal to Drag.
    (b) Lift is less than Weight, and Thrust is greater than Drag.
    (c) Lift is less than Weight, and Thrust is less than Drag.
    (d) Lift is greater than Weight, and Thrust is less than Drag.

24. The climb performance of a heavy aeroplane compared to when it is light is (better/worse/the same).

25. The climb performance of an aeroplane with low power set compared to high power is (better/worse/the same).

26. The climb performance of an aeroplane flown at a non-recommended climbing speed is (better than/worse than/the same as) the climb performance when flown at the recommended speed for the desired type of climb.

27. A prolonged en route climb is best flown:
    (a) at a relatively low airspeed to gain height quickly.
    (b) at a relatively low airspeed for better engine cooling and improved visibility.
    (c) at a relatively high airspeed for better engine cooling.

28. The take-off ground run may be shortened by using a small flap extension, but once in-flight, the climb angle through the air is (steeper/flatter/the same) when compared to a clean (un-flapped) aeroplane.

29. The angle of climb through the air and the rate of climb of an aeroplane are not affected by wind. What is affected is the f..... p... relative to the gr.... .

EXERCISES 12 — DESCENDING.

1. In a glide, 3 of the 4 main forces are acting on the aeroplane. They are .... ?

2. In a steady glide the aeroplane (is/is not) in equilibrium.

3. In a glide the Weight is balanced by the ... and .... .

4. In a descent, a component of the Weight acts along the flight path, counteracting the Drag and contributing to the aeroplanes forward speed. (True/False)?

5. If Drag is increased, the glide becomes (steeper/shallower).

6. If power is added, the descent becomes (steeper/shallower).

7. If flaps are lowered, the Drag is (increased/decreased).

8. If flaps are lowered, the descent becomes (steeper/shallower).

9. A heavy aeroplane will glide (further/not as far/the same distance), compared with when it is light. To glide the same distance as when it is light, a heavy aeroplane will need a (higher/lower) airspeed on descent.

10. A headwind will (increase/decrease) glide distance over the ground.

11. A tailwind will (increase/decrease) glide distance over the ground.

12. If you glide with a Rate of Descent of 500 fpm, then how long will it take you to descend 3000 ft?

13. If you have a RoD of 500 fpm, how long will it take you to descend 3000 ft in a 20 kt headwind?

14. If ice forms on the aeroplane, the Drag will (increase/decrease).

15. Increased Drag will make the glide (steeper/shallower).

16. Ice accretion will make a glide (steeper/shallower).

17. The addition of power will (steepen/flatten) the descent.

18. Adding power will (increase/decrease/not alter) the rate of descent.

19. Flying faster than or slower than the correct descent speed will (steepen/flatten) the descent angle through the air.

20. Lowering flap in a glide will (steepen/flatten/not alter) the descent angle through the air.

21. The rate of descent will (increase/decrease/remain the same) when descending into wind.

22. Wind does not affect descent through the air, but it does affect flight path o... the gr.... .

23. Reduced Weight does not change the glide angle, but (increases/reduces) the best gliding speed.

EXERCISES 13 — TURNING.

1. The force that causes turning is called the Cen....... Force.

.2. For a turning aeroplane, the centripetal force is provided by banking the aeroplane and tilting the L... force produced by the wings.

3. The Pilot banks the aeroplane by using the a......s.

4. To retain a vertical component to balance the Weight, the Lift force required in a level turn must be (greater than/equal to/less than) the Lift required when straight and level.

5. To develop the increased Lift force required in a turn at the same speed, the a.... of ...... must be increased by the Pilot applying back pressure to the control column.

6. The steeper the level turn, the greater the L... force required, the greater the A.... of A..... needed to produce it, and the greater the B... pressure the Pilot needs to apply to the control column.

7. Load Factor is the ratio of L... produced by the wings/aircraft W......

8. If the Load Factor when straight and level is 1 (which it must be), then the Load Factor in a level turn will be (greater than/equal to/less than) 1.

9. In a 60 degree level banked turn, the required Lift is twice that in straight and level flight. The load factor is ....?

10. Rudder is used by the Pilot to b...... the turn.

11. In a turn, due to the requirement for increased Lift, there is also increased D... .

12. To maintain airspeed in a turn, the Pilot must apply p.... to overcome the increased Drag.

13. At the same airspeed, the a.... o. a..... is greater in a turn than in straight and level flight.

14. In a turn, for the same airspeed the angle of attack is higher, and therefore the stalling angle of attack will be reached at (a higher/a lower/the same) airspeed as in straight and level flight.

15. In straight and level turns there is a tendency to (overbank/underbank).

16. In climbing turns, there is a tendency to (overbank/underbank).

17. In descending turns, there (is/is not) a strong tendency to underbank or overbank.

18. The ball out to the left means more (left/right) rudder pedal pressure from the Pilot is required to balance the turn.

19. Angle of bank is controlled by the a......s .

20. Nose position and height are controlled by the e........ .

21. The turn is balanced by keeping the ball in the centre with the r..... .

EXERCISES 14 — STALLING.

1. Stalling occurs at high angles of attack when the airflow around the aerofoil is unable to remain streamline, separates from the aerofoil surface and becomes T........ .

2. Turbulent flow upsets the formation of the areas of low S..... pressure so necessary to the production of L... .

3. The lowering of the lifting ability of the wing beyond this critical or stalling angle of attack is described as (increasing/decreasing) the Coefficient of Lift.

4. At angles of attack beyond the stalling angle, the Lift force produced by the wing is markedly (lower/higher).

5. Beyond the stalling angle, the Centre of Pressure for the diminished Lift force moves (rearwards/forwards), causing the nose to drop.

6. If the wings stall, the turbulent airflow over the tailplane may cause control b..... .

7. The stalling angle on a typical light training aircraft could be (0/4/16) degrees angle of attack.

8. Stalling is associated with a particular a.... of a..... .

9. Write down the formula that summarises neatly for us the factors involved in the production of Lift. LIFT = C$_{Lift}$ x ....

10. Of the factors involved in the production of Lift, the Pilot can change A.... of A..... and I........ A.. S.... .

11. Stalling occurs at a particular angle and is associated with an A.... of A..... , but in straight and level flight at a given weight, every angle of attack is associated with a particular I........ A.. S.... .

12. Lift is a direct function of (airspeed/airspeed-squared).

13. Airspeed is a direct function of (Lift/the square root of Lift).

14. S....... s..... depends upon the square root of the Lift required.

15. Lift required depends upon the W..... and/or the L... F..... .

16. If the Weight is lower, the Lift required is (higher/lower) and the stalling speed straight and level is (higher/lower).

17. If the weight of an aeroplane was increased in-flight, say by the formation of ice, its stalling speed would (increase/decrease).

18. If the Lift required from the wings increased due to the Pilot banking the aeroplane and applying back pressure to the control column to maintain height, then the stalling speed compared to that straight and level will (increase/stay the same/decrease).

19. In a banked turn at a constant height, the load factor is (increased/decreased/equal to 1).

20. The steeper the turn, the (greater/smaller) the load factor.

21. The steeper the turn, the (higher/lower) the stalling speed.

22. Stalling speed (increases/decreases/remains unaltered) with an increase in angle of bank.

23. Pulling out of a fast and steep dive, the load factor (is increased/is decreased/remains at 1 as in smooth straight and level flight).

24. Pulling out of a fast and steep dive, the stalling speed (is increased/is decreased/remains the same as straight and level).

25. If the angle of bank is 30 degrees, using the graphs in our notes, determine the increase in stalling speed over that for straight and level.

26. In a 60 degrees steep turn, the stalling speed will be ..% greater than that for straight and level.

27. Using the 'g-factor' graph, what percentage increase in stalling speed would you expect if you pulled out of a dive and experienced 4g?

28. Stalling Speed varies with the square root of the L... force required to be generated by the wings.

29. At higher weights, the wings need to produce (more/less/the same) Lift.

30. At higher weights, the Stalling Speed straight and level is (higher/the same/lower).

31. Stalling occurs at a critical ..... for an aerofoil.

32. Lift is a function of *'angle of attack'* and *'Indicated Air Speed'*. If the aeroplane flies at different altitudes, its Lift requirement straight and level at the same weight remains the same. Therefore at the stalling angle of attack the Indicated Air Speed will be (the same/higher/lower) at all altitudes.

33. The stalling IAS (varies/does not vary) with altitude.

34. If the aeroplane approaches the stalling angle with a lot of power on, the slipstream adds a lot of kinetic energy to the airflow and separation and stalling is delayed. The stalling speed power-on is (less than/the same as/greater than) the power-off stalling speed.

35. It is preferable to have a wing designed so that it stalls first near the (wingtip/wing root/trailing edge).

36. Washout designed into a wing (causes/does not cause) the inner section of the wing to stall first.

37. Stalling first towards the inner section of the wing is preferable because:
    (a) it sends turbulent air over the tailplane causing buffet which acts as a warning to the Pilot before the whole wing stalls.
    (b) the tendency for the aeroplane to roll is less if one wing stalls ahead of the other.
    (c) the ailerons may not lose their effectiveness as early.
    (d) all of the above.

38. Flaps (lower/increase) the stalling speed.

39. Stalling Indicated Air Speed when flying into a head wind is (higher/lower/the same) as stalling IAS when flying in a tail wind.

40. If the aeroplane is flying at a high angle of attack near the stall and a wing drops, then:
    (a) the dropped wing will have a smaller angle of attack and a greater possibility of stalling.
    (b) the dropped wing will have a higher angle of attack and a greater possibility of stalling.
    (c) the dropped wing will have a higher angle of attack and a lesser possibility of stalling.
    (d) the dropped wing will have a smaller angle of attack and a lesser possibility of stalling.

41. Attempting to pick-up a dropped wing with aileron near the stall on some aeroplanes can:
    (a) stall the dropped wing by increasing its angle of attack beyond the stalling angle.
    (b) stall the upper wing by increasing its angle of attack beyond the stalling angle.
    (c) stall the upper wing by decreasing its angle of attack.

42. During the entry to a spin, the angle of attack of the dropping wing (increases/decreases) and that of the rising wing (increases/decreases).

FOR YOUR OWN SUMMARY.

Draw diagrams to indicate:

1. Camber.

2. Aspect Ratio.

3. Relative Airflow.

4. Angle of Attack.

5. Angle of Incidence.

6. Chord.

7. Span.

8. Lift.

9. Thrust.

10. Centre of Pressure.

11. Centre of Gravity.

12. Dihedral.

13. *'Pendulum'* Effect.

14. Sweepback.

15. Indicated Air Speed, IAS.

16. True Air Speed, TAS.

17. Stalling angle of attack.

18. Stalling speed straight and level.

19. Stalling speed with increased Load Factors – turning, pulling out.

20. Stalling speed at higher weights.

21. Induced drag.

22. Parasite drag.

23. Primary flight controls.

24. The major axes of movement.

25. Initial and further effects of the primary flight controls.

26. The effect of lowering flap on Lift, Drag, attitude, and approach angle, of an aeroplane in flight.

27. The function of trim tabs.

28. The Lift curve as angle of attack increases.

29. The Drag curve.

30. The effect on stalling speed of weight, angle of bank, load factor, power, flap setting and height.

31. The effect on **climb performance** resulting from changes in weight, power, airspeed, wind and flap setting.

32. Repeat the same for **descent performance.**

33. Aileron drag.

EXERCISES 15 — THE AIRFRAME.

1. The main structural component of the wing is the ....

2. The aerofoil shape of the wing surface is due to the .... .

3. The most usual form of fuselage construction in training aeroplanes where the skin covers a light structure and carries much of the stress is called ....

4. Should an aeroplane be tied down so that ropes are taut?

5. Should pitot covers be used when overnight parking?

6. A Flight Control surface lock is used:
   (a) to lock the Flight Control in a fixed position when the aircraft is parked to prevent damage by strong and/or gusty winds.
   (b) to lock the Flight Control in a fixed position during steady straight and level flight.
   (c) to lock Trim Tabs into a fixed position.

7. Recall suggested actions in handling a cabin fire.

8. Recall suggested actions following an engine fire in flight.

9. Ventilating air (should/need not) always be used.

10. Air from a heat exchanger around the (engine air intake/exhaust manifold) is used in many light aircraft cabin heating systems.

11. Regular inspections of the engine exhaust system should be made to ensure that there are no leaks or cracks in the heat exchanger/exhaust manifold area that might allow dangerous exhaust gases such as .... into the cabin.

12. If a leak of engine gases into the cabin heating system is suspected the cabin heating air should be turned (*FULL ON/OFF*) and the ventilation air (reduced/increased).

EXERCISES 16 — THE AEROPLANE ENGINE.

1. Name the four strokes of a piston engine commencing with the Induction stroke.

2. During the induction stroke the i.... valve is open to allow the fuel/air mixture into the c........ .

3. During most of the compression stroke the inlet valve is ...... and the exhaust valve is ....

4. During most of the power stroke the inlet valve is ...... and the exhaust valve is ....

5. During most of the exhaust stroke the inlet valve is ...... and the exhaust valve is .... .

6. TDC and BDC refer to ... . and .... of the piston movement in the cylinder.

7. The inlet valve opening just prior to TDC and the commencement of the induction stroke is called v.... l... .

8. The inlet valve not closing until just after BDC on the completion of the induction stroke is called v.... l.. .

9. The exhaust valve opens just (before/after) BDC and the commencement of the exhaust stroke.

10. The exhaust valve closes just (before/after) TDC and the completion of the exhaust stroke.

11. The period when both inlet and exhaust valves are open simultaneously is called v.... o...... .

12. Compressing a gas causes its pressure to (increase/decrease/remain the same).

13. Compressing a gas causes its temperature to (increase/decrease/remain the same).

14. Ignition occurs in each cylinder just before the end of the .... stroke.

15. Ignition occurs in each cylinder just (as/before/after) the piston reaches Top Dead Centre.

16. The function of the piston aeroplane engine is to:
    (a) convert chemical energy to heat energy to mechanical energy.
    (b) use a mixture of fuel and air and the process of combustion to create power.
    (c) burn fuel only without the air being necessary to create power.
    (d) both (a) and (b) are correct.

17. To ignite the fuel/air mixture in the cylinder, just prior to TDC and the commencement of the power stroke there is a high-voltage s.... .

18. The s.... is produced by the i....... system.

19. Two important components of the ignition system are the m...... and d.......... .

20. Each cylinder receives a spark and fires (once/twice) in every two revolutions of the crankshaft.

21. Most aircraft have (one/two) magneto systems.

22. The magnetos are engine-driven and act as self-contained generators of electrical power to the spark plugs. (True/False)?

23. If one of the magneto switches is turned to *OFF,* there (should/should not) be an rpm drop.

24. Two separate ignition systems provide a higher level of s..... and more efficient c......... in the combustion chamber.

25. Switching the ignition *OFF* connects the magneto systems to *Earth*. (True/False)?

26. If a magneto earth wire is broken, switching the ignition to *OFF* (will/will not) stop the magneto producing electrical power.

27. The primary winding of a magneto is earthed when the ignition switch is placed to:
    (a) *START.*
    (b) *ON.*
    (c) *OFF.*

28. If a magneto earth wire comes loose in flight, the engine (will/will not) stop.

29. The spark plugs in a piston engine are provided with a high energy (or *high tension*) electrical supply from:
    (a) the battery at all times.
    (b) the magnetos, which each have a self-contained generation and distribution system.
    (c) the battery at start-up, and then the magnetos.

30. Moving the Ignition Switch in the cockpit to *START:*
    (a) directly completes the starter circuit connecting the Battery to the Starter Motor.
    (b) energises a solenoid-operated switch which completes the starter circuit connecting the Battery to the Starter Motor.
    (c) earths the Starter Motor.

31. Compared to the current flow through the starter circuit that connects the Battery to the Starter Motor, the current flow through the Ignition Switch in the *START* position is (low/high/the same).

32. The heavy duty starter circuit is activated by a solenoid-activated switch remotely controlled from the cockpit through a low current circuit:
    (a) to avoid the energy losses that would occur in additional heavy duty cable to the cockpit.
    (b) to avoid the extra weight of heavy duty cable to the cockpit.
    (c) to avoid an unnecessary fire risk caused by heavy current in the cockpit.
    (d) all of the above.

33. Because of the very low revs as you start the engine the spark needs to be delayed. This is done automatically in some magnetos by an i...... c....... .

34. If the starter relay sticks after the starter switch has been released, the starter motor (will/will not) remain engaged and the starter warning light (will/will not) remain illuminated.

35. The Pilot should monitor oil pressure when an engine is started up. If the engine is cold prior to start-up, the engine should be:
    (a) shut down immediately if oil pressure does not rise immediately upon start-up.
    (b) shut down, if oil pressure is not seen to rise within approximately 30 seconds of start-up.
    (c) shut down, if oil pressure has not reached normal limits by the time the aeroplane is ready for take-off.
    (d) operated normally, since it may take 10 minutes for oil pressure to rise.

36. It is important that there are no leaks in the exhaust system which may allow (oxygen/carbon monoxide/carbon dioxide), which is a colourless, odourless and dangerous gas into the cabin.

37. If an engine failure is accompanied by mechanical noise and the propeller stops rotating, the cause of the engine failure is most likely:
    (a) fuel starvation.
    (b) failure of a magneto.
    (c) break-up of a piston or valve.

38. Following a sudden and complete loss of power from the engine, there is no mechanical noise and the propeller continues to windmill. The likely cause of the power loss is:
    (a) fuel starvation.
    (b) failure of a magneto.
    (c) break-up of a piston or valve.

EXERCISES 17 — THE CARBURETTOR.

1. The fuel and air need to be mixed in a reasonably correct ratio to burn properly and this may be done by a c.......... .

2. A carburettor is used to supply:
   (a) air to the engine cylinders.
   (b) fuel to the engine cylinders.
   (c) a fuel/air mixture to the engine cylinders.

3. The amount of fuel that flows through the carburettor is directly controlled by the:
   (a) fuel pump.
   (b) accelerator pump.
   (c) throttle.
   (d) airflow through the carburettor venturi.

4. In a 'chemically-correct' mixture, following combustion all of the fuel and all of the air in the combustion chamber (is/is not) burned.

5. In a rich mixture, following combustion excess .... remains.

6. In a lean mixture, following combustion excess ... remains.

7. Moving the throttle in the cockpit moves the b........ v..... in the carburettor.

8. To give a little squirt of fuel to match the increased airflow when the throttle is opened quickly, a carburettor has an a.......... p... built into it.

9. The accelerator pump on a carburettor is used to:
   (a) control the fuel/air mixture during the cruise.
   (b) shut the engine down.
   (c) prevent an over-lean mixture, or even a 'weak-cut', if the throttle is opened quickly.

10. To ensure sufficient fuel is fed to the cylinders when idling at low rpm, the carburettor has an i..... j.. .

11. As air density decreases the weight of fuel introduced into the cylinder needs to be (increased/reduced) to match the decreased weight of air. This is done from the cockpit using the m...... c...... , which is usually a r.. knob.

12. The mixture control is used to:
   (a) alter the fuel flow to the main jet of the carburettor.
   (b) increase the volume of air through the carburettor.
   (c) increase the fuel flow through the accelerator pump.
   (d) alter the level of fuel in the float chamber.

13. As an aeroplane climbs to higher altitudes with the mixture control set in RICH, the fuel/air mixture:
   (a) does not change.
   (b) becomes leaner.
   (c) becomes richer.

14. For take-off at sea level and +15°C, the mixture control should normally be in f... r... .

15. An over-rich mixture may cause a loss of p...., high f... consumption, fouling of the s.... p.... and formation of c..... deposits on the piston heads and valves.

16. The extra fuel in a rich mixture causes extra (heating/cooling) in the cylinder by its evaporation.

17. A too-lean mixture may lead to excessively (high/low) cylinder head temperatures and explosive d......... .

18. The usual method of shutting an engine down is to pull the mixture control out into the i... cut-off position.

19. This (leaves, does not leave) fuel in the system, which would not be the case if the engine was shut down by switching the ignition OFF.

20. Progressive burning that commences prior to the ignition spark is called p..-i....... .

21. A great danger to correct functioning of the carburettor, especially in moist conditions, is c.......... i.. .

22. Ice can form in the .... even at high Outside Air Temperatures, due to expansion and cooling as evaporation of fuel occurs.

23. The remedy for suspected carburettor ice is to apply c.......... h... .

24. The pressure drop (and consequent temperature drop) near the throttle butterfly is **greatest** at (large/small) throttle openings, causing a greater likelihood of carburettor ice forming.

25. The correct procedure to achieve the best fuel/air mixture when cruising at altitude is to move the mixture control towards *LEAN* until the engine rpm:
    (a) drops to a minimum value.
    (b) reaches a peak value.
    (c) passes through a peak value at which point the mixture control is returned to a slightly richer position.
    (d) reaches a minimum value.

26. Normally a Pilot should avoid using carburettor heat during ground operations because the hot air source is ....

27. An engine that does not have a carburettor, but rather metered fuel that is fed under pressure into the induction manifold, is said to have:
    (a) fuel injection.
    (b) supercharging.
    (c) metered carburation.

28. If, during start-up, a fire occurs in the engine air intake, a generally-suitable procedure is to:
    (a) place the starter switch to *OFF*.
    (b) continue with a normal start.
    (c) keep turning the engine, but move the mixture control to *IDLE CUT-OFF* and open the throttle.

EXERCISES 18 — THE FUEL SYSTEM.

1. Some aeroplanes have auxiliary fuel boost pumps to provide fuel at the required p...... , to purge the fuel lines of any v....., to p.... the cylinders for start-up, and to supply fuel if the e.....-driven fuel pump fails.

2. A cold engine needs to be primed for start-up. The fuel Priming Pump operated by the Pilot delivers fuel:
    (a) through the carburettor to the induction manifold or inlet valve ports.
    (b) through the carburettor and directly into each of the cylinders.
    (c) to the induction manifold or inlet valve ports, bypassing the carburettor.

3. Using a fuel of lower grade than specified may lead to d......... .

4. Using a fuel of higher grade than specified may lead to l...-fouling of the spark p...., and the exhaust valves and their sealing faces could be e..... by the higher performance fuel exhausting.

5. Motor gasoline (should/should not) be used.

6. Motor fuel is more prone to p..-i....... and d......... .

7. Motor fuel contains higher amounts of l... .

8. Motor fuel may cause l...-fouling of the spark plugs and a strong possibility of d......... .

9. Fuel should be checked for contamination, especially water, prior to the f.... flight of the day, and after each re-f....... .

10. Water tends to collect at the (highest/lowest) points in the fuel system.

11. To minimise condensation of water in the fuel tanks when the aeroplane is parked, especially in cold conditions
    (a) the fuel tanks should be kept full.
    (b) the fuel tanks should be kept as empty as possible.

12. Regular checks for water in the fuel system are important since the presence of water in the fuel may cause:
    (a) a loss of engine power because of contamination of the fuel system.
    (b) a loss of engine power because of carburettor icing.
    (c) freezing of the fuel at high altitudes and/or low temperatures.

13. Aviation gasoline can be distinguished from aviation turbine fuel (kerosene) by col... and s.... .

14. 100/130 fuel is coloured g.... .

15. 100 LL (low lead) is b... .

16. AVGAS equipment should normally be coloured ...., whilst AVTUR equipment should normally be coloured ..... .

17. If the fuel strainer drain valve is left open following the pre-flight inspection of a low-wing aeroplane:
    (a) the fuel tanks will empty.
    (b) the effect will be negligible.
    (c) the engine-driven fuel pump may not be able to supply sufficient fuel to the engine, resulting in fuel starvation unless an electric fuel pump is in use.

18. Recall the advantages and disadvantages of refilling aircraft fuel tanks prior to overnight parking.

19. Recall the precautions that should be taken when refuelling an aircraft directly from fuel company sources (i.e. tanker, bowser) or from drums.

EXERCISES 19 — THE OIL SYSTEM.

1. Oil lowers friction between moving parts and so prevents high t........... and what heat is formed can to some extent be carried away by circulating o.. .

2. Oil is used both for lubrication and cooling. (True/False)?

3. Oil is circulated around an engine by:
    (a) an engine-driven pressure pump.
    (b) a scavenge pump.
    (c) a vacuum pump.
    (d) an electric pump.

4. Oil grades (may/may not) be mixed.

5. The same oil grade, but of different brand-names, (may/may not) be mixed.

6. Impurities in the oil should be removed by the o.. f..... .

7. If the oil filter clogs up, then the unfiltered oil is forced through an o..-f..... b.-p... valve. Dirty and contaminated oil (is/is not) better than no oil at all.

8. To aid in cooling the oil, most systems have an oil-c..... .

9. With too little oil, you may observe a (high/low) oil temperature and/or a (high/low) oil pressure.

10. If the oil quantity is too great, excess oil may be forced out through various parts of the e...... such as the front shaft s.... .

11. On start-up of a cold engine, the oil pressure gauge should indicate a rise (immediately/within 5 seconds/within 30 seconds/within 5 minutes).

EXERCISES 20 — THE COOLING SYSTEM.

1. Most aero-engines have cooling-f... to aid in cooling.

2. High airspeeds allow (better/worse) cooling.

3. Low airspeeds cause (worse/better) cooling.

4. Lean mixture leads to (higher/lower) temperatures.

5. A blocked oil cooler leads to (higher/lower) oil temperatures.

6. A high power setting leads to (higher/lower) temperatures.

7. Open cowl flaps encourage (better/poorer) cooling.

8. High OATs lead to (higher/lower) temperatures.

EXERCISES 21 — HANDLING.

1. If the oil quantity gauge suddenly dropped to zero, immediately monitor the o.. t.......... g.... .

2. If the oil temperature gauge showed a rapid increase in temperature, then there (may/may not) be a serious loss of oil.

3. If the oil temperature remained normal, there is probably (sufficient/insufficient) oil circulating.

4. If you suspect a serious loss of oil, then consideration should be given to (an immediate landing/a landing at the next suitable aerodrome which is say half an hour away).

5. Increasing power with a Constant Speed Unit, increase rpm first followed by Manifold Pressure. (True/False)?

6. Decreasing power with a CSU, decrease MP first, followed by rpm. (True/False)?

7. Prior to shutting an engine down, you should allow a brief c...... period.

8. Why do most engine manufacturers recommend that the use of carburettor heat during ground operations be minimised?

EXERCISES 22 — THE ELECTRICAL SYSTEM.

1. Normal in-flight electrical power is provided by an a........ or g........ .

2. A distribution point for electrical power to various services is called a:
   (a) circuit breaker.
   (b) fuse.
   (c) distributor.
   (d) bus bar.

3. Electrical power for start-up and as an emergency source of electrical power is the b...... .

4. An a........ requires an initial current from the b...... to activate it.

5. A typical lead-acid battery contains a solution of weak s.......... acid.

6. When the engine is stopped, the main source of electrical power is the:
   (a) battery.
   (b) magneto.
   (c) generator or alternator.
   (d) circuit breaker.

7. When the engine is running, the main source of electrical power is the:
   (a) battery.
   (b) magneto.
   (c) generator or alternator.
   (d) circuit breaker.

8. An ammeter measures (current in amps/voltage).

9. A centre-zero ammeter measures current in and out of the b......, whereas a left-zero ammeter measures only the o..... of the alternator. It has zero amps on the l... end of the scale and increases in amps to the right end of the scale.

10. Immediately after starting, ammeter indication will be (high/low) as the battery is re-charged.

11. An alternator is capable of a (high/low) output, and there (is/is not) a risk that the charging rate of a partially-flat battery could cause damage to the battery.

12. The ammeter reading zero may mean that the alternator is not supplying electrical power. (True/False)?

13. The illumination of a warning light for the electrical system may mean that the alternator is not supplying electrical power. (True/False)?

14. A split master switch controls the b...... and the ....

15. A voltage regulator maintains correct output v...... from the alternator.

16. Electrical circuits are protected by f.... and c...... b....... .

17. Fuses and circuit breakers are protection against excessive electrical (current/voltage).

18. A blown fuse (may/should not) be replaced by a fuse of a higher rating so that it will not blow again.

19. A popped CB **may** be reset, or a blown fuse replaced by one of the same value, while the aircraft is in flight. It is not necessary to wait until the aircraft has landed to replace the fuse. (True/False)?

20. Blown fuses or popped CBs (should/should not) be replaced more than once.

21. If the alternator (or generator) fails in flight, the electrical loads (should/need not) be reduced to a minimum and an early landing (should/need not) be made.

22. A 28 volt DC electrical system in an aircraft has a 24 volt battery:
    (a) for no particular reason.
    (b) to allow the alternator to fully recharge the battery once the engine is running.
    (c) so that the battery will not burn the alternator out.

23. A battery rated at 15 amp-hours is capable of providing 5 amps for a period of ... hours without recharging.

24. If the alternator fails in flight
    (a) the electrical system will not be affected.
    (b) the battery will be able to supply normal electrical power to all services, even if the flight is of long duration.
    (c) electrical services (such as lighting and unnecessary radios) should be reduced to a minimum to conserve battery power, and an early landing considered.

25. During engine start, a large current-draw (is/is not) made on the battery.

26. The battery master switch should be turned to *OFF* after the engine is stopped to avoid the battery discharging through:
    (a) the magnetos.
    (b) the alternator or generator.
    (c) electrical services connected to it.
    (d) the ignition switch.

27. Which of the following instruments and gauges would normally be electrically powered? Air Speed Indicator, Altimeter, Vertical Speed Indicator, Attitude Indicator, Turn Co-ordinator, Direction Indicator, Fuel Quantity Gauges, Engine RPM Gauge, Oil Temperature Gauge. (Check for your own particular aeroplane).

EXERCISES 23 — THE VACUUM SYSTEM.

1. The vacuum system induces, or draws, a high-speed airflow onto the 'buckets' on the edge of the gyro rotors causing them to spin. (True/False)?

2. The suction (or vacuum) gauge reads the pressure (above/below) atmospheric pressure.

3. A vacuum pump may be used to operate the (gyroscopic/engine/pitot-static) instruments.

4. A vacuum pump (draws/blows) air through the suction-operated flight instruments to operate (gyro rotors/pressure valves/regulators).

5. The vacuum pump, if fitted to a modern aeroplane, is most likely to be (electrically/engine/hydraulically)-driven.

6. Air-driven gyro rotors are prevented from spinning too fast by the (air filter/vacuum relief valve/suction gauge).

7. A zero reading on the suction gauge when the engine is running could indicate:
   (a) a failure of the vacuum pump.
   (b) a failure of the gauge itself.
   (c) either of the above.

8. A reading of 2"Hg (2 inches of mercury) on the suction gauge indicates a (low/normal/high) vacuum and a (low/normal/high) airflow.

9. Insufficient suction (may/will not) cause gyroscopic instruments (such as the Artificial Horizon or the Direction Indicator) to indicate incorrectly, erratically, or respond slowly.

10. A reading of 5"Hg on the suction gauge indicates a (low/normal/high) vacuum and a (low/normal/high) airflow.

11. Gyroscopic instruments driven by 'suction' created in an externally mounted Venturi-tube will be usable:
    (a) immediately the engine starts.
    (b) as soon as the aeroplane rolls for take-off.
    (c) if there is any airflow through the venturi caused by wind.
    (d) not until after the aircraft has been at flying speed for several minutes after take-off.

12. Name the two methods used to provide suction for the vacuum systems found in aircraft.

EXERCISES 24 — LANDING GEAR, TYRES AND BRAKES.

1. A cracked or severely corroded landing gear strut found by a Pilot during his Pre-Flight Inspection (should/need not) be inspected by a qualified Engineer before the aeroplane flies.

2. The damping agent used to dampen the rebound action in the oleo-pneumatic unit following a shock is the (compressed air/oil).

3. The oleo strut will extend (further/the same/less) in flight than on the ground.

4. The state of charge of the oleo-pneumatic unit (is/is not) indicated by how much of the strut extends while the nosewheel is supporting its normal load on the ground.

5. Why should mud or dirt noticed in a Pre-Flight Inspection be cleaned off the polished section of an oleo strut prior to taxying?

6. The nosewheel is held aligned with a ...... link and nosewheel oscillations either side of centre are damped by a ....

7. A nosewheel which is free to turn, but is not connected to the cockpit by any control rods or cables for turning is said to be of the .... type.

8. Nosewheel steering in light aircraft is usually operated by:
   (a) control rods or cables operated by the rudder pedals.
   (b) a steering wheel.
   (c) the brakes.

9. A castoring nosewheel can be made to turn by:
   (a) a steering wheel.
   (b) differential braking.
   (c) control rods or cables connected to the rudder pedals.

10. The relative movement between the tyre and the wheel flange is called ....

11. If a tyre has moved so that the creep marks are out of alignment, then:
   (a) it is serviceable.
   (b) it should be inspected and possibly re-fitted or replaced.
   (c) tyre pressure should be checked.
   (d) the brakes will be unserviceable.

12. A tyre that has some shallow cuts in the sidewalls and a number of small stones embedded in its tread (should/need not) be rejected by a Pilot.

13. A tyre that has a deep cut that exposes the casing cords (should/need not) be rejected for further flight.

14. A tyre with a large bulge in one of its sidewalls (should/need not) be rejected for further flight.

15. Braking of an individual main wheel is known as:
   (a) individual braking.
   (b) directional braking.
   (c) differential braking.

16. Most light aircraft braking systems are operated:
   (a) by cables.
   (b) pneumatically.
   (c) hydraulically.
   (d) electrically.

17. Hydraulic fluid leaks from the brake lines or other parts of the brake system (are/are not) acceptable.

18. A severely corroded or pitted brake disc (will/will not) be structurally weak and (will/will not) reduce braking efficiency.

19. The brake pads may suffer unnecessary wear if:
   (a) the tyre pressure is too high.
   (b) the tyre pressure is too low.
   (c) the parking brake is left on overnight.
   (d) the brake disc is corroded or pitted.

20. Wheel brakes (should/should not) be tested early in the taxi.

EXERCISES 25 — PRESSURE INSTRUMENTS.

1. Pressure instruments make use of static pressure and/or total or p.... pressure.

2. The altimeter requires ...... pressure.

3. Static pressure is sensed by the (pitot tube/static vent/static tube).

4. The pitot tube senses (total pressure/static pressure/dynamic pressure).

5. Some aeroplanes are fitted with an electrical P.... H..... as a precaution against ice forming in the pitot tube.

6. The pitot cover, used to prevent water, insects, dust, etc., accumulating in the pitot tube (should/should not) be removed prior to flight.

7. Water that has entered the pitot-static system lines (could/will not) cause incorrect readings on the pressure instruments.

8. From static pressure and pitot (total) pressure, we can obtain d...... pressure.

9. The ASI uses p.... (total) pressure and s..... pressure to find dynamic pressure, to which Indicated Air Speed is closely related.

10. The VSI measures the rate of change of (static/dynamic/total) pressure.

11. If a static vent ices over, the altimeter will show (an increasing/a decreasing/the same) altitude.

12. The altimeter has a subscale on which to set a pressure datum. (True/False)?

13. The VSI has a subscale on which to set a pressure datum. (True/False)?

14. With QNH set, the altimeter reads height:
    (a) Above Mean Sea Level (AMSL).
    (b) Above Aerodrome Level (AAL).
    (c) above the 1013 mb(hPa) pressure level.

15. With QFE set, the altimeter reads height:
    (a) Above Mean Sea Level (AMSL).
    (b) Above Aerodrome Level (AAL).
    (c) above the 1013 mb(hPa) pressure level.

16. When landing at an aerodrome other than the one of departure, a new QFE pressure setting (is/is not) required.

17. The altimeter subscale of a parked aeroplane is turned until the altimeter reads zero. The subscale setting will be the aerodrome (QFE/QNH/elevation).

18. The altimeter subscale of a parked aeroplane is turned until the altimeter reads the aerodrome's elevation. The subscale setting will be the aerodrome (QFE/QNH/pressure altitude).

19. The altimeter subscale is wound to 1013. The altimeter will indicate:
    (a) elevation.
    (b) height.
    (c) pressure altitude.
    (d) flight level.

20. V$_{NE}$ is known as the .... speed and is marked on the ASI with a ....-coloured line.

21. The stalling speed, wings-level and full flap extended, is indicated on the ASI as the (high/low) speed end of the (white/green/yellow) arc.

22. The stalling speed, wings-level and no flap extended, is indicated on the ASI as the (high/low) speed end of the (white/green/yellow) arc.

23. V$_{NO}$ is known as the .... speed and is indicated on the ASI as the (high/low) speed end of the (white/green/yellow) arc.

24. Which instruments are connected to the static source?

25. Which instrument is connected to the pitot tube, where the *total pressure* (i.e. dynamic plus static) is sensed?

EXERCISES 26 — GYROSCOPIC INSTRUMENTS.

1. The gyroscopic Directional Indicator should be regularly re-aligned with the magnetic c...... .

2. A vacuum pump fitted to an aeroplane may operate the (ASI/VSI/AI/DI/Compass/Turn Co-ordinator).

3. Slip or skid is indicated on the:
   (a) Turn Co-ordinator.
   (b) Balance Ball.
   (c) Attitude Indicator.
   (d) Direction Indicator.

4. A low vacuum may be indicated by a low suction reading and slow or erratic gyroscopic instruments. (True/False)?

5. Failure of the electrical supply to an electrically-driven Attitude Indicator may be indicated by:
   (a) a low ammeter reading.
   (b) a red warning flag.
   (c) low suction.

6. The Turn Indicator provides information resulting from the precession of a gyro that has its spin axis (vertical/horizontal).

7. The Attitude Indicator has a gyro with a (vertical/horizontal) spin axis.

EXERCISES 27 — THE MAGNETIC COMPASS.

1. The lubber line of the magnetic compass indicates:
   (a) True North.
   (b) Magnetic North.
   (c) the magnetic heading of the aeroplane.
   (d) the true heading of the aeroplane.
   (e) the track of the aeroplane over the ground.

2. The difference between True North and Magnetic North is called V........ .

3. Corrections that need to be made to an individual magnetic compass to obtain its magnetic heading can be found in the cockpit on the d........ card.

4. May magnetic materials be placed near the compass?

5. Is a magnetic compass more reliable near the Equator or near the Poles?

6. In the Northern Hemisphere, turning through North you should .... the magnetic heading.

7. In the Northern Hemisphere, you should .... the magnetic heading turning through South.

8. In the Northern Hemisphere, accelerating on a westerly heading will cause an apparent turn to the ..... .

9. Recall the Pilot serviceability checks on a magnetic compass.

10. Runway 32 at a particular aerodrome in the UK could have a bearing of:
    (a) 032°M.
    (b) 322°M.
    (c) 322°T.
    (d) 032°T.

EXERCISES 28 — AIRWORTHINESS.

1. The document to show that an aircraft is registered is the Certificate of ....

2. The document issued to indicate that a particular aeroplane complies with the appropriate airworthiness requirements is the C.......... of ....

3. The CofA is issued for a specified period. (True/False)?

4. Any maintenance required by the approved Maintenance Schedule that forms part of the aeroplane's Certificate of Airworthiness (must/need not) be completed for the CofA to become valid again.

5. May spins and loops be carried out in an aeroplane in the **Normal** category?

6. The Flight Manual (must/need not) be carried in the aircraft, while the Pilot's Operating Handbook (must/need not) remain with it.

7. The CAA Supplement takes precedence over the manufacturer's Flight Manual. (True/False)?

8. Placards in the cockpit have the same status as instructions in the .... and should be adhered to.

9. The time remaining to the next major inspection can be determined from:
   (a) the Certificate of Airworthiness.
   (b) the Flight Manual.
   (c) the Certificate of Maintenance Review.
   (d) Air Navigation (General) Regulations.

10. A Daily Inspection shall be carried out:
    (a) before the first flight of the day.
    (b) at least daily, not necessarily before the first flight of the day.

11. Should the oil quantity be checked in a Daily Inspection?

12. Should tyre inflation and their condition be checked in the Daily Inspection?

13. Minor maintenance and replacements that can be performed by a qualified Pilot are listed in the:
    (a) Flight Manual.
    (b) CAA Supplement to the Flight Manual.
    (c) Certificate of Airworthiness.
    (d) Air Navigation (General) Regulations.
    (e) Maintenance Schedule.
    (f) Pilot's Operating Handbook.

14. Aeroplanes on which a qualified Pilot can perform minor maintenance tasks must be:
    (a) less than 5700 kg and not used for aerial work.
    (b) less than 5700 kg.
    (c) less than 2730 kg and not used for public transport.
    (d) less than 2730 kg.

15. The legal responsibility to ensure that the aeroplane's maintenance documents are in order prior to flight is the:
    (a) Engineer's.
    (b) Pilot's.
    (c) Chief Flying Instructor's.
    (d) CAA's.

16. Defects requiring maintenance after flight should be entered by the Pilot in the:
    (a) Technical Log.
    (b) Certificate of Airworthiness.
    (c) Flight Manual.
    (d) Certificate of Maintenance release.

17. Can a Pilot legally replace a landing gear tyre?

18. Can a Pilot legally change the engine oil?

19. Can a Pilot legally change the spark plugs and set their gaps?

20. May a Pilot who is not qualified as an aero-engineer replace a propeller?

21. Having completed approved maintenance, the Pilot:
    (a) need not record it.
    (b) should record it in the appropriate place, but not sign for it.
    (c) should record it in the appropriate place and certify it with his signature and licence number.
    (d) should notify the CAA.

22. Aircraft performance data is contained in the ....

23. Some aircraft in the Normal Category are permitted to operate in the Utility Category and perform limited aerobatics provided:
    (a) certain weight and CG limitations are satisfied.
    (b) the weight is less than 3000 kg.
    (c) stalls are not performed.
    (d) a Flying Instructor is on board.

24. Specify the conditions that must be satisfied before a Pilot can sign the second part of a Duplicate Inspection for a flight or engine control system.

EXERCISES 29 — AIRFRAME LIMITATIONS.

Define the following:

1. Maximum Take-Off Weight.

2. Maximum Landing Weight.

3. Normal Operating Limit Speed.

4. Never Exceed Speed.

5. Manoeuvring Speed.

6. Turbulence Penetration Speed.

7. Severe turbulence (can/will not) cause limit load factors to be exceeded and result in structural damage or failure.

8. At speeds in excess of the manoeuvring speed, full backward movement of the control column can cause the limit load factor to be exceeded. (True/False)?

9. At speeds in excess of the manoeuvring speed (V_A), the Pilot should avoid abrupt or large control movements mainly because:
    (a) the aeroplane will stall.
    (b) the limit load factor may be exceeded.
    (c) the aeroplane will be out-of-balance.

10. The normal operating limit speed (V_{NO}) should:
    (a) only be exceeded in smooth air.
    (b) never be exceeded.
    (c) is less than the manoeuvring speed (V_A.)

11. List the specific items that a Pilot or an Engineer should check on an aeroplane following a heavy landing.

EXERCISES 30 — THE ATMOSPHERE.

1. What are the three main constituents of the Earth's atmosphere?

2. High humidity causes air density to (increase/decrease/remain the same).

3. The amount of water vapour in the air is called:
    (a) dampness.
    (b) relative humidity.
    (c) humidity.
    (d) the degree of saturation.

4. The amount of water vapour that the air is actually carrying compared to what it is capable of carrying at that temperature is called:
   (a) dampness.
   (b) relative humidity.
   (c) humidity.
   (d) the degree of saturation.

5. As the temperature of a parcel of air drops, its relative humidity:
   (a) increases.
   (b) decreases.
   (c) stays the same.
   (d) gradually falls to zero.

6. If the temperature of a given parcel of air increases at a constant pressure, the density of the air:
   (a) increases.
   (b) decreases.
   (c) stays the same.

7. If the temperature increases, the Take-Off Distance Required:
   (a) increases.
   (b) decreases.
   (c) stays the same.

8. Compared to a sea level aerodrome, the Take-Off Distance Required at a high elevation aerodrome is:
   (a) greater.
   (b) less.
   (c) the same.

9. Engine performance and airframe aerodynamic performance are poorer at high altitudes mainly because of:
   (a) the lower temperature.
   (b) the higher pressure.
   (c) the lower density.
   (d) the higher relative humidity.

10. If the pressure altitude increases, the Take-Off Distance Required:
    (a) increases.
    (b) decreases.
    (c) stays the same.

11. As air expands, its pressure and density:
    (a) remain the same.
    (b) increase.
    (c) decrease.

12. Aeroplane performance deteriorates at (high/low) temperatures.

13. The lower the air density 'Rho' the (poorer/better) the performance of the airframe and the engine.

14. The 'measuring stick' for atmospheric variables such as pressure, temperature, density is the Inter........ St...... At........ .

15. ISA Mean Sea Level standard pressure is ...... mb(hPa).

16. ISA MSL temperature is .. degrees Celsius.

17. Pressure in the ISA falls at approximately 1 mb(hPa) per .. ft

18. Temperature in the ISA falls at approximately . degrees C per 1,000 ft gain in altitude.

19. If MSL atmospheric pressure is 1013 mb(hPa), what is the pressure at:
    (1) 30 ft AMSL
    (2) 60 ft AMSL
    (3) 3,000 ft AMSL?

20. What is the ISA temperature at the following pressure altitudes:
    (1) PA 2,000 ft
    (2) PA 5,000 ft
    (3) PA 10,000 ft?

21. Convert 15°C to °F and write down the formula to use.

22. Convert 77°F to °C and write down the formula to use.

EXERCISES 31 — TAKE-OFF AND LANDING PERFORMANCE.

1. Take-off distance is established on a h.... surface that is ...... and .... .

2. Higher weights (increase/decrease) take-off distance required.

3. Higher temperatures (increase/decrease) take-off distance required.

4. Higher aerodrome elevations, with their decreased air density, result in poorer aerodynamic and engine performance, and require (increased/decreased) take-off distances.

5. A tailwind (increases/decreases) take-off distances.

6. A 10 kt wind at 60 degrees off the runway heading gives a (0/4/9) kt crosswind.

7. A 20 kt wind at 60 degrees off the runway gives a (0/9/18) kt crosswind.

8. A 10 kt wind at 30 degrees off the runway heading gives a (0/5/9) kt crosswind component.

9. A 20 kt wind at 30 degrees off the runway heading gives a (0/5/10) kt crosswind component.

10. In crosswind conditions, the headwind or tailwind component (should/need not) be applied when calculating the Take-Off or Landing Distances.

11. A 10 kt wind at 30 degrees off the runway heading gives a (0/5/9) kt headwind component.

12. A 20 kt wind at 30 degrees off the runway heading gives a (0/5/18) kt headwind component.

13. Take-Off Distance is measured to:
    (a) the lift-off point on the runway.
    (b) to 100 ft above the runway level.
    (c) to 50 ft above the runway level.

14. Soft, sandy surfaces may (increase/decrease) take-off distance.

15. Up-slope will (increase/decrease) take-off distance.

16. A 10% increase in aircraft weight is likely to cause an increase in Take-Off Distance to a Height of 50 ft of ....%, i.e. a factor of ..... .

17. An increase of 1000 ft in Aerodrome Elevation is likely to cause an increase in Take-Off Distance to a Height of 50 ft of ....%, i.e. a factor of ..... .

18. An increase of 10°C in Ambient Temperature is likely to cause an increase in Take-Off Distance to a Height of 50 ft ....%, i.e. a factor of ..... .

19. Short dry grass under 5 inches is likely to cause an increase in Take-Off Distance to a Height of 50 ft of ....%, i.e. a factor of ..... .

20. Long dry grass between 5 and 10 inches is likely to cause an increase in Take-Off Distance to a Height of 50 ft ....%, i.e. a factor of ..... .

21. Short wet grass under 5 inches is likely to cause an increase in Take-Off Distance to a Height of 50 ft of ....%, i.e. a factor of ..... .

22. Long wet grass between 5 and 10 inches is likely to cause an increase in Take-Off Distance to a Height of 50ft of ....%, i.e. a factor of ..... .

23. Soft ground or snow is likely to cause an increase in Take-Off Distance to a Height of 50 ft of at least ....%, i.e. a factor of at least ..... .

24. A 2% uphill slope is likely to cause an increase in Take-Off Distance to a Height of 50 ft of ....%, i.e. a factor of ..... .

25. A tailwind component of 10% of Lift-Off Speed is likely to cause an increase in Take-Off Distance to a Height of 50 ft of ....%, i.e. a factor of ..... .

26. For Private flights, the CAA recommends that, after taking account of all relevant variables, a safety factor of .... be applied for take-off.

27. The Measured Take-Off Distance for an aeroplane at a given weight and flap setting extracted from a Manual is 370 metres at sea level and 10°C. For this particular aeroplane type, the CAA has imposed a mandatory 5% increase in published distances. What is the Recommended Minimum Take-Off Distance for the aeroplane at an aerodrome elevation 1000 ft AMSL; 2% upslope; a short grass surface that is wet; a temperature of +20°C; and a tailwind of 5 kt (lift-off speed is 50 kt)?

28. Measured Take-Off Distance from the Manual is 400 metres; Take-Off Aerodrome elevation 1000 ft; a wet long-grass strip with 2% upslope; +20°C; tailwind component 5 kt (lift-off speed 50 kt). Mandatory CAA limitation: nil.

29. Clearway (must/need not) be a clear ground surface.

30. Stopway (must/need not) be an unobstructed ground surface.

31. Headwind (increases/decreases/does not affect) take-off distance.

32. Tailwind (increases/decreases/does not affect) take-off distance.

33. Tailwind (increases/decreases/does not affect) lift-off IAS.

34. Tailwind (increases/decreases/does not affect) lift-off GS.

35. Headwind (increases/decreases/does not affect) lift-off IAS.

36. Headwind (increases/decreases/does not affect) lift-off GS.

37. Landing distance is measured from .. ft over the ground, power (off/on), to a stop.

38. Increased weights mean (increased/decreased) landing distances.

39. High elevations mean (increased/decreased) landing distance.

40. High temperatures mean (increased/decreased) landing distances.

41. Tailwind means (increased/decreased) landing distances.

42. Tailwind means (higher/lower/the same) IAS on approach.

43. Tailwind means (higher/lower/the same) GS on approach.

44. Wet and slippery runway surfaces mean (increased/decreased) landing distances.

45. Down-slope means (increased/decreased) landing distances.

46. Flap means (increased/decreased) approach speeds.

47. Use of flap means (shorter/longer) landing distances.

48. A 10% increase in aircraft weight is likely to cause an increase in Landing Distance from a Height of 50 ft of ....%, i.e. a factor of ..... .

49. An increase of 1000 ft in Aerodrome Elevation is likely to cause an increase in Landing Distance from a Height of 50 ft of ....%, i.e. a factor of ..... .

50. An increase of 10°C in Ambient Temperature is likely to cause an increase in Landing Distance from a Height of 50 ft of ....%, i.e. a factor of ..... .

51. Short dry grass under 5 inches is likely to cause an increase in Landing Distance from a Height of 50 ft of ....%, i.e. a factor of ..... .

52. Long dry grass is likely to cause an increase in Landing Distance from a Height of 50 ft of ....%, i.e. a factor of ..... .

53. Short wet grass under 5 inches is likely to cause an increase in Landing Distance to a Height of 50 ft of ....%, i.e. a factor of ..... .

54. Long wet grass above 5 inches is likely to cause an increase in Landing Distance from a Height of 50 ft of ....%, i.e. a factor of ..... .

55. Snow is likely to cause an increase in Landing Distance from a Height of 50 ft of at least ....%, i.e. a factor of at least ..... .

56. A 2% downhill slope is likely to cause an increase in Landing Distance from a Height of 50 ft of ....%, i.e. a factor of ..... .

57. A tailwind component of 10% of Landing Speed is likely to cause an increase in Landing Distance from a Height of 50 ft of ....%, i.e. a factor of ..... .

58. For Private flights, the CAA recommends that, after taking account of all relevant variables, a safety factor of .... be applied for landing.

59. The Measured Landing Distance from 50 ft for an aeroplane at a given weight extracted from a Manual is 370 metres at sea level and 10°C. What is the Recommended Landing Distance for the aeroplane at an aerodrome elevation 1000 ft amsl, 2% downslope, a short grass surface that is wet, a temperature of +20°C, and a tailwind of 5 kt (Landing Speed is 50 kt)?

60. Performance data (is/is not) found in the Flight Manual and its associated CAA Supplement.

EXERCISES 32 — EN ROUTE PERFORMANCE.

1. Flying for **Range** is flying to achieve the best (distance over the ground/time in the air) for a given amount of fuel.

2. Another way of expressing 'flying for range' is to say that you want to achieve the (least/greatest) fuel burn-off for a given **Distance**.

3. Flying for best range, the Pilot wants to achieve the greatest number of (nautical miles/minutes in the air) for the given fuel.

4. Flying the aeroplane so that it can stay in the air for the longest **Time** possible is called (endurance/range) flying.

5. To achieve best endurance, the fuel flows should be kept as (high/low) as possible for safe flight.

6. Fuel flow in a piston engine aeroplane depends upon the power being produced, so for best **Endurance** and lowest fuel flow you should choose a speed for (minimum/maximum) power.

7. When flying at a given airspeed, an aeroplane loaded to a Gross Weight of 2000 lb will fly at (a greater/the same/a lesser) angle of attack compared to when it is loaded to a Gross Weight of 1500 lb.

8. The power required to maintain cruising speed for a particular aeroplane when it is heavily laden is (the same as/greater than/less than) the power required when it is light.

EXERCISES 33 — WEIGHT AND BALANCE.

1. The weight that includes the weight of the airframe, engine, fixed equipment, unusable fuel, full oil is called the B.... E.... W..... .

2. The weight of the aeroplane plus Pilot, passengers, baggage, cargo, ballast, but excluding only the usable fuel, is called the ....

3. The maximum allowable gross weight permitted for take-off is the M...... T...-O.. W..... .

4. Sometimes a high obstacle in the take-off flight path or a short runway or some other performance consideration restricts the weight that you may take- off at to something less than the structural MTOW. This reduced TOW is called a P..........-Limited Take-Off Weight.

5. The maximum permitted landing weight is called the M...... L....... W..... .

6. A short runway may not allow us to land at the MLW (structural), but at a P..........-L....... Landing Weight.

7. Landing Weight = Take-Off Weight – B...-o.. .

8. List the items that must be weighed in determining the load of an aeroplane.

9. The turning effect or turning moment of a force depends on two things, its (magnitude/temperature) and its (pressure/moment arm).

10. The longer the moment arm from the Centre of Gravity the (greater/smaller) the turning effect of a given force.

11. The CG Datum is used as a reference from which to measure moment arm. (True/False)?

12. The Pilot has the legal responsibility to ensure that the aeroplane will be operated within the weight and balance limitations. (True/False)?

13. Calculate the moment of 250 lb of fuel in a fuel tank whose moment arm is 20 inches from the datum.

14. Calculate the moment of 30 Imperial Gallons of AVGAS in a fuel tank whose moment arm is 80·2 inches from the datum. The Specific Gravity of AVGAS is 0·72, so 1 Imp. Gallon weighs 7·2 lb.

15. A Pilot would normally check the CG position of ...... Weight and .... Weight prior to flight.

16. It is possible in some aeroplanes that full fuel tanks and a full passenger and baggage load would exceed the maximum weight limits. An appropriate solution would be to:
    (a) operate over the maximum weight limit.
    (b) reduce the fuel on board, even though it will be insufficient for the flight plus reserves.
    (c) reduce the fuel on board, but to not less than that required for the flight plus reserves, and then, if necessary, off-load baggage and/or passengers.
    (d) Off-load baggage and/or passengers, so that a full fuel load can be carried.

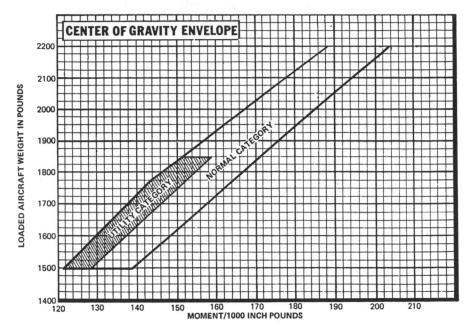

Fig.5. Centre of Gravity Envelope.

The next questions refer to the Centre of Gravity Envelope shown above.

17. The combination(s) of Weight and Total Moment which are acceptable for flight in the Normal Category are:
    (a) 1900 lb and 170,000 inch.pounds (or pound.inches).
    (b) 1900 lb and 180,000 inch.pounds.
    (c) 1640 lb and 180,000 inch.pounds.
    (d) 1640 lb and 138,000 inch.pounds.
    (e) 1640 lb and 130,000 inch.pounds.
    (f) 2125 lb and 196,000 inch.pounds.

18. The combination(s) of Weight and Total Moment which are acceptable for flight in the Utility Category are:
    (a) 1900 lb and 170,000 inch.pounds (or pound.inches).
    (b) 1900 lb and 180,000 inch.pounds.
    (c) 1640 lb and 180,000 inch.pounds.
    (d) 1640 lb and 138,000 inch.pounds.
    (e) 1640 lb and 130,000 inch.pounds.
    (f) 2125 lb and 196,000 inch.pounds.

19. Having calculated the Take-Off Weight and CG position, a Pilot can calculate a Zero Fuel Weight and CG position by subtracting the weight and moment of the (total usable fuel/estimated burn-off).

20. Having calculated the Take-Off Weight and CG position, a Pilot can calculate a Landing Weight and CG position by subtracting the weight and moment of the (total usable fuel/estimated fuel consumed).

EXERCISES 34 — WAKE TURBULENCE.

1. The static air pressure beneath a wing is (greater than/less than) the static air pressure above the wing.

2. The air beneath a wing of an aeroplane in flight tends to leak around the wingtip and into the lower static pressure area above the wing. This leaves a trail of invisible w...... v......s behind.

3. These wingtip vortices can be very strong behind a heavy aeroplane flying slowly at a high a.... of a....., such as on take-off and landing.

4. Wingtip vortices tend to drift (up/down).

5. Wingtip vortices tend to drift (downwind/upwind, remain stationary over the ground even in steady winds).

6. You should (disregard/avoid) wake turbulence behind a heavy jet that has just taken-off.

7. The most dangerous area for wake turbulence behind a heavy jet is (at the start of his take-off run/just past his point of rotation and on his climb-out).

8. Wake turbulence (is different to/the same as) 'jet blast'.

EXERCISES 35 — GROUND EFFECT.

1. The better **'flyability'** of an aeroplane near the ground or some other surface is called g..... e..... .

2. When an aeroplane is flying close to the ground the ground surface will restrict the airflow around the wings in a number of ways. The surface will restrict u. wash and d... wash and also restrict the formation of w...... vortices.

3. Ground effect will cause an increase in **'lifting ability'**. The more technical name for this is C.......... of L... .

4. Ground effect will not allow as great a formation of wingtip vortices as in **'free air'** and therefore ground effect causes a reduction in i...... drag.

5. As an aeroplane climbs out of ground effect on take-off its climb performance will tend to (increase/decrease).

6. In ground effect the Air Speed Indicator and the Altimeter (will/may not) read accurately.

EXERCISES 36 — WINDSHEAR.

1. Any change in the wind speed and/or the wind direction as you move from one point to another is called a w...sh... .

2. The effect of a windshear that causes an aeroplane to fly above the desired flight path and/or to increase its speed is called o...shoot effect.

3. The effect of a windshear that causes an aeroplane to fly below the desired flight path and/or to decrease its speed is called u....shoot effect.

4. If the initial effect of a windshear is reversed as the aeroplane travels further along its flight path (say on approach to land), then the overall influence of the windshear on the aeroplane is called a windshear r....... effect.

ANSWERS —
The Aeroplane - technical

ANSWERS 1 —
THE FORCES . . .
1. Weight.
2. Lift.
3. Thrust.
4. Drag.
5. Lift, Thrust.
6. greater.

ANSWERS 2 —
WEIGHT.
1. Centre of Gravity.
2. wing loading = weight of the aeroplane/wing area.
3. 15 lb/sq.ft.

ANSWERS 3 —
AEROFOIL — LIFT.
1. Lift.
2. boundary layer.
3. streamline.
4. turbulent.
5. Bernoulli.
6. in all directions.
7. due to motion.
8. constant.
9. static dynamic.
10. decrease.
11. increase.
12. decrease.
13. decreases.
14. speed up.
15. decrease.
16. Camber.
17. Mean Camber Line.
18. Chord Line.
19. Chord.
20. Thickness.
21. decreases.
22. less than.
23. Lift.
24. Drag.
25. total reaction, Lift, Drag.
26. angle of attack.
27. decrease, Lift.
28. increases.
29. decreases.
30. Centre of Pressure.
31. moves forwards.
32. rearwards.
33. wing shape, angle of attack, air density (Rho), velocity of airflow, wing area (S).
34. ability.
35. Coefficient of Lift.
36. Dynamic Pressure.
37. L = C$_{Lift}$ x ½ Rho V-squared x S
38. angle of attack.
39. increases.
40. lower.
41. will.
42. zero.
43. (c).
44. increases.
45. 90.
46. angle of attack.
47. increases.
48. (a).

ANSWERS 4 —
DRAG.
1. opposes.
2. parallel to.
3. Thrust.
4. Thrust.
5. parallel to, opposite to.
6. induced, parasite.
7. skin friction, form drag, interference drag.
8. skin friction.
9. skin friction.
10. increases.
11. separates, turbulent.
12. delayed.
13. form drag.
14. interference drag.
15. increases.
16. induced drag.
17. lower.
18. lower, vortices.
19. outwards towards the wingtip.
20. inwards towards the root.
21. vortices.
22. high.
23. high.
24. low.
25. low.
26. (a).
27. high, washout.
28. long span and a short chord.

29. wingtip.
30. low.
31. high.
32. at a speed where the Parasite Drag and Induced Drag are equal.
33. Thrust.
34. Induced Drag, greater.
35. Parasite Drag, greater.
36. (c).
37. (a).

ANSWERS 5 — LIFT/DRAG RATIO.

1. 12:1
2. induced drag, 5:1
3. parasite, 6:1
4. 15:1.
5. most.
6. minimum.
7. minimum.
8. (d).

ANSWERS 6 — THRUST . . .

1. Thrust.
2. aerofoil.
3. blade angle.
4. twisted.
5. hub.
6. tip.
7. propeller tip.
8. Thrust .
9. rpm, airspeed.
10. fine.
11. coarse.
12. power.
13. yaw, rudder.
14. roll left and yaw left.
15. (a).
16. (b).

ANSWERS 7 — STABILITY.

1. nose-down.
2. nose-up.
3. pitch down.
4. tailplane, horizontal stabiliser.
5. (b).
6. will.
7. without.
8. longitudinal, rolling.
9. lateral, pitching.
10. normal, yawing.
11. tailplane.
12. forward.
13. forward.

14. CP is behind the CG, tailplane generates a downward force.
15. (b).
16. large, vertical.
17. dihedral.
18. low.
19. sideslip, yaw.
20. roll.
21. roll and yaw.
22. forward.
23. aft.
24. is not.

ANSWERS 8 — CONTROL.

1. elevator.
2. lateral.
3. down.
4. up.
5. (d).
6. fall.
7. ailerons.
8. longitudinal.
9. left.
10. go down.
11. up.
12. higher.
13. higher, more.
14. away from.
15. adverse aileron yaw.
16. differential ailerons, frise-type ailerons.
17. greater than.
18. lowered, lesser.
19. rudder.
20. normal.
21. increase, roll.
22. rise.
23. roll.
24. (b).
25. increases.
26. more.
27. increases.
28. elevator, rudder.
29. True.
30. (d).
31. elevator trim tab, elevator trim wheel.
32. trim tabs.
33. large.
34. will.
35. (a).
36. may, lateral.
37. (a).
38. (a).
39. (b).
40. (b).

ANSWERS 9 —
FLAPS.

1. increase.
2. lower.
3. lowers.
4. lower.
5. Drag.
6. Lift, Drag.
7. less.
8. steeper.
9. lower.
10. lower.
11. better, lower.
12. shortens.
13. slower, shorter.
14. (a).
15. (b).
16. decrease.
17. delay.
18. True.

ANSWERS 10 —
STRAIGHT AND LEVEL.

1. is.
2. Lift, Drag, Weight and Thrust.
3. equal.
4. equal.
5. (b).
6. L = C$_{Lift}$ x ½ Rho V-squared x S.
7. Indicated Air Speed.
8. angle of attack.
9. angle of attack, IAS, decrease.
10. reduced.
11. increased.
12. high.
13. low.
14. low.
15. high.
16. Lift.
17. decrease.
18. lower.
19. lower.
20. Thrust.
21. Thrust.
22. high.
23. high.
24. high.
25. high.
26. Indicated Air Speed.
27. angle of attack.
28. increase.
29. increasing.

ANSWERS 11 —
CLIMBING.

1. exceed.
2. Weight.

3. Drag.
4. less.
5. feet per minute.
6. 350 fpm.
7. 350 fpm.
8. 400.
9. 500 fpm.
10. 500 fpm.
11. 600 fpm.
12. vertical speed indicator.
13. drag.
14. ceiling.
15. better.
16. worse.
17. 500 ft.
18. best rate of climb speed.
19. best gradient (angle).
20. cruise-climb speed.
21. yes.
22. yes.
23. (b).
24. worse.
25. worse.
26. worse than.
27. (c).
28. flatter.
29. flight path over the ground.

ANSWERS 12 —
DESCENDING.

1. Lift, Drag, Weight
2. is.
3. Lift and Drag.
4. True.
5. steeper.
6. shallower.
7. increased.
8. steeper.
9. the same distance, higher airspeed.
10. decrease.
11. increase.
12. 6 mins.
13. 6 mins.
14. increase.
15. steeper.
16. steeper.
17. flatten.
18. decrease.
19. steepen.
20. steepen.
21. stay the same.
22. over the ground.
23. reduces.

ANSWERS 13 —
TURNING.
1. Centripetal.
2. Lift.
3. ailerons.
4. greater than.
5. angle of attack.
6. Lift, angle of attack, backwards.
7. Lift/Weight.
8. greater than.
9. 2.
10. balance.
11. Drag.
12. power.
13. angle of attack.
14. a higher.
15. overbank.
16. overbank.
17. is not.
18. left.
19. ailerons.
20. elevators.
21. rudder.

ANSWERS 14 —
STALLING.
1. turbulent.
2. static, Lift.
3. decreasing.
4. lower.
5. rearwards.
6. control buffet.
7. 16.
8. angle of attack.
9. $L = C_{Lift} \times \frac{1}{2}$ Rho V-squared x S
10. angle of attack, Indicated Air Speed.
11. angle of attack, Indicated Air Speed.
12. airspeed-squared.
13. square root of Lift.
14. stalling speed.
15. weight, load factor.
16. lower, lower.
17. increase.
18. increase.
19. increased.
20. greater.
21. higher.
22. increases.
23. is increased.
24. is increased.
25. 7%.
26. 41%.
27. 100%, i.e. stall speed is doubled.
28. Lift.

29. more.
30. higher.
31. angle.
32. same.
33. does not.
34. less than.
35. wing root.
36. causes.
37. (d).
38. lower.
39. the same.
40. (b).
41. (a).
42. increases (dropping wing), decreases (rising wing).

ANSWERS 15 —
THE AIRFRAME.
1. spar.
2. ribs.
3. semi-monocoque.
4. no.
5. yes.
6. (a).
7 & 8 *refer to the text.*
9. should.
10. exhaust manifold.
11. carbon monoxide.
12. *OFF,* increased.

ANSWERS 16 —
THE AEROPLANE ENGINE.
1. induction or intake, compression, power, exhaust.
2. inlet, cylinder.
3. closed, closed.
4. closed, closed.
5. closed, open.
6. top dead centre, bottom dead centre.
7. valve lead.
8. valve lag.
9. before.
10. after.
11. valve overlap.
12. increase.
13. increase.
14. compression.
15. before.
16. (d).
17. spark.
18. spark, ignition.
19. magneto, distributor.
20. once.
21. two.
22. True.
23. should.

24. safety, combustion.
25. True.
26. will not.
27. (c).
28. will not.
29. (b).
30. (b).
31. low.
32. (d).
33. impulse coupling.
34. will, will.
35. (b).
36. carbon monoxide.
37. (c).
38. (a).

ANSWERS 17 —
THE CARBURETTOR.

1. carburettor.
2. (c).
3. (d) Note: It is indirectly controlled by the throttle, which varies the butterfly valve position. This affects the airflow, but it is the airflow which directly controls the amount of fuel taken into the airstream.
4. is.
5. fuel.
6. air.
7. butterfly valve.
8. accelerator pump.
9. (c).
10. idling jet.
11. reduced, mixture control, red.
12. (a).
13. (c).
14. full rich.
15. power, fuel, spark plugs, carbon.
16. cooling.
17. high CHTs, detonation.
18. idle cut-off or cut-out.
19. does not.
20. pre-ignition.
21. carburettor ice.
22. carburettor.
23. carburettor heat.
24. small.
25. (c).
26. unfiltered.
27. (a).
28. (c).

ANSWERS 18 —
THE FUEL SYSTEM.

1. pressure, vapour, prime, engine-driven.

2. (c).
3. detonation.
4. lead-fouling, spark plugs, eroded.
5. should not.
6. pre-ignition, detonation.
7. lead.
8. lead-fouling, detonation.
9. first flight of the day, each re-fuelling.
10. lowest.
11. (a).
12. (a).
13. colour and smell.
14. green.
15. blue.
16. AVGAS – red; AVTUR – black.
17. (c).
18 & 19 *refer to the text.*

ANSWERS 19 —
THE OIL SYSTEM.

1. temperatures, oil.
2. True.
3. (a).
4. may not.
5. may.
6. oil filter.
7. oil filter by-pass valve, is.
8. oil-cooler.
9. high temperature, low pressure.
10. engine, seals
11. 30 seconds.

ANSWERS 20 —
THE COOLING SYSTEM.

1. fins.
2. better.
3. worse.
4. higher.
5. higher.
6. higher.
7. better.
8. higher.

ANSWERS 21 —
ENGINE HANDLING.

1. oil temperature gauge.
2. may.
3. sufficient.
4. immediate landing.
5. True.
6. True.
7. cooling.
8. Because the hot air is unfiltered.

ANSWERS 22 —
THE ELECTRICAL SYSTEM.
1. alternator, generator.
2. (d).
3. battery.
4. alternator, battery.
5. sulphuric.
6. (a).
7. (c).
8. current in amps.
9. battery, output, left.
10. high.
11. high, is.
12. True.
13. True.
14. battery, alternator.
15. voltage.
16. fuses, circuit breakers.
17. current.
18. should not.
19. True.
20. should not.
21. should, should.
22. (b).
23. 3 hours.
24. (c).
25. is.
26. (c).
27. ASI, Altimeter and VSI are pitot-static instruments and are not electrically powered (although there may be an electrical Pitot Heater to avoid icing); the gyroscopic instruments (AI, TC and DI) may be electrically powered or powered from the Vacuum System – a typical arrangement is a vacuum-powered AI and DI with an electrical TC; the Fuel Quantity Gauges and Oil Temperature Gauge (if fitted) will probably be electrically-powered; the RPM Gauge is self-powered directly off the engine.

ANSWERS 23 —
THE VACUUM SYSTEM.
1. True.
2. below.
3. gyroscopic.
4. draws, gyro rotors.
5. engine-driven.
6. Vacuum Relief Valve.
7. (c).
8. low, low.
9. may.

10. high, high.
11. (d).
12. Engine-driven Vacuum Pumps and externally mounted Venturi-tubes.

ANSWERS 24 —
LANDING GEAR, TYRES AND BRAKES.
1. should.
2. oil.
3. further.
4. is.
5. To avoid rapid wearing of the seals during taxying and ground manoeuvres as the strut telescopes in and out.
6. torque link, shimmy-damper.
7. castoring.
8. (a).
9. (b).
10. creep.
11. (b).
12. need not.
13. should.
14. should.
15. (c).
16. (c).
17. are not.
18. will, will.
19. (d).
20. should.

ANSWERS 25 —
PRESSURE INSTRUMENTS.
1. pitot.
2. static.
3. static vent.
4. total pressure.
5. pitot heater.
6. should.
7. could.
8. dynamic.
9. pitot, static.
10. static.
11. same.
12. True.
13. False.
14. (a).
15. (b).
16. is.
17. QFE.
18. QNH.
19. (c).
20. never-exceed speed, red.
21. low, white.
22. low, green.

23. normal operating limit speed, high speed end of the green arc.
24. Altimeter, Vertical Speed Indicator, Air Speed Indicator.
25. Air Speed Indicator.

ANSWERS 26 — GYROSCOPIC INSTRUMENTS.

1. compass.
2. AI, DI, TC.
3. (b).
4. True.
5. (b).
6. horizontal.
7. vertical.

ANSWERS 27 — THE MAGNETIC COMPASS.

1. (c).
2. variation.
3. deviation.
4. no.
5. near the Equator.
6. undershoot.
7. overshoot.
8. North.
9. *refer to the text.*
10. (b).

ANSWERS 28 — AIRWORTHINESS.

1. Registration.
2. Certificate of Airworthiness.
3. True.
4. must.
5. no.
6. must, need not.
7. True.
8. Flight Manual.
9. (c).
10. (a) before the first flight of the day.
11. yes.
12. yes.
13. (d), ANR(GEN).
14. (c).
15. (b).
16. (a).
17. yes.
18. yes.
19. yes.
20. no.
21. (c).
22. Flight Manual and CAA Supplement.
23. (a).
24. *refer to the text.*

ANSWERS 29 — AIRFRAME LIMITATIONS.

1 – 6. *refer to the text.*
7. can.
8. True.
9. (b).
10. (a).
11. *refer to the text.*

ANSWERS 30 — THE ATMOSPHERE.

1. nitrogen, oxygen and water vapour.
2. decrease.
3. (c).
4. (b).
5. (a).
6. (b).
7. (a).
8. (a).
9. (c).
10. (a).
11. (c).
12. high.
13. poorer.
14. International Standard Atmosphere.
15. 1013·2 mb(hPa).
16. 15.
17. 30.
18. 2.
19. 1012, 1011, 913.
20. +11, +5, −5.
21. 59°F, °F = $\frac{9}{5}$ × °C + 32.
22. 25°C, °C = $\frac{5}{9}$ × (°F − 32).

ANSWERS 31 — TAKE-OFF AND LANDING PERFORMANCE.

1. hard surface that is level and dry.
2. increase.
3. increase.
4. increased.
5. increases.
6. 9.
7. 18.
8. 5.
9. 10.
10. should.
11. 9.
12. 18.
13. (c).
14. increase.
15. increase.
16. 20%, 1·2.
17. 10%, 1·1.
18. 10%, 1·1.
19. 20%, 1·2.
20. 25%, 1·25.
21. 25%, 1·25.
22. 30%, 1·3.
23. at least 25%, at least 1·25.

24. 10%, 1·1.
25. 20%, 1·2.
26. 1·33.
27. Minimum Recommended Take-Off Distance = 370 x mandatory 1·05 x 1·1 x 1·1 x 1·25 x 1·1 x 1·2 x 1·33 = 1032 metres.
28. Recommended Take-Off Distance = 400 x 1·1 x 1·1 x 1·3 x 1·1 x 1·2 x 1·33 = 1105 metres.
Note the significant increase in distance when the various factors are applied. Good airmanship would suggest that a take-off in the opposite direction would be preferable, taking advantage of a downslope and a headwind.
29. need not.
30. must.
31. decreases.
32. increases.
33. does not affect.
34. increases.
35. does not affect.
36. decreases.
37. 50, power off.
38. increased.
39. increased.
40. increased.
41. increased.
42. the same.
43. higher.
44. increased.
45. increased.
46. decreased.
47. shorter.
48. 10%, 1·1.
49. 5%, 1·05.
50. 5%, 1·05.
51. 20%, 1·2.
52. 30%, 1·3.
53. 30%, 1·3.
54. 40%, 1·4.
55. at least 25%, at least 1·25.
56. 10%, 1·1.
57. 20%, 1·2.
58. 1·43.
59. 370 x 1·05 x 1·1 x 1·3 x 1·05 x 1·2 x 1·43 = 1001 metres.
60. is.

ANSWERS 32 — EN ROUTE PERFORMANCE.

1. distance over the ground.
2. least.
3. nautical miles.
4. endurance.
5. low.
6. minimum power.
7. greater.
8. greater than.

ANSWERS 33 — WEIGHT AND BALANCE.

1. Basic Empty Weight.
2. Zero Fuel Weight.
3. Maximum Take-off Weight.
4. performance.
5. Maximum Landing Weight.
6. performance-limited.
7. burn-off.
8. *refer to the text.*
9. magnitude, moment arm.
10. greater
11. True.
12. True.
13. 5000 lb. in.
14. 216 lb x 80·2 in = 17,323·2 lb in.
15. Take-off Weight, Zero Fuel Weight.
16. (c).
17. (a), (d), (f).
18. (d).
19. total usable fuel.
20. estimated fuel consumed.

ANSWERS 34 — WAKE TURBULENCE.

1. greater.
2. wingtip vortices.
3. angle of attack.
4. down.
5. downwind.
6. avoid.
7. point of rotation and climb out.
8. different to.

ANSWERS 35 — GROUND EFFECT.

1. ground effect.
2. upwash, downwash, wingtip vortices.
3. Coefficient of Lift.
4. induced drag.
5. decrease.
6. may not.

ANSWERS 36 — WINDSHEAR.

1. windshear.
2. overshoot effect.
3. undershoot effect.
4. windshear reversal effect.

INDEX